"Shawn R. Tucker's well-conceived sourcebook on *The Virtues and the Vices in the Arts* fills an important niche, and will be especially helpful for students just embarking on their study of the art and literature of European civilization. It represents a very useful compilation of key texts and illustrative artworks that document the historical conversation and debate about the moral life that has shaped the different cultures springing from Greco-Roman and Judeo-Christian antiquity."

—**DWIGHT D. ALLMAN**
Baylor University

"Shawn Tucker has done a great service bringing together a variety of texts and images from the rich tradition surrounding the vices and virtues, texts as different as Plato's *Republic* and Hildegard of Bingen's *Ordo Virtutum*, and images as varied as Brueghel's engravings of lust and anger and Paul Cadmus's paintings of envy and pride. This anthology will be a welcome resource for students of history, philosophy, literature, and art."

—**HOLLY JOHNSON**
Mississippi State University

"In *The Virtues and the Vices in the Arts*, Shawn Tucker has brought together important works on the vices and virtues that outline the trajectories of the development, diversification, and sometimes reversal, of these lively concepts over more than two thousand years of human thinking about morals and ethics. . . . The sources gathered here present both nonspecialists and specialists with enough material to appreciate the diversity and vitality of the long-lasting debate on the nature of vice and virtue in Western culture."

—**RHONDA L. MCDANIEL**
Middle Tennessee State University

The Virtues and Vices in the Arts

A Sourcebook

The Virtues and Vices in the Arts

A Sourcebook

Edited and with Introductions by
SHAWN R. TUCKER

CASCADE *Books* • Eugene, Oregon

THE VIRTUES AND VICES IN THE ARTS
A Sourcebook

Cascade Books
An Imprint of Wipf and Stock Publishers
199 W. 8th Ave., Suite 3
Eugene, OR 97401

www.wipfandstock.com

ISBN 13: 978-1-62564-718-4

Cataloguing-in-Publication data:

The virtues and vices in the arts : a sourcebook / edited by Shawn R. Tucker.

xii + 288 p. ; 23 cm. Includes bibliographical references and index.

ISBN 13: 978-1-62564-718-4

1. Vices in Art. 2. Virtues in Art. 3. Vices in Literature. 4. Virtues in Literature. I. Tucker, Shawn R. II. Title.

N7831 V60 2015

Manufactured in the U.S.A. 01/22/2015

Contents

Figures

Acknowledgments

THANK YOU TO THOSE at Cascade Books who helped to bring this project to fruition. Your professionalism and generosity were invaluable in this process. Thank you to the student reviewers who helped out in the process, including Rebecca Brackett, Erin Day, Elizabeth Dobbins, Yvonne Hsu, Alana Morro, Catherine Reynolds, John Stovall, Molly Strayer, and Christine Zimmerman. I am also grateful to the many students who took my seminar over the years dealing with the Virtues and Vices. Your feedback on portions of the manuscript and your enthusiasm and courage in addressing this material were an inspiration to me.

I also extend my very heartfelt gratitude to Elon University. This wonderful institution, where I am proud to be able to teach and work, offered tremendous support for this project. That support included the scholarship assistance to help fund the necessary permissions. Without that essential help, this would be a pamphlet. Elon also provided me with the sabbatical during which much of this material was assembled and written.

And finally, to Nicole, my wife, your constant support means the world to me.

Introduction

A HOUSE DIVIDED

There's a shadow just behind me,
Clouding every step I take,
Making every promise empty,
Pointing every finger at me,
Waiting like a stalking butler . . .

(Tool, "Sober," Undertow, 1993)[1]

The vices have always had a bad rap, especially when they get reclassified as "sins," that is, as offenses not only against taste and social propriety but against God himself. But then again, isn't it obvious that these so-called sins are in fact the very stuff of life, the hot, puffy, humiliating, pathetic, but essential ingredients in that human comedy that began with the expulsion from the Garden of Eden?

—Robert C. Solomon[2]

We live in a house divided. The same culture that deals with the tragedy of an average of two alcohol-related traffic deaths every hour finds its sporting events saturated in beer advertisements. While the latest pop singer proclaims her willingness to be "A Slave 4 U," parents, teachers, and coaches work tirelessly to instill real independence and value in young girls. We tell our children to "just say no" to the very things that many popular public figures embrace. We celebrate our cultural freedoms to sing and sell and persuade while grieving their excessive and disastrous consequences.

1. Excerpts from "Sober" are reprinted with the permission of Hal Leonard Corporation.
2. Solomon, *Wicked Pleasures*, 1.

That virtue and vice are powerful cultural forces is nothing new. Solomon's quotation above sets the beginning of such a tragicomedy at least back at Eden. What might make our current moment unique is the ambiguity about what exactly constitutes a virtue and a vice. In recasting the vices as "the very stuff of life," Solomon echoes a common idea that the vices often seem more vital or living than the virtues. Our cultural house is divided not only by virtue and vice but by the very meaning of *virtue* and *vice.*

Of course not everyone seems so unsure, so divided, and those clear-sighted and confident people earn our respect and admiration. And they scare us. Such people stand up, go to jail, make personal sacrifices, and even stare down death for what they believe. But what is the basis for such a powerful personal conviction? Is it the power of truth born of integrity, or does it show how, to use Yeats's phrase from "The Second Coming," "the worst / Are full of passionate intensity"? The same Robert Solomon quoted above warns how traditional virtues and vices can make powerful and dangerous combinations; "When anger, envy, and justice join forces, watch out!"[3]

Added to the mix of all of this ambiguity is yet another force, an undertow (to borrow the title of the Tool CD mentioned in the epigraph above). There is an increasingly common cultural location—the addiction meeting or the rehabilitation clinic. In rehab, the vices are not the "stuff of life" or the "essential ingredients in that human comedy." At an AA meeting there are no bonus points for uncertainty. As the Tool quote asserts, vice can be an ever-stalking, ever-clouding, and ever-accusing force that becomes so powerful that it makes every promise empty. One unique feature in the Tool song is that there are shifts in the narration, not exactly what one would expect in heavy-metal rock music. At one point the speaker seems to be vice itself, warning,

> I am just a worthless liar.
> I am just an imbecile.
> I will only complicate you.
> Trust in me and fall as well.
> I will find a center in you.
> I will chew it up and leave,
> I will work to elevate you
> Just enough to bring you down.

Those overcome by vice find their integrity "complicated" and compromised, their center chewed up and dissolved. Victims of vice find that this worthless liar poisons life instead of adding spice; it is corrosive, not a condiment. In the end, vice is a solvent that eats away every aspiration, every plan, and finally every relationship.

So in our divided house we have those collapsed by addictions and those paralyzed by fear of doing anything that might not fit someone else's idea of virtuousness. While some suffer because of uncertainty, and some suffer (ignorantly perhaps)

3. Ibid., 7.

because of certainty, others thrive on uncertainty and still others on certainty. The divided house, inhabited by so many contrasting residents, is a house whose very framework is formed by the virtues and vices, since this house is built from those moral and ethical ideals found in many of our culture's important philosophical, religious, and artistic works. Those works can be didactic or critical or satirical. Some are clear and expository, some elusive and mystical, while others are ambiguous and even paradoxical. The virtues and vices may be reverenced, like alchemy, as holding ancient, magical secrets, even transcendent power, or they can be playfully profaned.

This book, far from seeking to harmonize different concepts or expressions of virtue and vice, provides some of the source documents that have helped establish the philosophical, religious, social, and artistic discussion about virtue and vice. This book includes those works central to a particular house, what we could roughly and inaccurately call Western civilization. It is outside of its scope to trace the virtues and vices in other traditions. This anthology begins with the Greco-Roman and Judeo-Christian antecedents of the virtues and vices. The second section provides documents related to their codification in the early so-called Christian era. The apex of their cultural importance is the material in the third section. The fourth section's documents show the variety of ways that Renaissance thinkers and artists engaged the tradition, while the last section shows transformations of the virtues and vices up to the present.[4] The power or "virtue" of this book is not its ability to provide definitive answers to questions that surround the virtues and vices, but to provide some of the original ways that they have been presented. While it cannot reunite the house divided, it can inspire its occupants to explore its footings and foundations, as well as its fractures and fissures.

VIRTUES, VICES, SINS, AND GIFTS OF THE SPIRIT

I am a professor, and when I teach Dante's *Divine Comedy* students often wonder why some sinners are in hell while others are in purgatory. I respond by asking what they can do with moldy cheese commonly found in college refrigerators. Some insists that moldy cheese must be sent immediately to Chernobyl by someone in full hazmat gear. Brighter students answer with a question: how much mold is there? When I ask what difference it makes, they explain that if there is a little mold, then you can just cut that portion off, while if there is too much mold to separate it from the cheese, then there is no salvaging the cheese. And that is also the difference between Dante's sinners in hell and purgatory. For those who have committed transgressions that sit, metaphorically, on the surface of their souls, some purgative sin removal is called for. But for those completely contaminated and overcome by sin, like cheese filled with mold, the only option is hell. When sin cannot be separated from soul, that soul goes to eternal Chernobyl, so to speak.

4. Unless I've indicated otherwise, all footnotes within anthologized works are my own.

This comparison points toward the difference between sin and vice. Vice, which comes from the Latin word *vitium*, meaning "fault" or "defect," is a characteristic, a habit so ingrained that it has come to dominate. A sin is an individual act of transgression. While the vicious will necessarily sin often as a consequence of the state of their souls, otherwise virtuous people may commit isolated sinful acts. According to elements of the Christian tradition, sins are deadly to the degree, either that they manifest a vicious nature, or that they inevitably lead to more sins. That is not to say that every author or artist or thinker is completely consistent, but, in general, the "deadlier" sins reveal a soul's depravity and lead to more character decay.

Tracing the roots of what we now call the seven deadly sins is an important thread through this book. Someone new to the history of the virtues and vices may be surprised to find that they are not specifically listed in the Bible. This book contains some of their biblical antecedents, but our common list of virtues and vices does not emerge until long after the formation of the Bible. It is also important to note that the specific number of vices and the specific vices themselves fluctuate over time. Prudentius (348–413 CE), for example, listed eight main vices as well as an entire evil entourage to accompany them. Evagrius (345–399 CE) often listed eight, though he sometimes added a ninth, and Gregory the Great (540–604 CE) shuffled those lists to form one with pride as the principle vice followed by seven sinful attendants. Even this list was slightly altered before Dante (1265–1321 CE) penned his *Purgatory*. The chart below gives lists of vices presented in chronological order according to different authors or artists.

VICES				
Prudentius	*Evagrius*	*Gregory*	*Dante (seven deadly sins)*	*Giotto*
Worship-of-the-Old-Gods	Gluttony	Pride	Pride	Foolishness
Lust	Fornication	Vain Glory	Envy	Inconstancy
Wrath	Avarice	Envy	Anger	Ire
Pride	Sadness	Anger	Sloth	Injustice
Indulgence (and entourage)	Anger	Melancholy	Avarice	Idolatry
Greed (and entourage)	Acedia	Avarice	Gluttony	Envy
Thrift (Greed in disguise)	Vainglory	Gluttony	Lust	Despair
Discord or Heresy	Jealousy	Lust		
	Pride			

Standing across the field from the vices in the battle for the soul are the virtues. These also change over time, and in Prudentius's work there are eleven with prominent roles, though more are named. But Prudentius's list of virtues, like his vices, did not become a fixed standard, and Gregory the Great generated his own lists. In one part of his commentary on Job, Gregory gives the list commonly drawn from Isaiah. These are traditionally called the gifts of the Spirit and are often adapted as contrasts or remedies for the vices. Gregory also provided the most common list of virtues. This list was developed from the four cardinal, classical, or humanistic virtues: prudence, temperance, fortitude, and justice. These derive from Greco-Roman culture. To these four were added the three theological virtues drawn from Paul: faith, hope, and charity or love. This list becomes the standard list of virtues.

VIRTUES					
Plato	*Paul*	*Prudentius*	*Evagrius*	*Gregory (Gifts of Spirit)*	*Gregory, Dante, Giotto*
Wisdom	Faith	Faith	Abstinence	Wisdom	Faith
Courage	Hope	Chastity	Chastity	Understanding	Hope
Temperance	Love	Long-Suffering	Freedom from Possessions	Counsel	Charity
Justice		Lowliness	Joy	Fortitude	Prudence
		Hope	Patience	Knowledge	Temperance
		Sobriety	Perseverance	Piety	Fortitude
		Reason	Freedom from Vainglory	Fear	Justice
		Good Works	Freedom from Jealousy		
		Concord	Humility		
		Peace			
		Wisdom			

A couple of features come to the fore when we examine these lists. Evagrius set up the basic cast of the vices, Gregory made modifications, and then by Dante's time one further modification had been made. Giotto's list seems quite different, because his standard was the then rather stable seven virtues; Giotto created seven vices in opposition. In other contexts the seven deadly sins are the standard, with variations on the gifts of the Spirit acting as healing contrasts.

Another element of these charts is the words themselves. The vice on Evagrius's list given as *acedia* is worth pausing over. The Greek roots of this word mean "an absence of care." For monks who take vows, flee the world, and live in the desert, *acedia* means "carelessness," or "a lack of concern about spiritual things." Acedia is the indifference and apathy that leads devotees to abandon their vows. Over the centuries, as the vices moved from cells and monasteries to the public sphere, this spiritual aridity became sloth. In Dante's work this sloth means a lack of enthusiastic love toward God and toward the good. In our time, sloth means laziness. The best expression of this modern version of *acedia* is the song "Sloth" in Kurt Weill and Bertolt Brecht's *The Seven Deadly Sins*. In this song the brothers worry that Anna will lapse in her dedication to building the family fortune; they complain that she "was always a bit strange and easygoing," and that "if you didn't throw her out of bed / that lazy piece wouldn't get up in the morning."[5] Imagine that heinous crime against capitalism: being easygoing and not getting up all morning!

Acedia is not the only interesting term on the charts. Many different words can be used for what seems to be the same vice or virtue. Sometimes *fortitude* is *strength*, *courage*, *might*, *prowess*, or *perseverance*. Any of the virtues or vices can evoke a number of synonyms. A word like the Latin *luxuria* may be translated as "indulgence," "excess," "dissipation," or even "lust." And finally, the word for positive qualities, virtues, has its Latin root in *vir* or "man." *Virtus* not only means "virtue": it can also mean "manliness," "excellence," "worth," "goodness," "courage," or "bravery." The general idea is supposed to be that vices are flaws, while virtues are excellences. The virtues are the quintessential traits of a "man," or of human beings at their best and embodying their fullest potential. In contrast, the vices are the various contaminants that, like mold, can overcome, dominate, and debilitate. These fatal flaws, the vices, subvert human potential or "unman" the man.

CONSTELLATIONS

As a kid I was always frustrated by constellations. I just could not see how those little lights were supposed to be a lion or a hunter or twins. The only ones I could see were the pots or the ladles or whatever. It really takes quite an imaginative leap to outline figures from the vast array of stars. And of course those shapes are not actually "written in the stars" but are our own projections onto them. Had the evening sky been obscured by clouds throughout human history until the very recent past, I wonder what constellations we would recognize. Would we recognize Ferrari instead of Pegesus, or Elvis instead of Orion?

Just as constellations are collections of stars assembled to make recognizable or meaningful images, so the works collected in this anthology can be grouped in different and useful ways. The anthology itself is chronological with introductions that provide historical context. Although this book groups the anthologized texts chronologically, below are five constellations or clusters of ideas that can be used to link various works. These constellations can be used group the works in interesting ways, to identify meaningful patterns, and even to suggest new connections. While there may seem to be a certain naturalness about either the selection or the chronological

5. Kurt Weill and London Symphony Orchestra, *The Seven Deadly Sins*, 15.

arrangement of these works in this anthology (or both) and about the connections and patterns that emerge based on the selection and arrangement, the apparent naturalness should not obscure the very real arbitrariness of either the selection or the chronological arrangement of these works.

Competing Cosmologies

Stan and Barbara have a son who had once been a very happy and easygoing child. One day, almost out of the blue, that now-teenage son started to become moody and withdrawn, quarrelsome and confrontational. His schoolwork dropped off, as did his interest in family, social, spiritual, and cultural activities. He began staying up late (and doing who knows what) and sleeping until midday; so many of his normal patterns seemed to have changed. What most parents would conclude about all of these symptoms is that the teenager is, of course, perfectly normal. But what if your child's changes were not normal, did not fit the patterns of other teenagers, and were more dramatic and severe? You may rightly conclude that your child has a problem. She or he may show symptoms of depression. What would you do?

Depression is an interesting cultural phenomenon, because its complexity tests many of our current views of the world. Our scientific view may explain depression as a chemical problem, as a physiological phenomenon, or as a psychological or sociological conflict. The depressed may have a chemical imbalance, may lack proper psychological tools for dealing with reality, or may be victims of overwhelming social forces. According to another view, the depressed may suffer from a spiritual emptiness, perhaps caused by sin or vice, or from the spiritual vacuum of a materialistic culture. The depressed suffer from a lack of God or a lack of the spiritual. Another cultural force may tell the depressed that they need a better job, a better house, better clothes, or a better brand of beer. (They need a little "retail therapy.") So what is depression, and what do the depressed need? Here are some answers our current culture (and divided house) may provide: they need a pill, therapy, a better diet and more exercise, better friends, prayer, a spiritual sanctuary, less anxiety about what car they drive, or a new car.

What the issue of depression brings out is the different worldviews that exist in the same culture and how those different and even contradictory views attempt to make sense of such an important issue. This multiplicity of views is not unique to our culture. One of the most valuable things about examining the virtues and vices is to see different worldviews at play in the same work. Such an examination allows us to see how worldviews can come together, split apart, and twist around one another in their harmonious and conflictive coexistence.

The early Christian writer Tertullian (160–225 CE) once asked the rhetorical question: "what indeed has Athens to do with Jerusalem?" Tertullian was contrasting the worldview of the Greeks and Romans with the view developed by Christians working out of the Jewish tradition. The Greco-Roman view focuses on human beings and how humans live in a world of other humans. That world has human-made problems that call for human solutions. This is therefore called a humanistic view. The Greek word *cosmos* means "order," and Tertullian was critical of the Greco-Roman cosmology, or method of making sense of, or of ordering, the universe. Tertullian envisioned a clear split between the Greco-Roman and the Judeo-Christian cosmologies. The Judeo-Christian cosmology is theocentric or God-centered. God is the ultimate creator and sustainer of all, and is the judge of what is right and wrong, what is virtue and vice. According to this view, real success in mortality and blessings in the afterlife come from living with God as the center of one's life.

The contrasts and conflicts between the humanistic and the theocentric are woven through this anthology. This book's first section shows the contrast with documents from (so to speak) Athens and Jerusalem. Prudentius, Gregory, Giotto and others attempt to synthesize these cosmologies using different approaches and yielding different results. Some, like Franklin, take a more humanistic view, while others, like Lewis, adapt a decidedly more theocentric one. Machiavelli and Nietzsche use the humanistic to tacitly or explicitly criticize the theocentric. One way to discern the humanistic from the theocentric in a given work is to find how it backs up its claims about virtue and vice. Theocentric works refer to the authority of God or other supernatural sources, while humanistic ones use human experience and insight as the standard.

If the central comparison of the humanistic and theocentric is the rivalry between Athens and Jerusalem, then the contrasting images for the organic and the mechanistic world-views are the plant and the machine. These views emphasize that the world is made of parts that function together. The contrast is that the machine functions universally, forever, and with absolute predictability. The laws of thermodynamics, for example, were not just enacted and have no statute of limitations. In contrast, the organic view of the world emphasizes the way that phenomena grow out of others, emerging, blooming, wilting, dying, and then setting the stage for another birth, another life. The organic view places an accent on flux and unpredictability. While the trees of virtue and of vice found in the *Speculum Virginum* give the most obvious example of the organic, it is perhaps the dreamy, fluid, and somewhat open or even unpredictable quality of Langland's *Piers Plowman* that makes this work the best expression of the organic approach. Franklin's project to improve his character, his formula to better his moral machine, reveals most clearly the mechanical worldview. The mechanical worldview can reinforce the stable, the absolute qualities in the virtues and vices, where the organic could make space for doubt, indeterminacy, and even grace.

A powerful view of the world, of human social and economic interaction, and one that came to prominence in the nineteenth and twentieth centuries, is Marxism. This worldview examines, among other things, the ways that capitalism influences every aspect of life, including social interactions. Kurt Weill and Bertolt Brecht's *The Seven Deadly Sins* gives compelling expression to this view and the ways capitalism configures virtue and vice. A Marxist cosmology can also be applied to works that predate its emergence to explore otherwise hidden or ulterior views or interactions. Could Machiavelli's *The Prince* show how capitalism transforms social and economic realities, forcing a prince to use whatever means necessary to keep control? What ulterior motives or agendas might be hidden under the virtuous and vicious imagery in Lorenzetti's murals in the Palazzo Pubblico?

Cosmologies are ways that people make sense of reality, how they find or make meaning, or how they discern significant patterns among the otherwise undistinguished data or "stars" of reality. With an issue as important as depression or virtue and vice, the cosmologies often come into sharp and powerful relief. The competition between different cosmologies is another heated indication of the divisions of our cultural house. But such competitions can also reveal the limitations of any single view. By seeing the inherent limitations in any cosmology, those engaged in important debates may embrace the humility sufficient for real dialogue and for the emergence of any issue's best synthetic solution.

Public or Private

The virtues and vices are normative, or, in other words, they are like building codes. Building codes are standards that every builder must conform to when creating a structure. The idea behind building codes is that they ensure that the structure is safe for all of its occupants. Building codes in tropical areas, for example, make specific requirements about walls and windows to ensure that the structure will survive hurricane-force winds and flooding. A house in a colder climate would be built according to codes designed to ensure protection against freezing and snowy conditions. These codes are readily available, and they establish certain expectations.

The virtues and vices are also meant to establish certain public norms for proper and safe conduct and character. They set up expectations for social interaction, such as social equality and justice. These public norms can be used to establish one's status as a citizen. Good citizens live by the norms; bad ones do not. The virtues and vices can be used as personal and internal standards to establish one's scruples and for self-evaluation. To the degree that this standard of virtue and vice is of divine authorship or inspiration and authority, it can also establish one's "rightness" with God.

In order for building codes to work, they must be as public as possible. The same holds true for the normative function of the virtues and vices. From the first document here, Plato's *Republic*, and then prevalent in many subsequent works, there is a connection between virtue, vice, and education. Plato's ideal world would not only include a mandatory education in virtue for its most important citizens, but it would severely limit the art that might subvert such an education and have a dangerous moral impact upon the whole society. Cicero gives his son specific instructions on virtue that are not unlike those of Proverbs. Jesus and Paul indicate to their listeners the path of virtue as does the father in Rejlander's *The Two Ways of Life* or as do the panels that contrast virtues and vice at Amiens Cathedral and in Giotto's frescoes. Sometimes this inculcation in the virtues and vices takes a more decidedly public cast, as in Siena's Palazzo Pubblico, whereas in other cases this education is both public and private, as in Franklin's *Autobiography*.

Part of what makes Franklin's work more private is that it involves the more individual and solitary act of reading. Large public images, like frescoes in the town hall or sculptural decorations on the cathedral, invite a more public reception. At the other end of the continuum of public and private are Evagrius's reflective and meditative tracts. In the solitary confines of the desert cell, the monk uses Evagrius's writings to discern the evil influences that would assail the soul. Other written documents fall more toward the public side. Prudentius's *Psychomachia* reaches out to a broader audience to give a graphic and dramatic representation of virtue and vice's battle for the soul. This battle becomes more public with illustrations. Dante's work is even more general and public than Prudentius's, but it still inspires individual self-reflection. Perhaps Brueghel's prints, which could be readily reproduced and therefore in wide circulation, fall right between the public and the private. While they are widely available, they are of a smaller and more intimate scale than sculpted panels, large-scale paintings, or murals. They depict a large number of figures in the entire panorama of virtue and vice but can still strike a chord with an individual's struggle with those conflictive forces.

As the virtues and vices are normative, they not only set public and private standards, but they also set the stage for one of their most powerful artistic expressions—satire. For satire to be effective and entertaining, it must reverse commonly held expectations. Homer Simpson is funny because he reverses many expectations of a good father, husband, neighbor, and employee. The satirical elements of *Piers Plowman* and other works play on the tension created by the norms established by the standards of virtue and vice, and the gross or ironic or humorous betrayal of those norms. Nowhere is this reversal clearer and more striking than in Kurt Weill and Bertolt Brecht's satirical swipe at capitalism in *The Seven Deadly Sins*.

If the virtues and vices are like building codes, then a variety of public and private authorities often act as inspectors. For Plato, inspection should be constant, public, and in the hands of those most qualified to enforce the proper standards. Part of that enforcement is censorship. Standards of virtue and vice form the basis of censorship from at least Plato all the way to the present. While it is beyond the scope of this book to include the many codes, regulations, and ratings systems, as well as the lively debates around them, such censorship standards and contests inevitably invoke questions of public and private expression and reception, circling back to various ideas about virtue and vice.

Power or Peace

If you were visited by a wish-granting fairy and told that you could have either immense power or a deep and abiding peace, which would you choose? Think about this carefully before you answer. What do you want, control or serenity? Perhaps power and peace are complements. After all, what kind of real power do people possess if they are in turmoil, especially if they have a constant fear of losing that power? And what sort of peace does not include a certain sense of predictability, reliability, or security?

Many works included in this volume address peace and/or power. In his dialogue about an ideal state, Plato discusses the emergence of social conflict when people are no longer satisfied with having their basic needs met. Plato's utopian republic would be a state where peace is secured by the moorings of power in the hands of those best equipped to look out for everyone. Machiavelli, on the other hand, presents a real-world or realpolitik perspective of a leader's need to exploit the ignorance and fear of the masses to maintain dominance. Nietzsche extends some of these elements in his critique of the various ways that people abdicate their power to others. In these three works there are the powerful and the powerless, some who hold power while others are held by their power. This struggle for control, or at least the effort to authorize one's power, can also be read into works like the murals in Siena's Palazzo Pubblico and in Pollaiuolo and Raphael's panels for the Florentine Mercanzia.

In these examples power is public, but the battle for internal control is perhaps even more important in works about the virtues and vices. Jesus's account of the blessed and the interior battles described by Paul, Tertullian, Prudentius, and Langland illustrate the soul's innermost power struggle. And that struggle is variously illustrated in *Psychomachia* manuscripts and by Bruegel, among others. Even Dante's poem and Chaucer's tale show the gradual process whereby the power of vice is painstakingly identified, confronted, and finally overcome.

At the end of the battle scenes in Prudentius's version of the soul's internal fight for power, the narrator describes how "a fair and happy state of circumstance and life has been established over all." This is a place where all of the faculties or the "peaceable Sentiments can dwell in security under the protection of guard-post and rampart," and where the soul can "find relief and relaxation." The struggle for control of the soul turns out to be a battle for peace. For Prudentius, peace comes from the absolute harmony of the faculties. This peace is not unlike the stillness that Evagrius holds aloft as the soul's highest end. For both of these writers, the vices are spirits, forces, or "thoughts" of disorder, disintegrating the harmony that should reign in the soul. Such dissonant forces are cast from the Garden of Virtue in Mantegna's painting and are gruesomely depicted in Cadmus's panels.

From these works we could get the impression that peace and power are two sides of the same coin, and maybe they are. Power and peace are central to the qualities of

Isaiah's promised Messiah. Maybe one cannot go wrong in picking either one when the wish-granting fairy finally shows up. But it is still hard to square certain notions of power with Jesus's promise that the meek would inherit the earth. In our daily lives, we see Machiavellian individuals in all political and social organizations, even in families, where members may exert power with vicious means like dishonesty, fraud, blackmail, passive aggression, and coercion. When will their (meek) victims come into that inheritance? We know powerful people who have a dramatic influence because of their goodness, their integrity, and their courage. Think of Mother Teresa and Martin Luther King Jr. But we also know the power of those who work in hate, who foment fear, and who twist otherwise good ideas for very destructive ends. Many of the texts in this book ask and variously answer questions about the relationship between virtue, vice, power, and peace, and about the many ways to negotiate those relationships.

Firmness (and Pliability)

There is a universally recognized list of virtues and vices. The virtues are faith, hope, love, wisdom, courage, temperance, and justice. The first three are the theological virtues, which come from the Judeo-Christian tradition via Paul. (Oh, by the way, there are other lists of Judeo-Christian virtues in Proverbs and Isaiah, and in other places in Paul's writing. And there are also the Beatitudes, and you could easily draw some virtues from the Ten Commandments.) The last four virtues we listed are the cardinal, classical, or humanistic virtues. They are wisdom, courage, temperance, and justice. (Well, those are the four that Plato listed, but sometimes prudence takes the place of wisdom; fortitude—or just strength—takes the place of Courage; and while temperance seems pretty common, Plato's concept of justice is actually less like fairness and equality, and more like doing right or secular "righteousness." And Aristotle had a whole slew of other virtues that he listed, and Benjamin Franklin tried to live by thirteen virtues. Ben of course failed—maybe he should have pared his list down.)

There is an equally precise, concrete, and universally recognized list of vices. They are pride, anger, envy, sloth, greed, gluttony, and lust. Actually Aristotle had two vices for each of the many virtues he listed, and Paul had a few lists of sinful qualities. By the way, Evagrius had a list of eight vices, which sometimes climbed to nine, and which included *acedia* and sadness. (Imagine that: depression as a vice!) Oh, and Prudentius has a different set of vices to go with his different set of virtues. And when the builders of the French Gothic cathedrals in places like Paris, Amiens, and Chartres set the virtues and vices in stone, they used twelve of each.

The list of virtues and vices is set, firm, and stable, and that means the whenever you mention them, everyone knows exactly what you mean. (Unless, of course, you mean the virtues and/or vices according to Plato or Jesus or Paul or Evagrius or Prudentius or . . . With each of these writers and with every work in this book there is pliability, to varying degrees, about the virtues and vices.)

Because the virtues and vices are set, firm, and universally recognized, they communicate unequivocally. If you see a statue or painting of a woman looking into a mirror, for example, you know that she is a figure of Wisdom, who embodies the Greco-Roman ideal that true understanding is to "know thyself." (Or she could be a figure of Vanity, who is consumed with either herself or mere "appearance.") Wisdom often has the head of Janus, showing that she sees past, present, and future. (Or you could be looking at a symbol of the two faces of Fraud or Duplicity.) It is even more telling if she has the snake and apple, further connoting Wisdom. (Unless it is a figure of Eve.) All other vices and virtues have an equally stable and universal set of symbols or attributes. (Vagaries abound.)

Besides making works of art recognizable, and thus eliminating the need for supplemental texts to explain or names to designate, everyone everywhere knows exactly what is virtuous and vicious, no matter what the situation is. (Well this just falls apart almost immediately. Most of the works included here have titles or texts or even labels right there, so that you know that the naked lady with the sword is Justice (or maybe Fortitude or Strength or Perseverance) and not Anger or Fury or Violence or War. And of course there is a huge difference between Nietzsche's and Lewis's worldview, and subsequently their view of virtue and vice.)

What makes the virtues and vices so interesting is their firmness—and their pliability. They are canonized in sacred texts, etched in stone, inculcated in the young, used for confession and self-examination, and become a universal moral standard, pointing toward absolute values like a compass. (Yah, like a compass in a magnet factory!)

Because the virtues and vices have such a universal validity, one should learn about them and incorporate them. (And one should, with suspicion and sympathy, be inspired to respond to them in every way.) Their stony inflexibility (and lively liquidity) can charge one's approach to life, to others, and to creativity. It is the concreteness (and fluidity) of the virtues and vices that make them so compelling.

Do the Virtues and Vices Work?

I think that Benjamin Franklin was genuinely confused that his noble project for moral improvement did not work. The excerpt included in this book from his *Autobiography* describes his very deliberate plan for self-improvement. We must assume that Ben really tried, but somehow failed. Ben's failure raises the above question: do the virtues and vices really work?

Since at least Evagrius, we can see the list of virtues and vices as a sort of moral diet. Even Cicero recommends daily doses of goodness for his growing son. Our culture knows plenty about diets, and perhaps drawing such a comparison raises some interesting questions. Is a regimen of the virtues and vices a useful or even doable character diet? Did Franklin fail because he just had the wrong diet? Did Ben need the moral Weight Watchers (or the Evagrian Evil-Thought Watchers) or the Psychomachia South Beach instead of his Enlightenment Atkins? Did he miss two important virtues—perseverance and patience—and therefore never see their fruit? Was Ben so focused on food, on individual acts, that he lost sight of the larger goal—a healthy character? Another point which some writers and artists in this book may make is that Ben's attempt to change his character amounted to an attempt to save himself without recourse to God. Did Ben fail because, in his pride, he made himself his own god? Someone like Nietzsche may retort that this idea is just more moral Munchausen syndrome to encourage sickness and dependence instead of power and independence. Suddenly Ben's moral flabbiness becomes everyone's concern.

This question of the power, the *virtus*, of the virtues and vices can seem rather hypothetical if not comical. The question becomes real when you or someone you care about feels a compelling need to overcome a vice and/or acquire an important virtue. Eradicating vice and embracing virtue is not cocktail-party banter for the people included in this book. How does one come to grips with the true nature of virtue and vice and how does one live in the healthiest way possible is a deadly serious issue in most of the works included here, even in cases where that brass-knuckles seriousness is cloaked in the velvet glove of satire.

PART I

Foundations

It is the simple yet profound question of human nature: are humans naturally good? Are truth, wisdom, and virtue already inside of us, just waiting for the proper conditions to grow and flourish? Is the default state of human moral character set at the right balance and only loses its equilibrium by accident? Or are we fulfilled and right when we are properly aligned with something higher, larger, or deeper? Are humans born complete, or at least very potentially complete in themselves, or is there a "God-shaped hole" in everyone? This question has a direct connection with virtue and vice. It also helps us understand the works in this book's first section.

HUMAN POTENTIAL AND PROTECTION I

Plato, Aristotle, and Cicero would generally agree that humans have within them all of the tools that they need to live a fully satisfying life. There is even a phrase that we use with Plato's writing to describe how humans have all they need within them and that they merely need to develop those aspects. That phrase is the Maieutic method, and it is derived from the Greek word for midwife. Socrates, the speaker in Plato's writings, describes himself as a midwife who is there to assist in the "birth" or emergence of truth that is already inside the learner. *The Republic* is an extended birthing session, where Socrates coaxes his learners through the sometimes difficult and even painful process of bringing the truth to light. What is brought to light is how the ideal state is based upon people following their best innate inclinations. Those inclinations are for everyone to do what they are best equipped to do, with those best equipped to look after the entire state acting as social guardians and facilitators.

Aristotle has a similarly optimistic view of human beings. His idea is that with proper training, one can acquire the habits of a virtuous life. In fact, Aristotle's view sounds like what we generally think of when we think of Eastern medicine. The emphasis with both is on the proper balance. For humans to be successful, they must have the properly balanced response to any human experience or impulse. Everyone, for example, experiences fear, but the courageous respond to it properly. Those who are overly confident in the face of fear are rash or foolhardy, while those who are overly afraid are cowards. Aristotle catalogs the whole gamut of human experience and impulses to show how deficiencies and excesses make one morally unhealthy in the same way that an excess or deficiency of protein, iron, or calcium would make one physically ill. Rational self-examination with an eye on the healthiest individuals can help one see where those excesses or deficiencies lie, and then it is fully within one's power to correct them by finding the proper balance. Of course rational self-examination requires proper training. Children, for example, do not know how to find a proper balance, but with the right training people can form the best habits to bring to life their innate potential.

What does not come through in the excerpts from Plato and Aristotle is that sometimes life just stinks. There is pain, suffering, and difficulties. There are ironic reversals, where just when everything seemed to be just right, it all falls apart. A view of life's excruciating reversals, not to mention its utter unreliability, must have been especially clear to Romans like Cicero. In the face of so much social and personal decline and disappointment, Romans like Cicero adapted a fierce devotion to what they could control—themselves. The emphasis on personal integrity, a steady resilience and fortitude in spite of all, and a levelheadedness in the face of any potential persuasions by pleasure or pain are the hallmarks of the approach known as Stoicism. If Plato and Aristotle's view is human expansion, human development from the growth of latent powers, Cicero's outlook is virtue's fortress in the midst of a siege, a soul that can remain still and safe with its internal resources and integrity.

HUMAN POTENTIAL AND PROTECTION II

The first three works in this section are from Athens, so to speak: from the humanistic Greeks and Romans, who held the view of humans naturally following their best innate inclinations to achieve their highest potential. The last four works are from Jerusalem, from the theocentric Jewish and Christian cultures centered on belief that one's highest potential came from a proper relationship with God. God is the standard by which human potential is measured in the theocentric works. That Being is also the one who guarantees the specific theocentric promise: eternal life. It is the divine instead of the human foundation and standard of virtue and vice that distinguishes Jerusalem from Athens.

Proverbs are wise sayings precisely because they reinforce how real wisdom comes from a proper respect and reverence for God. These sayings set up the contrast between the wise, who submit their will and understanding to God via obedience, against those who deviate, who stray, or who believe that they know themselves. Peace, power, and protection come to those who live by the covenant no matter what the circumstance (like Joseph, who was sold into Egypt, and who is mentioned later on in this book, in the introduction to Proverbs). Isaiah extends this in his description of a great leader or Messiah, who, because of His faithfulness to the covenant, would embody the greatest human and divine qualities and would subsequently bless the entire human race.

The greatest contrast between Athens and Jerusalem comes in Jesus's description of the blessed. Aristotle's "blessed" are those whose ambition has combined with innate talents to make them powerful, magnanimous, and universally admired. Jesus asserts that the poor in spirit, the meek, and those who mourn are the ideal. In Paul's writings we find a similar contrast. In Athens being virtuous means following one's best tendencies and in being balanced and healthy. For Paul, being virtuous is a constant and heated battle, and it is a battle that requires weaponry that only God through the Spirit can provide. Paul's view of the Spirit's work against sin seems closer to Western medicine's view of antibodies, which destroy attacking viruses. Aristotle seeks balance, the golden mean between too much and too little, whereas Paul seeks absolute victory and triumph. Plato may hear the momentary cries of virtue's birth, but Paul hears the tumultuous clamor of virtue and vice's life-or-death struggle.

PLATO'S *THE REPUBLIC*

Introduction

Plato's *Republic* is haunted by sheep—fat, lazy, and stupidly obedient sheep. Behind those sheep are greedy and selfish shepherds who care for them, keeping them safe, happy, and well-fed long enough to let them reproduce, to sheer them, and to butcher them. The reason that sheep haunt the *Republic* is that the discussion that we are most interested in is about the nature of justice. What is justice? What does it mean to be just, and where can we find justice? And, to get to the problem, who does justice benefit—the rulers or the ruled? Could it be that what passes for justice is simply a cover that the powerful use to take advantage of the powerless? Is justice the shepherd's crook that oppressive rulers use to keep the herded masses stupid and subservient to their selfish ends?

We hear the ghost sheep in the first book of *The Republic*. *The Republic* is a discussion between Socrates and various speakers, and in the first book we meet Thrasymachus, someone who seems to really have it in for Socrates. Thrasymachus can hardly contain himself as the discussion of justice begins. When he finally gets a chance to interrupt, he calls Socrates an immature, snot-nosed child who does not know how the world really works. He offers this lesson:

> You fancy that the shepherd or neatherd [cowherd] fattens or tends the sheep or oxen with a view to their own good and not to the good of himself or his master; and you further imagine that the rulers of states, if they are true rulers, never think of their subjects as sheep, and that they are not studying their own advantage day and night. Oh, no; and so entirely astray are you in your ideas about the just and unjust as not even to know that justice and the just are in reality another's good; that is to say, the interest of the ruler and stronger, and the loss of the subject and servant; whereas the reverse holds in the case of injustice; for the unjust is lord over the truly simple and just: he is the stronger, and his subjects do what is for his interest, and minister to his happiness, which is very far from being their own. (Book I, 343 b–c)[1]

Thrasymachus's flippant, sarcastic, and condescending attitude only adds more spit and vinegar to his argument. Rulers are fat shepherds who keep their sheep safe while plotting that which will serve only the rulers' ends. If those rulers have a key precept, it is justice. Thrasymachus pulls back the curtain, or pulls the wool from Socrates's eyes, to reveal that what is really going on is that the unjust take advantage of the just. The irony that Thrasymachus reveals is how what seems to be a virtue, a positive quality, is actually detrimental to those who possess it in the greatest abundance: the vast, obedient, and abused masses.

The excerpts given below are haunted by those sheep. Socrates's entire discussion of justice can be seen as an attempt to refute several aspects of Thrasymachus's accusations. Thrasymachus proposes that justice is relative, that what determines whether something is just or unjust is the degree to which it serves the powerful. Socrates puts forward that justice exists independent of the self-interests of the powerful. Where Thrasymachus sees what passes for justice as a means of oppression, Socrates views justice as the essential healthiness or right relation of the state and of individuals in the state. Socrates also refutes Thrasymachus's idea that the unjust are better off than the just.

If the dramatic contest at the center of Plato's *Republic* is over the nature of justice, then modern readers may be a bit puzzled by Socrates's approach. Socrates does not refute Thrasymachus directly, but instead engages in a discussion wherein he has the truth speak for itself. Socrates believes that people have knowledge within them, and that knowledge just needs to be coaxed out through thoughtful discussions. The philosopher's job is to act as a sort of attendant or midwife who helps along in the painful process of giving birth to truth. So Socrates's approach is to ask questions in such a way that the true nature of justice emerges. The questions begin with an effort to come to a consensus view of an ideal community or state. Everyone can agree on what a good society should look like and how it should function. But partway into this discussion, one of the speakers interjects extras, superfluous additions to Socrates's utopia. Whether it is the extras, the frills, that cause conflicts, or just the maintenance

1. Plato, *The Republic*, 609.

of the state, is unclear, but what we find is that such a state needs protection. That protection comes in the form of an elite class of guardians. When Socrates describes these guardians, we get our first glimpse of four key qualities or classical virtues. Guardians must be quick to see, must know how to use the tools of their job, and must be able to discern friends from enemies. Guardians must be wise. They must also show valor and strength in the face of danger, which is courage. A good guardian is "full of spirit" or passion, but that passion must be controlled, must be deployed within proper constraints. A guardian needs both a "great spirit" and a "gentle nature," and the proper balance of these traits is temperance. Such a guardian will bring all of these qualities to bear in the job that must be done, and in properly doing that job, eschewing all others, the guardian is just.

The concept of justice in *The Republic* is broader than we might expect, because the Greek word commonly translated as "justice" has a larger meaning. The Greek word for justice, *dikaiosynē* or *dikaiosunē*, can also be translated "doing right," "righteousness," "right standing," or "right behavior," as well as by words such as "fairness" and "morality." In order to develop this essential rightness in guardians, Socrates goes into a lengthy discussion about education in his ideal state. Each guardian must develop as a "great spirit," with training that would include physical strength through gymnastics as well music and literature to train the mind. Socrates is very proscriptive about the types of music and the content of the literature taught to the guardians. Strict censorship in the ideal state ensures that while the imagination is engaged, through somewhat fanciful and false stories, the mind is not corrupted by fundamentally flawed ideas about the gods. Socrates places such an emphasis on this because humans take their moral cues from the behavior of the gods and should not get the wrong cues.

The ideal state Socrates depicts provides a framework and an illustration of the four essential qualities, for the four most fundamental traits of fully functioning communities and individuals. The state is wise in its discernment of friends and enemies and in its understanding of what encourages and hinders its well-being. The state is courageous and strong in defending itself from others and in defending its principles against false ideas, ignorance, and corruption. What this community also shows is a harmony among all of its parts, the sense of control and restraint that is temperance. Here the lower drives or desires are kept in check by the higher goals and faculties. True justice in the state is in people doing what is right or proper to them, in doing their job well, and in not meddling in what is not proper to them. The state does not have busybodies sticking their noses where they do not belong, nor does it have people taking what is not rightfully theirs. And this proper standing of each individual with relation to the state corresponds to a similar rightness within each individual. Citizens do not have conflicts within themselves between competing interests or desires, since such an internal civil war would indicate injustice and a lack of proper self-discipline or temperance. What Socrates describes is a perfectly harmonious integration of desires and abilities born of justice, temperance, courage, and wisdom.

Plato's *Republic* demonstrates the close connection between virtue, theology, art, and education. As I mentioned above, the work calls for social control of the arts so that they inculcate the proper views of the gods and inspire correct behavior. The artistic representation of the virtues and vices is almost always tied to larger views of reality and behavior, to philosophy, religion, and psychology. What *The Republic* also shares with other works is the affirmation of a political connection between virtue and vice, specifically the idea that an elite group with a special endowment of virtue should be exemplars, teachers, and enforcers of virtue for the entire community. That endowment comes from the pure nature of the elites augmented by their specific training or nurture. These elite form a sort of moral police and secular priesthood. Such an idea may make modern readers uncomfortable. Where Plato sees the noble protection of nurturing guardians, we may hear the buzz of sheers and the bleating of sheep.

From Book II (371e–380c)[2]

And now, Adeimantus, is our State matured and perfected?

I think so.

Where, then, is justice, and where is injustice, and in what part of the State did they spring up?

Probably in the dealings of these citizens with one another. I cannot imagine that they are more likely to be found anywhere else.

I dare say that you are right in your suggestion, I said; we had better think the matter out, and not shrink from the enquiry. Let us then consider, first of all, what will be their way of life, now that we have thus established them. Will they not produce corn, and wine, and clothes, and shoes, and build houses for themselves? And when they are housed, they will work, in summer, commonly, stripped and barefoot, but in winter substantially clothed and shod. They will feed on barley-meal and flour of wheat, baking and kneading them, making noble cakes and loaves; these they will serve up on a mat of reeds or on clean leaves, themselves reclining the while upon beds strewn with yew or myrtle. And they and their children will feast, drinking of the wine which they have made, wearing garlands on their heads, and hymning the praises of the gods, in happy converse with one another. And they will take care that their families do not exceed their means; having an eye to poverty or war.

But, said Glaucon, interposing, you have not given them a relish to their meal.

True, I replied, I had forgotten; of course they must have a relish-salt, and olives, and cheese, and they will boil roots and herbs such as country people prepare; for a dessert we shall give them figs, and peas, and beans; and they will roast myrtle-berries

2. From Plato, *The Republic*, in *The Dialogues of Plato*, vol. 1, trans. Benjamin Jowett (2 vols., New York: Random House, 1937), 635–44, 690–99, 705–9.

and acorns at the fire, drinking in moderation. And with such a diet they may be expected to live in peace and health to a good old age, and bequeath a similar life to their children after them.

Yes, Socrates, he said, and if you were providing for a city of pigs, how else would you feed the beasts?

But what would you have, Glaucon? I replied.

Why, he said, you should give them the ordinary conveniences of life. People who are to be comfortable are accustomed to lie on sofas, and dine off tables, and they should have sauces and sweets in the modern style.

Yes, I said, now I understand: the question which you would have me consider is, not only how a State, but how a luxurious State is created; and possibly there is no harm in this, for in such a State we shall be more likely to see how justice and injustice originate. In my opinion the true and healthy constitution of the State is the one which I have described. But if you wish also to see a State at fever-heat, I have no objection. For I suspect that many will not be satisfied with the simpler way of life. They will be for adding sofas, and tables, and other furniture; also dainties, and perfumes, and incense, and courtesans, and cakes, all these not of one sort only, but in every variety; we must go beyond the necessaries of which I was at first speaking, such as houses, and clothes, and shoes: the arts of the painter and the embroiderer will have to be set in motion, and gold and ivory and all sorts of materials must be procured.

True, he said.

Then we must enlarge our borders; for the original healthy State is no longer sufficient. Now will the city have to fill and swell with a multitude of callings which are not required by any natural want; such as the whole tribe of hunters and actors, of whom one large class have to do with forms and colors; another will be the votaries of music—poets and their attendant train of rhapsodists, players, dancers, contractors; also makers of divers kinds of articles, including women's dresses. And we shall want more servants. Will not tutors be also in request, and nurses wet and dry, tirewomen and barbers, as well as confectioners and cooks; and swineherds, too, who were not needed and therefore had no place in the former edition of our State, but are needed now? They must not be forgotten: and there will be animals of many other kinds, if people eat them.

Certainly.

And living in this way we shall have much greater need of physicians than before?

Much greater.

And the country which was enough to support the original inhabitants will be too small now, and not enough?

Quite true.

Then a slice of our neighbors' land will be wanted by us for pasture and tillage, and they will want a slice of ours, if, like ourselves, they exceed the limit of necessity, and give themselves up to the unlimited accumulation of wealth?

That, Socrates, will be inevitable.

And so we shall go to war, Glaucon. Shall we not?

Most certainly, he replied.

Then without determining as yet whether war does good or harm, thus much we may affirm, that now we have discovered war to be derived from causes which are also the causes of almost all the evils in States, private as well as public.

Undoubtedly.

And our State must once more enlarge; and this time the enlargement will be nothing short of a whole army, which will have to go out and fight with the invaders for all that we have, as well as for the things and persons whom we were describing above.

Why? he said; are they not capable of defending themselves?

No, I said; not if we were right in the principle which was acknowledged by all of us when we were framing the State: the principle, as you will remember, was that one man cannot practice many arts with success.

Very true, he said.

But is not war an art?

Certainly.

And an art requiring as much attention as shoemaking?

Quite true.

And the shoemaker was not allowed by us to be a husbandman, or a weaver, a builder—in order that we might have our shoes well made; but to him and to every other worker was assigned one work for which he was by nature fitted, and at that he was to continue working all his life long and at no other; he was not to let opportunities slip, and then he would become a good workman. Now nothing can be more important than that the work of a soldier should be well done. But is war an art so easily acquired that a man may be a warrior who is also a husbandman, or shoemaker, or other artisan; although no one in the world would be a good dice or draught player who merely took up the game as a recreation, and had not from his earliest years devoted himself to this and nothing else? No tools will make a man a skilled workman, or master of defense, nor be of any use to him who has not learned how to handle them, and has never bestowed any attention upon them. How then will he who takes up a shield or other implement of war become a good fighter all in a day, whether with heavy-armed or any other kind of troops?

Yes, he said, the tools which would teach men their own use would be beyond price.

And the higher the duties of the guardian, I said, the more time, and skill, and art, and application will be needed by him?

No doubt, he replied.

Will he not also require natural aptitude for his calling?

Certainly.

Then it will be our duty to select, if we can, natures which are fitted for the task of guarding the city?

It will.

And the selection will be no easy matter, I said; but we must be brave and do our best.

We must.

Is not the noble youth very like a well-bred dog in respect of guarding and watching?

What do you mean?

I mean that both of them ought to be quick to see, and swift to overtake the enemy when they see him; and strong too if, when they have caught him, they have to fight with him.

All these qualities, he replied, will certainly be required by them.

Well, and your guardian must be brave if he is to fight well?

Certainly.

And is he likely to be brave who has no spirit, whether horse or dog or any other animal? Have you never observed how invincible and unconquerable is spirit and how the presence of it makes the soul of any creature to be absolutely fearless and indomitable?

I have.

Then now we have a clear notion of the bodily qualities which are required in the guardian.

True.

And also of the mental ones; his soul is to be full of spirit?

Yes.

But are not these spirited natures apt to be savage with one another, and with everybody else?

A difficulty by no means easy to overcome, he replied.

Whereas, I said, they ought to be dangerous to their enemies, and gentle to their friends; if not, they will destroy themselves without waiting for their enemies to destroy them.

True, he said.

What is to be done then? I said; how shall we find a gentle nature which has also a great spirit, for the one is the contradiction of the other?

True.

He will not be a good guardian who is wanting in either of these two qualities; and yet the combination of them appears to be impossible; and hence we must infer that to be a good guardian is impossible.

I am afraid that what you say is true, he replied.

Here feeling perplexed I began to think over what had preceded. My friend, I said, no wonder that we are in a perplexity; for we have lost sight of the image which we had before us.

What do you mean? he said.

I mean to say that there do exist natures gifted with those opposite qualities.

And where do you find them?

Many animals, I replied, furnish examples of them; our friend the dog is a very good one: you know that well-bred dogs are perfectly gentle to their familiars and acquaintances, and the reverse to strangers.

Yes, I know.

Then there is nothing impossible or out of the order of nature in our finding a guardian who has a similar combination of qualities?

Certainly not.

Would not he who is fitted to be a guardian, besides the spirited nature, need to have the qualities of a philosopher?

I do not apprehend your meaning.

The trait of which I am speaking, I replied, may be also seen in the dog, and is remarkable in the animal.

What trait?

Why, a dog, whenever he sees a stranger, is angry; when an acquaintance, he welcomes him, although the one has never done him any harm, nor the other any good. Did this never strike you as curious?

The matter never struck me before; but I quite recognize the truth of your remark.

And surely this instinct of the dog is very charming;—your dog is a true philosopher.

Why?

Why, because he distinguishes the face of a friend and of an enemy only by the criterion of knowing and not knowing. And must not an animal be a lover of learning who determines what he likes and dislikes by the test of knowledge and ignorance?

Most assuredly.

And is not the love of learning the love of wisdom, which is philosophy?

They are the same, he replied.

And may we not say confidently of man also, that he who is likely to be gentle to his friends and acquaintances, must by nature be a lover of wisdom and knowledge?

That we may safely affirm.

Then he who is to be a really good and noble guardian of the State will require to unite in himself philosophy and spirit and swiftness and strength?

Undoubtedly.

Then we have found the desired natures; and now that we have found them, how are they to be reared and educated? Is not this enquiry which may be expected to throw light on the greater enquiry which is our final end—How do justice and injustice grow up in States? for we do not want either to omit what is to the point or to draw out the argument to an inconvenient length.

Adeimantus thought that the enquiry would be of great service to us.

Then, I said, my dear friend, the task must not be given up, even if somewhat long.

Certainly not.

Come then, and let us pass a leisure hour in story-telling, and our story shall be the education of our heroes.

By all means.

And what shall be their education? Can we find a better than the traditional sort?—and this has two divisions, gymnastics for the body, and music for the soul.

True.

Shall we begin education with music, and go on to gymnastics afterwards?

By all means.

And when you speak of music, do you include literature or not?

I do.

And literature may be either true or false?

Yes.

And the young should be trained in both kinds, and we begin with the false?

I do not understand your meaning, he said.

You know, I said, that we begin by telling children stories which, though not wholly destitute of truth, are in the main fictitious; and these stories are told them when they are not of an age to learn gymnastics.

Very true.

That was my meaning when I said that we must teach music before gymnastics.

Quite right, he said.

You know also that the beginning is the most important part of any work, especially in the case of a young and tender thing; for that is the time at which the character is being formed and the desired impression is more readily taken.

Quite true.

And shall we just carelessly allow children to hear any casual tales which may be devised by casual persons, and to receive into their minds ideas for the most part the very opposite of those which we should wish them to have when they are grown up?

We cannot.

Then the first thing will be to establish a censorship of the writers of fiction, and let the censors receive any tale of fiction which is good, and reject the bad; and we will desire mothers and nurses to tell their children the authorized ones only. Let them fashion the mind with such tales, even more fondly than they mould the body with their hands; but most of those which are now in use must be discarded.

Of what tales are you speaking? he said.

You may find a model of the lesser in the greater, I said; for they are necessarily of the same type, and there is the same spirit in both of them.

Very likely, he replied; but I do not as yet know what you would term the greater.

Those, I said, which are narrated by Homer and Hesiod, and the rest of the poets, who have ever been the great story-tellers of mankind.

But which stories do you mean, he said; and what fault do you find with them?

A fault which is most serious, I said; the fault of telling a lie, and, what is more, a bad lie.

But when is this fault committed?

Whenever an erroneous representation is made of the nature of gods and heroes,—as when a painter paints a portrait not having the shadow of a likeness to the original.

Yes, he said, that sort of thing is certainly very blamable; but what are the stories which you mean?

First of all, I said, there was that greatest of all lies, in high places, which the poet told about Uranus, and which was a bad lie too,—I mean what Hesiod says that Uranus did, and how Cronus retaliated on him. The doings of Cronus, and the sufferings which in turn his son inflicted upon him, even if they were true, ought certainly not to be lightly told to young and thoughtless persons; if possible, they had better be buried in silence. But if there is an absolute necessity for their mention, a chosen few might hear them in a mystery, and they should sacrifice not a common [Eleusinian] pig, but some huge and unprocurable victim; and then the number of the hearers will be very few indeed.

Why, yes, said he, those stories are extremely objectionable.

Yes, Adeimantus, they are stories not to be repeated in our State; the young man should not be told that in committing the worst of crimes he is far from doing anything outrageous; and that even if he chastises his father when he does wrong, in whatever manner, he will only be following the example of the first and greatest among the gods.

I entirely agree with you, he said; in my opinion those stories are quite unfit to be repeated.

Neither, if we mean our future guardians to regard the habit of quarrelling among themselves as of all things the basest, should any word be said to them of the wars in heaven, and of the plots and fightings of the gods against one another, for they are not true. No, we shall never mention the battles of the giants, or let them be embroidered on garments; and we shall be silent about the innumerable other quarrels of gods and heroes with their friends and relatives. If they would only believe us we would tell them that quarrelling is unholy, and that never up to this time has there been any quarrel between citizens; this is what old men and old women should begin by telling children; and when they grow up, the poets also should be told to compose for them in a similar spirit. But the narrative of Hephaestus binding Here his mother, or how on another occasion Zeus sent him flying for taking her part when she was being beaten, and all the battles of the gods in Homer—these tales must not be admitted into our State, whether they are supposed to have an allegorical meaning or not. For a young person cannot judge what is allegorical and what is literal; anything that he receives into his mind at that age is likely to become indelible and unalterable; and therefore it is most important that the tales which the young first hear should be models of virtuous thoughts.

There you are right, he replied; but if any one asks where are such models to be found and of what tales are you speaking—how shall we answer him?

I said to him, You and I, Adeimantus, at this moment are not poets, but founders of a State: now the founders of a State ought to know the general forms in which poets should cast their tales, and the limits which must be observed by them, but to make the tales is not their business.

Very true, he said; but what are these forms of theology which you mean?

Something of this kind, I replied:—God is always to be represented as he truly is, whatever be the sort of poetry, epic, lyric or tragic, in which the representation is given.

Right.

And is he not truly good? and must he not be represented as such?

Certainly.

And no good thing is hurtful?

No, indeed.

And that which is not hurtful hurts not?

Certainly not.

And that which hurts not does no evil?

No.

And can that which does no evil be a cause of evil?

Impossible.

And the good is advantageous?

Yes.

And therefore the cause of well-being?

Yes.

It follows therefore that the good is not the cause of all things, but of the good only?

Assuredly.

Then God, if he be good, is not the author of all things, as the many assert, but he is the cause of a few things only, and not of most things that occur to men. For few are the goods of human life, and many are the evils, and the good is to be attributed to God alone; of the evils the causes are to be sought elsewhere, and not in him.

That appears to me to be most true, he said.

Then we must not listen to Homer or to any other poet who is guilty of the folly of saying that two casks "Lie at the threshold of Zeus, full of lots, one of good, the other of evil lots," and that he to whom Zeus gives a mixture of the two "Sometimes meets with evil fortune, at other times with good;" but that he to whom is given the cup of unmingled ill, "Him wild hunger drives o'er the beauteous earth."

And again—"Zeus, who is the dispenser of good and evil to us." And if any one asserts that the violation of oaths and treaties, which was really the work of Pandarus, was brought about by Athene and Zeus, or that the strife and contention of the gods was instigated by Themis and Zeus, he shall not have our approval; neither will we allow our young men to hear the words of Aeschylus, that "God plants guilt among men when he desires utterly to destroy a house." And if a poet writes of the sufferings of Niobe—the subject of the tragedy in which these iambic verses occur—or of the house of Pelops, or of the Trojan War or on any similar theme, either we must not permit him to say that these are the works of God, or if they are of God, he must devise some explanation of them such as we are seeking; he must say that God did what was just and right, and they were the better for being punished; but that those who are punished are miserable, and that God is the author of their misery—the poet is not to be permitted to say; though he may say that the wicked are miserable because they require to be punished, and are benefited by receiving punishment from God; but that God being good is the author of evil to any one is to be strenuously denied, and not to be said or sung or heard in verse or prose by any one whether old or young in any well-ordered commonwealth. Such a fiction is suicidal, ruinous, impious.

I agree with you, he replied, and am ready to give my assent to the law.

From Book IV (427d–434d)

But where, amid all this, is justice? Son of Ariston, tell me where. Now that our city has been made habitable, light a candle and search, and get your brother and Polemarchus and the rest of our friends to help, and let us see where in it we can discover justice and where injustice, and in what they differ from one another, and which of them the man who would be happy should have for his portion, whether seen or unseen by gods and men.

Nonsense, said Glaucon: did you not promise to search yourself, saying that for you not to help justice in her need would be an impiety?

I do not deny that I said so, and as you remind me, I will be as good as my word; but you must join.

We will, he replied.

Well, then, I hope to make the discovery in this way: I mean to begin with the assumption that our State, if rightly ordered, is perfect.

That is most certain.

And being perfect, is therefore wise and valiant and temperate and just.

That is likewise clear.

And whichever of these qualities we find in the State, the one which is not found will be the residue?

Very good.

If there were four things, and we were searching for one of them, wherever it might be, the one sought for might be known to us from the first, and there would be no further trouble; or we might know the other three first, and then the fourth would clearly be the one left.

Very true, he said.

And is not a similar method to be pursued about the virtues, which are also four in number?

Clearly.

First among the virtues found in the State, wisdom comes into view, and in this I detect a certain peculiarity.

What is that?

The State which we have been describing is said to be wise as being good in counsel?

Very true.

And good counsel is clearly a kind of knowledge, for not by ignorance, but by knowledge, do men counsel well?

Clearly.

And the kinds of knowledge in a State are many and diverse?

Of course.

There is the knowledge of the carpenter; but is that the sort of knowledge which gives a city the title of wise and good in counsel?

Certainly not; that would only give a city the reputation of skill in carpentering.

Then a city is not to be called wise because possessing a knowledge which counsels for the best about wooden implements?

Certainly not.

Nor by reason of a knowledge which advises about brazen pots, I said, nor as possessing any other similar knowledge?

Not by reason of any of them, he said.

Nor yet by reason of a knowledge which cultivates the earth; that would give the city the name of agricultural?

Yes.

Well, I said, and is there any knowledge in our recently-founded State among any of the citizens which advises, not about any particular thing in the State, but about the whole, and considers how a State can best deal with itself and with other States?

There certainly is.

And what is this knowledge, and among whom is it found? I asked.

It is the knowledge of the guardians, he replied, and is found among those whom we were just now describing as perfect guardians.

And what is the name which the city derives from the possession of this sort of knowledge?

The name of good in counsel and truly wise.

And will there be in our city more of these true guardians or more smiths?

The smiths, he replied, will be far more numerous.

Will not the guardians be the smallest of all the classes who receive a name from the profession of some kind of knowledge?

Much the smallest.

And so by reason of the smallest part or class, and of the knowledge which resides in this presiding and ruling part of itself, the whole State, being thus constituted according to nature, will be wise; and this, which has the only knowledge worthy to be called wisdom, has been ordained by nature to be of all classes the least.

Most true.

Thus, then, I said, the nature and place in the State of one of the four virtues has somehow or other been discovered.

And, in my humble opinion, very satisfactorily discovered, he replied.

Again, I said, there is no difficulty in seeing the nature of courage; and in what part that quality resides which gives the name of courageous to the State.

How do you mean?

Why, I said, every one who calls any State courageous or cowardly, will be thinking of the part which fights and goes out to war on the State's behalf.

No one, he replied, would ever think of any other.

The rest of the citizens may be courageous or may be cowardly but their courage or cowardice will not, as I conceive, have the effect of making the city either the one or the other.

Certainly not.

The city will be courageous in virtue of a portion of herself which preserves under all circumstances that opinion about the nature of things to be feared and not to be feared in which our legislator educated them; and this is what you term courage.

I should like to hear what you are saying once more, for I do not think that I perfectly understand you.

I mean that courage is a kind of salvation.

Salvation of what?

Of the opinion respecting things to be feared, what they are and of what nature, which the law implants through education; and I mean by the words 'under all circumstances' to intimate that in pleasure or in pain, or under the influence of desire or fear, a man preserves, and does not lose this opinion. Shall I give you an illustration?

If you please.

You know, I said, that dyers, when they want to dye wool for making the true sea-purple, begin by selecting their white color first; this they prepare and dress with much care and pains, in order that the white ground may take the purple hue in full perfection.

The dyeing then proceeds; and whatever is dyed in this manner becomes a fast color, and no washing either with lyes or without them can take away the bloom. But, when the ground has not been duly prepared, you will have noticed how poor is the look either of purple or of any other color.

Yes, he said; I know that they have a washed-out and ridiculous appearance.

Then now, I said, you will understand what our object was in selecting our soldiers, and educating them in music and gymnastics; we were contriving influences which would prepare them to take the dye of the laws in perfection, and the color of their opinion about dangers and of every other opinion was to be indelibly fixed by their nurture and training, not to be washed away by such potent lyes as pleasure—mightier agent far in washing the soul than any soda or lye; or by sorrow, fear, and desire, the mightiest of all other solvents. And this sort of universal saving power of true opinion in conformity with law about real and false dangers I call and maintain to be courage, unless you disagree.

But I agree, he replied; for I suppose that you mean to exclude mere uninstructed courage, such as that of a wild beast or of a slave—this, in your opinion, is not the courage which the law ordains, and ought to have another name.

Most certainly.

Then I may infer courage to be such as you describe?

Why, yes, said I, you may, and if you add the words 'of a citizen,' you will not be far wrong;—hereafter, if you like, we will carry the examination further, but at present we are seeking not for courage but justice; and for the purpose of our enquiry we have said enough.

You are right, he replied.

Two virtues remain to be discovered in the State—first temperance, and then justice which is the end of our search.

Very true.

Now, can we find justice without troubling ourselves about temperance?

I do not know how that can be accomplished, he said, nor do I desire that justice should be brought to light and temperance lost sight of; and therefore I wish that you would do me the favor of considering temperance first.

Certainly, I replied, I should not be justified in refusing your request.

Then consider, he said.

Yes, I replied; I will; and as far as I can at present see, the virtue of temperance has more of the nature of harmony and symphony than the preceding.

How so? he asked.

Temperance, I replied, is the ordering or controlling of certain pleasures and desires; this is curiously enough implied in the saying of 'a man being his own master;' and other traces of the same notion may be found in language.

No doubt, he said.

There is something ridiculous in the expression 'master of himself;' for the master is also the servant and the servant the master; and in all these modes of speaking the same person is denoted.

Certainly.

The meaning is, I believe, that in the human soul there is a better and also a worse principle; and when the better has the worse under control, then a man is said to be master of himself; and this is a term of praise: but when, owing to evil education or association, the better principle, which is also the smaller, is overwhelmed by the greater mass of the worse—in this case he is blamed and is called the slave of self and unprincipled.

Yes, there is reason in that.

And now, I said, look at our newly-created State, and there you will find one of these two conditions realized; for the State, as you will acknowledge, may be justly called master of itself, if the words 'temperance' and 'self-mastery' truly express the rule of the better part over the worse.

Yes, he said, I see that what you say is true.

Let me further note that the manifold and complex pleasures and desires and pains are generally found in children and women and servants, and in the freemen so called who are of the lowest and more numerous class.

Certainly, he said.

Whereas the simple and moderate desires which follow reason, and are under the guidance of mind and true opinion, are to be found only in a few, and those the best born and best educated.

Very true.

These two, as you may perceive, have a place in our State; and the meaner desires of the many are held down by the virtuous desire and wisdom of the few.

That I perceive, he said.

Then if there be any city which may be described as master of its own pleasures and desires, and master of itself, ours may claim such a designation?

Certainly, he replied.

It may also be called temperate, and for the same reasons?

Yes.

And if there be any State in which rulers and subjects will be agreed as to the question who are to rule, that again will be our State?

Undoubtedly.

And the citizens being thus agreed among themselves, in which class will temperance be found—in the rulers or in the subjects?

In both, as I should imagine, he replied.

Do you observe that we were not far wrong in our guess that temperance was a sort of harmony?

Why so?

Why, because temperance is unlike courage and wisdom, each of which resides in a part only, the one making the State wise and the other valiant; not so temperance, which extends to the whole, and runs through all the notes of the scale, and produces a harmony of the weaker and the stronger and the middle class, whether you suppose them to be stronger or weaker in wisdom or power or numbers or wealth, or anything else. Most truly then may we deem temperance to be the agreement of the naturally superior and inferior, as to the right to rule of either, both in states and individuals.

I entirely agree with you.

And so, I said, we may consider three out of the four virtues to have been discovered in our State. The last of those qualities which make a state virtuous must be justice, if we only knew what that was.

The inference is obvious.

The time then has arrived, Glaucon, when, like huntsmen, we should surround the cover, and look sharp that justice does not steal away, and pass out of sight and escape us; for beyond a doubt she is somewhere in this country: watch therefore and strive to catch a sight of her, and if you see her first, let me know.

Would that I could! but you should regard me rather as a follower who has just eyes enough to see what you show him—that is about as much as I am good for.

Offer up a prayer with me and follow.

I will, but you must show me the way.

Here is no path, I said, and the wood is dark and perplexing; still we must push on.

Let us push on.

Here I saw something: Halloo! I said, I begin to perceive a track, and I believe that the quarry will not escape.

Good news, he said.

Truly, I said, we are stupid fellows.

Why so?

Why, my good sir, at the beginning of our enquiry, ages ago, there was justice tumbling out at our feet, and we never saw her; nothing could be more ridiculous. Like people who go about looking for what they have in their hands—that was the way with us—we looked not at what we were seeking, but at what was far off in the distance; and therefore, I suppose, we missed her.

What do you mean?

I mean to say that in reality for a long time past we have been talking of justice, and have failed to recognize her.

I grow impatient at the length of your exordium.

Well then, tell me, I said, whether I am right or not: You remember the original principle which we were always laying down at the foundation of the State, that one man should practise one thing only, the thing to which his nature was best adapted;—now justice is this principle or a part of it.

Yes, we often said that one man should do one thing only.

Further, we affirmed that justice was doing one's own business, and not being a busybody; we said so again and again, and many others have said the same to us.

Yes, we said so.

Then to do one's own business in a certain way may be assumed to be justice. Can you tell me whence I derive this inference?

I cannot, but I should like to be told.

Because I think that this is the only virtue which remains in the State when the other virtues of temperance and courage and wisdom are abstracted; and, that this is the ultimate cause and condition of the existence of all of them, and while remaining in them is also their preservative; and we were saying that if the three were discovered by us, justice would be the fourth or remaining one.

That follows of necessity.

If we are asked to determine which of these four qualities by its presence contributes most to the excellence of the State, whether the agreement of rulers and subjects, or the preservation in the soldiers of the opinion which the law ordains about the true nature of dangers, or wisdom and watchfulness in the rulers, or whether this other which I am mentioning, and which is found in children and women, slave and freeman, artisan, ruler, subject,—the quality, I mean, of every one doing his own work, and not being a busybody, would claim the palm—the question is not so easily answered.

Certainly, he replied, there would be a difficulty in saying which.

Then the power of each individual in the State to do his own work appears to compete with the other political virtues, wisdom, temperance, courage.

Yes, he said.

And the virtue which enters into this competition is justice?

Exactly.

Let us look at the question from another point of view:

Are not the rulers in a State those to whom you would entrust the office of determining suits at law?

Certainly.

And are suits decided on any other ground but that a man may neither take what is another's, nor be deprived of what is his own?

Yes; that is their principle.

Which is a just principle?

Yes.

Then on this view also justice will be admitted to be the having and doing what is a man's own, and belongs to him?

Very true.

Think, now, and say whether you agree with me or not. Suppose a carpenter to be doing the business of a cobbler, or a cobbler of a carpenter; and suppose them to exchange their implements or their duties, or the same person to be doing the work of both, or whatever be the change; do you think that any great harm would result to the State?

Not much.

But when the cobbler or any other man whom nature designed to be a trader, having his heart lifted up by wealth or strength or the number of his followers, or any like advantage, attempts to force his way into the class of warriors, or a warrior into that of legislators and guardians, for which he is unfitted, and either to take the implements or the duties of the other; or when one man is trader, legislator, and warrior all in one, then I think you will agree with me in saying that this interchange and this meddling of one with another is the ruin of the State.

Most true.

Seeing then, I said, that there are three distinct classes, any meddling of one with another, or the change of one into another, is the greatest harm to the State, and may be most justly termed evil-doing?

Precisely.

And the greatest degree of evil-doing to one's own city would be termed by you injustice?

Certainly.

This then is injustice; and on the other hand when the trader, the auxiliary, and the guardian each do their own business, that is justice, and will make the city just.

I agree with you.

From Book IV (441d–445b)

And the individual will be acknowledged by us to be just in the same way in which the State is just?

That follows of course.

We cannot but remember that the justice of the State consisted in each of the three classes doing the work of its own class?

We are not very likely to have forgotten, he said.

We must recollect that the individual in whom the several qualities of his nature do their own work will be just, and will do his own work?

Yes, he said, we must remember that too.

And ought not the rational principle, which is wise, and has the care of the whole soul, to rule, and the passionate or spirited principle to be the subject and ally?

Certainly.

And, as we were saying, the united influence of music and gymnastics will bring them into accord, nerving and sustaining the reason with noble words and lessons, and moderating and soothing and civilizing the wildness of passion by harmony and rhythm?

Quite true, he said.

And these two, thus nurtured and educated, and having learned truly to know their own functions, will rule over the concupiscent, which in each of us is the largest part of the soul and by nature most insatiable of gain; over this they will keep guard, lest, waxing great and strong with the fulness of bodily pleasures, as they are termed, the concupiscent soul, no longer confined to her own sphere, should attempt to enslave and rule those who are not her natural-born subjects, and overturn the whole life of man?

Very true, he said.

Both together will they not be the best defenders of the whole soul and the whole body against attacks from without; the one counselling, and the other fighting under his leader, and courageously executing his commands and counsels?

True.

And he is to be deemed courageous whose spirit retains in pleasure and in pain the commands of reason about what he ought or ought not to fear?

Right, he replied.

And him we call wise who has in him that little part which rules, and which proclaims these commands; that part too being supposed to have a knowledge of what is for the interest of each of the three parts and of the whole?

Assuredly.

And would you not say that he is temperate who has these same elements in friendly harmony, in whom the one ruling principle of reason, and the two subject ones of spirit and desire are equally agreed that reason ought to rule, and do not rebel?

Certainly, he said, that is the true account of temperance whether in the State or individual.

And surely, I said, we have explained again and again how and by virtue of what quality a man will be just.

That is very certain.

And is justice dimmer in the individual, and is her form different, or is she the same which we found her to be in the State?

There is no difference in my opinion, he said.

Because, if any doubt is still lingering in our minds, a few commonplace instances will satisfy us of the truth of what I am saying.

What sort of instances do you mean?

If the case is put to us, must we not admit that the just State, or the man who is trained in the principles of such a State, will be less likely than the unjust to make away with a deposit of gold or silver? Would any one deny this?

No one, he replied.

Will the just man or citizen ever be guilty of sacrilege or theft, or treachery either to his friends or to his country?

Never.

Neither will he ever break faith where there have been oaths or agreements?

Impossible.

No one will be less likely to commit adultery, or to dishonor his father and mother, or to fail in his religious duties?

No one.

And the reason is that each part of him is doing its own business, whether in ruling or being ruled?

Exactly so.

Are you satisfied then that the quality which makes such men and such states is justice, or do you hope to discover some other?

Not I, indeed.

Then our dream has been realized; and the suspicion which we entertained at the beginning of our work of construction, that some divine power must have conducted us to a primary form of justice, has now been verified?

Yes, certainly.

And the division of labor which required the carpenter and the shoemaker and the rest of the citizens to be doing each his own business, and not another's, was a shadow of justice, and for that reason it was of use?

Clearly.

But in reality justice was such as we were describing, being concerned, however, not with the outward man, but with the inward, which is the true self and concernment of man: for the just man does not permit the several elements within him to interfere with one another, or any of them to do the work of others—he sets in order his own inner life, and is his own master and his own law, and at peace with himself; and when he has bound together the three principles within him, which may be compared to the higher, lower, and middle notes of the scale, and the intermediate intervals—when he has bound all these together, and is no longer many, but has become one entirely temperate and perfectly adjusted nature, then he proceeds to act, if he has to act, whether in a matter of property, or in the treatment of the body, or in some affair of politics or private business; always thinking and calling that which preserves and co-operates with this harmonious condition, just and good action, and the knowledge which presides over it, wisdom, and that which at any time impairs this condition, he will call unjust action, and the opinion which presides over it ignorance.

You have said the exact truth, Socrates.

Very good; and if we were to affirm that we had discovered the just man and the just State, and the nature of justice in each of them, we should not be telling a falsehood?

Most certainly not.

May we say so, then?

Let us say so.

And now, I said, injustice has to be considered.

Clearly.

Must not injustice be a strife which arises among the three principles—a meddlesomeness, and interference, and rising up of a part of the soul against the whole, an assertion of unlawful authority, which is made by a rebellious subject against a true prince, of whom he is the natural vassal—what is all this confusion and delusion but injustice, and intemperance and cowardice and ignorance, and every form of vice?

Exactly so.

And if the nature of justice and injustice be known, then the meaning of acting unjustly and being unjust, or, again, of acting justly, will also be perfectly clear?

What do you mean? he said.

Why, I said, they are like disease and health; being in the soul just what disease and health are in the body.

How so? he said.

Why, I said, that which is healthy causes health, and that which is unhealthy causes disease.

Yes.

And just actions cause justice, and unjust actions cause injustice?

That is certain.

And the creation of health is the institution of a natural order and government of one by another in the parts of the body; and the creation of disease is the production of a state of things at variance with this natural order?

True.

And is not the creation of justice the institution of a natural order and government of one by another in the parts of the soul, and the creation of injustice the production of a state of things at variance with the natural order?

Exactly so, he said.

Then virtue is the health and beauty and well-being of the soul, and vice the disease and weakness and deformity of the same?

True.

And do not good practices lead to virtue, and evil practices to vice?

Assuredly.

Still our old question of the comparative advantage of justice and injustice has not been answered: Which is the more profitable, to be just and act justly and practise virtue, whether seen or unseen of gods and men, or to be unjust and act unjustly, if only unpunished and unreformed?

In my judgment, Socrates, the question has now become ridiculous. We know that, when the bodily constitution is gone, life is no longer endurable, though pampered with all kinds of meats and drinks, and having all wealth and all power; and shall we be told that when the very essence of the vital principle is undermined and corrupted, life is still worth having to a man, if only he be allowed to do whatever he likes with the single exception that he is not to acquire justice and virtue, or to escape from injustice and vice; assuming them both to be such as we have described?

Yes, I said, the question is, as you say, ridiculous.

ARISTOTLE'S *THE NICOMACHEAN ETHICS*

Introduction

At the end of *Star Wars*, Luke Skywalker must carefully maneuver his fighter through a sort of channel in the Death Star in order to fire the missiles that finally destroy it. Aristotle would have loved this climactic scene, as it could symbolize Aristotle's notion of virtue as the mean. Luke must fly close to the Death Star while not colliding with it and then must stay in the middle of the channel in ways similar to what characters must do in stories Aristotle himself would know: Odysseus must carefully maneuver between Scylla and Charybdis or even Daedalus's advises his son Icarus to fly neither too high nor too low. Aristotle would happily join in the applause of Luke's efforts, his excellence, and his virtue in the film's closing ceremonial scene.

What we now have as Aristotle's *Nicomachean Ethics* are probably the philosopher's lecture notes. These lectures were for wealthy younger men, and for that reason I have kept the gendered language in the excerpt. There are several points that Aristotle would want these young men to understand through his lecture. The first point is that happiness is the objective of life. Before those young men could turn to a companion and say, "well duh," Aristotle would help them understand the nature of that happiness. For Aristotle, happiness is associated with real satisfaction, or, to be more precise, happiness comes when one functions properly. The central question is what is one's proper function? Aristotle answers this question by using analogies and with reference to his view of human nature. Aristotle lists several occupations, including flute-player, sculptor, artist, carpenter, and tanner to show that all people who work in these occupations have a function. Even body parts and organs have specific functions. He then lists three faculties—growth, perception, and rational thought. Humans have all of these faculties, but some are higher, are more valuable, and are exclusive to humans. Even plants have a propensity to grow, and animals share with humans the ability to perceive. It is the rational faculty that makes humans unique and helps define their function. Aristotle concludes that real human happiness comes from functioning at the highest possible level by harmoniously using all of one's faculties.

The Greek word Aristotle uses for doing what is particular or what is a characteristic activity is *ergon*. But in order to really be happy, one must do these activities in the best way possible or with the highest level of excellence. The Greek word for "excellence" is also the word for "virtue," *arête*. Our current English usage still has a vestige of this when we extol the virtues of a fine meal or book. True human virtue means doing with excellence what is intrinsic to human function. For Aristotle, virtue is not a passion that you feel or a faculty that you can use; virtue is the condition of your character. Anyone can feel angry or momentarily unafraid just as anyone has the capacity for rational thought and action, but it is one's inherent disposition toward the right actions that makes one virtuous.

After he has set out how happiness comes from functioning at the highest level possible or with excellence, Aristotle elaborates on what that excellence is. What makes something excellent is that it is just the right amount—not too much or too little. Since virtue is just the right amount, there are actually two vices for each virtue, with one vice being an excess and the other being a deficiency. And each virtue or excellence has its own particular sphere.

This idea that virtue is the right amount, while there are two vices, one an excess and the other a deficiency, is clearer when we look at an example. One sphere is the area of fear and confidence. The virtue in this sphere is to feel them in the right amount and in the right way, and the word for that is *courage*. The vices on either extreme are (on the one hand) rashness, overconfidence, or excessive courage; and (on the other hand) cowardice, not enough courage. With all spheres there is a virtue that is the mean between two vices. Aristotle warns that the response of excellence to one situation may be easier for one person than another, so finding that proper mean can be more difficult depending upon the person and the sphere. The remainder of the excerpt given below from *The Nicomachean Ethics* elaborates on defining virtue and the mean with relation to bodily pleasure and pain. The right response in that sphere is temperance.

Aristotle's significant and lasting contribution to the Western notion of virtue and vice is his idea of virtue or excellence as the right amount or proper response in any given sphere of life. Aristotle believed that with proper training and by developing the proper habits, people could learn to avoid excesses and deficiencies, they could steer clear of the dangers of too much and too little, and they could find happiness in fulfilling the functions inherent to them. All it took was a little Aristotelian (or perhaps Jedi) training.

Book I, Chapters 5–6[3]

But leaving this subject for the present let us revert to the good of which we are in quest and consider what its nature may be. For it is clearly different in different actions or arts; it is one thing in medicine, another in strategy, and so on. What then is the good in each of these instances? It is presumably that for the sake of which all else is done. This in medicine is health, in strategy, victory, in domestic architecture, a house, and so on. But in every action and purpose it is the end, as it is for the sake of the end that people all do everything else. If then there is a certain end of all action, it will be this which is the practicable good, and if there are several such ends it will be these.

Our argument has arrived by a different path at the same conclusion as before, but we must endeavor to elucidate it still further. As it appears that there are more ends than one and some of these, e.g. wealth, flutes, and instruments generally, we desire as means to something else, it is evident that they are not all final ends. But the highest good is clearly something final. Hence if there is only one final end, this will be the object of which we are in search, and if there are more than one, it will be the most final of them. We speak of that which is sought after for its own sake as more final than that which is sought after as a means to something else; we speak of that which is never desired as a means to something else as more final than the things which are desired both in themselves and as means to something else; and we speak of a thing as absolutely final, if it is always desired in itself and never as a means to something else.

It seems that happiness preeminently answers to this description, as we always desire happiness for its own sake and never as a means to something else, whereas we desire honor, pleasure, intellect, and every virtue, partly for their own sakes (for we should desire them independently of what might result from them) but partly also as being means to happiness, because we suppose they will prove the instruments of happiness. Happiness, on the other hand, nobody desires for the sake of these things, nor indeed as a means to anything else at all.

We come to the same conclusion if we start from the consideration of self-sufficiency, if it may be assumed that the final good is self-sufficient. But when we speak of self-sufficiency, we do not mean that a person leads a solitary life all by himself, but that he has parents, children, wife, and friends, and fellow-citizens in general, as man is naturally a social being. But here it is necessary to prescribe some limits; for if the circle be extended so as to include parents, descendants, and friends' friends, it will go on indefinitely. Leaving this point, however, for future investigation, we define the

3. From Aristotle, *The Nicomachean Ethics of Aristotle*, trans. J. E. C. Welldon (London: Macmillan, 1930), 12–16, 34–6, 43–53,55–57. It should be noted that Welldon's translation uses gender-specific language. The impulse to change this language so that it fits a wider audience has been avoided. That decision was made to maintain Welldon's original and specific language and because it seems reasonable to assume that Aristotle assumed a male audience. For that reason, the narrowly gendered language, with all of its problems, has been retained.

self-sufficient as that which, taken by itself, makes life desirable, and wholly free from want, and this is our conception of happiness.

Again, we conceive happiness to be the most sublime of all things, and that not merely as one among other good things. If it were one among other good things, the addition of the smallest good would increase its desirability; for the accession makes a superiority of goods, and the greater of two goods is always the most desirable. It appears then that happiness is something final and self-sufficient, being the end of all action.

Perhaps, however, it seems a truth which is commonly admitted, that happiness is the supreme good, what is wanted is to define its nature a little more clearly. The best way of arriving at such a definition will probably be to ascertain the function of Man. For, as with a flute-player, a statuary, or any artisan, or in fact anybody who has a definite function and action, his goodness, or excellence seems to lie in his function, so it would seem to be with Man, if indeed he has a definite function. Can it be said then that, while a carpenter and a cobbler have definite functions and actions, Man, unlike them, is naturally functionless? The reasonable view is that, as the eye, the hand, the foot, and similarly each several parts of the body has a definite function, so Man may be regarded as having a definite function apart from all these. What then, can this function be? It is not life; for life is apparently something which humanity shares with the plants, and it is something peculiar to humanity that we are looking for. We must exclude therefore the life of nutrition and increase. There is next what may be called the life of sensation. But this too, is apparently shared by humanity with horses, cattle, and all other animals. There remains what I may call the practical life of the rational part of Man's being. But the rational part is twofold; it is rational partly in the sense of being obedient to reason, and partly in the sense of possessing reason and intelligence. The practical life too may be conceived of in two ways, either as a moral state, or as a moral activity; but we must understand by it the life of activity, as this seems to be the truer form of the conception.

The function of Man then is an activity of soul in accordance with reason, or not independently of reason. Again the functions of a person of a certain kind, and of such a person who is good of his kind e.g. of a harpist and a good harpist, are in our view generally the same, and this view is true of people of all kinds without exception, the superior excellence being only an addition to the function; for it is the function of a harpist to play the harp, and of a good harpist to play the harp well. This being so, if we define the function of Man as a kind of life, and this life as an activity of soul, or a course of action in conformity with reason, if the function of a good man is such activity or action of a good and noble kind, and if everything is successfully performed when it is performed in accordance with its proper excellence, it follows that the good of Man is an activity of soul in accordance with virtue or, if there are more virtues than one, in accordance with the best and most complete virtue. But it is necessary to add the words "in a complete life." For as one swallow or one day does not make a spring, so one day or a short time does not make a fortunate or happy person.

Book II, Chapter 1

Virtue or excellence being twofold, partly intellectual and partly moral, intellectual virtue is both originated and fostered mainly by teaching; it therefore demands experience and time. Moral virtue on the other hand is the outcome of habit, and accordingly its name is derived by a slight deflection of habit. From this fact it is clear that no moral virtue is implanted in us by nature; a law of nature cannot be altered by habituation. Thus, a stone naturally tends to fall downwards, and it cannot be habituated or trained to rise upwards, even if we were to habituate it by throwing it upwards ten thousand times; nor again can fire be trained to sink downwards, nor anything else that follows one natural law be habituated or trained to follow another. It is neither by nature then nor in defiance of nature that virtues are implanted in us. Nature gives us the capacity of receiving them, and that capacity is perfected by habit.

Again, if we take the various natural powers which belong to us, we first acquire the proper faculties and afterwards display the activities. It is clearly so with the senses. It was not by seeing frequently or hearing frequently that we acquired the senses of seeing or hearing; on the contrary it was because we possessed the senses that we made use of them, not by making use of them that we obtained them. But the virtues we acquire by first exercising them, as is the case with all the arts, for it is by doing what we ought to do when we have learnt the arts that we learn the arts themselves; we become, for example, builders by building and harpists by playing the harp. Similarly it is by doing just acts that we become just, by doing temperate acts that we become temperate, by doing courageous acts that we become courageous. The experience of states is a witness to this truth, for it is by training the habits that legislators make the citizens good. This is the object which all legislators have at heart; if a legislator does not succeed in it, he fails of his purpose, and it constitutes the distinction between a good polity and a bad one.

Again, the causes and means by which any virtue is produced and by which it is destroyed are the same; and it is equally so with any art; for it is by playing the harp that both good and bad harpists are produced and the case of builders and all other artisans is similar, as it is by building well that they will be good builders and by building badly that they will be bad builders. If it were not so, there would be no need of anybody to teach them; they would all be born good or bad in their several trades. The case of the virtues is the same. It is by acting in such transactions as take place between man and man that we become either just or unjust. It is by acting in the face of danger and by habituating ourselves to fear or courage that we become either cowardly or courageous. It is much the same with our desires and angry passions. Some people become temperate and gentle, others become licentious and passionate according as they conduct themselves in one way or another way in particular circumstances. In a word moral states are the results of activities corresponding to the moral states themselves. It is our duty therefore to give a certain character to the activities, as the moral states depend upon the differences of the activities. Accordingly, the difference between one training of the habits and another from early days is not a light matter, but is serious and all-important.

Book II, Chapter 4–7,9

We have next to consider the nature of virtue.

Now, as the qualities of the soul are three, namely, emotions, faculties and moral states, it follows that virtue must be one of the three. By the "emotions" I mean desire, anger, fear, courage, envy, joy, love, hatred, regret, emulation, pity—in a word whatever is attended by pleasure or pain. I call those "faculties" in respect of which we are said to be capable of experiencing these emotions, for example, capable of getting angry or being pained or feeling pity. And I call those "moral states" in respect of which we are well or ill-disposed towards the emotions, ill-disposed, for example, towards the passion of anger, if our anger be too violent or too feeble, and well-disposed if it be duly moderated, and similarly towards the other emotions.

Now neither the virtues nor the vices are emotions; for we are not called good or evil in respect of our emotions but in respect of our virtues or vices. Again, we are not praised or blamed in respect of our emotions; a person is not praised for being afraid or being angry, nor blamed for being angry in an absolute sense, but only for being angry in a certain way; but we are praised or blamed in respect of our virtues or vices. Again, whereas we are angry or afraid without deliberate purpose, the virtues are in some sense deliberate purposes, or do not exist in the absence of deliberate purpose. It may be added that while we are said to be moved in respect of our emotions, in respect of our virtues or vices we are not said to be moved but to have a certain disposition.

These reasons also prove that the virtues are not faculties. For we are not called either good or bad, nor are we praised or blamed, as having an abstract capacity for emotion. Also while Nature gives us our faculties, it is not Nature that makes us good or bad, but this is a point which we have already discussed. If then the virtues are neither emotions nor faculties, it remains that they must be moral states.

The nature of virtue has been now generically described. But it is not enough to state merely that virtue is a moral state, we must also describe the character of that moral state.

It must be laid down then that every virtue or excellence has the effect of producing a good condition of that of which it is a virtue or excellence, and of enabling it to perform its function well. Thus the excellence of the eye makes the eye good and its function good, as it is by the excellence of the eye that we see well. Similarly, the excellence of the horse makes a horse excellent and good at racing, at carrying its rider and at facing the enemy.

If then this is universally true, the virtue or excellence of man will be such a moral state as makes a man good and able to perform his proper function well. We have already explained how this will be the case, but another way of making it clear will be to study the nature or character of this virtue.

Now in everything, whether it be continuous or discrete, it is possible to take a greater, a smaller, or an equal amount, and this either absolutely or in relation to ourselves, the equal being a mean between excess and deficiency. By the mean in respect of the thing itself, or the absolute mean, I understand that which is equally distinct from both extremes and this is one and the same thing for everybody. By the mean considered relatively to ourselves I understand that which is neither too much nor too little; but this is not one thing, nor is it the same for everybody. Thus if 10 be too much and 2 too little we take 6 as a mean in respect of the thing itself; for 6 is as much greater than 2 as it is less than 10, and this is a mean in arithmetical proportion. But the mean considered relatively to ourselves must not be ascertained in this way. It does not follow that if 10 pounds of meat be too much and 2 be too little for a man to eat, a trainer will order him 6 pounds, as this may itself be too much or too little for the person who is to take it; it will be too little, for example, for Milo, but too much for a beginner in gymnastics. It will be the same with running and wrestling; the right amount will vary with the individual. This being so, everybody who understands his business avoids alike excess and deficiency; he seeks and chooses the mean, not the absolute mean, but the mean considered relatively to ourselves.

Every science then performs its function well, if it regards the mean and refers the works which it produces to the mean. This is the reason why it is usually said of successful works that it is impossible to take anything from them or to add anything to them, which implies that excess or deficiency is fatal to excellence but that the mean state ensures it. Good artists too, as we say, have an eye to the mean in their works. But virtue, like Nature herself, is more accurate and better than any art; virtue therefore will aim at the mean; I speak of moral virtue, as it is moral virtue which is concerned with emotions and actions, and it is these which admit of excess and deficiency and the mean. Thus it is possible to go too far, or not to go far enough, in respect of fear, courage, desire, anger, pity, and pleasure and pain generally, and the excess and the deficiency are alike wrong; but to experience these emotions at the right times and on the right occasions and towards the right persons and for the right causes and in the right manner is the mean or the supreme good, which is characteristic of virtue. Similarly there may be excess, deficiency, or the mean, in regard to actions. But virtue is concerned with emotions and actions, and here excess is an error and deficiency a fault, whereas the mean is successful and laudable, and success and merit are both characteristics of virtue.

It appears then that virtue is a mean state, so far at least as it aims at the mean.

Again, there are many different ways of going wrong; for evil is in its nature infinite, to use the Pythagorean figure, but good is finite. But there is only one possible way of going right. Accordingly the former is easy and the latter difficult; it is easy to miss the mark but difficult to hit it. This again is a reason why excess and deficiency are characteristics of vice and the mean state a characteristic of virtue: "For good is simple, evil manifold." Virtue then is a state of deliberate moral purpose consisting in a mean that is relative to ourselves, the mean being determined by reason, or as a prudent man would determine it.

It is a mean state firstly as lying between two vices, the vice of excess on the one hand, and the vice of deficiency on the other, and secondly because, whereas the vices either fall short of or go beyond what is proper in the emotions and actions, virtue not only discovers but embraces the mean.

Accordingly, virtue, if regarded in its essence or theoretical conception, is a mean state, but, if regarded from the point of view of the highest good, or of excellence, it is an extreme.

But it is not every action or every emotion that admits of a mean state. There are some whose very name implies wickedness, as for example, malice, shamelessness, and envy, among emotions, or adultery, theft, and murder, among actions. All these, and others like them, are censured as being intrinsically wicked, not merely the excesses or deficiencies of them. It is never possible then to be right in respect of them; they are always sinful. Right or wrong in such actions as adultery does not depend on our committing them with the right person, at the right time or in the right manner; on the contrary it is sinful to do anything of the kind at all. It would be equally wrong then to suppose that there can be a mean state or an excess or deficiency in unjust, cowardly or licentious conduct; for, if it were so, there would be a mean state of an excess or of a deficiency, an excess of an excess and a deficiency of a deficiency. But as in temperance and courage there can be no excess or deficiency because the mean is, in a sense, an extreme, so too in these cases there cannot be a mean or an excess or deficiency, but, however the acts may be done, they are wrong. For it is a general rule that an excess or deficiency does not admit of a mean state, nor a mean state of an excess or deficiency. But it is not enough to lay down this as a general rule; it is necessary to apply it to particular cases, as in reasonings upon actions, general statements, although they are broader, are less exact than particular statements. For all action refers to particulars, and it is essential that our theories should harmonize with the particular cases to which they apply.

We must take particular virtues then from the catalogue of virtues.

In regard to feelings of fear and confidence, courage is a mean state. On the side of excess, he whose fearlessness is excessive has no name, as often happens, but he whose confidence is excessive is foolhardy, while he whose timidity is excessive and whose confidence is deficient is a coward.

In respect of pleasures and pains, although not indeed of all pleasures and pains, and to a less extent in respect of pains than of pleasures, the mean state is temperance, the excess is licentiousness. We never find people who are deficient in regard to pleasures; accordingly such people again have not received a name, but we may call them insensible.

As regards the giving and taking of money, the mean state is liberality, the excess and deficiency are prodigality and illiberality. Here the excess and deficiency take opposite forms; for while the prodigal man is excessive in spending and deficient in taking, the illiberal man is excessive in taking and deficient in spending.

(For the present we are giving only a rough and summary account of the virtues, and that is sufficient for our purpose; we will hereafter determine their character more exactly.)

In respect of money there are other dispositions as well. There is the mean state which is magnificence; for the magnificent man, as having to do with large sums of money, differs from the liberal man who has to do only with small sums; and the excess corresponding to it is bad taste or vulgarity, the deficiency is meanness. These are different from the excess and deficiency of liberality; what the difference is will be explained hereafter.

In respect of honor and dishonor the mean state is high-mindedness, the excess is what is called vanity, the deficiency little-mindedness. Corresponding to liberality, which, as we said, differs from magnificence as having to do not with great but with small sums of money, there is a moral state which has to do with petty honor and is related to high-mindedness which has to do with great honor; for it is possible to aspire to honor in the right way, or in a way which is excessive or insufficient, and if a person's aspirations are excessive, he is called ambitious, if they are deficient, he is called unambitious, while if they are between the two, he has no name. The dispositions too are nameless, except that the disposition of the ambitious person is called ambition. The consequence is that the extremes lay claim to the mean or intermediate place. We ourselves speak of one who observes the mean sometimes as ambitious, and at other times as unambitious; we sometimes praise an ambitious, and at other times an unambitious person. The reason for our doing so will be stated in due course, but let us now discuss the other virtues in accordance with the method which we have followed hitherto.

Anger, like other emotions, has its excess, its deficiency, and its mean state. It may be said that they have no names, but as we call one who observes the mean gentle, we will call the mean state gentleness. Among the extremes, if a person errs on the side of excess, he may be called passionate and his vice passionateness, if on that of deficiency, he may be called impassive and his deficiency impassivity.

There are also three other mean states with a certain resemblance to each other, and yet with a difference. For while they are all concerned with intercourse in speech and action, they are different in that one of them is concerned with truth in such intercourse, and the others with pleasantness, one with pleasantness in amusement and the other with pleasantness in the various circumstances of life. We must therefore discuss these states in order to make it clear that in all cases it is the mean state which is an object of praise, and the extremes are neither right nor laudable but censurable. It is true that these mean and extreme states are generally nameless, but we must do our best here as elsewhere to give them a name, so that our argument may be clear and easy to follow.

In the matter of truth, then, he who observes the mean may be called truthful, and the mean state truthfulness. Pretence, if it takes the form of exaggeration, is boastfulness, and one who is guilty of pretence is a boaster; but if it takes the form of depreciation it is irony, and he who is guilty of it is ironical.

As regards pleasantness in amusement, he who observes the mean is witty, and his disposition wittiness; the excess is buffoonery, and he who is guilty of it a buffoon, whereas he who is deficient in wit may be called a boor and his moral state boorishness.

As to the other kind of pleasantness, namely, pleasantness in life, he who is pleasant in a proper way is friendly, and his mean state friendliness. But he who goes too far, if he has no ulterior object in view, is obsequious, while if his object is self-interest, he is a flatterer, and he who does not go far enough and always makes himself unpleasant is a quarrelsome and morose sort of person.

There are also mean states in the emotions and in the expression of the emotions. For although modesty is not a virtue, yet a modest person is praised as if he were virtuous. For here too one person is said to observe the mean and another to exceed it, as for example, the bashful man who is never anything but modest, whereas a person who has insufficient modesty or no modesty at all is called shameless, and one who observes the mean modest.

Righteous indignation, again, is a mean state between envy and malice. They are all concerned with the pain and pleasure which we feel at the fortunes of our neighbors. A person who is righteously indignant is pained at the prosperity of the undeserving; but the envious person goes further and is pained at anybody's prosperity, and the malicious person is so far from being pained that he actually rejoices at misfortunes.

It has now been sufficiently shown that moral virtue is a mean state, and in what sense it is a mean state; it is a mean state as lying between two vices, a vice of excess on the one side and a vice of deficiency on the other, and as aiming at the mean in the emotions and actions.

That is the reason why it is so hard to be virtuous; for it is always hard work to find the mean in anything, for example, it is not everybody, but only a man of science, who can find the mean or center of a circle. So too anybody can get angry—that is an easy matter—and anybody can give or spend money, but to give it to the right persons, to give the right amount of it and to give it at the right time and for the right cause and in the right way, this is not what anybody can do, nor is it easy. That is the reason why it is rare and laudable and noble to do well. Accordingly one who aims at the mean must begin by departing from that extreme which is the more contrary to the mean; he must act in the spirit of Calypso's advice, "Far from this smoke and swell you keep your bark," for of the two extremes one is more sinful than the other. As it is difficult then to hit the mean exactly, we must take the second best course, as the saying goes, and choose the lesser of two evils, and this we shall best do in the way that we have described, that is, by steering clear of the evil which is further from the mean. We must also observe the things to which we are ourselves particularly prone, as different natures have different inclinations, and we may ascertain what these are by a consideration of our feelings of pleasure and pain. And then we must drag ourselves in the direction opposite to them; for it is by removing ourselves as far as possible from what is wrong that we shall arrive at the mean, as we do, when we pull a crooked stick straight.

But in all cases we must especially be on our guard against what is pleasant and against pleasure, as we are not impartial judges of pleasure. Hence our attitude towards pleasure must be like that of the elders of the people in the *Iliad* towards Helen, and we must never be afraid of applying the words they use; for if we dismiss pleasure as they dismissed Helen, we shall be less likely to go wrong. It is by action of this kind, to put it summarily, that we shall best succeed in hitting the mean.

It may be admitted that this is a difficult task, especially in particular cases. It is not easy to determine, for example, the right manner, objects, occasions, and duration of anger. There are times when we ourselves praise people who are deficient in anger, and call them gentle, and there are other times when we speak of people who exhibit a savage temper as spirited. It is not however one who deviates a little from what is right, but one who deviates a great deal, whether on the side of excess or of deficiency, that is censured; for he is sure to be found out. Again, it is not easy to decide theoretically how far and to what extent a man may go before he becomes censurable, but neither is it easy to define theoretically anything else within the region of perception; such things fall under the head of particulars, and our judgment of them depends upon our perception.

So much then is plain, that the mean state is everywhere laudable, but that we ought to incline at one time towards the excess and at another towards the deficiency; for this will be our easiest manner of hitting the mean, or in other words of attaining excellence.

CICERO'S *OF DUTIES*

Introduction

Try to hold two pictures in your mind at one time. In one picture is a wise old man. In the other is a wild young man. The old man is diligently writing, trying to get it all down. He seems to be sending one last message. The young man should be in class, should be reading and studying and discoursing. Instead he has been drinking, and drinking so much that the ship painted inside his drinking basin is beginning to look like it is actually floating. Or it is sinking. The old man is in a villa in the Italian countryside, but he cannot enjoy the bucolic setting. He has seen his dream of an ideal Roman republic end in violence and chaos. His political enemies are hunting him down. The young man lives with the other students in Athens, but he has the bonus of plenty of money. The young man has two things from the old man, his father, but of those things, the light of wisdom from the old man's letter has been eclipsed by the glare of the old man's money.

To read Cicero's *Of Duties* is to hear an aged father give advice to one who may have been totally deaf to it. For Cicero it is duty that gives meaning to life. Duty gives weight, substance, and gravity to a life which would otherwise float away or even sink. Duty is pleasure's counterweight and remedy. In order to develop the contours of duty, or one's role and obligation to the state and to others, Cicero refashioned and developed Greek ideals about wisdom, justice, fortitude, and temperance. As a well-educated public servant, Cicero was a typical Roman in his high regard for practical wisdom, for nature, for manliness, and for magnificence. When he writes about wisdom, for example, he warns against wasting time on issues that do not have any clear practical application. He asserts that humans naturally want genuine understanding of the world around them, and that by nature humans will act correctly toward one another. As a Roman man, Cicero asserts that his son should act in a strong, manly way. The Latin word for man, *vir* is at the root of the English word *virtue*, with the Latin word *virtú* meaning "manliness." And if to be virtuous is to be manly, then for Cicero proper ambition that leads to prestige, wealth, and influence affirm the sort of magnificence of character that one could expect from a successful Roman.

While Cicero affirms the high importance of duty, he is not a buzzkill. Well, okay, maybe he was a buzzkill. And, come to think of it, it is funny that a man who seems to know so much about virtue is now almost powerless, chased around the Italian countryside while so much of his society seems to be falling apart. He had a dream, a vision that made him excited, giddy, buzzed, but that had all come to naught. Perhaps that is the reason why he embraced Stoicism. What Cicero gained from Stoicism was the idea that personal integrity could ensure genuine internal success. Cicero teaches his son the value of indifference to outward circumstances. This would be especially acute to him, since his outward circumstances were so dire. Through it all, Cicero could still see the value in his life's guiding principles, in wisdom, justice, fortitude, and temperance. But I wonder if his son, still buzzed by youth and pleasure, would see the value of those principles, the value of indifference to outward circumstances, or the value of duties.

Book I: V–VIII The Four Virtues[4]

V.

You see here, Marcus, my son, the very form and as it were the face of Moral Goodness; "and if," as Plato says, "it could be seen with the physical eye, it would awaken a marvelous love of wisdom." But all that is morally right rises from some one of four sources: it is concerned either (1) with the full perception and intelligent development of the true; or (2) with the conservation of organized society, with rendering to every man his due, and with the faithful discharge of obligations assumed; or (3) with the greatness and strength of a noble and invincible spirit; or (4) with the orderliness and moderation of everything that is said and done, wherein consist temperance and self-control.

Although these four are connected and interwoven, still it is in each one considered singly that certain definite kinds of moral duties have their origin: in that category, for instance, which was designated first in our division and in which we place wisdom and prudence, belong the search after truth and its discovery; and this is the peculiar province of that virtue. For the more clearly anyone observes the most essential truth in any given case and the more quickly and accurately he can see and explain the reasons for it, the more understanding and wise he is generally esteemed, and justly so. So, then, it is truth that is, as it were, the stuff with which this virtue has to deal and on which it employs itself.

Before the three remaining virtues, on the other hand, is set the task of providing and maintaining those things on which the practical business of life depends, so that the relations of man to man in human society may be conserved, and that largeness and nobility of soul may be revealed not only in increasing one's resources and acquiring advantages for one's self and one's family but far more in rising superior to these very things. But orderly behavior and consistency of demeanor and self-control and the like have their sphere in that department of things in which a certain amount of physical exertion, and not mental activity merely, is required. For if we bring a certain amount of propriety and order into the transactions of daily life, we shall be conserving moral rectitude and moral dignity.

4. From Cicero, *Of Duties*, trans. Walter Miller (Loeb Classical Library; Cambridge: Harvard University Press, 1913), 17–29, 63–71, 95–103, 155–65. It should be noted that Miller's translation uses gender-specific language. The impulse to change this language so that it fits a wider audience has been avoided. That decision was made to maintain Miller's original and specific language and because it seems reasonable to assume that Cicero assumed a male audience. For that reason, the narrowly gendered language, with all of its problems, has been retained.

VI.

Now, of the four divisions which we have made of the essential idea of moral goodness, the first, consisting in the knowledge of truth, touches human nature most closely. For we are all attracted and drawn to a zeal for learning and knowing; and we think it glorious to excel therein, while we count it base and immoral to fall into error, to wander from the truth, to be ignorant, to be led astray. In this pursuit, which is both natural and morally right, two errors are to be avoided: first, we must not treat the unknown as known and too readily accept it; and he who wishes to avoid this error (as all should do) will devote both time and attention to the weighing of evidence. The other error is that some people devote too much industry and too deep study to matters that are obscure and difficult and useless as well.

If these errors are successfully avoided, all the labor and pains expended upon problems that are morally right and worth the solving will be fully rewarded. Such a worker in the field of astronomy, for example, was Gaius Sulpicius, of whom we have heard; in mathematics, Sextus Pompey, whom I have known personally; in dialectics, many; in civil law, still more. All these professions are occupied with the search after truth; but to be drawn by study away from active life is contrary to moral duty. For the whole glory of virtue is in activity; activity, however, may often be interrupted, and many opportunities for returning to study are opened. Besides, the working of the mind, which is never at rest, can keep us busy in the pursuit of knowledge even without conscious effort on our part. Moreover, all our thought and mental activity will be devoted either to planning for things that are morally right and that conduce to a good and happy life, or to the pursuits of science and learning.

With this we close the discussion of the first source of duty.

VII.

Of the three remaining divisions, the most extensive in its application is the principle by which society and what we may call its "common bonds" are maintained. Of this again there are two divisions—justice, in which is the crowning glory of the virtues and on the basis of which men are called "good men"; and, close akin to justice, charity, which may also be called kindness or generosity.

The first office of justice is to keep one man from doing harm to another, unless provoked by wrong; and the next is to lead men to use common possessions for the common interests, private property for their own.

There is, however, no such thing as private ownership established by nature, but property becomes private either through long occupancy (as in the case of those who long ago settled in unoccupied territory) or through conquest (as in the case of those who took it in war) or by due process of law, bargain, or purchase, or by allotment. On this principle the lands of Arpinum are said to belong to the Arpinates, the Tusculan lands to the Tusculans; and similar is the assignment of private property. Therefore, inasmuch as in each case some of those things which by nature had been common property became the property of individuals, each one should retain possession of that which has fallen to his lot; and if anyone appropriates to himself anything beyond that, he will be violating the laws of human society.

But since, as Plato has admirably expressed it, we are not born for ourselves alone, but our country claims a share of our being, and our friends a share; and since, as the Stoics hold, everything that the earth produces is created for man's use; and as men, too, are born for the sake of men, that they may be able mutually to help one another; in this direction we ought to follow Nature as our guide, to contribute to the general good by an interchange of acts of kindness, by giving and receiving, and thus by our skill, our industry, and our talents to cement human society more closely together, man to man.

The foundation of justice, moreover, is good faith;—that is, truth and fidelity to promises and agreements. And therefore we may follow the Stoics, who diligently investigate the etymology of words; and we may accept their statement that "good faith" is so called because what is promised is "made good," although some may find this derivation rather farfetched.

There are, on the other hand, two kinds of injustice—the one, on the part of those who inflict wrong, the other on the part of those who, when they can, do not shield from wrong those upon whom it is being inflicted. For he who, under the influence of anger or some other passion, wrongfully assaults another seems, as it were, to be laying violent hands upon a comrade; but he who does not prevent or oppose wrong, if he can, is just as guilty of wrong as if he deserted his parents or his friends or his country. Then, too, those very wrongs which people try to inflict on purpose to injure are often the result of fear: that is, he who premeditates injuring another is afraid that, if he does not do so, he may himself be made to suffer some hurt. But, for the most part, people are led to wrong-doing in order to secure some personal end; in this vice, avarice is generally the controlling motive.

VIII.

Again, men seek riches partly to supply the needs of life, partly to secure the enjoyment of pleasure. With those who cherish higher ambitions, the desire for wealth is entertained with a view to power and influence and the means of bestowing favors; Marcus Crassus, for example, not long since declared that no amount of wealth was enough for the man who aspired to be the foremost citizen of the state, unless with the income from it he could maintain an army. Fine establishments and the comforts of life in elegance and abundance also afford pleasure, and the desire to secure it gives rise to the insatiable thirst for wealth. Still, I do not mean to find fault with the accumulation of property, provided it hurts nobody, but unjust acquisition of it is always to be avoided.

The great majority of people, however, when they fall a prey to ambition for either military or civil authority, are carried away by it so completely that they quite lose sight of the claims of justice. For Ennius says:"There is no fellowship inviolate, / No faith is kept, when kingship is concerned"; and the truth of his words has an uncommonly wide application. For whenever a situation is of such a nature that not more than one can hold preeminence in it, competition for it usually becomes so keen that it is an extremely difficult matter to maintain a "fellowship inviolate." We saw this proved but now in the effrontery of Gaius Caesar, who, to gain that sovereign power which by a depraved imagination he had conceived in his fancy, trod underfoot all laws of gods and men. But the trouble about this matter is that it is in the greatest souls and in the most brilliant geniuses that we usually find ambitions for civil and military authority, for power, and for glory, springing up; and therefore we must be the more heedful not to go wrong in that direction.

But in any case of injustice it makes a vast deal of difference whether the wrong is done as a result of some impulse of passion, which is usually brief and transient, or whether it is committed wilfully and with premeditation; for offences that come through some sudden impulse are less culpable than those committed designedly and with malice aforethought.

But enough has been said on the subject of inflicting injury.

Book I: XVIII, 61 to XX Fortitude's Virtue and Virility

We must realize, however, that while we have set down four cardinal virtues from which as sources moral rectitude and moral duty emanate, that achievement is most glorious in the eyes of the world which is won with a spirit great, exalted, and superior to the vicissitudes of earthly life. And so, when we wish to hurl a taunt, the very first to rise to our lips is, if possible, something like this: "For ye, young men, show a womanish soul, yon maiden a man's"; and this: "Thou son of Salmacis, win spoils that cost nor sweat nor blood."

When, on the other hand, we wish to pay a compliment, we somehow or other praise in more eloquent strain the brave and noble work of some great soul. Hence there is an open field for orators on the subjects of Marathon, Salamis, Plataea, Thermopylae, and Leuctra, and hence our own Cocles, the Decii, Gnaeus and Publius Scipio, Marcus Marcellus, and countless others, and, above all, the Roman People as a nation are celebrated for greatness of spirit. Their passion for military glory, moreover, is shown in the fact that we see their statues usually in soldier's garb.

XIX.

But if the exaltation of spirit seen in times of danger and toil is devoid of justice and fights for selfish ends instead of for the common good, it is a vice; for not only has it no element of virtue, but its nature is barbarous and revolting to all our finer feelings. The Stoics, therefore, correctly define courage as "that virtue which champions the cause of right." Accordingly, no one has attained to true glory who has gained a reputation for courage by treachery and cunning; for nothing that lacks justice can be morally right.

This, then, is a fine saying of Plato's: "Not only must all knowledge that is divorced from justice be called cunning rather than wisdom," he says, "but even the courage that is prompt to face danger, if it is inspired not by public spirit, but by its own selfish purposes, should have the name of effrontery rather than of courage." And so we demand that men who are courageous and high-souled shall at the same time be good and straightforward, lovers of truth, and foes to deception; for these qualities are the center and soul of justice.

But the mischief is that from this exaltation and greatness of spirit spring all too readily self-will and excessive lust for power. For just as Plato tells us that the whole national character of the Spartans was on fire with passion for victory, so, in the same way, the more notable a man is for his greatness of spirit, the more ambitious he is to be the foremost citizen, or, I should say rather, to be sole ruler. But when one begins to aspire to pre-eminence, it is difficult to preserve that spirit of fairness which is absolutely essential to justice. The result is that such men do not allow themselves to be constrained either by argument or by any public and lawful authority; but they only too often prove to be bribers and agitators in public life, seeking to obtain supreme power and to be superiors through force rather than equals through justice. But the greater the difficulty, the greater the glory; for no occasion arises that can excuse a man for being guilty of injustice.

So then, not those who do injury but those who prevent it are to be considered brave and courageous. Moreover, true and philosophic greatness of spirit regards the moral goodness to which Nature most aspires as consisting in deeds, not in fame, and prefers to be first in reality rather than in name. And we must approve this view; for he who depends upon the caprice of the ignorant rabble cannot be numbered among the great. Then, too, the higher a man's ambition, the more easily he is tempted to acts of injustice by his desire for fame. We are now, to be sure, on very slippery ground; for scarcely can the man be found who has passed through trials and encountered dangers and does not then wish for glory as a reward for his achievements.

XX.

The soul that is altogether courageous and great is marked above all by two characteristics: one of these is indifference to outward circumstances; for such a person cherishes the conviction that nothing but moral goodness and propriety deserves to be either admired or wished for or striven after, and that he ought not to be subject to any man or any passion or any accident of fortune. The second characteristic is that, when the soul is disciplined in the way above mentioned, one should do deeds not only great and in the highest degree useful, but extremely arduous and laborious and fraught with danger both to life and to many things that make life worth living.

All the glory and greatness and, I may add, all the usefulness of these two characteristics of courage are centered in the latter; the rational cause that makes men great, in the former. For it is the former that contains the element that makes souls pre-eminent and indifferent to worldly fortune. And this quality is distinguished by two criteria: (1) if one account moral rectitude as the only good; and (2) if one be free from all passion. For we must agree that it takes a brave and heroic soul to hold as slight what most people think grand and glorious, and to disregard it from fixed and settled principles. And it requires strength of character and great singleness of purpose to bear what seems painful, as it comes to pass in many and various forms in human life, and to bear it so unflinchingly as not to be shaken in the least from one's natural state of the dignity of a philosopher. Moreover, it would be inconsistent for the man who is not overcome by fear to be overcome by desire, or for the man who has shown himself invincible to toil to be conquered by pleasure. We must, therefore, not only avoid the latter, but also beware of ambition for wealth; for there is nothing so characteristic of narrowness and littleness of soul as the love of riches; and there is nothing more honorable and noble than to be indifferent to money, if one does not possess it, and to devote it to beneficence and liberality, if one does possess it.

As I said before, we must also beware of ambition for glory; for it robs us of liberty, and in defence of liberty a high-souled man should stake everything. And one ought not to seek military authority; nay, rather it ought sometimes to be declined, sometimes to be resigned.

Again, we must keep ourselves free from every disturbing emotion, not only from desire and fear, but also from excessive pain and pleasure, and from anger, so that we may enjoy that calm of soul and freedom from care which bring both moral stability and dignity of character. But there have been many and still are many who, while pursuing that calm of soul of which I speak, have withdrawn from civic duty and taken refuge in retirement. Among such have been found the most famous and by far the foremost philosophers and certain other earnest, thoughtful men who could not endure the conduct of either the people or their leaders; some of them, too, lived in the country and found their pleasure in the management of their private estates. Such men have had the same aims as kings—to suffer no want, to be subject to no authority, to enjoy their liberty, that is, in its essence, to live just as they please.

Book I: XXVII–XXVIII Temperance

XXVII.

We have next to discuss the one remaining division of moral rectitude. That is the one in which we find considerateness and self-control, which give, as it were, a sort of polish to life; it embraces also temperance, complete subjection of all the passions, and moderation in all things. Under this head is further included what, in Latin, may be called decorum (Propriety); . . . Such is its essential nature, that it is inseparable from moral goodness; for what is proper is morally right, and what is morally right is proper. The nature of the difference between morality and propriety can be more easily felt than expressed. For whatever propriety may be, it is manifested only when there is pre-existing moral rectitude. And so, not only in this division of moral rectitude which we have now to discuss but also in the three preceding divisions, it is clearly brought out what propriety is. For to employ reason and speech rationally, to do with careful consideration whatever one does, and in everything to discern the truth and to uphold it—that is proper. To be mistaken, on the other hand, to miss the truth, to fall into error, to be led astray—that is as improper as to be deranged and lose one's mind. And all things just are proper; all things unjust, like all things immoral, are improper.

The relation of propriety to fortitude is similar. What is done in a manly and courageous spirit seems becoming to a man and proper; what is done in a contrary fashion is at once immoral and improper.

This propriety, therefore, of which I am speaking belongs to each division of moral rectitude; and its relation to the cardinal virtues is so close, that it is perfectly self-evident and does not require any abstruse process of reasoning to see it. For there is a certain element of propriety perceptible in every act of moral rectitude; and this can be separated from virtue theoretically better than it can be practically. As comeliness and beauty of person are inseparable from the notion of health, so this propriety of which we are speaking, while in fact completely blended with virtue, is mentally and theoretically distinguishable from it.

The classification of propriety, moreover, is twofold:

(1) we assume a general sort of propriety, which is found in moral goodness as a whole;

(2) there is another propriety, subordinate to this, which belongs to the several divisions of moral goodness.

The former is usually defined somewhat as follows: "Propriety is that which harmonizes with man's superiority in those respects in which his nature differs from that of the rest of the animal creation." And they so define the special type of propriety which is subordinate to the general notion, that they represent it to be that propriety which harmonizes with Nature, in the sense that it manifestly embraces temperance and self-control, together with a certain deportment such as becomes a gentleman.

XXVIII.

That this is the common acceptation of propriety we may infer from that propriety which poets aim to secure. Concerning that, I have occasion to say more in another connection. Now, we say that the poets observe propriety, when every word or action is in accord with each individual character. For example, if Aeacus or Minos said, "Let them hate, if only they fear," or: "The father is himself his children's tomb," that would seem improper, because we are told that they were just men. But when Atreus speaks those lines, they call forth applause; for the sentiment is in keeping with the character. But it will rest with the poets to decide, according to the individual characters, what is proper for each; but to us Nature herself has assigned a character of surpassing excellence, far superior to that of all other living creatures, and in accordance with that we shall have to decide what propriety requires.

The poets will observe, therefore, amid a great variety of characters, what is suitable and proper for all—even for the bad. But to us Nature has assigned the roles of steadfastness, temperance, self-control, and considerateness of others; Nature also teaches us not to be careless in our behavior towards our fellow men. Hence we may clearly see how wide is the application not only of that propriety which is essential to moral rectitude in general, but also of the special propriety which is displayed in each particular subdivision of virtue. For, as physical beauty with harmonious symmetry of the limbs engages the attention and delights the eye, for the very reason that all the parts combine in harmony and grace, so this propriety, which shines out in our conduct, engages the approbation of our fellow men by the order, consistency, and self-control it imposes upon every word and deed.

We should, therefore, in our dealings with people show what I may almost call reverence toward all men—not only toward the men who are the best, but toward others as well. For indifference to public opinion implies not merely self-sufficiency, but even total lack of principle. There is, too, a difference between justice and considerateness in one's relations to one's fellow men. It is the function of justice not to do wrong to one's fellow men; of considerateness, not to wound their feelings; and in this the essence of propriety is best seen.

With the foregoing exposition, I think it is clear what the nature is of what we term propriety.

Further, as to the duty which has its source in propriety, the first road on which it conducts us leads to harmony with Nature and the faithful observance of her laws. If we follow Nature as our guide, we shall never go astray, but we shall be pursuing that which is in its nature clear-sighted and penetrating (Wisdom), that which is adapted to promote and strengthen society (Justice), and that which is strong and courageous (Fortitude). But the very essence of propriety is found in the division of virtue which is now under discussion (Temperance). For it is only when they agree with Nature's laws that we should give our approval to the movements not only of the body, but still more of the spirit.

Now we find that the essential activity of the spirit is twofold: one force is appetite . . . , which impels a man this way and that; the other is reason, which teaches and explains what should be done and what should be left undone. The result is that reason commands, appetite obeys.

Book I: XLIII–XLV Resolving Conflicting Duties Demanded by the Virtues

XLIII.

Now, I think I have explained fully enough how moral duties are derived from the four divisions of moral rectitude. But between those very actions which are morally right, a conflict and comparison may frequently arise, as to which of two actions is morally better—a point overlooked by Panaetius. For, since all moral rectitude springs from four sources (one of which is prudence; the second, social instinct; the third, courage; the fourth, temperance), it is often necessary in deciding a question of duty that these virtues be weighed against one another.

My view, therefore, is that those duties are closer to Nature which depend upon the social instinct than those which depend upon knowledge; and this view can be confirmed by the following argument: (1) suppose that a wise man should be vouchsafed such a life that, with an abundance of everything pouring in upon him, he might in perfect peace study and ponder over everything that is worth knowing, still, if the solitude were so complete that he could never see a human being, he would die. . . (2) Again, that wisdom which I have given the foremost place is the knowledge of things human and divine, which is concerned also with the bonds of union between gods and men and the relations of man to man. If wisdom is the most important of the virtues, as it certainly is, it necessarily follows that that duty which is connected with the social obligation is the most important duty. And (3) service is better than mere theoretical knowledge, for the study and knowledge of the universe would somehow be lame and defective, were no practical results to follow. Such results, moreover, are best seen in the safeguarding of human interests. It is essential, then, to human society; and it should, therefore, be ranked above speculative knowledge.

Upon this all the best men agree, as they prove by their conduct. For who is so absorbed in the investigation and study of creation, but that, even though he were working and pondering over tasks never so much worth mastering and even though he thought he could number the stars and measure the length and breadth of the universe, he would drop all those problems and cast them aside, if word were suddenly brought to him of some critical peril to his country, which he could relieve or repel? And he would do the same to further the interests of parent or friend or to save him from danger.

From all this we conclude that the duties prescribed by justice must be given precedence over the pursuit of knowledge and the duties imposed by it; for the former concern the welfare of our fellow men; and nothing ought to be more sacred in men's eyes than that.

XLIV.

And yet scholars, whose whole life and interests have been devoted to the pursuit of knowledge, have not, after all, failed to contribute to the advantages and blessings of mankind. For they have trained many to be better citizens and to render larger service to their country. So, for example, the Pythagorean Lysis taught Epaminondas of Thebes; Plato, Dion of Syracuse; and many, many others. As for me myself, whatever service I have rendered to my country—it, indeed, I have rendered any—I came to my task trained and equipped for it by my teachers and what they taught me. And not only while present in the flesh do they teach and train those who are desirous of learning, but by the written memorials of their learning they continue the same service after they are dead. For they have overlooked no point that has a bearing upon laws, customs, or political science; in fact, they seem to have devoted their retirement to the benefit of us who are engaged in public business. The principal thing done, therefore, by those very devotees of the pursuits of learning and science is to apply their own practical wisdom and insight to the service of humanity. And for that reason also much speaking (if only it contain wisdom) is better than speculation never so profound without speech; for mere speculation is self-centered, while speech extends its benefits to those with whom we are united by the bonds of society.

And again, as swarms of bees do not gather for the sake of making honeycomb but make the honeycomb because they are gregarious by nature, so human beings—and to a much higher degree—exercise their skill together in action and thought because they are naturally gregarious. And so, if that virtue [Justice] which centers in the safeguarding of human interests, that is, in the maintenance of human society, were not to accompany the pursuit of knowledge, that knowledge would seem isolated and barren of results. In the same way, courage [Fortitude], if unrestrained by the uniting bonds of society, would be but a sort of brutality and savagery. Hence it follows that the claims of human society and the bonds that unite men together take precedence of the pursuit of speculative knowledge.

And it is not true, as certain people maintain, that the bonds of union in human society were instituted in order to provide for the needs of daily life; for, they say, without the aid of others we could not secure for ourselves or supply to others the things that Nature requires; but if all that is essential to our wants and comfort were supplied by some magic wand, as in the stories, then every man of first-rate ability could drop all other responsibility and devote himself exclusively to learning and study. Not at all. For he would seek to escape from his loneliness and to find someone to share his studies; he would wish to teach, as well as to learn; to hear, as well as to speak. Every duty, therefore, that tends effectively to maintain and safeguard human society should be given the preference over that duty which arises from speculation and science alone.

XLV.

The following question should, perhaps, be asked: whether this social instinct, which is the deepest feeling in our nature, is always to have precedence over temperance and moderation also. I think not. For there are some acts either so repulsive or so wicked, that a wise man would not commit them, even to save his country. Posidonius has made a large collection of them; but some of them are so shocking, so indecent, that it seems immoral even to mention them. The wise man, therefore, will not think of doing any such thing for the sake of his country; no more will his country consent to have it done for her. But the problem is the more easily disposed of because the occasion cannot arise when it could be to the state's interest to have the wise man do any of those things.

This, then, may be regarded as settled: in choosing between conflicting duties, that class takes precedence which is demanded by the interests of human society. [And this is the natural sequence; for discreet action will presuppose learning and practical wisdom; it follows, therefore, that discreet action is of more value than wise (but inactive) speculation.]

So much must suffice for this topic. For, in its essence, it has been made so clear, that in determining a question of duty it is not difficult to see which duty is to be preferred to any other. Moreover, even in the social relations themselves there are gradations of duty so well defined that it can easily be seen which duty takes precedence of any other: our first duty is to the immortal gods; our second, to country; our third, to parents; and so on, in a descending scale, to the rest.

From this brief discussion, then, it can be understood that people are often in doubt not only whether an action is morally right or wrong, but also, when a choice is offered between two moral actions, which one is morally better. This point, as I remarked above, has been overlooked by Panaetius. But let us now pass on to what remains.

PROVERBS

Introduction

Her husband's name was Potiphar, and she is one of the original desperate housewives. She has her eye on the Israelite servant who is the household steward. His name is Joseph, and he was purchased by her husband after Joseph's brothers took his coat, threw him in a pit, debated whether to kill him or not, and finally sold him. If you did not know this was the Bible, and the very first book of the Bible, you might think it was the backstory for an episode of a trashy daytime talk show. (Oh, and just imagine Joseph, his brothers, Potiphar, and Potiphar's wife on a trashy daytime talk show!) But when Potiphar's wife tries to reenact her favorite daytime drama with the servant, he rebuffs her, saying, "How then can I do this great wickedness, and sin against God?" (Genesis 39:9). For Joseph, having an affair is not just betraying his master's trust; it is betraying God. What makes this element of the story of Joseph's life so important for Israelite culture is that Joseph could have felt betrayed and abandoned by God, could have made any number of excuses, presumably could have gotten away with what Potiphar's wife proposed, and could have at least avoided some prison time. But Joseph remained true to the central defining feature of his life and culture; his covenant with God. Every element of Joseph's life was triangulated through his relationship with God, making this otherwise solitary indiscretion a "sin against God." Proverbs reflects this theocentric or God-centered view, but creates an interesting overlap between worldly outcomes and transcendent consequences.

Whether these proverbs or gems of wisdom are from the actual King Solomon or not is not as important as what they tell us about Israelite culture. The prologue to the book makes clear that real wisdom is based in the covenant relation, in a true and humble reverence for God. The writings establish a clear binary between the foolish who despise God's wisdom and those wise and obedient enough to follow correct precepts. Poetic parallelisms reinforce this binary. Calamity overtakes the foolish because "they hated knowledge / and did not choose to fear the Lord" and owing to the fact that "they would not accept [Wisdom's] advice / and spurned [Wisdom's] rebuke." Those same people "will eat the fruit of their ways / and be filled with the fruit of their schemes." Nothing seems to happen to the foolish or the wise without a necessary and reinforcing doubling.

The excerpt from Proverbs given below also warns against adultery, but those warnings include the human and divine consequences of transgression. Some of the warnings seem right out of a trashy daytime talk show, one where the betrayed husband will be violently angry and will accept no form of compensation. Another warning shows an early use of the destructive fire imagery so often associated with lust. The deeper central message is that the proper relation with God is the foundation of correct actions and real understanding, or, as Joseph's story shows, to sin is to sin against God. This fundamental meaning is woven into the entire book, and it comes through somewhat in the phrase, "But a man who commits adultery has no sense / whoever does so destroys himself." One of the hallmarks of Hebrew Wisdom literature is how it bridges the human and the divine realms.

The book of Proverbs is also important for our purposes, as it shows the tendency to assign virtuous or vicious qualities to animals. The "sluggish" is encouraged to "Go to the ant," to "consider its ways and to be wise." This parallelism makes the abstract qualities of industriousness concrete and visible. While this brings the abstract to the concrete, it could also train the mind to look for the abstract in the concrete, in the otherwise mundane. The sluggard will now not only know what industriousness and diligence are by considering the ant, but when such sluggards see ants they would be reminded and warned anew. This valuable reciprocity is found in various Bible parables and in medieval bestiaries, and it carries through in works like Spenser's *The Faerie Queene.*

Proverbs has another important antecedent; it gives a list of vices, or, better stated, a list of seven propensities that the Lord hates. We could summarize those as pride, dishonesty, malicious violence, fraud, evil deeds, perjury, and dissension. Except for pride, here the arrogance of "haughty eyes," none of these vices makes their way onto any of the key early lists. Paul picks up a couple when he warns against dissensions, factions, and fits of rage in his comparison of a life with the Spirit and one without. Perhaps what may be most important about this list is how it shows a tendency to innumerate sinful character traits, the very tendency that is this book's subject.

Proverbs 1 (NIV)[5]

Purpose and Theme

1 The proverbs of Solomon son of David, king of Israel:
2 for gaining wisdom and discipline;
  for understanding words of insight;
3 for receiving instruction in prudent behavior,
  doing what is right and just and fair;
4 for giving prudence to those who are simple,
  knowledge and discretion to the young—
5 let the wise listen and add to their learning,
  and let the discerning get guidance—
6 for understanding proverbs and parables,
  the sayings and riddles of the wise.
7 The fear of the LORD is the beginning of knowledge,
  but fools despise wisdom and instruction.

Exhortations to Embrace Wisdom

Warning against the Invitation of Sinful Men

8 Listen, my son, to your father's instruction
  and do not forsake your mother's teaching.
9 They are a garland to grace your head
  and a chain to adorn your neck.

5. From The Holy Bible, New International Version®, NIV® Copyright © 1973, 1978, 1984, 2011 by Biblica, Inc.® Used by permission. All rights reserved worldwide.

10 My son, if sinful men entice you,
do not give in to them.
11 If they say, "Come along with us;
let's lie in wait for innocent blood,
let's ambush some harmless soul;
12 let's swallow them alive, like the grave,
and whole, like those who go down to the pit;
13 we will get all sorts of valuable things
and fill our houses with plunder;
14 throw in your lot with us,
and we will all share the loot"—
15 my son, do not go along with them,
do not set foot on their paths;
16 for their feet rush into evil,
they are swift to shed blood.
17 How useless to spread a net
where every bird can see it!
18 These men lie in wait for their own blood;
they ambush only themselves!
19 Such are the paths of all who go after ill-gotten gain;
it takes away the life of those who get it.

Wisdom's Rebuke

20 Out in the open wisdom calls aloud,
she raises her voice in the public square;
21 on top of the wall she cries out,
at the city gate she makes her speech:
22 "How long will you who are simple love your simple ways?
How long will mockers delight in mockery
and fools hate knowledge?
23 Repent at my reubke!
Then I will pour out my thoughts to you,
I will make known to you my teachings.
24 But since you refuse to listen when I call
and no one pays any attention when I stretch out my hand,
25 since you ignore all my advice
and do not accept my rebuke,
26 I in turn will laugh when disaster strikes you;
I will mock when calamity overtakes you—
27 when calamity overtakes you like a storm,

when disaster sweeps over you like a whirlwind,
when distress and trouble overwhelm you.
28 "Then they will call to me but I will not answer;
they will look for me but will not find me,
29 since they hated knowledge
and did not choose to fear the LORD.
30 Since they would not accept my advice
and spurned my rebuke,
31 they will eat the fruit of their ways
and be filled with the fruit of their schemes.
32 For the waywardness of the simple will kill them,
and the complacency of fools will destroy them;
33 but whoever listens to me will live in safety
and be at ease, without fear of harm."

Proverbs 6 (NIV)

Warnings against Folly

1 My son, if you have put up security for your neighbor,
if you have shaken hands in pledge for a stranger,
2 you have been trapped by what you said,
ensnared by the words of your mouth.
3 So do this, my son, to free yourself,
since you have fallen into your neighbor's hands:
Go—to the point of exhaustion—;
and give your neighbor no rest!
4 Allow no sleep to your eyes,
no slumber to your eyelids.
5 Free yourself, like a gazelle from the hand of the hunter,
like a bird from the snare of the fowler.
6 Go to the ant, you sluggard;
consider its ways and be wise!
7 It has no commander,
no overseer or ruler,
8 yet it stores its provisions in summer
and gathers its food at harvest.
9 How long will you lie there, you sluggard?
When will you get up from your sleep?
10 A little sleep, a little slumber,
a little folding of the hands to rest—

11 and poverty will come on you like a thief
    and scarcity like an armed man.
12 A troublemaker and a villain,
    who goes about with a corrupt mouth,
13 who winks maliciously with his eye,
    signals with his feet
    and motions with his fingers,
14 who plots evil with deceit in his heart—
    he always stirs up conflict.
15 Therefore disaster will overtake him in an instant;
    he will suddenly be destroyed—without remedy.
16 There are six things the Lord hates,
    seven that are detestable to him:
17 haughty eyes,
    a lying tongue,
    hands that shed innocent blood,
18 a heart that devises wicked schemes,
    feet that are quick to rush into evil,
19 a false witness who pours out lies
    and a person who stirs up conflict in the community.

Warning against Adultery

20 My son, keep your father's command
    and do not forsake your mother's teaching.
21 Bind them always upon your heart;
    fasten them around your neck.
22 When you walk, they will guide you;
    when you sleep, they will watch over you;
    when you awake, they will speak to you.
23 For this command is a lamp,
    this teaching is a light,
    and correction and instruction
    are the way to life,
24 keeping you from your neighbor's wife,
    from the smooth talk of a wayward woman.
25 Do not lust in your heart after her beauty
    or let her captivate you with her eyes.
26 For a prostitute can be had for a loaf of bread,
    but another man's wife preys on your very life.
27 Can a man scoop fire into his lap

without his clothes being burned?
28 Can a man walk on hot coals
without his feet being scorched?
29 So is he who sleeps with another man's wife;
no one who touches her will go unpunished.
30 People do not despise a thief if he steals
to satisfy his hunger when he is starving.
31 Yet if he is caught, he must pay sevenfold,
though it costs him all the wealth of his house.
32 But a man who commits adultery has no sense;
whoever does so destroys himself.
33 Blows and disgrace are his lot,
and his shame will never be wiped away.
34 For jealousy arouses a husband's fury,
and he will show no mercy when he takes revenge.
35 He will not accept any compensation;
he will refuse a bribe, however great it is.

Proverbs 9:1–10 (NIV)

Invitations of Wisdom and of Folly

1 Wisdom has built her house;
she has set up its seven pillars.
2 She has prepared her meat and mixed her wine;
she has also set her table.
3 She has sent out her servants, and she calls
from the highest point of the city,
4 "Let all who are simple come to my house!"
To those who have no sense she says,
5 "Come, eat my food
and drink the wine I have mixed.
6 Leave your simple ways and you will live;
walk in the way of insight.
7 "Whoever corrects a mocker invites insult;
whoever rebukes a wicked man incurs abuse.
8 Do not rebuke a mockers or they will hate you;
rebuke the wise and they will love you.
9 Instruct the wise and they will be wiser still;
teach the righteous and they will add to their learning.
10 The fear of the LORD is the beginning of wisdom,
and knowledge of the Holy One is understanding.

ISAIAH

Introduction

The biblical prophet Isaiah was a man with a down-to-earth sense of the world, of political events, and of daily realities. He also possessed tremendous spiritual and mystical insight. Evidence from the book of Isaiah and from tradition indicate that he was an advisor to several rulers of the kingdom of Judah. Isaiah lived through tremendous social and political turmoil, and his life ended, according to tradition, with his martyrdom. In his writings Isaiah is keenly aware of the social injustices of his time. He powerfully describes the vanity, corruption, and oppression of his time, accusing unjust leaders of "crushing" the people and "grinding the faces of the poor" (Isaiah 3:15). The central message of the book of Isaiah, and of all Hebrew prophetic writings, is that happiness and blessings come from complete devotion to the covenant, and that despair and calamity are the consequences of its betrayal. Yet Isaiah is also a key source for the majestic promises of the glorious reign of a Messiah. It is that Messiah and his reign that provide key antecedents for our notions of virtue.

The eleventh chapter of Isaiah contains messianic prophecies. For those of the Christian tradition, this prophesied Messiah is Jesus Christ, while Jews still await this prophesied Messiah. The section of Isaiah given below begins with the organic image of a shoot emerging from the stump of Jesse. This Jesse is traditionally the father of King David. That shoot is identified as one endowed with what have traditionally been called the gifts of the Spirit. After giving this list of special capacities from the Spirit of the Lord, the prophet then explains how this leader would judge beyond mere surface appearances. This ability to see the moral reality of someone or of a situation brings to mind the original offspring of Jesse. In the first book of Samuel we find the Israelite God giving counsel to Samuel about how to choose a king to succeed Saul. Samuel is told not to be impressed with the external qualities of rulers like Saul: "Do not consider his appearance or his height, for I have rejected him. The Lord does not look at the things people look at. People look at the outward appearance, but the Lord looks at the heart" (1 Samuel 16:7).

Isaiah describes how the promised leader would have this and other divine qualities that would fit like royal vestments. This leader's righteous rule would usher in a paradisiacal era marked by natural harmony, by a superabundance of divine understanding, and by peace. It is easy to see the power and appeal of such prophecies. The promise of reliable leadership, of sound judgment, harmony, and peace would have spoken as forcefully to Isaiah's socially and politically tumultuous time as it might our own. Ever since these prophecies were given, numberless leaders have tried to possess or at least appear to possess this great leader's divine qualities at the same time that they have tried to initiate a similar utopian age.

The qualities of this promised leader, as stated above, have traditionally been called the gifts of the Spirit. Those gifts, at least from the time of Gregory the Great's commentary on Job, are listed as wisdom, understanding, counsel, power or fortitude, knowledge, piety, and fear of the Lord. Piety seems to be drawn from how the leader would "delight" in the humble and reverent attitude toward God. It gives us one more quality, to bump the number up to seven. This prophecy also hints at Jesus's Beatitudes, as this leader would righteously "judge the needy" and would make decisions in favor of "the poor of the earth." Finally, Isaiah's description of a leader's ideal virtues and subsequent social harmony connect it with Plato's "guardians" in his ideal republic.

Isaiah 11:1–10: Gifts of the Holy Spirit (NIV)[6]

The Branch from Jesse

1 A shoot will come up from the stump of Jesse;
from his roots a Branch will bear fruit.
2 The Spirit of the LORD will rest on him—
the Spirit of wisdom and of understanding,
the Spirit of counsel and of might,
the Spirit of the knowledge and the fear of the LORD—

3 and he will delight in the fear of the LORD.
He will not judge by what he sees with his eyes,
or decide by what he hears with his ears;
4 but with righteousness he will judge the needy,
with justice he will give decisions for the poor of the earth.
He will strike the earth with the rod of his mouth;
with the breath of his lips he will slay the wicked.
5 Righteousness will be his belt
and faithfulness the sash around his waist.
6 The wolf will live with the lamb,
the leopard will lie down with the goat,
the calf and the lion and the yearling together;
and a little child will lead them.

7 The cow will feed with the bear,
their young will lie down together,
and the lion will eat straw like the ox.

8 The infant will play near the cobra's den,
and the young child put its hand into the viper's nest.

6. From The Holy Bible, New International Version®, NIV® Copyright © 1973, 1978, 1984, 2011 by Biblica, Inc.® Used by permission. All rights reserved worldwide.

9 They will neither harm nor destroy
on all my holy mountain,
for the earth will be full of the knowledge of the Lord
as the waters cover the sea.
10 In that day the Root of Jesse will stand as a banner for the peoples; the nations will
rally to him, and his resting place will be glorious.

MATTHEW

Introduction

As I stated in the introduction to this book, the seven virtues are not in the Bible. This might surprise you. One would think that with a book that fat you could find at least the seven virtues, the seven opposite vices, and maybe a good recipe for chicken fettuccini Alfredo. What you do find are many antecedents to the seven virtues, including the Beatitudes. At the beginning of what is perhaps Jesus's most important set of teachings, the so-called Sermon on the Mount, is a list describing the qualities of the blessed. The list describes the "blessed," and the Latin word is *beatu*, so the list is called the Beatitudes. What the list gives are the traits of those who would be worthy of the kingdom of heaven, with certain specific blessings corresponding to each attribute.

Keep in mind that while this list today may seem common, even clichéd, in its original context it may have been very dramatic and revolutionary. In fact, it can be seen as an almost point-for-point refutation of qualities that the Greeks and Romans would celebrate. Certainly both Plato and Aristotle valued a strong and vibrant "spirit" and confidence. They would probably have very different ideas about meekness, about a deeply felt need for righteousness, and for mercy. What would they do with the concept of purity of heart or being a peacemaker? They surely would not be persuaded that a reward in heaven would merit persecution now. While later we will see efforts to fuse the Judeo-Christian and the Greco-Roman, perhaps for now the best way to see the Beatitudes in a fresh way is by their contrast with the humanistic traditions. Or maybe in contrast with some of the values in culture right now.

Matthew 5:1–12 (NIV): The Beatitudes[7]

Introduction to the Sermon on the Mount

1 Now when Jesus saw the crowds, he went up on a mountainside and sat down. His
disciples came to him, 2 and he began to teach them.

7. From The Holy Bible, New International Version®, NIV® Copyright © 1973, 1978, 1984, 2011 by Biblica, Inc.® Used by permission. All rights reserved worldwide.

The Beatitudes

He said:
3 "Blessed are the poor in spirit,
for theirs is the kingdom of heaven.
4 Blessed are those who mourn,
for they will be comforted.
5 Blessed are the meek,
for they will inherit the earth.
6 Blessed are those who hunger and thirst for righteousness,
for they will be filled.
7 Blessed are the merciful,
for they will be shown mercy.
8 Blessed are the pure in heart,
for they will see God.
9 Blessed are the peacemakers,
for they will be called children of God.
10 Blessed are those who are persecuted because of righteousness,
for theirs is the kingdom of heaven.
11 Blessed are you when people insult you, persecute you and falsely say all kinds of
evil against you because of me. 12 Rejoice and be glad, because great is your reward
in heaven, for in the same way they persecuted the prophets who were before you."

PAUL'S LETTERS

Introduction

In order to understand Paul's ideas about virtue and vice, imagine the ancient teacher opening a driving school. At Paul's driving school, students would begin by learning all of the traffic laws and rules. He would carefully show them how to keep their hands at "ten and two." As students learned and gained confidence, Paul would place less emphasis on the rules, and more on being a good driver. He might tell students that good driving is less about staying in the lines and more about being focused on both where you are going and on what other drivers are doing. Good drivers are therefore vigilant, always on the look out for people in their blind spots, people trying to merge, or people on the phone. Yet good drivers are also at ease, finding a certain reassurance and calm born of skill and experience. Good driving therefore is about being vigilant, yet at ease.

The principles of Paul's driving school apply to one's moral life. While the virtuous life is one of constant vigilance, it should also go beyond mere rule keeping and legal righteousness. Life is not just about staying in the lines. Paul describes living a life where the demands of the law become overcome or superseded as one lives "by the Spirit." Focusing on the road ahead, on one's destination, allows one to live for a larger purpose instead of just living to avoid traps, pitfalls, ditches, or oncoming traffic. Of course Paul does not use driving imagery, but his image of the soul securely armed against the assaults of sin is one of his most powerful and long-lasting. For Paul, the virtuous life seems to be one that is lived vigilantly, yet at ease.

Paul himself may have felt an internal battle or conflict between a righteousness that comes from abiding by the law and a righteousness that comes by virtue of living one's life in harmony with God. In Paul's letter to those of Galatia, he affirms that real harmony with God allows one to supersede the law. Righteousness is more than just not breaking the law; it is embracing and living by the divine. This life of the Spirit is made possible by Christ's expiatory sacrifice, which changes one's nature, allowing one to enjoy a harmony with the divine, thereby keeping the law as a matter of course.

Just as Paul's Letter to the Galatians offers a contrast between the law and the Spirit, so Paul's First Letter to the Corinthians offers a contrast between the mortal life's incompleteness and the fullness of the next life. In this life, where humans know, see, and understand incompletely (similar to seeing "a reflection as in a mirror" [1 Corinthians 13:12]), gifts like prophecy and tongues are very important. But at some point, when all is known and revealed, such gifts will become obsolete. At that point, the only gift that will still be valuable will be love. Paul's description of love is one of the most famous and profound. This is an unselfish love, typified by a kindness and patience that neither envies nor holds on to past offenses. As this love always protects, trusts, hopes, and perseveres, it mirrors God's own benevolent care. While temporary gifts like tongues and prophecy have an important place in the partiality of time, love is the deeper and more fundamental gift and motivation throughout both time and eternity. Paul places this virtue with faith and hope to form the traditional triumvirate, but he gives love the sovereign place. The loving enjoy a special, harmonious relation with God; they are the ones truly driving in the center of their lane toward their divine destination. Though the loving must be vigilant to guard such a relation from relentless attacks by sin and temptation, they can find peace and comfort in the relationship with God and others.

Though modern scholarship raises doubts about the authenticity of some of these letters, what have been traditionally understood as Paul's writings have had an undeniable and powerful impact on Western ideas about virtue and vice. The image that has had the greatest impact is the image of putting on the armor of God in order to combat and defeat evil. Such armor provides both protection from evil and power to do good. This image from Paul's Letter to the Ephesians is adapted by Tertullian and developed by Prudentius, and it becomes a very important and prominent metaphor in almost all subsequent art dealing with the struggle between virtue and vice.

Galatians 5:16–26 (NIV)[8]

16 So I say, walk by the Spirit, and you will not gratify the desires of the flesh. 17 For
the flesh desires what is contrary to the Spirit, and the Spirit what is contrary to the
flesh. They are in conflict with each other, so that you do not do what you want. 18 But
if you are led by the Spirit, you are not under the law.

19 The acts of the flesh are obvious: sexual immorality, impurity and debauchery;
20 idolatry and witchcraft; hatred, discord, jealousy, fits of rage, selfish ambition, dissensions, factions 21 and envy; drunkenness, orgies, and the like. I warn you, as I did
before, that those who live like this will not inherit the kingdom of God.

22 But the fruit of the Spirit is love, joy, peace, patience, kindness, goodness,
faithfulness, 23 gentleness and self-control. Against such things there is no law. 24
Those who belong to Christ Jesus have crucified the flesh with its passions and desires.
25 Since we live by the Spirit, let us keep in step with the Spirit. 26 Let us not become
conceited, provoking and envying each other.

1 Corinthians 13 (NIV): Love

1 If I speak in the tongues of men or of angels, but do not have love, I am only a
resounding gong or a clanging cymbal. 2 If I have the gift of prophecy and can fathom
all mysteries and all knowledge, and if I have a faith that can move mountains, but do
not have love, I am nothing. 3 If I give all I possess to the poor possess to the poor and
give over my body to hardship that I may boast, but do not have love, I gain nothing.

4 Love is patient, love is kind. It does not envy, it does not boast, it is not proud.
5 It does not dishonor others, it is not self-seeking, it is not easily angered, it keeps no
record of wrongs. 6 Love does not delight in evil but rejoices with the truth. 7 It always
protects, always trusts, always hopes, always perseveres.

8 Love never fails. But where there are prophecies, they will cease; where there
are tongues, they will be stilled; where there is knowledge, it will pass away. 9 For we
know in part and we prophesy in part, 10 but when completeness comes, what is in
part disappears. 11 When I was a child, I talked like a child, I thought like a child, I
reasoned like a child. When I became a man, I put the ways of childhood behind me.
12 For now we see only a reflection as in a mirror; then we shall see face to face. Now
I know in part; then I shall know fully, even as I am fully known.

13 And now these three remain: faith, hope and love. But the greatest of these is
love.

Ephesians 6:10–18 (NIV)

The Armor of God

10 Finally, be strong in the Lord and in his mighty power. 11 Put on the full armor of
God, so that you can take your stand against the devil's schemes. 12 For our struggle
is not against flesh and blood, but against the rulers, against the authorities, against
the powers of this dark world and against the spiritual forces of evil in the heavenly
realms. 13 Therefore put on the full armor of God, so that when the day of evil comes,
you may be able to stand your ground, and after you have done everything, to stand.
14 Stand firm then, with the belt of truth buckled around your waist, with the breastplate of righteousness in place, 15 and with your feet fitted with the readiness that
comes from the gospel of peace. 16 In addition to all this, take up the shield of faith,
with which you can extinguish all the flaming arrows of the evil one. 17 Take the
helmet of salvation and the sword of the Spirit, which is the word of God. 18 And pray
in the Spirit on all occasions with all kinds of prayers and requests. With this in mind,
be alert and always keep on praying for all the Lord's people.

PART II

Codification of the Virtues and Vices

If people like Plato, Aristotle, and Cicero as well as Isaiah, Matthew, Paul, and the author of Proverbs provided the raw materials, it was people like Prudentius, Evagrius, and Gregory the Great who developed those materials into the virtues and vices. The Classical and Judeo-Christian worlds provided the principles, while subsequent thinkers refined them into the "building codes," the commonly agreed upon standards of upright moral goodness and downright badness. This process of assembling such codes into the list of virtues and vices did not happen all at once. The story of the codification of the virtues and vices has many interesting twists and turns.

The first important character in this story is Quintus Septimius Florens Tertullianus, or simply Tertullian (160–225 CE). An excerpt from Tertullian's *The Shows* is the first item in this section. Tertullian's part in the story of the virtues and vices is that he continued and elaborated Paul's idea of a moral battle between good and evil. While he did not set up a well-developed list of virtues and vices, Tertullian's battle imagery found its way into Prudentius's elaborate epic poem of the battle within the soul (or *psychomachy*). Prudentius (348–413 CE) did give a remarkable list of virtues and vices, and his dramatic personification of each offers a stirring and engaging discussion of their nature. The epic battle pits Faith against Idolatry, Chastity against Lust, Long-Suffering against Wrath, Lowliness and Hope opposite Pride, Sobriety confronting Indulgence, and Reason and Good Works defeating greed. The work has a final triumph of the Virtues overcoming Discord and building a temple to Wisdom. Though the *Psychomachia* was a tremendously popular text throughout the medieval period, Prudentius's list did not become the standard code of virtues and vices.

Prudentius seems to have developed virtues and vices that would suit his dramatic and moral purposes, and there does not seem to be one clear source for his selection.

The next principal character in the development of the virtues and vices is Evagrius of Pontus (345–399 CE). Evagrius is important because he developed a list of vices or evil spirits that must be overcome. This list was drawn up as part of the spiritual meditation for the Christians who had fled the world seeking moral purity in the harsh isolation of the Egyptian desert. This list formed the basis of the vices and seven deadly sins, and it includes gluttony, fornication, avarice, anger, sadness, *acedia*, vainglory, and pride.

Perhaps the single most important person not included in this section is John Cassian (360–435 CE). Cassian was Evagrius's pupil, and he elaborated on his teacher's list of vices in his book *Institutes*. This book brought the vices from Egypt to France, and it became required reading for Benedictine monks. Cassian's list also became the basis for penitential manuals, which are handbooks that priests used to help identify and eliminate sins in the souls of those seeking absolution through confession. For Cassian and Evagrius, the vices were the evil spirits or thoughts to be overcome, and the virtues were those God-given powers that could overcome them.

While this list of vices developed in the Egyptian deserts, the virtues came together in a different location and context. Most Christians living in the Roman world were careful to distinguish themselves from pagans, yet they nevertheless recognized and incorporated the humanistic virtues they saw around them. People like Saint Augustine saw the Roman Empire as an important yet inherently limited precursor to the emerging "city of God," or Christian empire. Such Christians admired the humanistic Roman values. Perhaps the most important step toward transforming humanistic values into Christian virtues was made by the fourth-century bishop of Milan, Saint Ambrose (340–397 CE). In about 375 CE, Ambrose wrote *Paradise*, and in it he compared the cardinal or classical virtues to the four rivers of the Edenic paradise. This comparison allowed Ambrose to explain that these "rivers" flowed from one common source, Christ, thereby allowing their combination with the theological virtues.

TERTULLIAN'S *THE SHOWS*

Introduction

In the small North Carolina town where I live we have some batting cages. Batting cages, if you do not know, are places where machines pitch baseballs at people who want to practice their swing. I believe that the cages are owned locally, and they have a sign in front that can be changed to make announcements. In May of 2006 the sign admonished people to not see the movie *The Da Vinci Code*. Given the cultural environment, I believe that this plea was made on account of the movie's controversial depictions of religion, specifically Christianity and Catholicism. Tertullian would have been happy with this sign, but possibly not happy enough. He probably would have discouraged people from seeing most any movie or from going to theater productions, watching television, or attending sporting events.

Tertullian lived in North Africa (modern-day Tunisia) from about 160 until 225 CE. And he would probably not like that I use the abbreviation *CE* (which stands for the Common Era) instead of *AD* (which stands for the Latin phrase *anno domine*—"year of our Lord"); he would likely see the use of *CE* as a further diminishment of Christian devotion. Tertullian was fiercely devoted to Christianity at a ferocious time. His hometown of Carthage did not have batting cages, so the Carthaginians would round up people and make them fight to the death in gladiatorial arenas. Tertullian was outraged with this on several levels. He himself may have seen Christians martyred in this way, and at least knew that Christians had indeed undergone martyrdom, so he was beside himself to see Christians attend such horrific, bloodlust spectacles. Not only did they encourage the worst instincts and feed the most base desires, but they had pagan roots and were patronized by so-called Christians. And so he wrote against this practice in his work *Of Shows* or *De Spectaculis*. In this work Tertullian uses his sharp rhetorical skills to persuade his audience that such shows as well as violent and vulgar theatrical performances seduce Christians away from God and only serve demonic purposes.

Though Tertullian himself rejected (pagan) Greek philosophy, going so far as to ask, "what has Athens to do with Jerusalem or the Academy with the Church?" (*De praescriptione*, vii.), he would agree with Plato on the power of art and the need to control that power. Part of Tertullian's argument is that the very power of these shows would have a damaging impact upon Christians. What Tertullian also says is that Christians should look at the real battle, the real "fightings and wrestlings" between the virtues and the vices. Instead of being distracted by sinful and eternally meaningless temporal battles, the true Christian should be keenly aware of the battle between good and evil. In this respect Tertullian continues Paul's martial imagery of the Christian soul in constant warfare. He also lays the groundwork for Prudentius's extended treatment of the *psychomachia* or the battle in (and for) the soul.

Chapter XXIX.[1]

But now, if you think we are to pass this interval of life here in delights, why are you so ungrateful as not to find enough in the great pleasures, the many pleasures, given you by God, and not to recognize them? What has more joy in it than reconciliation with God, the Father and Lord, than the revelation of truth, the recognition of error, and forgiveness for all the great sins of the past? What greater pleasure is there than disdain for pleasure, than contempt for the whole world, than true liberty, than a

1. From Tertullian, *De Spectaculis,* trans. T. R. Glover (Loeb Classical Library; Cambridge: Harvard University Press, 1931), 295–97.

clean conscience, than life sufficient, than the absence of all fear of death? than to find yourself trampling underfoot the gods of the Gentiles, expelling demons, effecting cures, seeking revelations, living to God? These are the pleasures, the spectacles of Christians, holy, eternal, and free. Here find your games of the circus,—watch the race of time, the seasons slipping by, count the circuits, look for the goal of the great consummation, battle for the companies of the churches, rouse up at the signal of God, stand erect at the angel's trump, triumph in the palms of martyrdom. If the literature of the stage delight you, we have sufficiency of books, of poems, of aphorisms, sufficiency of songs and voices, not fable, those of ours, but truth; not artifice but simplicity. Would you have fightings and wrestlings? Here they are—things of no small account and plenty of them. See impurity overthrown by chastity, perfidy slain by faith, cruelty crushed by pity, impudence thrown into the shade by modesty; and such are the contests among us, and in them we are crowned. Have you a mind for blood? You have the blood of Christ.

PRUDENTIUS'S *PSYCHOMACHIA*

Introduction

I still scratch my head at the concept of Christian rock. I know that on a certain level it makes sense. Music is sounds, rhythms, melodies, particular instruments, maybe lyrics, and in that respect music is amoral. And music, like any of the arts, can powerfully convey content, and for that reason Plato calls for its strict public control. So if music can have such a powerful impact, why could not Christians harness the same sounds, rhythms, melodies and particular instruments of other rock bands? Of course Christian rock bands do just that, but it has always seemed like an odd fit to me. Maybe I just have not heard enough successful Christian rock. Maybe it's because so much rock music seems so decidedly irreligious or even antireligion, or maybe it is because the original term, *rock and roll*, seems to evoke images of (illicit) sexual activity sufficient to shake the entire Chevy van. If he were alive today, I suspect that Prudentius would be in a Christian rock band, blending Tertullian and Paul with Pink Floyd and Pearl Jam. What Prudentius did was the fifth-century equivalent, incorporating elements of martial Roman culture in a Christian psychological and spiritual drama. In addition, Prudentius *Psychomachia* is a crucial text for the virtues and vices, establishing key conflicts and iconographies.

Aurelius Prudentius Clemens (348–413 CE) lived most of his life in Roman-controlled Spain. His most famous work, the *Psychomachia*, begins with a preface and frame narrative about Abraham and Lot. Abraham, the father of the faithful, is a model of one who fights with the armor of faith, and who shows his total devotion to God by being willing to sacrifice the thing he loved most—in this case, his son. In that same frame narrative, Lot, Abraham's nephew, is described as one who was taken captive by barbarian kings. In contrast with the ever-faithful Abraham, Lot becomes an embodiment of all souls who, since Adam's fall, are overcome by the savage vices. And just as Lot is freed when Abraham overcomes his captors, so are our souls freed by Christ the Victor.

With this preface in place, Prudentius begins his epic with an evocation of his muse, Christ, asking "our King" to tell of the forces furnished to the soul to overcome the evil passions. The poem ends with the virtues building a temple to house Wisdom. The bulk of the *Psychomachia* is given over to a variety of lively battle scenes. The chart below shows how those scenes can be divided into episodes. In almost every episode, one or two virtues battle a vice that may or may not be accompanied by partnering vices. Often a biblical example is given for the virtue described.

Episode	*Virtue*	*Example*	*Vice*	*Mode of Defeat*
One	Faith		Worship-of-the-Old-Gods	Strikes her down
Two	Chastity	Judith	Lust	Stone and sword
Three	Long-Suffering	Job	Wrath	Virtue's invincibility provokes Wrath's suicide
Four	Lowliness and Hope	David	Pride	Vice falls in pit, Lowliness beheads her
Five	Sobriety	Moses	Indulgence and entourage	Strikes with the Cross
Six A	Reason and Good Works		Greed and entourage	(Protection of Reason's shield)
Six B	Good Works		Thrift (Greed in disguise)	Strangles and stabs
Seven	Faith and others		Discord or Heresy	Strikes, tears to pieces

This chart reveals important clues about the context of the *Psychomachia*. Faith's struggle against idolatry represents Christianity's conflict with a paganism still very much alive in Prudentius's time. By contrast, at a later time Giotto casts Christianity's already-vanquished opponent symbolically as idol worship. Sexuality, faith, and paganism come together in Chastity's fight with Lust: Prudentius seems to see the same connection between sexual purity and faith that Paul so often calls for in his letters. Prudentius extends Paul's call for humility and sobriety in the next episode, even using an example that appears in the New Testament—of Moses as one who sacrificed for God worldly pleasure and comfort (Hebrews 11:24–27). In the conflict between Reason and Greed, Prudentius shows considerable insight, not only in how Reason can protect the faithful, but in how Greed disguised as Thrift is overcome by Good Works. Given the intense conflicts within the Christian world before, during, and after Prudentius's life, the final episode is perhaps understated, predictive, and overly optimistic, as Faith swiftly and decisively overcomes Discord and Heresy.

When the virtues and vices are placed on a chart like this, what also comes to the fore is what is not included. Charity, for example, never takes the field, except perhaps as Good Works, and the only place we find love (Amor) is in the guise of desire and as part of Indulgence's malicious entourage. Classical virtues like Justice and Fortitude never enter the fray by name, though Fortitude is implied in how the virtues struggle against the vices. Nor do we ever directly encounter Temperance, though here again it may be manifest as Sobriety and Reason over excesses like Indulgence and Greed. It is very telling that we never witness an attack of Envy. For as much as Prudentius gives us a battle inside the soul, the conflicts seem more external in light of Envy's absence. There is the battle with paganism, with sexual impurity, with excesses like pride, indulgence, and greed, but there is not a picture of an internal conflict (potentially between Christians) with envy. Nor does Prudentius seem attuned to the interior conflicts with sloth or sadness, or to *acedia*'s lack of concern about spiritual growth. These are internal battles that ascetics like Evagrius detect and describe.

What strikes many people who read the *Psychomachia* for the first time is how graphically Prudentius describes these metaphorical battles within and for control of the soul or psyche. In the very first episode, Faith

> smites her foe's head down, . . . lays in the dust that mouth that was sated with the blood of beasts, and tramples the eyes under foot, squeezing them out in death. The throat is choked and the scant breath confined by the stopping of its passage, and long gasps make a hard and agonizing death.[2]

Of course then the other virtues leap for joy! Clearly there is no "love your enemies" here. But the soul has no room for loving its enemies; it can give no quarter or take prisoners of an enemy that will never stand down. Prudentius's graphic battle provides a new version of Virgil's *Aeneid*, not set in the mythic past, but in the souls of those living in the Christian Roman present. Some portions of the battle seem like an awkward mixing of Virgil and Paul. Even on the most superficial level one finds that the Virtues are, in the Roman tradition, very virile and "manly" female embodiments of those abstract principles. The *Psychomachia* employs some of the imagery, language, and graphic martial descriptions that would have been popular with its original audience. Those Roman features combine with content inspired by Paul and Tertullian. It is up to the reader to determine how successful this version of fifth-century Christian rock is.

2. From Prudentius, *Psychomachia*, in *Prudentius*, trans. H. J. Thomson (Loeb Classical Library; Cambridge: Harvard University Press), 281.

Episodes IV and V[3]

It chanced that Pride was galloping about, all puffed up, through the widespread squadrons, on mettled steed which she had covered with a lion's skin, laying the weight of shaggy hair over its strong shoulders, so that being seated on the wild beast's mane she might make a more imposing figure as she looked down on the columns with swelling disdain. High on her head she had piled a tower of braided hair, laying on a mass to heighten her locks and make a lofty peak over her haughty brows. A cambric mantle hanging from her shoulders was gathered high on her breast and made a rounded knot on her bosom, and from her neck there flowed a filmy streamer that billowed as it caught the opposing breeze. Her charger also, too spirited to stand still, carries itself proudly, ill brooking to have its mouth curbed with the bit it is champing. This way and that it backs in its rage, since it is denied freedom to run off and is angered at the pressure of the reins. In such style does this boastful she-warrior display herself, towering over both armies as she circles round on her bedecked steed and with menacing look and speech eyes the force that confronts her; a force but small in number and scantily armed, that Lowliness had gathered for the war—a princess she, indeed, but standing in need of others's help and wanting trust in her own provision. She had made Hope her fellow, whose rich estate is on high and lifted up from the earth in a wealthy realm. Therefore Pride in her madness, after looking on Lowliness and her poor equipment of paltry arms that made no display, broke forth in speech with bitter words: "Are ye not ashamed, ye poor creatures, to challenge famous captains with troops of low degree, to take the sword against a race of proud distinction, whose valor in war has long won wealth for it, and given it power to impose its rule on hills where rich grass grows? And now—can it be?—a newcomer with nothing is trying to drive out the ancient princes! Behold the warriors who will have our sceptres become the spoil of their right hands, who seek to drive the furrow over lands that we have broken up, to ravage with a strangers's plough the soil our hands have taken, and with war expel its hardy cultivators! Absurd mob! Why, in the hour of birth we embrace the whole man, his frame still warm from his mother, and extend the strength of our power through the body of the new-born child, we are lords and masters all within the tender bones. What place in our abode was granted to you when the growing strength of our realm was matched by that of the sovereignty that was born with it? For both the house and its masters were born on the same day and we grew side by side as the years passed, since the time when the first man, going forth from the hedged bounds of Eden, went over into the wide world, and the venerable Adam clothed himself with skins, whereas he had been naked still, had he not followed our instruction. What foe is this that from shores unknown arises now to trouble us, a spiritless, luckless, base, insensate foe, who claims his rights so late, after banishment till now? Doubtless there will be trust in the silly dreams of the vain talk which bids poor wretches choose the

3. Ibid., 291–311.

hope of a good that 'may some day come to pass, so that its feckless consolations flatter their unmanly sloth with idle expectation! Ay, a nerveless hope it must be that flatters these raw troops, for in the dust of battle here the bray of the War-Queen's trumpet does not rouse them, and their courage is not hot enough to brace their unwarlike spirit. Is Chastity's cold stomach of any use in war, or Brotherly Love's soft work done by stress of battle? What shame it is, O god of war, O valorous heart of mine, to face such an army as this, to take the sword against such trumpery, and engage with troupes of girls, among them beggarly Righteousness and poverty-stricken Honesty, dried-up Soberness and white-faced Fasting, Purity with scarce a tinge of blood to color her cheeks, unarmed Simplicity exposed with no protection to every wound, and Lowliness humbling herself to the ground, with no freedom even in her own eyes, and whose agitation betrays her ignoble spirit! I shall have this feeble band trodden down like stubble; for we disdain to shatter them with our stark swords, to dip our blades in their frigid blood, and disgrace our warriors with a triumph that needs no manhood." Thus exclaiming she spurs on her swift charger and flies wildly along with loose rein, eager to upset her lowly enemy with the shock of her horse-hide shield and trample on her fallen body. But she falls headlong into a pit which as it chanced cunning Deceit had privily dug across the field—Deceit, one of those cursed plagues, the Vices, a crafty worker of trickery, who foreseeing the war had secretly broken the level earth with treacherous trenches on the enemy's side, that the ditch might catch their regiments in their onrush and the columns plunge into it and be swallowed up; and lest the army should be watchful and discover the pit that was set to deceive it, she had concealed the edges by covering them with branches and laying turf over them to simulate ground. But the lowly princess, though knowing nought of this, was still on the further side, and had not yet come up to Deceit's trap nor set foot on the craftily hidden pit that meant her ill. Into the snare has fallen that rider as she galloped in swift career, and suddenly revealed the secret gulf. Thrown forward, she clings around the horse's neck in its tumble; the weight of its breast comes down on her and she is tossed about among its broken legs. But the quiet, self-controlled Virtue, seeing the vain monster crushed and lying at the point of death, bends her steps calmly towards her, raising her face a little and tempering her joy with a look of kindliness. As she hesitates, her faithful comrade Hope comes to her side, holds out to her the sword of vengeance, and breathes into her the love of glory. Grasping her blood-stained enemy by the hair, she drags her out and with her left hand turns her, face upwards; then, though she begs for mercy, bends the neck, severs the head, lifts it and holds it up by the dripping locks. Hope with her pure lips upbraids the dead Vice: "An end to thy big talk! God breaks down all arrogance. Greatness falls; the bubble bursts; swollen pride is flattened. Learn to put away disdain, learn to beware of the pit before your feet, all ye that are overweening. Well known and true is the saying of our Christ that the lowly ascend to high places and the proud are reduced to low degree. We have seen how Goliath, terrible as he was in body and in valor, fell by a weak hand; it was but a boy's right hand that shot at him a little stone whizzing from his sling, and pierced a hole deep in his forehead. He, for all his stark menace, his boasting and his fierce and bitter speech, in the midst of his ungoverned pride and fearful raging, as he vaunted himself, affrighting the heavens with his shield, found what a little child's toy can do, and wild man of war as he was, fell to a lad of tender years. That day the lad, in the ripening of his valor, followed me; as his spirit came to its bloom he lifted it up towards my kingdom; because for me is kept a sure home at the feet of the all-powerful Lord, and when I call men on high the victors who have cut down the sins that stain them reach after me." With these words, striking the air with her gilded wings, the maid flies off to heaven. The Virtues marvel at her as she goes and lift up their hearts in longing, desiring to go with her, did not earthly warfare detain them in command. They join in conflict with the Vices and reserve themselves for their own due reward.

From the western bounds of the world had come their foe Indulgence, one that had long lost her repute and so cared not to save it; her locks perfumed, her eyes shifting, her voice listless, abandoned in voluptuousness she lived only for pleasure, to make her spirit soft and nerveless, in wantonness to drain alluring delights, to enfeeble and undo her understanding. Even then she was languidly belching after a night-long feast; for as it chanced dawn was coming in and she was still reclining by the table when she heard the hoarse trumpets, and she left the lukewarm cups, her foot slipping as she stepped through pools of wine and perfumes, and trampling on the flowers, and was making her drunken way to the war. Yet it was not on foot, but riding in a beauteous chariot that she struck and won the hearts of the admiring fighters. Strange warfare! No swift arrow is sped in flight from her bowstring, no lash-thrown lance shoots forth hissing, her hand wields no menacing sword; but as if in sport she throws violets and fights with rose-leaves, scattering baskets of flowers over her adversaries. So the Virtues are won over by her charms; the alluring breath blows a subtle poison on them that unmans their frames, the fatally sweet scent subduing their lips and hearts and weapons, softening their iron-clad muscles and crushing their strength. Their courage drops as in defeat; they lay down their javelins, their hands, alas! enfeebled, all to their shame struck dumb in their wonder at the chariot gleaming with flashing gems of varied hue, as with fixed gaze they look longingly at the reins with their tinkling gold-foil, the heavy axle of solid gold, so costly, the spokes, one after another, of white silver, the rim of the wheel holding them in place with a circle of pale electrum. And by this time the whole array, its standards turned about, was treacherously submitting of its own will to a desire to surrender, wishing to be the slaves of Indulgence, to bear the yoke of a debauched mistress, and be governed by the loose law of the pot-house. The stout-hearted Virtue Soberness mourned to see a crime so sore, her allies deserting the right wing, a band once invincible being lost without shedding of blood. Like the good leader she is, she had carried the standard of the cross at the head of her troops, and now she plants the spike in the ground and sets it up, and with biting words restores her unsteady regiment, mingling appeals with her reproaches to awake their courage: "What blinding madness is vexing your disordered minds? To what fate are you rushing? To whom are you bowing the neck? What bonds are these (for shame!) you long to bear on arms that were meant for weapons, these yellow garlands interspersed with bright lilies, these wreaths blooming with red-hued flowers? Is it to chains like these you will give up hands trained to war, with these bind your stout arms, to have your manly hair confined by a gilded turban with its yellow band to soak up the spikenard you pour on, and this after you have had inscribed with oil on your brows the signs whereby was given to you the king's anointing, his everlasting unction? To walk softly with a train sweeping the path you have trod? To wear flowing robes of silk on your enfeebled frames, after the immortal tunic that bountiful Faith wove with deft fingers, giving an impenetrable covering to cleansed hearts to which she had already given rebirth? And so to feasts that last into the night, where the great tankard spills out wasted floods of foaming wine, while the ladles drip on to the table, the couches are soaked with neat liquor, and their embossed ornaments still wet with the dew of yesterday? Have you forgotten, then, the thirst in the desert, the spring that was given to your fathers from the rock, when the mystic wand split the stone and brought water leaping from its top? Did not food that angels brought flow into your fathers' tents in early days, that food which now with better fortune, in the lateness of time, near the end of the world's day, the people eats from the body of Christ? And it is after tasting of this banquet that you let shameful debauchery carry you relentlessly to the drunken den of Indulgence, and soldiers whom no raging Wrath nor idols could force by war to yield have been prevailed on by a tipsy dancer! Stand, I pray you. Remember who ye are, remember Christ too. Ye should bethink yourselves of your nation and your fame, your God and King, your Lord. Ye are the high-born children of Judah and have come of a long line of noble ancestors that stretches down to the mother of God, by whom God himself was to become man. Let the renowned David, who never rested from the troubles of war, awake your noble spirits; and Samuel too, who forbids touching the spoil taken from a rich foe, nor suffers the uncircumcised king to live after his defeat, lest the captive, were he allowed to survive, summon the victor from his life of peace to a renewal of war. He counts it sin to spare the monarch even as a prisoner; but your desire, on the contrary, is to be conquered and submit. Repent, I beseech you by the fear of the high God, if at all it moves you, that you have desired to follow after this pleasant sin, committing a heinous betrayal. If ye repent, your sin is not deadly. Jonathan repented that he had broken the sober fast with the sweet honeycomb, tasting, alas! in an evil hour the savor of honey on his rod, when the tempting desire to be king charmed his young mind and broke the holy vow. Yet because he repented we do not have to lament the fate that was decreed, and the cruel sentence did not stain his father's axe. Lo, I, Soberness, if ye make ready to concert with me, open up a way for all the Virtues whereby the temptress Indulgence, for all her great train, shall pay the penalty, she and her regiment, under the judgment of Christ." So speaking, she holds up the cross of the Lord in face of the raging chariot-horses, thrusting the holy wood against their very bridles; and for all their boldness they have taken fright at its outspread arms and flashing top, and in the rout of blind panic career down a steep place. Their driver, leaning far back and pulling on the reins, is carried helplessly along, her dripping locks befouled with dust; then she is thrown out and the whirling wheels entangle her who was their mistress, for she falls forward under the axle and her mangled body is the brake that slows the chariot down. Soberness gives her the death-blow as she lies, hurling at her a great stone from the rock. As chance has put this weapon in the standard-bearer's way (for she carries no javelins in her hand, but only the emblem of her warfare), chance drives the stone to smash the breath-passage in the midst of the face and beat the lips into the arched mouth. The teeth within are loosened, the gullet cut, and the mangled tongue fills it with bloody fragments. Her gorge rises at the strange meal; gulping down the pulped bones she spews up again the lumps she swallowed. "Drink up now thine own blood, after thy many cups," says the maiden, upbraiding her. "Be these thy grim dainties, in place of the too much sweetness thou hast enjoyed in time past. The taste of bitter death in thy mouth, the savoring of this final, ghastly draught, turns to gall the wanton delights that allured thee in thy life." At the slaughter of its leader her company of triflers scatters and runs in a flutter of fear. Jest and Sauciness first cast away their cymbals; for it was with such weapons that they played at war, thinking to wound with the noise of a rattle! Desire turns his back in flight. Pale himself with fear, he leaves behind his poisoned darts, abandoning his bow where it has slipped from his shoulder, his quiver where it falls. Ostentation, that parader of empty grandeur, is stripped bare of her vain flowing robe. Allurement's garlands are torn and trail behind her, the gold on her neck and head unfastened, and jarring Strife disorders her jewels. Pleasure is content to go with injured feet through thorny brakes, for superior force makes her endure the painful flight, and the dread of danger hardens her tender soles to bear the torture of the way. Wherever the column turns, as it rushes this way and that in its agitated flight, lie things lost, a hairpin, ribbands, fillets, a brooch, a veil, a breast-band, a coronet, a necklace. These spoils Soberness and all the soldiers of Soberness refrain from handling; they trample under their chaste feet the cursed causes of offence, nor let their austere gaze turn a blind eye towards the joys of plunder.

EVAGRIUS OF PONTUS'S *ON THE EIGHT THOUGHTS*

Introduction

Stillness. Unsullied quiet. A peace that passes all understanding. The soul caught up in its rightful home, absorbed back into its proper abode. For ascetics like Evagrius of Pontus (345–399 CE), stillness or *hesychia* was the soul's proper objective and the end to which every element of one's life should be aimed. The virtues, like thermal winds under eagles' wings, could lift that soul up, while the vices, like lead, were dark, powerful forces keeping the soul down. In Evagrius's many writings on the virtues and vices we have a pithy and potent exploration of their nature.

Evagrius, it would seem, recognized the value of stillness because he experienced the soul's exile in chaos. He was born in northern Turkey, the son of a rural bishop, and evidently a bright young man who moved up the ranks, working with key people like Gregory of Nazianzus. He knew the spiritual chaos of his time, including the various doctrinal debates, but the real disorder of his soul may have come from his affair with a married aristocratic woman. What ended the affair was a terrifying dream he had in which he was only freed from prison by an angel with his promise to renounce the relationship. But even after ending his affair and fleeing to Jerusalem, he did not find peace. In Jerusalem he suffered a prolonged fever, leading his spiritual advisor to question the state of his soul. For Evagrius, his physical sickness was merely a manifestation of his real internal disease. In search of wholeness, Evagrius fled the world he was accustomed to and joined the ascetics in the deserts of Egypt.

In his writings, Evagrius dramatically describes the chaos as well as the stillness or the "impassability" that a soul can and should achieve. This achievement works in a logical progression. A monk—the audience Evagrius addresses—must learn the fundamental and practical spiritual skills. One must first recognize and overcome temptations of one's bodily passions, including gluttony, lust, and greed. In addition, one must properly harness psychic or emotional states, overcoming sadness, anger, and *acedia* with patience and courage. The rational faculty must also be properly yoked, eliminating vainglory and pride with prudence and humility. Evagrius thus lists eight temptations to be overcome. He does not call them sins or vices. Instead, he calls them "thoughts," or sometimes "demons," and the general picture that we get is that they are nefarious evil forces, each of which is a specialist in some area, but, in working together, they often lay the groundwork for each other. The evil thoughts assail one from outside, and do not rise from oneself. One is responsible, not for being tempted or attacked, but for one's response to that attack. The practical spiritual skills used to fend off these demons are the necessary groundwork for the sort of stillness one would need for proper prayer, meditation, and wholeness with God. This next spiritual level is reserved for the knowers, the gnostics, those ready for the higher mysteries of the knowledge of God.

Evagrius's writings were, for a long time, forgotten, neglected, or misassigned because he ended up on the wrong side of a key theological debate, leaving him essentially blacklisted. Evagrius's pupil, John Cassian, incorporated, with slight alteration, his teacher's list of eight temptations into his *Institutes*, which he brought from Egypt to France. This book became required reading for Benedictine monks and set the foundation for penitential manuals, thus setting the stage for an adapted version of Evagrius's eight evil thoughts to eventually become the seven deadly sins.

Evagrius's writings are not meant to be read quickly. If a monk has anything, he has time. These descriptions of evil temptations and their remedies will only give up their secrets when the reader gives them proper time and energy, in the form of deep meditation and contemplation. Read. Stop. Meditate. Be still.

ON THE EIGHT THOUGHTS[4]

1. Gluttony

1. Abstinence is the origin of fruitfulness, the blossom and beginning of the practical life.
2. He who controls the stomach diminishes the passions; he who is overcome by food gives increase to pleasures.
3. 'Amalek was the first of the nations' (Num. 24:20); and gluttony is the first of the passions.[5]
4. Wood is the matter used by fire, and food is the matter used by gluttony.[6]
5. A lot of wood raises a large flame; an abundance of food nourishes desire.
6. A flame grows dim when matter is wanting; a lack of food extinguishes desire.
7. He who seized the jawbone destroyed the foreign nations and easily tore asunder the bonds of his hands (Judg. 15:9–20).[7]
8. The (place called) Destruction of the Jawbone begat a spring of water;[8] and when gluttony was wiped out, it gave birth to practical contemplation.
9. A tent peg, passing unnoticed destroyed an enemy's jawbone (Judg. 4:21); and the principle of abstinence has put passion to death.[9]
10. Desire for food gave birth to disobedience and a sweet taste expelled from paradise (Gen. 3:6, 23).

4. From Evagrius of Pontus, "On the Eight Thoughts," in *Evagrius of Pontus*, trans. Robert E. Sinkewicz (Oxford Early Christian Studies; Oxford: Oxford University Press, 2003), 73–75, 80–81, 87–90. Used by permission. Notes selected from the original.

5. *Amalek*. After the exodus from Egypt Amalek was the first of the nations to attack Israel. According to Origen's allegorical reading, Amalek was called 'first of the nations' because he was a hostile power, the first to turn people to paganism.

6. *The matter used by gluttony*. The passions use sensible objects or the memories of such as the 'matter' or material to tempt human beings. The different passions have a greater or lesser range of material to draw upon for this purpose.

7. *he who seized the jawbone*. When Samson took revenge on the Philistines, they in turn attacked Judah. The men of Judah then captured Samson, bound his hands with ropes and handed him over to the Philistines. The Spirit of the Lord came upon Samson and the bonds caught fire and dropped from his hands. Samson then took the jawbone of an ass and slew a thousand Philistines. Throwing the jawbone away, he called the place 'Destruction of the Jawbone.' Since Samson was thirsty, God opened the wound of the jawbone (according to the LXX text) and water came forth from it.

8. *A spring of water*. Evagrius usually understand springs of water as the virtues from which flows gnosis (knowledge of God). Cf. S51-Prov. 4:21, '*So that your springs may not abandon you, guard them in your heart.*' He calls the virtues 'springs,' from which is begotten the 'living water' (John 4:11). Which is the knowledge of Christ'; cf. also S9-Ps 17:16 'He calls springs the virtues from which there issues knowledge.'

9. *A tent peg*. Jael killed Sisera by approaching quietly while he slept and driving a tent peg into his head.

11. Extravagance in foods pleases the throat, but it nourishes the unsleeping worm of licentiousness.

12. A stomach in want is prepared to spend vigils in prayers, but a full stomach induces a lengthy sleep.

13. Vigilant thinking is found in the driest regimen; a life of moist diet plunges the mind into the deep.

14. The prayer of one who fasts is like a young eagle soaring upwards, whereas that of a drunkard is born downwards under the weight of satiety.

15. The mind of one who fasts is like a radiant star in the clear night air; that of a drunkard is concealed in a moonless night.

16. Fog conceals the sun's rays; and heavy consumption of food darkens the mind.

17. A soiled mirror does not produce a clear image of the form that falls upon it; when the intellect is blunted by satiety, it does not receive the knowledge of God.

18. Land that has become barren produces thorns; and the mind of a glutton grows shameful thoughts.

19. It is not possible to find spices in the mud, nor the fragrance of contemplation in a glutton.

20. A glutton's eye is busy looking for dinner parties; the eye of the abstinent person is busy looking for meetings of the wise.

21. A glutton's soul rejoices at the commemorations of the martyrs;[10] that of the abstinent person imitates their lives.

22. A cowardly soldier shudders at the trumpet that announces the battle; the glutton shudders at the proclamation of abstinence.

23. The gluttonous monk, under the burden and scourge of his belly, demands a daily share of the spoils.

24. The speedy traveller will quickly gain the city, and the abstinent monk a state of peace.[11]

25. The slow traveller will have to make camp in the desert[12] under the sky, and the gluttonous monk will not attain the abode of impassibility.

26. The smoke of incense sweetens the air, and the prayer of the abstinent person presents a sweet odour to God (cf. Rev. 8:4).

10. *The commemorations of the martyrs.* Funeral banquets were held to commemorate the death of the martyrs. Such celebrations were often occasions for excesses in eating and drinking.

11. *A state of peace.* This is a synonym for *apatheia*, 'impassibility.'

12. *Make camp in the desert.* Evagrius interprets the desert as a symbol for 'the rational soul deprived of God.' *Egypt* signifies evil; the *desert,* the practical life; the land of *Judah,* the contemplations of the bodies; *Jerusalem,* that of the incorporeals; and *Zion* is the symbol of the Trinity.

27. If you give yourself over to the desire for food, nothing will suffice to fulfil your pleasure, for the desire for food is a fire that ever takes in and is ever in flames.

28. A sufficient measure fills a vessel; a full stomach does not say, 'Enough!'

29. An extension of hands put Amalek to flight (Exod. 17:11), and the raising of practical works subdues the passions of the flesh.

30. Exterminate from yourself every breath of wickedness and forcefully mortify the members of your flesh (cf. Col. 3:5). In the same way that an enemy destroyed can cause you no fear, so the mortified body will not trouble the soul.

31. A dead body does not experience the pain caused by fire, nor does the abstinent person experience the pleasure of desire that is dead.

32. If you strike an Egyptian, hide him in the sand (Exod. 2:11–12); and do not fatten the body with a vanquished passion, for as the hidden plant grows on fertile land, so does passion sprout afresh in a fat body.[13]

33. An extinguished flame lights again if it is given firewood; and a pleasure that has been extinguished is rekindled in a satiety of food.

34. Do not pity a body that is debilitated and in mourning, nor fatten it up with rich foods, for if it gains strength it will rebel against you and wage unrelenting war upon you, until it takes your soul captive and delivers you as a slave to the passion of fornication.

35. A docile horse, lean in body, never throws its rider, for the horse that is restrained yields to the bit and is compelled by the hand of the one holding the reins; the body is subdued with hunger and vigil and does not jump when a thought mounts upon it, nor does it snort when it is moved by an impassioned impulse.

4. *Anger*

1. Anger is a passion that leads to madness and easily drives those who possess it out of their senses; it makes the soul wild and moves it to shun all (human) encounter.

2. A fierce wind will not move a tower; irascibility cannot carry off a soul free from anger.

3. Water is driven by the force of the winds; the irascible person is troubled by senseless thoughts.

4. The angry monk, like a solitary wild boar, saw some people and gnashed his teeth.

---

13. *If you strike an Egyptian, hide him in the sand.* For Evagrius Egypt is the symbol of evil and the Egyptians a symbol for the disposition of evil. So the Egyptian buried in the sand is the evil passion buried in the sterile soil where it will wither and die.

5. The forming of a mist thickens the air; the movement of irascibility thickens the intellect of the angry person.
6. A passing cloud darkens the sun; a thought of resentment darkens the mind.
7. A lion in a cage continuously rattles the hinges; the irascible monk in his cell rattles thoughts of anger.
8. A calm sea is a delight to contemplate, but there is nothing more delightful than a state of peace. For dolphins go diving in a sea that is calm; thoughts worthy of God swim in a state of peace.
9. A patient monk is like a still spring offering a gentle drink to all, but the intellect of an angry person is always disturbed and provides no water to the thirsty, and if it does offer water it is muddy and useless.
10. The eyes of an angry person are irritated and bloodshot and are indicative of a troubled heart; the face of a patient person is composed, with gentle eyes looking downwards.
11. The gentleness of a man is remembered by God (cf. Ps. 131:1), and a soul without anger becomes a temple of the Holy Spirit.
12. Christ reclines his head on a patient spirit (cf. Matt. 8:20), and an intellect at peace becomes a shelter for the Holy Trinity.
13. Foxes find shelter in the resentful soul, and beasts make their lairs in a troubled heart.
14. A distinguished person avoids a shameful inn, and God avoids a resentful heart.
15. When a stone falls into water it troubles it; an evil word troubles a man's heart.
16. Remove thoughts of anger from your soul, and let not irascibility lodge in your heart, and you will not be troubled at the time of prayer. In the same way as the smoke from chaff irritates the eyes, so does resentment irritate the mind in the time of prayer.
17. The thoughts of the irascible person are a viper's offspring (cf. Matt. 3:7); they consume the heart that gave them birth.
18. The prayer of the irascible person is an abominable incense offering (cf. Isa. 1:13); the psalmody of an angry person is an irritating noise.
19. The gift of a resentful person is a blemished sacrifice (cf. Lev. 22:22) and does not approach the consecrated altar.
20. The irascible person sees disturbing nightmares, and an angry person imagines attacks of wild beasts.
21. A patient person has visions of encounters with holy angels, and one free from resentment discourses on spiritual matters and receives in the night the answers to mysteries.

8. Pride

1. Pride is a tumor of the soul filled with pus; when it has ripened, it will rupture and create a great disgusting mess.
2. A flash of lightning foretells the sound of thunder; vainglory announces the presence of pride.
3. The soul of a proud person mounts a great height, and casts him down from there into an abyss.
4. A rock broken off from a mountain descends in a quick rush; the person who has withdrawn from God quickly falls.
5. The one who has distanced himself from God suffers the disease of pride in ascribing his accomplishments to his own strength.
6. As he who mounts a spider web falls through and is born downwards, so he falls who is confident of his own strength.
7. A lot of fruit bends a tree's new branches; an abundance of virtue humbles a person's thinking.
8. Rotten fruit is useless to the farmer; the virtue of the proud person will be of no use to God.
9. The vine-prop supports the young branch weighed down with fruit; the fear of God the virtuous soul. As the weight of fruit knocks down the young branch, so does pride cast down the virtuous soul.
10. Do not give your soul to pride, and you will not see terrifying fantasies, for the soul of the proud person is abandoned by God and becomes a plaything of the demons: at night he imagines a multitude of wild beasts approaching and by day he is troubled by thoughts of cowardice; when he falls asleep he is continually jumping up and when he is awake he cowers at a bird's shadow; the sound of a leaf frightens the proud man and the noise of water breaks down his soul. He who a little while before set himself against God and rejected his help is later frightened by paltry fantasies.
11. Pride cast the archangel from heaven and made him fall to earth like lightning (cf. Isa. 14:12; Luke 10:18). Humility leads a person up to heaven and prepares him to dance with the angels.
12. Why do you put on airs, fellow, if you are mud and rot (cf. Job 4:19; 25:6)? Why do you puff yourself up and exalt yourself above the clouds? Consider your nature, that you are earth and ashes (cf. Gen. 18:27), and in a little while will dissolve into dust—a swaggerer now, but in a while a worm (cf. Ps. 21:7). Why do you raise your neck which in a while will turn to rot? A great thing is the human being who is helped by God; he is abandoned and then he realizes the weakness

of his nature. You have nothing good which you have not received from God (cf. 1 Cor. 4:7). Why then do you glory in another's (good) as if it were your own? Why do you pride yourself in the grace of God as if it were your own possession? Acknowledge the one who gave it and do not exalt yourself so much. You are a creature of God; do not reject the Creator. You receive help from God; do not deny your benefactor. You have mounted to the height of this way of life, but he has guided you. You have attained the accomplishments of virtue, but he has wrought this together with you. Confess the one who exalted you that you may remain secure on the heights. You are a human being; remain within the bounds of your nature. Acknowledge one of your own kind because he is of the same substance as you; do not deny the relationship because of vain boasting. Though he is humble and you are haughty, still the same Creator formed you both. Do not despise the humble person, for he stands more secure than you. He walks on the earth and does not quickly fall, but the haughty person will get bruised if he falls.

13. Pride is an unsound vehicle, and he who gets into it is quickly thrown. The humble person always stands firm and the foot of pride (Ps. 35:12) will never trip him.

14. The proud monk is a tree without roots; he will not bear the rush of the wind.

15. An attitude that is not puffed up is a walled city; he who lives in it will be unharmed.

16. A breath of wind sends straw into the air; an attack of presumption exalts the proud man.

17. When a bubble bursts it will disappear; the memory of the proud person perishes after his death.

18. The word of a humble person is a soothing ointment for the soul, but that of a proud person is filled with boasting.

19. The prayer of a humble person gets God's attention, but the supplication of the proud vexes God.

20. A precious stone is striking in a gold setting; a person's humility is resplendent among many virtues.

21. One celebrating Passover eats unleavened bread often (cf. Exod. 12:18–20); a virtuous soul is nourished on freedom from arrogance. For as leavened bread rises from the moment it is first near a fire, but unleavened bread remains in a lowly form, so virtue exalts the proud person but it does not puff up the humble person with presumption.

22. If you are fleeing Laban the Syrian, flee in secret and do not trust his promise to escort you, for through those means whereby he said he would escort you, he shall restrain you. For in escorting you with musicians, flutes, and drums,

he contrives to pull back the fleeing mind by beguiling it with the sound of music and by dissipating its moral resolve with the harmony of the melody (Gen. 31:20–7).

23. A staff is a symbol of instruction; he who holds it crosses the Jordan of life (cf. Gen. 32:10).

24. A staff in the hand of a traveller is useful for every purpose; instruction in the practical life directs a person's life.

25. A staff cast away becomes a serpent (Exod. 4:3); instruction that departs from the practical life becomes pleasure.

26. Do not let the serpent that crawls on the ground frighten you; nor the passion of pleasure that creeps among earthly material concerns. For if you grab it by the tail, it will again be a staff in your hand (Exod. 4:4); if you gain control of a passion it will again become instruction.

27. In the desert a serpent bites and kills the soul (cf. Num. 21:6); pleasure wounds and destroys the mind with ease.

28. He who looks at the bronze serpent escapes death (Num. 21:9); he who gazes upon the rewards of chastity shall live forever.

29. A serpent bites a horse's hoof (Gen. 49:17–18); the reason of chastity touches passion.[14]

30. A long-standing infection is cured with a cautery; a habit of vainglory by dishonor and sadness.

31. The scalpel and cautery cause a great deal of pain, but they restrict the spreading of the wound; on the one hand, dishonor pains the one being treated, but on the other, it puts a stop to the grievous passions, namely vainglory and pride.

32. Humility is the parapet of a housetop, and it keeps safe the one who gets up upon it (Deut. 22:8).[15] When you ascend to the height of the virtues, then you will have much need of security. He who falls at ground level gets up quickly, but he who falls from a high place is in danger of death.

14. *The reason of chastity.* The *logos* of chastity may refer either to the 'word' of counsel about chastity or the 'reason,' the ultimate principle, of chastity that dissolves passion. One manuscript extends the scriptural allusion: 'when the horse was bitten by a serpent, the horseman fell backwards (Gen. 49:17); the mind of one who loves pleasure inclined to evil when passion caught hold. The rider who fell backwards when the horse broke off waits for salvation from the Lord (Gen. 49:18); when the mind has fallen away it calls upon the help of God. An extension of hands put Amalek in flight (Exod. 17:11); actions directed upwards in truth mortify the passions.'

15. *The parapet of a housetop.* Deut. 22:8, "If you build a new house, you shall make a parapet on the housetop, and you will not be responsible for a death in your house if someone falls from it."

GREGORY THE GREAT'S *MORALS ON THE BOOK OF JOB*

Introduction

Pope Gregory the Great's massive *Morals on the Book of Job* is also called *An Extensive Consideration of Moral Questions* or the *Magna Moralia*, or *The Humungous Book of Moral Lessons that a Super Smart Guy Working for a Long Time (and without a Computer!) Drew from the Book of Job*. It could also be called *The Seven Degrees of Job*. If you have played the quirky and popular game Seven Degrees of Kevin Bacon, you know that the object is to take the most obscure thing and, by degrees, link it back to one common hub, like Kevin Bacon. Gregory uses the book of Job as his hub and then connects what seems like every historical, allegorical, and moral idea; every person, place, event; every biblical and nonbiblical religious precept back to Job, by degrees. So of course Gregory links Job with the seven gifts of the Spirit, the four cardinal virtues, the three theological virtues (plus one), and the seven—make that eight—vices. As Gregory plays Seven Degrees of Job, he brings together key ideas about virtue and vice, about their nature, and about their relationship to one another and to the soul. Gregory often draws an organic connection among the virtues and among the vices, while continuing the image of the martial conflict between virtue and vice. By bringing together so many ideas and vividly presenting their nature and interrelations, and doing it in a book that was extraordinarily popular throughout the medieval period, it is probably not an overstatement to say that Gregory is both the preserving link and the foundational source for ideas about virtue and vice.

When Gregory turns his keen mind to Job, he finds everything, including the virtues and vices. The first excerpt below is from Gregory's commentary on the second verse of Job. Here Gregory explores the symbolic or allegorical meaning of Job's seven sons and three daughters. Gregory takes Job as an allegory for the soul. In the soul are born seven sons, who in this case are the seven gifts of the Holy Spirit extrapolated from Isaiah. To these seven sons are added the three daughters of the three theological virtues, bringing the total to the "perfect ten." Gregory talks about how they "feast together," cooperating in the soul's nourishment and insight.

In this same excerpt Gregory develops the idea that just as Job has feared for the possible sins of his children, so the soul must be vigilant about the corruption of its virtues. In order to show how prayer is the soul's proper security system, Gregory uses the example of Ishbosheth. In this rather obscure Bible story, Ishbosheth failed to post a sufficiently vigilant guard, thereby allowing his enemies to enter his home and kill him while he was asleep (2 Samuel 4). With the example of Ishbosheth Gregory continues to play the Seven Degrees of Job via a Bible story that illustrates an allegorical and moral truth.

Gregory also links verses from Job with the cardinal virtues. In the second excerpt Gregory takes as his point of departure the verse about the wind blasting the four corners of the house where Job's children ate. Gregory identifies those four corners with the four supports of Prudence, Temperance, Fortitude, and Justice. He further connects them with the four rivers of Paradise as Saint Ambrose had done. Gregory mentions how these four rivers can water the heart. He also warns that those four, to return to the previous metaphor, can be attacked by whirlwinds of vice, leaving the virtues exposed to sin and causing the whole structure to collapse and devastate the moral character. He explores the relationship between the four cardinal virtues and the seven gifts of the Holy Spirit, and then further shows how even the attack and apparent collapse of the entire structure could be ultimately beneficial. From such a collapse the soul could learn true vigilance, humility, and complete reliance on God.

Where Job encounters the miserable comforts of his three friends, Gregory finds how the vices can come cloaked as virtues. The reverent and humble may initially see the vices for what they are, but even those vices may attempt deeper deceptions. Just as Job was able to see through their fraud, so the vigilant soul can see the truth and transform potential vices into powerful virtues.

The power and nature of vice is the last excerpt's central subject. Gregory connects a battle image from Job with the vices' tremendous assaults. Pride first takes control of the heart and then gives the field to generals, the seven principal vices: Vain Glory, Envy, Anger, Melancholy, Avarice, Gluttony, and Lust. Each general in turn brings lieutenants and captains in the form of accompanying vices. Gregory develops the interrelatedness of the vices, and then explores how the vices attempt to use reason to continue their devastation of the "conquered heart."

There is an element of the virtues and vices tradition that comes into sharp focus in these excerpts that should be noted. Gregory mentions how important it is for the soul to have proper vigilance to prevent the corruption or the overthrow of its virtues. He also mentions the wrong security system—women. He makes a point of how a woman had fallen asleep when she was supposed to be guarding Ishbosheth's house. As he explores the allegorical and moral meaning of this, Gregory concludes that women lack the proper manly skills, the virtue of a *vir* (or man) to ensure safety. This shows how the virtues can be used in a gendered way, or at least in a specifically gendered way that would place an accent on male moral superiority. There is a fundamental sexism at work here, as virtue can mean a moral excellence that women do not possess. It is also interesting to note that Pride is the "queen" of sins, conquering the heart for her generals, and opposed by the clearly masculine Redeemer of the soul. Gregory's influential text, purposefully or not, perpetuates a sexism that is part of the virtues and vices tradition.

Gregory's lists of virtues and vices are not original. He draws upon the gifts of the Spirit, and the cardinal and theological virtues while adapting Evagrius's list of the evil thoughts. As mentioned in this section's introduction, Gregory would have indirectly encountered that list through John Cassian, whose writings were part of the Benedictine canon. The genius of Gregory is to connect all these traditions to one text, the book of Job. Gregory builds on the work of previous thinkers, preserving the insights of the past while giving a lively and compelling depiction that would be a key source for the various virtues and vices in the Western world. In the end, in order to discuss the virtues and vices in the Western world one is compelled to go back to the *Morals on the Book of Job*, or to, in some ways, play the Seven Degrees of Gregory.

First Part, Book I, Sections 38 and 44 through 49[16]

Job 1:2, And there were born unto him seven sons and three daughters.
38. For there are seven sons born to us, when by the conception of good intent the seven virtues of the holy Spirit spring up in us. Thus the Prophet particularizes this inward offspring, when the Spirit renders the mind fruitful, in these words; And the Spirit of the Lord shall rest upon Him, the spirit of wisdom and understanding, the spirit of counsel and might, the spirit of knowledge and piety, and the spirit of the fear of the Lord shall fill him. [Isa. 11:2] So when by the coming of the Holy Spirit there is engendered in each of us, 'wisdom, understanding, counsel, might, knowledge, piety, and the fear of the Lord,' something like a lasting posterity is begotten in the mind, which preserves the stock of our nobility that is above unto life, for so much the longer as it allies it with the love of eternity. Yet surely the seven sons have in us three sisters, forasmuch as all that manly work which these virtuous affections do, they unite with faith, hope, and charity. For the seven sons never attain the perfection of the number ten, unless all that they do be done in faith, hope, and charity . . .

Ver. 4. And his sons went and feasted in their houses, every one his day.
44. 'The sons feast in their houses,' when the several virtues feed the mind after their proper sort; and it is well said, Everyone his day, for each son's day is the shining of each virtue. Briefly to unfold then these same gifts of sevenfold grace, wisdom has one day, understanding another day, counsel another, fortitude another, knowledge another, piety another, fear another, for it is not the same thing to be wise that it is to understand; for many indeed are wise in the things of eternity, but cannot in any sort understand them. Wisdom therefore gives a feast in its day in that it refreshes the mind with the hope and assurance of eternal things. Understanding spreads a feast in its day, forasmuch as, in that it penetrates the truths heard, refreshing the heart, it lights up its darkness. Counsel gives a feast in its day, in that while it stays us from acting precipitately, it makes the mind to be full of reason. Fortitude gives a feast in its day, in that whereas it has no fear of adversity, it sets the viands of confidence before the alarmed soul. Knowledge prepares a feast in her day, in that in the mind's belly, she overcomes the emptiness of ignorance. Piety sets forth a feast in its day, in that it satisfies the bowels of the heart with deeds of mercy. Fear makes a feast in its day, in

16. From Gregory the Great, *Morals on the Book of Job*, vol. 1, trans. J. H. Parker (Oxford: Oxford University Press, 1844–50), 52–53, 56–60, 118–23, 174–76; ibid., 5th part, book 31, 489–92,

that whereas it keeps down the mind, that it may not pride itself in the present things, it strengthens it with the meat of hope for the future.

45. But I see that this point requires searching into in this feasting of the sons, viz. that by turns they feed one another. For each particular virtue is to the last degree destitute, unless one virtue lends its support to another. For wisdom is less worth if it lacks understanding, and understanding is wholly useless if it be not based upon wisdom, in that whilst it penetrates the higher mysteries without the counterpoise of wisdom, its own lightness is only lifting it up to meet with the heavier fall. Counsel is worthless, when the strength of fortitude is lacking thereto, since what it finds out by turning the thing over, from want of strength it never carries on so far as to the perfecting in deed; and fortitude is very much broken down, if it be not supported by counsel, since the greater the power which it perceives itself to have, so much the more miserably does this virtue rush headlong into ruin, without the governance of reason. Knowledge is nought if it hath not its use for piety; for whereas it neglects to put in practice the good that it knows, it binds itself the more closely to the Judgment: and piety is very useless, if it lacks the discernment of knowledge, in that while there is no knowledge to enlighten it, it knows not the way to shew mercy. And assuredly unless it has these virtues with it, fear itself rises up to the doing of no good action, forasmuch as while it is agitated about every thing, its own alarms renders it inactive and void of all good works. Since then by reciprocal ministrations virtue is refreshed by virtue, it is truly said that the sons feast with one another by turns; and as one aids to relieve another, it is as if the numerous offspring to be fed were to prepare a banquet each his day. It follows;

And sent and called for their three sisters, to eat and to drink with them.

46. When our virtues invite faith, hope, and charity into every thing they do, they do, as sons employed in labor, call their three sisters to a feast; that faith, hope, and charity may rejoice in the good work, which each virtue provides; and they as it were gain strength from that meat, whilst they are rendered more confident by good works, and whereas after meat they long to imbibe the dew of contemplation, they are as it were from the cup inebriated.

47. But what is there that we do, in this life, without some stain of defilement, howsoever slight? For sometimes by the very good things we do we draw near to the worse part, since while they beget much in the mind, they at the same time engender a certain security, and when the mind enjoys security, it unlooses itself in sloth; and sometimes they defile us with some self-elation, and set us so much the lower with God, as they make us bigger in our own eyes. Hence it is well added,

Ver. 5. And it was so, when the days of their feasting were gone about, that Job sent and sanctified them.

47. For, when the round of the days of feasting is gone about, to send to his sons and to sanctify them, is after the perception of the virtues to direct the inward intention, and

to purify all that we do with the exact sifting of a reexamination, lest things be counted good which are evil, or at least such as are truly good be thought enough when they are imperfect. For thus it very often happens that the mind is taken in, so that it is deceived either in the quality of what is evil or the quantity of what is good. But these senses of the virtues are much better ascertained by prayers than by examinings. For the things which we endeavor to search out more completely in ourselves, we oftener obtain a true insight into by praying than by investigating. For when the mind is lifted up on high by the kind of machine of compunction, all that may have been presented to it concerning itself, it surveys the more surely by passing judgment upon it beneath its feet. Hence it is well subjoined,

And rose up early in the morning and offered burnt offerings, according to the number of them all.

48. For we rise up early in the morning, when being penetrated with the light of compunction we leave the night of our human state, and open the eyes of the mind to the beams of the true light, and we offer a burnt offering for each son, when we offer up the sacrifice of prayer for each virtue, lest wisdom may uplift; or understanding, while it runs nimbly, deviate from the right path; or counsel, while it multiplies itself, grow into confusion; that fortitude, while it gives confidence, may not lead to precipitation, lest knowledge, while it knows and yet has no love, may swell the mind; lest piety, while it bends itself out of the right line, may become distorted; and lest fear, while it is unduly alarmed, may plunge one into the pit of despair. When then we pour out our prayers to the Lord in behalf of each several virtue, that it be free from alloy, what else do we but according to the number of our sons offer a burnt offering for each? for an holocaust is rendered 'the whole burnt.' Therefore to pay a 'holocaust' is to light up the whole soul with the fire of compunction, that the heart may burn on the altar of love, and consume the defilements of our thoughts, like the sins of our own offspring,

49. But none know how to do this saving those, who, before their thoughts proceed to deeds, restrain with anxious circumspection the inward motions of their hearts. None know how to do this saving they who have learnt to fortify their soul with a manly guard. Hence Ishbosheth is rightly said to have perished by a sudden death, whom holy Scripture at the same time testifies to have had not a man for his doorkeeper but a woman, in these words; And the sons of Rimmon the Beerothite, Rechab and Baanah, went and came about the heat of the day to the house of Ishbosheth, who lay on a bed at noon; and they came thither into the midst of the house:, and the portress of the house was fallen asleep, winnowing wheat. And they came privily into the house fetching ears of wheat, and they smote him in the groin (2 Sam 4:5–7). The portress winnows the wheat, when the wardkeeping of the mind distinguishes and separates the virtues from the vices; but if she falls asleep, she lets in conspirators to her master's destruction, in that when the cautiousness of discernment is at an end, a way is set open for evil spirits to slay the soul. They enter in and carry off the ears, in

that they at once bear off the germs of good thoughts; and they smite in the groin, in that they cut off the virtue of the soul by the delights of the flesh. For to smite in the groin is to pierce the life of the mind with the delights of the flesh. But this Ishbosheth would never have perished by such a death, if he had not set a woman at the entrance to his house, i.e. set an easy guard at the way of access to the mind. For a strong and manly activity should be set over the doors of the heart, such as is never surprised by sleep of neglect, and never deceived by the errors of ignorance; and hence he is rightly named Ishbosheth, who is exposed by a female guard to the swords of his enemies, for Ishbosheth is rendered 'a man of confusion.' And he is 'a man of confusion,' who is not provided with a strong guard over his mind, in that while he reckons himself to be practising virtues, vices stealing in kill him unawares. The entrance to the mind then must be fortified with the whole sum of virtue, lest at any time enemies with insidious intent penetrate into it by the opening of heedless thought. Hence Solomon says, Keep thy heart with all diligence, for out of it are the issues of life (Prov. 4:23). It is meet then that we form a most careful estimate of the virtues that we practise, beginning with the original intent, lest the acts which they put forth, even though they be right, may proceed from a bad origin: and hence it is rightly subjoined in this place;

First Part, Book II, Sections 76 through 79

Ver. 18, 19. While he was yet speaking, there came also another, and said, Thy sons and thy daughters were eating and drinking wine in their eldest brother's house: And, behold, there came a great wind from the wilderness, and smote the four corners of the house, and it fell upon the young men, and they are dead; and I only am escaped alone to tell thee.

76. As we have before said, 'the wilderness' is the deserted multitude of impure spirits, which when it forsook the felicity of its Creator, as it were lost the hand of the cultivator. And from the same there came a strong wind, and overthrew the house; in that strong temptation seizes us from the unclean spirits, and overturns the conscience from its settled frame of tranquillity. But this house stands by four corners for this reason, that the firm fabric of our mind is upheld by Prudence, Temperance, Fortitude, Justice. This house is grounded on four corners, in that the whole structure of good practice is raised in these four virtues. And hence do four rivers of Paradise water the earth. For while the heart is watered with these four virtues, it is cooled from all the heat of carnal desires. Yet sometimes when idleness steals on the mind, prudence waxes cold; for when it is weary and turns slothful, it neglects to forecast coming events. Sometimes while some delight is stealing on the mind, our temperance decays. For in whatever degree we are led to take delight in the things of this life, we are the less temperate to forbear in things forbidden. Sometimes fear works its way into the heart and confounds the powers of our fortitude, and we prove the less able to encounter adversity, the more excessively we love some things that we dread to part with. And sometimes self-love invades the mind, makes it swerve by a secret declension from

the straight line of justice: and in the degree that it refuses to refer itself wholly to its Maker, it goes contrary to the claims of justice. Thus 'a strong wind smites the four corners of the house,' in that strong temptation, by hidden impulses, shakes the four virtues; and the corners being smitten, the house is as it were uprooted; in that when the virtues are beaten, the conscience is brought to trouble.

77. Now it is within these four corners of the house that the sons are feasting, because it is within the depths of the mind, which is carried up to the topmost height of perfection in these four virtues especially, that the others like a kind of offspring of the heart take their food together. For the gift of the Spirit, which, in the mind It works on, forms first of all Prudence, Temperance, Fortitude, Justice, in order that the same mind may be perfectly fashioned to resist every species of assault, doth afterwards give it a temper in the seven virtues, so as against folly to bestow Wisdom, against dulness, Understanding, against rashness, Counsel, against fear, Courage, against ignorance, Knowledge, against hardness of heart, Piety, against pride, Fear.

78. But sometimes, whilst the mind is sustained with the plenitude and richness of a gift so large, if it enjoys uninterrupted security in these things, it forgets from what source it has them, and imagines that it derives that from itself, which it sees to be never wanting to it. Hence it is that this same grace sometimes withdraws itself for our good, and shews the presumptuous mind how weak it is in itself. For then we really learn whence our good qualities proceed, when, by seemingly losing them, we are made sensible that they can never be preserved by our own efforts. And so for the purpose of tutoring us in lessons of humility, it very often happens that, when the crisis of temptation is upon us, such extreme folly comes down upon our wisdom, that the mind being dismayed, knows nothing how to meet the evils that are threatened, or how to make ready against temptation. But by this very folly, the heart is wisely instructed; forasmuch as from whatever cause it turns to folly for a moment, it is afterwards rendered by the same the more really, as it is the more humbly, wise; and by these very means, whereby wisdom seems as if lost, it is held in more secure possession. Sometimes when the mind lifts itself up in pride on the grounds of seeing high things, it is dulled with a remarkable obtuseness in the lowest and meanest subjects; that he, who with rapid flight penetrated into the highest things, should in a moment see the very lowest closed to his understanding. But this very dulness preserves to us, at the very time that it withdraws from us, our power of understanding. For whereas it abases the heart for a moment, it strengthens it in a more genuine way to understand the loftiest subjects. Sometimes while we are congratulating ourselves that we do every thing with grave deliberation, some piece of chance takes us in the nick, and we are carried off with a sudden precipitancy; and we, who believed ourselves always to have lived by method, are in a moment laid waste with an inward confusion. Yet by the discipline of this very confusion we learn not to attribute our counsels to our own powers; and we hold to gravity with the more matured endeavors, that we return to the same as if once lost. Sometimes while the mind resolutely defies adversity, when

adverse events rise up, she is struck with violent alarm. But when agitated thereby, she learns to Whom to attribute it, that on any occasion she stood firm; and she afterwards holds fast her fortitude the more resolutely, as she sees it now gone as it were out of her hand the moment that terror came upon her. Sometimes whilst we are congratulating ourselves that we know great things, we are stunned with a blindness of instantaneous ignorance. But in so far as the eye of the mind is for a moment closed by ignorance, it is afterwards the more really opened to admit knowledge, in that in fact being instructed by the stroke of its blindness, it may know also from whom it has its very knowing. Sometimes while ordering all things in a religious spirit, when we congratulate ourselves that we have in abundant measure the bowels of pious tenderness, we are struck with a sudden fit of hardness of heart. But when thus as it were hardened, we learn to Whom to ascribe the good dispositions of piety which we have; and the piety, which has been in a manner extinguished, is recovered with more reality, seeing that it is loved with fuller affection as having been lost. Sometimes while the mind is overjoyed that it is bowed under the fear of God, it suddenly waxes stiff under the temptations of pride. Yet immediately conceiving great fears that it should have no fear, it speedily turns back again to humility, which it recovers upon a firmer footing, in proportion as it has felt the weight of this virtue by seeming to let it go.

79. When the house, then, is overthrown, the sons perish; because when the conscience is disturbed under temptation, the virtues that are engendered in the heart, for any advantage from ourselves knowing them, are speedily and in the space of a moment overwhelmed. Now these sons live inwardly by the Spirit, though they perish outwardly in the flesh; because, forsooth, although our virtues in the time of temptation be disordered in a moment, and fall from the safety of their seat, yet by perseverance in endeavor they hold on unimpaired in the root of the mind. With these the three sisters likewise are slain, for in the heart, sometimes Charity is ruffled by afflictions, Hope shaken by fear, Faith beaten down by questionings. For oftentimes we grow dull in the love of our Creator, while we are chastened with the rod beyond what we think suitable for us. Often while the mind fears more than need be, it weakens the confidence of its hopes. Often while the intellect is exercised with endless questionings, faith being staggered grows faint, as though it would fail. But yet the daughters live, who die when the house is struck. For notwithstanding that in the seat of the conscience the disorder by itself tells that Faith, Hope, and Charity, are almost slain, yet they are kept alive in the sight of God, by perseverance in a right purpose of mind; and hence a servant escapes alone to tell these things, in that discretion of mind remains unhurt even amid temptations. And the servant is the cause that Job recovers his sons by weeping, whilst the mind, being grieved at what discretion reports, keeps by penitence the powers which it had in a manner begun to part with. By a marvellous dispensation of Providence are we thus dealt with, so that our conscience is at times struck with the smitings of guilt. For a person would count himself possessed of great powers indeed, if he never at any time within the depth of his mind felt the

failure of them. But when the mind is shaken by the assaults of temptation, and is as it were more than enough disheartened, there is shewn to it the defence of humility against the arts of its enemy, and from the very occasion, whence it fears to sink powerless, it receives strength to stand firm. But the person tempted not only learns from Whom he has his strength, but is made to understand with what great watchfulness he must preserve it. For oftentimes one, whom the conflict of temptation had not force to overcome, has been brought down in a worse way by his own self-security. For when anyone awearied relaxes himself at his ease, he abandons his mind without restraint to the corrupter. But if, by the dispensations of mercy from above, the stroke of temptation falls upon him, not so as to overwhelm him with a sudden violence, but to instruct him by a measured approach, then he is awakened to foresee the snares, so that with a cautious mind he girds himself to face the enemy in fight. And hence it is rightly subjoined,

First Part, Book III, Sections 65 through 70

65. Yet it very often happens, that whilst we are striving to stay ourselves in this fight of temptation by exalted virtues, certain vices cloak themselves to our eyes under the garb of virtues, and come to us as it were with a smooth face, but how adverse to us they are we perceive upon examination. And hence the friends of blessed Job as it were come together for the purpose of giving comfort, but they burst out into reviling, in that vices that plot our ruin assume the look of virtues, but strike us with hostile assault. For often immoderate anger desires to appear justice, and often dissolute remissness, mercy; often fear without precaution would seem humility, often unbridled pride, liberty. Thus the friends come to give consolation, but fall off into words of reproach, in that vices, cloaked under the guise of virtues, set out indeed with a smooth outside, but confound us by a bitter hostility. And it is rightly said,

Ver. 11. For they had made an appointment together to come to mourn with him and to comfort him.

66. For vices make an appointment together under the cloak of virtues; in that there are certain ones, which are banded together against us by a kind of agreement, such as pride and anger, remissness and fear. For anger is neighbor to pride, and remissness to cowardice. Those then come together by agreement, which are allied to one another in opposition to us, by a kind of kinship in iniquity; but if we acknowledge the toilsomeness of our captivity, if we grieve in our inmost soul from love of our eternal home, the sins that steal upon the inopportunely joyful, will not be able to prevail against the opportunely sad. Hence it is well added,

Ver. 12. And when they lifted up their eyes afar off, and knew him not, they lifted up their voice, and wept.

67. For the vices do not know us in our afflictions, in that so soon as they have knocked at the dejected heart, being reproved they start back, and they, which as it were knew us in our joy, because they made their way in, cannot know us in our sadness, in that they break their edge on our very rigidity itself. But our old enemy, the more he sees that he is himself caught out in them, and that with a good courage, cloaks them with so much the deeper disguise under the image of virtues; and hence it is added, They lifted up their voice, and wept; and they rent every one his mantle, and sprinkled dust upon their heads toward heaven.

Ver. 13. So they sat down with him upon the ground seven days and seven nights.
68. For by the weeping pity is betokened, discretion by the cutting of the garments, the affecting of good works by the dust upon the head, humility by the sitting. For sometimes the enemy in plotting against us feigns somewhat that is full of pity, that he may bring us down to an end of cruelty. As is the case, when he prevents a fault being corrected by chastisement, that that, which is not suppressed in this life, may be stricken with the fire of hell. Sometimes he presents the form of discretion to the eyes, and draws us on to snares of indiscretion, which happens, when at his instigation we as it were from prudence allow ourselves too much nourishment on account of our weakness, while we are imprudently raising against ourselves assaults of the flesh. Sometimes he counterfeits the affecting of good works, yet hereby entails upon us restlessness in labors, as it happens, when a man cannot remain quiet, and, as it were, fears to be judged for idleness. Sometimes he exhibits the form of humility, that he may steal away our affecting of the useful, as is the case when he declares to some that they are weaker and more useless than indeed they are, that whereas they look upon themselves as too unworthy, they may fear to administer the things wherein they might be able to benefit their neighbors.

69. But these vices which the old enemy hides under the semblance of virtues, are very minutely examined by the hand of compunction. For he that really grieves within, resolutely foredetermines what things are to be done outwardly, and what are not. For if the virtue of compunction moves us in our inward parts, all the clamoring of evil dictates is made mute; and hence it follows,

And none spake a word unto him; for they saw that his grief was very great.
70. For if the heart feels true sorrow, the vices have no tongue against it. And when the life of uprightness is sought with an entire aim, the fruitless prompting of evil is closed up. But oftentimes if we brace ourselves with strong energy against the incitements of evil habits, we turn even those very evil habits to the account of virtue. For some are possessed by anger, but while they submit this to reason, they convert it into service rendered to holy zeal. Some are lifted up by pride. But whilst they bow down the mind to the fear of God, they change this into the free tone of unrestrained authority in defence of justice. Strength of the flesh is a snare to some; but whilst they bring under the body by practising works of mercy, from the same quarter, whence they were

exposed to the goading of wickedness, they purchase the gains of pitifulness. And hence it is well that this blessed Job, after a multitude of conflicts, sacrifices a victim for his friends. For those whom he has for long borne as enemies by their strife, he one day makes fellow-countrymen by his sacrifice, in that whilst we turn all evil thoughts into virtues, bringing them into subjection, by the offering of the intention, we as it were change the hostile aims of temptation into friendly dispositions.

Fifth Part, Book 31, Sections 87 through 91

87. For the tempting vices, which fight against us in invisible contest in behalf of the pride which reigns over them, some of them go first, like captains, others follow, after the manner of an army. For all faults do not occupy the heart with equal access. But while the greater and the few surprise a neglected mind, the smaller and the numberless pour themselves upon it in a whole body. For when pride, the queen of sins, has fully possessed a conquered heart, she surrenders it immediately to seven principal sins, as if to some of her generals, to lay it waste. And an army in truth follows these generals, because, doubtless, there spring up from them importunate hosts of sins. Which we set forth the better, if we specially bring forth in enumeration, as we are able, the leaders themselves and their army. For pride is the root of all evil, of which it is said, as Scripture bears witness; Pride is the beginning of all sin. But seven principal vices, as its first progeny, spring doubtless from the poisonous root, namely, vain glory, envy, anger, melancholy, avarice, gluttony, lust. For, because He grieved that we were held captive by those seven sins of pride, therefore our Redeemer came to the spiritual battle of our liberation, full of the spirit of sevenfold grace.

88. But these several sins have each their army against us. For from vain glory there arise disobedience, boasting, hypocrisy, contentions, obstinacies, discords, and the presumptions of novelties. From envy there spring hatred, whispering, detraction, exultation at the misfortunes of a neighbor, and affliction at his prosperity. From anger are produced strifes, swelling of mind, insults, clamor, indignation, blasphemies. From melancholy there arise malice, rancour, cowardice, despair, slothfulness in fulfilling the commands, and a wandering of the mind on unlawful objects. From avarice there spring treachery, fraud, deceit, perjury, restlessness, violence, and hardnesses of heart against compassion. From gluttony are propagated foolish mirth, scurrility, uncleanness, babbling, dulness of sense in understanding. From lust are generated blindness of mind, inconsiderateness, inconstancy, precipitation, self-love, hatred of God, affection for this present world, but dread or despair of that which is to come. Because, therefore, seven principal vices produce from themselves so great a multitude of vices, when they reach the heart, they bring, as it were, the band of an army after them. But of these seven, five namely are spiritual, and two are carnal.

89. But they are, each of them, so closely connected with other, that they spring only the one from the other. For the first offspring of pride is vain glory, and this,

when it hath corrupted the oppressed mind, presently begets envy. Because doubtless while it is seeking the power of an empty name, it feels envy against any one else being able to obtain it. Envy also generates anger; because the more the mind is pierced by the inward wound of envy, the more also is the gentleness of tranquillity lost. And because a suffering member, as it were, is touched, the hand of opposition is therefore felt as if more heavily impressed. Melancholy also arises from anger, because the more extravagantly the agitated mind strikes itself, the more it confounds itself by condemnation; and when it has lost the sweetness of tranquility, nothing supports it but the grief resulting from agitation. Melancholy also runs down into avarice; because, when the disturbed heart has lost the satisfaction of joy within, it seeks for sources of consolation without, and is more anxious to possess external goods, the more it has no joy on which to fall back within. But after these, there remain behind two carnal vices, gluttony and lust. But it is plain to all that lust springs from gluttony, when in the very distribution of the members, the genitals appear placed beneath the belly. And hence when the one is inordinately pampered, the other is doubtless excited to wantonness.

90. But the leaders are well said to exhort, the armies to howl, because the first vices force themselves into the deluded mind as if under a kind of reason, but the countless vices which follow, while they hurry it on to every kind of madness, confound it, as it were, by bestial clamor. For vain glory is wont to exhort the conquered heart, as if with reason, when it says, Thou oughtest to aim at greater things, that, as thou hast been able to surpass many in power, thou mayest be able to benefit many also. Envy is also wont to exhort the conquered heart, as if with reason, when it says, In what are thou inferior to this or that person? Why then are thou not either equal or superior to them? What great things art thou able to do, which they are not able to do! They ought not then be either superior, or even equal, to thyself. Anger is also wont to exhort the conquered heart, as if with reason, when it says, the things that are done to thee cannot be borne patiently; nay rather, patiently to endure them is a sin; because if thou dost not withstand them with great indignation, they are afterwards heaped upon thee without measure. Melancholy is also wont to exhort the conquered heart as if with reason, when it says, What ground hast thou to rejoice, when thou endurest so many wrongs from thy neighbors? Consider with what sorrow all must be looked upon, who are turned to such gall of bitterness against thee. Avarice is wont to exhort the conquered mind, as if with reason, when it says, It is a very blameless thing, that thou desirest some things to possess; because thou seekest not to be increased, but art afraid of being in want; and that which another retains for no good, thou thyself expendest to better purpose. Gluttony is also wont to exhort the conquered heart, as if with reason, when it says, God has created all things clean, in order to be eaten, and he who refuses to fill himself with food, what else does he do but gainsay the gift that has been granted him. Lust also is wont to exhort the conquered heart, as if with reason, when it says, Why enlargest thou not thyself now in pleasure, when thou knowest not what may follow thee? Thou oughtest not to lose in longings the time

thou hast received; because thou knowest not how speedily it may pass by. For if God had not wished man to be united in the pleasure of coition, He would not, at the first beginning of the human race, have made them male and female. This is the exhortation of leaders, which, when incautiously admitted into the secrecy of the heart, too familiarly persuades to wrong. And this a howling army in truth follows, because when the hapless soul, once captured by the principal vices, is turned to madness by multiplied iniquities, it is now laid waste with brutal cruelty.

PART III

The Medieval Apex

IT MIGHT BE A slight exaggeration, but the virtues and vices were the medieval traffic light. Most everyone today, even a small child, knows what a traffic light means. There is no doubt that red means stop, green means go, and yellow means go faster. (Or does it mean caution, slow down, stop, or make sure there are no police around as you go?) Inspired by the ideas of Tertullian, Prudentius, Evagrius, and Gregory the Great, artists and thinkers for the next thousand years or so used virtue and vice as a similarly clear (and occasionally ambiguous) set of ideas and symbols. We can track this use with four paths or trajectories: Divine Endowment, the Struggle, Contraries Cured by Contraries, and the Summa.

DIVINE ENDOWMENT

As the example of Prudentius's *Psychomachia* shows, early Christians adapted their beliefs to their culture. This is true in the visual arts as well as in literature. The manuscript illustrations for the *Psychomachia* developed the text's martial Roman theme with Roman visual vocabulary. Virtues were dressed as Roman matrons, battle scenes followed Roman artistic conventions for showing conflict, and some manuscripts even used Roman mythological figures like Eros. When Christians wanted to show virtue, especially as a divine gift, they also drew upon classical models.

Christians showed a divine gift or endowment of virtue in various ways. In the *Vienna Dioscurides* from the fifth century, the artist continued the Roman practice of showing people with mythological or abstract figures. This work has a dedicatory portrait of Anicia Julia with figures of Magnanimity and Prudence on either side. Carolingian artists used the same approach, as seen in the portraits of rulers accompanied by the cardinal virtues. It is in these ninth-century works that we find the basic set of symbols associated with those virtues. Prudence holds a book, Justice has a scale, Fortitude is duly armed, and Temperance bears a torch while pouring water from a jug. Prudence, Justice, and Fortitude's symbols persist over time, but Temperance's symbols change. Where in this image Temperance extinguishes the flame of desire or inordinate passion, later versions will show her pouring liquid from one vessel to another, a symbol of diluted wine and therefore moderation.

While images of the virtues may accompany individuals to show their divine endowment, there is another way that medieval artists show virtue as a divine gift. Virtue, meaning both goodness and power, is taken to a higher level in the frontispiece of the *Floreffe Bible* in the British Library (Figure 1). This image, inspired by Gregory's *Commentary*, shows redemption stretching back into the past and reaching toward the future. At the center of the frontispiece are two concentric circles. Against the gold background of the centermost circle stand the full length figures of Faith, Hope, and Charity. Around them are eight medallions set in the larger circle. Seven of these medallions show the Gifts of the Spirit, each with a small banner inscribed with a scriptural phrase. The illustration's top register shows Job's sacrifice blessed by the hand of God. Seated at the large table below Job are his ten children at a feast. On the left side of the central circle is Paul, David stands on the right, and the Twelve Apostles sit in two groups of six below them. We find some of the Acts of Mercy in the bottom register; feeding the hungry, giving drink to the thirsty, clothing the naked, sheltering the homeless, and visiting the imprisoned and the sick. The illustration works chronologically from top to bottom, with Old Testament figures Job, his children, and David giving way to Paul and the Apostles. We see the Works of Mercy, commended throughout time but re-emphasized with Christ, at the bottom. The power of the virtues radiates from the center of the work, exuding God's gracious endowment to the past, present, and future.

Finally, there is an even more common way that we see virtue moving out over time past, present, and future. Numerous medieval objects, like shrines, doors, reliquaries, chalices, crowns, and baptisteries have similar images of the virtues. Such images reinforce the power of the possessors of those objects or the rituals associated with them. Images of the virtues on these objects, not unlike a police officer's badge or shield, visually authorize or show the authority of the possessor or object. Where the officer's badge validates the ticket you just got for not making that yellow light, images of the virtues on various medieval objects validate the rituals associated with them and evidence an endowment of divine authority.

THE STRUGGLE

It is easy to see why a king would want the virtues on his crown. The virtues give him the "green light" to go, to move forward with confidence in his endowment of virtue. We do not want any ambiguous "yellow lights" on the crown—the wearer's virtue may be ambiguous enough! But one place we might appreciate ambiguity, or at least the tension caused by a pitched struggle, is in images of the soul's internal battle between good and evil. In this respect we see many medieval images of conflict though with varying degrees of dramatic tension.

The many manuscripts of Prudentuis's *Psychomachia* provide an obvious example of medieval struggle imagery. Such images seem to have inspired those artists and architects who decorated the Romanesque churches in places like western France. Many of these churches have large, highly visible, and important images of virtues defeating vices. The church of Saint Pierre in Aulney features six figures of the virtues defeating the vices. The figures are in the half-circular bands above the doors, and they are identified by inscriptions. They show, going from left to right, Patience over Anger, Chastity over Lust, Humility over Pride, Giving Alms over Greed, Faith over Idolatry, and Concord over Discord. This list clearly shows the inspiration of Prudentius. These images would reinforce for pilgrims and churchgoers how the virtues can overcome the vices.

In the one hundred or so years between (on the one hand) these images at Aulney and (on the other hand) the cathedral decorations at Amiens, Paris, and Chartres, the virtues slide down the building so that the conflict is at eye level. Where Aulney has large, standing figures, the cathedrals have seated virtues set within a frame. The virtues are still placed above the vices, but additional pairs have been added and some couples have been changed. What remains constant is the struggle, though here again the power of the virtues, conveyed by their being above the vices and by their confident restraint, never seems to be in doubt. The same could be said for Giotto's depictions of the seven virtues contrasted with seven vices in Padua. Placed at eye level, like the cathedral decorations, Giotto's depictions place viewers in the middle of the conflict.

These images of struggle are fairly static; in all of them the virtues handily defeat the vices. In the many medieval images of ladders of virtue, the battle involves the viewer more directly and is not resolved. The inspiration for these images is John Climacus' *Ladder of Virtues*, a book written for monks who would reach, step by step, the highest spiritual heights by overcoming sinful impulses and acquiring heavenly virtues. Eleventh-century illustrations of this ladder, with figures attempting to climb with angelic help and in spite of demonic attacks, show that this image was in circulation before it was adapted for the *Speculum Virginum*. But perhaps the most dramatic medieval depiction of this struggle is Hildegard's theatrical presentation of the soul's struggle in her *Ordo Virtutum*. This work is the great drama of the soul, moving from Edenic innocence through the sinfulness of the fall to a final redemption, all in a pattern that is meant to show every soul's conflictive journey.

There is one last struggle between virtue and vice that we should touch on, and this is instances when virtue seems to be losing. And virtue really is losing in most of the *Roman de Fauvel*! The story tells of the political and social ascendency of a fallow-colored horse named Fauvel, whose name stands for Flattery, Avarice,

Villainy, Variability (Duplicity), Envy, and Cowardice (Lascheté). When Fauvel attempts to secure his place by marrying Fortune, he's given the hand of Vain Glory instead. While Fauvel and Vain Glory's vicious offspring fill the world, the text ends optimistically with a tournament where the virtues, with angelic help, overcome the vices. As a critique of social, political, and religious corruption in France, this work uses the standard of virtues to level that critique. In this respect, the *Roman de Fauvel* is like Ambrogio Lorenzetti's paintings in Siena's Palazzo Pubblico. Both works offer examples of corruption and the rule of vice. Lorenzetti uses another mural to show a clear view of the contrasting rule of virtue, but Fauvel's audience does not need such a blatant contrast, since its own internalized standard of virtue reveals the discrepancy.

CONTRARIES CURED BY CONTRARIES

Images of the struggle between virtue and vice are often pedagogical, even therapeutic. These images seek to teach the viewer how to avoid vice and embrace virtue. A key medieval principle for doing just that is the idea of how contraries cure contraries. Here is an example: you start to feel sluggish and tired, so you decide to go for a brisk walk. You start to feel upset, so you put on some soothing music and examine why you feel angry. You find yourself preoccupied with your neighbor's new car, so you . . . sneak into his garage at night and set it on fire. No! You try to think about all of the great things that you have. In each case you use a contrary to cure a contrary, whether it is activity to cure lethargy, calm music and reason to cure anger, or gratitude to cure envy.

This notion of how contraries cure contraries, something we see today, is central to the virtues and vices tradition, especially in penitential manuals. A penitential manual is a book used by someone with the authority to help heal others. These manuals, like *The Penitential of Cummean*, were strongly influenced by John Cassian's classification of the seven deadly sins. Thus there is a section for the slothful, and the manual stipulates that they are to be given additional work. Gluttons are to fast, the lustful to abstain, and the proud are to humble themselves. These manuals, like legal documents, can also be very specific about intention, circumstances, and duration, clearly establishing the appropriate virtuous cure for its vicious contrary.

Penitential manuals are very important to the virtues and vices tradition. Not only did these manuals preserve and promote the insights of people like Evagrius, but they gave people a framework or standard by which to examine themselves. Individuals could thereby perform a sort of spiritual diagnostics by comparing their souls with the standards provided by the virtues and vices. The church recognized the importance of such an examination. In 1213 Pope Innocent III assembled the Fourth Council of the Lateran. Among the canons or important decisions arrived at during this meeting was Canon 21, mandating that everyone who had reached the "years of discretion" or who was old enough to know better, must confess his or her sins to a priest at least once a year. Confession and penance were based on principles established by penitential manuals. In turn, as this mandated confession filtered down into society, it became necessary for church leaders to train people how to confess. This led to an explosion of tracts and sermons meant to train people on the principles of penance, contrition, confession, and satisfaction or absolution. "The Parson's Tale" is an excellent example of all of these elements. Finally, contrasting images like the *Tree of Virtue* and the *Tree of Vice* or even the many pairings of virtue and vice visually demonstrate how contraries can clarify and cure contraries.

THE SUMMA

The summa is one of the crowning achievements of the medieval world. For our purposes, a summa is a compendium, an encyclopedic bringing together and harmonizing. Summas can be philosophical and theological texts, and a famous example is Saint Thomas Aquinas's *Summa Theologica*. As a compendium of religious knowledge, Saint Thomas's *Summa* has an entire section on habits, and another on virtues, and vices, with a carefully worked out examination of all of their aspects. Medieval thinkers favored the image of the mirror or "speculum" as a metaphor for how all knowledge can come together and can reflect the workings of a supreme Creator. We could even consider the great cathedrals, with their attempt to bring together and harmonize intellectual and spiritual truth, as a summa.

Excellent visual representations of this effort to combine and harmonize truth include images of the *Wheel of Sevens* (Figures 2 and 3). These wheels have seven concentric circles divided into seven sections. Each ring features a subject or theological concept. Starting with the outermost ring and moving to the innermost ring, the rings show the seven elements of the Lord's Prayer, the seven sacraments, the seven gifts of the spirit, the seven weapons of justice, the seven acts of mercy, the seven virtues, and the corresponding vices. It is not by coincidence that these rings look like the geocentric cosmos. This diagram is supposed to show the largest "macro" truths as well as the most individual "micro" truths, bringing together and harmonizing them all.

Though they are different, Dante's *Purgatorio* and Langland's *Piers Plowman* can be seen as summas, or compendiums of various elements of the virtues and vices. Both works affirm virtue as a gift, as a divine endowment. Sinners on Dante's mountain of Purgatory are blessed by virtuous stars and by images of virtue to inspire their ascent. Everyone in the world of *Piers Plowman* is given abilities and spiritual gifts as well as the "seeds" of the cardinal virtues. There is also a pitched struggle in both books. Dante's sinners fight to overcome their vices, and Piers battles the forces of evil and the often evil disposition of everyday people. Both texts also use satirical elements to critique the everyday vices of their contemporary world. Dante's is a powerful example of how contraries cure contraries, and both texts bring together social, political, philosophical, and theological truths into a powerful and harmonious whole. In the works of Dante, Langland, and others we have the apex of the artistic and cultural importance and power of the virtues and vices.

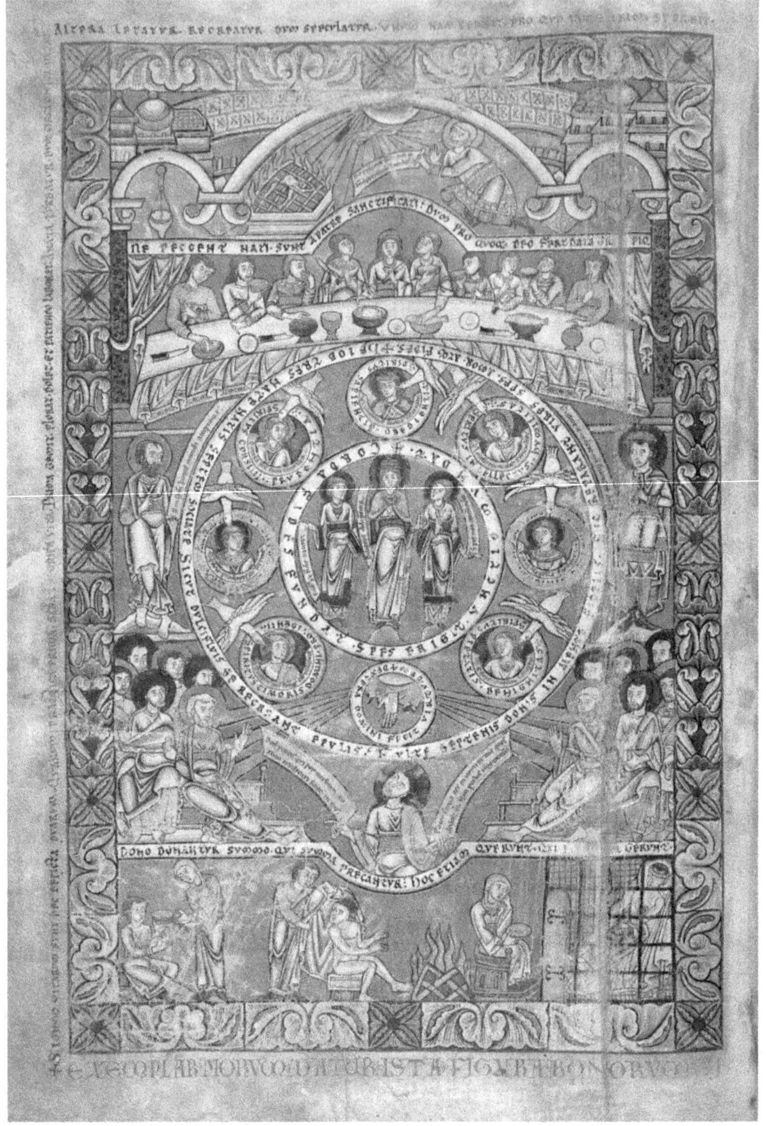

Figure 1. Anonymous about 1170: Frontispiece. *Floreffe Bible.* Add MS 17738, f. 3v, London: British Library.

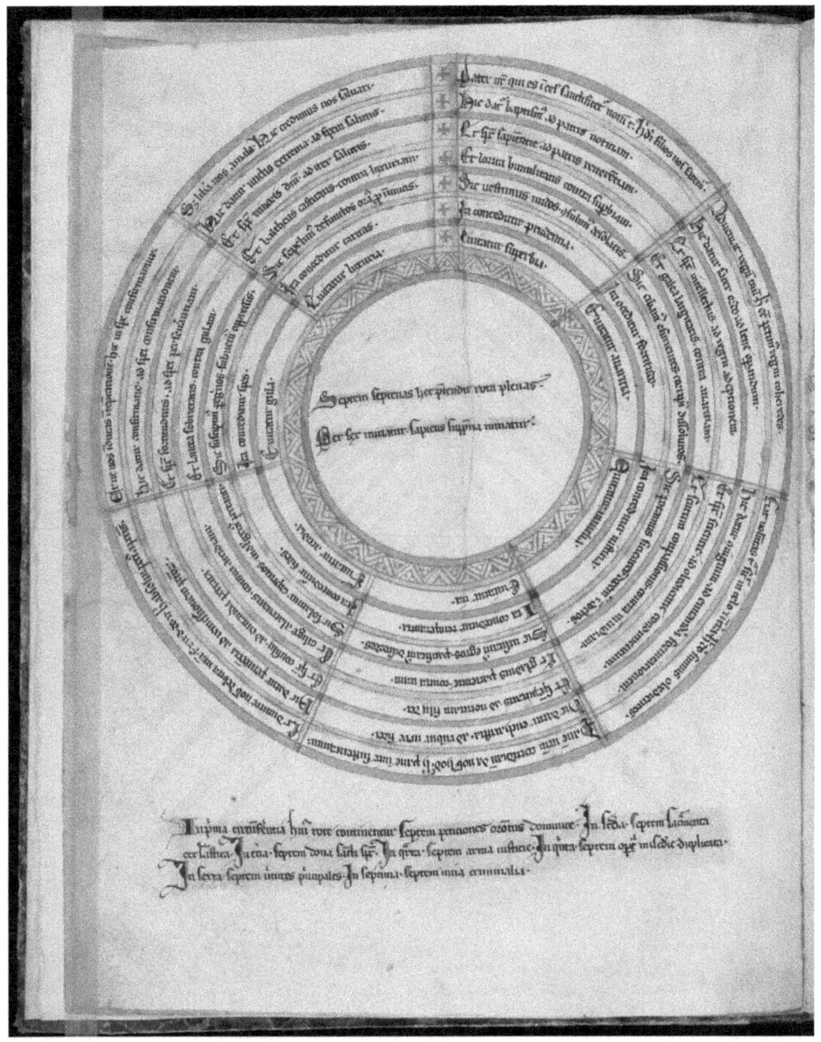

Figure 2. Anonymous late 13th century or early 14th century: *Wheel of Sevens. Speculum Theologiae*, Beinecke MS 416, Yale University.

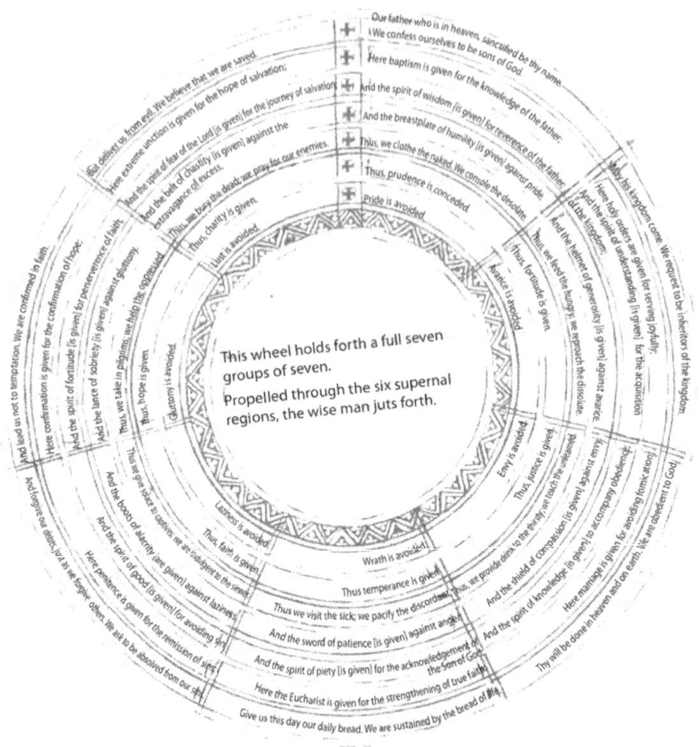

In the first circumference of this wheel are the seven petitions of prayer to the Lord. In the second are the ecclesiastical sacraments. In the third are the seven gifts of the Holy Spirit. In the fourth are the seven arms of justice. In the fifth are the seven works of mercy, doubled. In the sixth are the seven principle virtues. In the seventh are the seven criminal vices.

Figure 3. Diagram of Anonymous late 13th century or early 14th century: *Wheel of Sevens*. Translation by Brian Noell. *Speculum Theologiae*, Beinecke MS 416, Yale University.

PSYCHOMACHIA ILLUSTRATIONS

One exam option I give when I teach Prudentius's *Psychomachia* is to ask students to create an artistic response to the text. As students often find the poem's graphic imagery inspiring, this is a fairly popular option. More than one student has attempted a film adaptation. This seems like a good idea until those students try to find a female willing to be thrown headfirst off of a horse falling into a pit. It can be just as difficult to find someone willing to stick a "missile" into the ground for the "unnatural" purpose of killing herself. Equally challenging is finding an actor for Patience willing to be assailed on all sides by the weapons of the vicious, as is finding a Faith positively disposed to going into battle topless. The best I have had for this option are trailers for such an adaptation, with scenes very carefully chosen.

The *Psychomachia*'s graphic imagery apparently began inspiring artistic responses almost immediately. Despite countless lost works, there still exist sixteen manuscripts of the *Psychomachia* dated from the ninth century to 1289 that contain between two and ninety illustrations. Those illustrations, sampled here, show the poem's popularity through medieval times, attest to its powerful resonance, and establish some of the standard ways that the virtues, the vices, and their conflict are artistically rendered. The illustrations included here are from two of those manuscripts. Scholars believe that all the existing manuscripts derive from a distant common source developed soon after the poem was written. Such conclusions originate because all the existing manuscripts have generally the same arrangement of figures and show the same portions of the text. Those figures all use the same weapons in every manuscript. Though they come from a common source, scholars divide the manuscripts into roughly two groups, and give them the imaginative scholarly names Group 1 and Group 2. The first two examples here, the Paris images, are from Group 1, while the Bern manuscript is from Group 2.

The first two works are from the Bibliothèque Nationale in Paris. This manuscript was completed in the tenth century in France. The first scene shows Pride flying in to attack, or at least to trash talk. She assails the figure of Humility. These two figures show features common to Group 1 manuscripts: both wear long garments, and each wears a mantle on her head. Humility's mantle clings to hear body because she stands still, composed, and controlled. (Humility looks like a Roman matron, and the Paris manuscript best preserves the antique style of what scholars believe was the original.) Pride's mantle billows toward Humility in haughty speed and arrogance. (The way Pride's mantle billows behind her is reminiscent of Roman depictions of water or sky gods.)

The second work from Paris shows Pride falling into the pit. The scene below explains Pride's fall, as it shows Fraud digging the pit. Two matronly virtues observe from a safe distance. The final register is Humility and Hope preparing to behead Pride. In these illustrations, as in the others from Paris, the artist takes liberties with scale and placement of figures. In the first scene, Pride seems like she's an adult on a hobbyhorse, while Humility seems larger and closer. In the second illustration, we see that when the text and scene run together, the artist uses double lines to frame the scene.

These images show the play of peace and power. Pride approaches at a breakneck and haughty pace, her horse lunging forward and her drapery billowing. She seems to move with showy strength and confidence. Humility stands serenely, her understated shield forward and her sword resting casually. She is poised, serene, matronly, and secure in her inward integrity and peace. The stately and gently curving verticals of this figure contrast sharply with the jumble of lines, drapery, and horseflesh in the next scene of Pride's fall. This contrast is further reinforced in the remaining scenes, where the horse's frantic lines and Pride's jumbled contours contrast sharply with the calm dignity of Hope and Humility.

The last example is from the Burgerbibliothek in Bern, Switzerland. This ninth-century manuscript is from Group 2. Manuscripts from this group usually show the

Virtues as warriors wearing mail and helmets. The Vices enter the fray in short costumes and skirts, often sporting disheveled, flame-like hair. While the illustrations in Group 2 often have features even more reminiscent of the ancient model, they also seem to have come from a version of the *Psychomachia* that shows the influence of manuscripts from Reims. The flame-like hair, the exaggeratedly curved postures, and even the placement of the figures make them look like those of the famous *Utrecht Psalter*.

The image from the Bern manuscript shows Wrath's violent attack. Though Patience is protected by a helmet and mail, Patience's shield is lowered with the spear rested at ease. As Patience looks on, unperturbed, Wrath lunges forward, with flaming hair flowing back, only to find its sword breaking to pieces. To the left of Patience, Wrath's fury and failure culminate in its suicide, a death graphically driven home by the spear point protruding from Wrath's back.

These early illustrations of the battle for the soul emerge naturally from the very graphic nature of the *Psychomachia*. The poem itself seems to call for such a gripping visual rendition. While the number and quality of the illustrations and manuscripts attest to the poem's power and popularity, the intense contrasts in many of the illustrations reinforce virtue and vice's desperate internal battle for the soul.

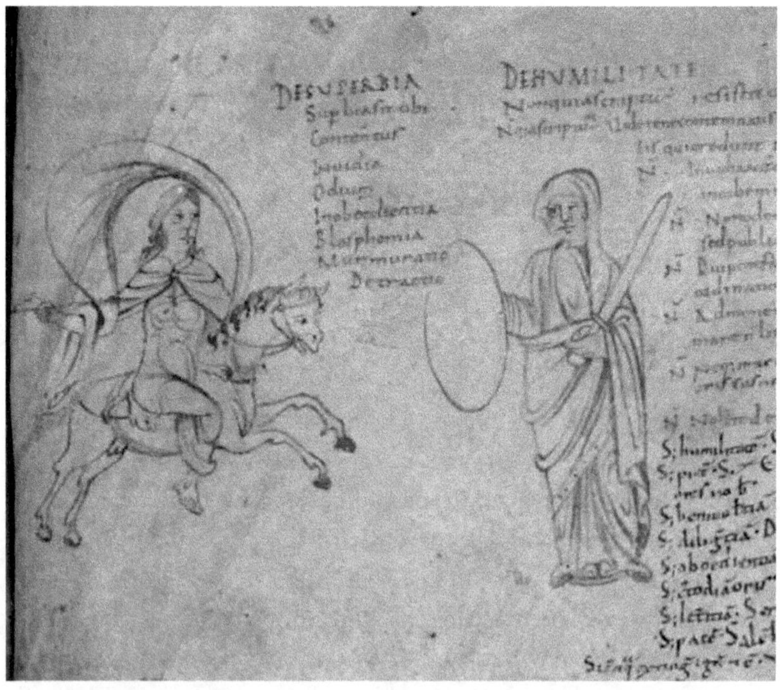

Figure 4. Anonymous from Paris, 10th century: *Pride Attacking Humility. Recueil factice composé de 4 manuscrits ou fragments de manuscrits différents: I. Arator Subdiaconus, Historia apostolica (f. 3–48). — II. Aurelius Clementis Prudentius, Psychomachia (f. 49–64). — III. Venantius Fortunatus, Carmina (f. 65–71). — IV. Aldhelmus, Carmina ecclesiastica (f. 73–80),* 53r Paris, Bibliothèque Nationale. Found at http://gallica.bnf.fr/ark:/12148/btv1b84238395.r=%28text%3Aprudentius%29.langFR/.

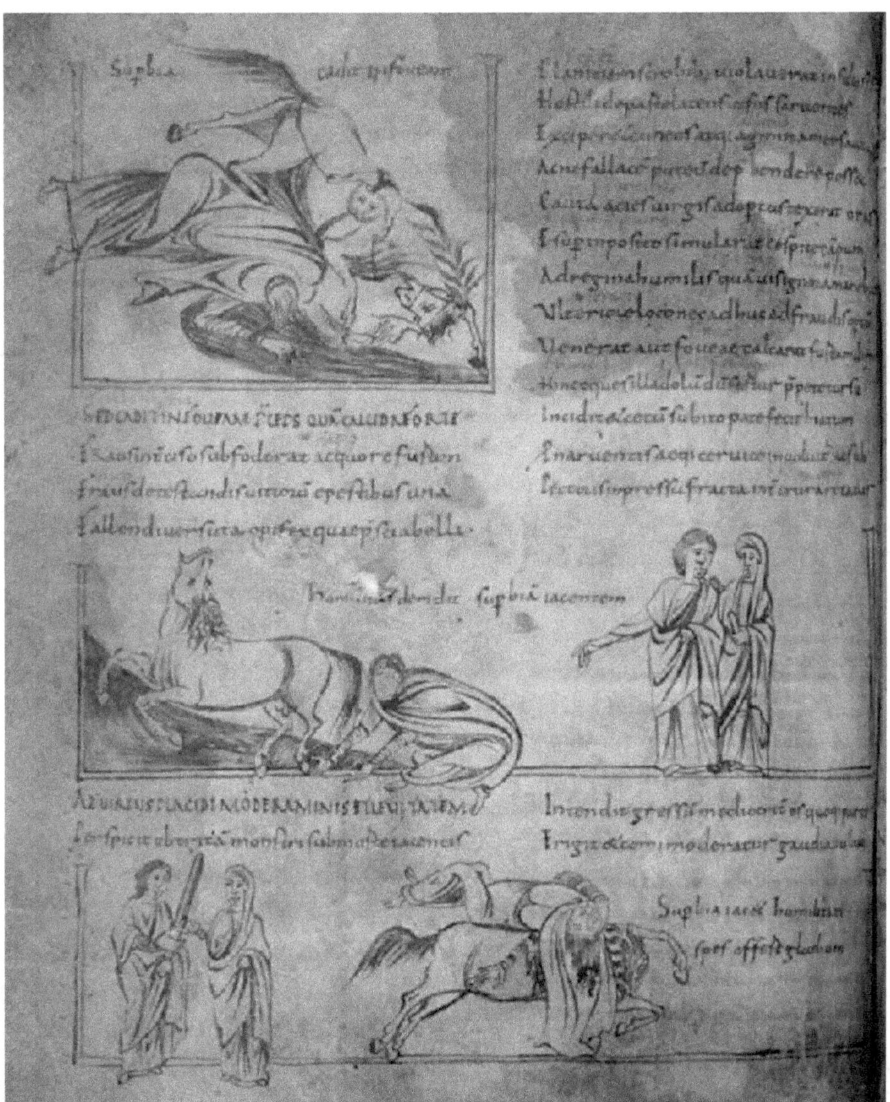

Figure 5. Anonymous from Paris, 10th century: *The Fall of Pride, Fraud Digs a Pit, Humility and Hope Prepare to Behead Pride. Recueil factice composé de 4 manuscrits ou fragments de manuscrits différents: I. Arator Subdiaconus, Historia apostolica (f. 3–48). — II. Aurelius Clementis Prudentius, Psychomachia (f. 49–64). — III. Venantius Fortunatus, Carmina (f. 65–71). — IV. Aldhelmus, Carmina ecclesiastica (f. 73–80),* 51v Paris, Bibliothèque Nationale. Found at: http://gallica.bnf.fr/ark:/12148/btv1b84238395.r=%28text%3Aprudentius%29.langFR/.

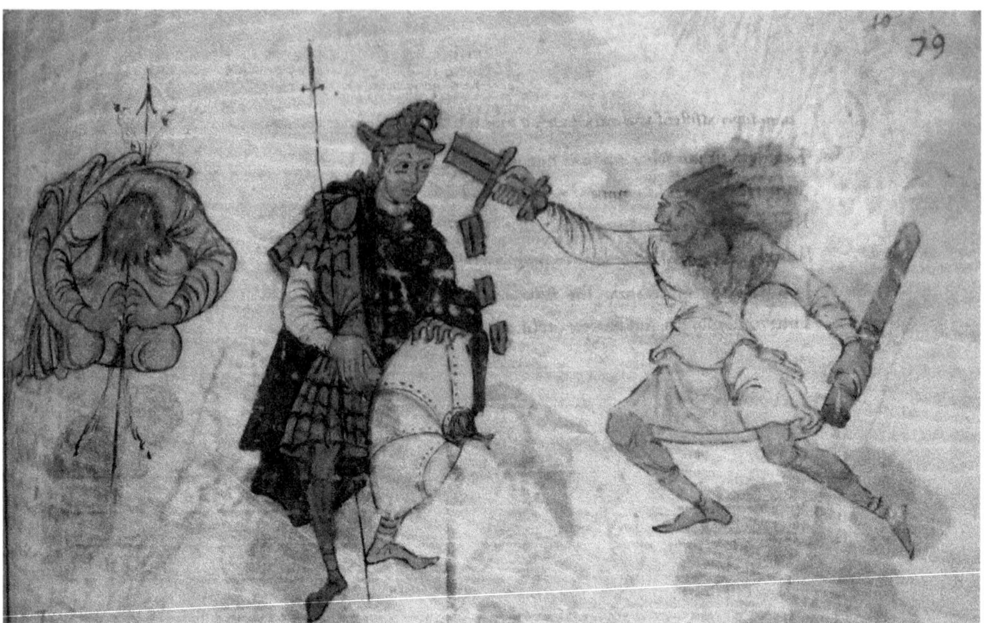

Figure 6. Anonymous 9th century: *Wrath's Suicide, Patience Withstanding Wrath's Assault.* Burgerbibliothek Bern, Cod. 264, p. 79, Bern, Burgerbibliothek.

ILLUSTRATIONS OF THE *SPECULUM VIRGINUM*

"Mirror, mirror, on the wall, who's the fairest of them all?" In her pride, the evil queen in the story of Snow White and the Seven Dwarfs wants to be the fairest of all. Eventually her envy comes together with deceit and violence in a remarkably vicious combination. The medieval devotion manual *Speculum Virginum*, or *Mirror of Virgins*, warns female devotees of the danger of pride and all of its consequences. This mirror also shows humility's positive powers with the overarching goal of revealing and encouraging piety in its audience.

The *Speculum Virginum*, which was created around 1140 CE, should not be thought of as a work to be passively read; it is more like a script, with characters dramatically engaged in a developing plot. During its time, the very nuns it ostensibly addresses would have probably read it aloud. And with this script comes some essential scenery in the form of images to ponder while listening to the dialogue. The *Speculum's* dialogue involves a "virgin in Christ," Theodora, and her spiritual advisor, Peregrinus, or "Pilgrim." They start by talking about the devoted life, and how such a life should lead to a true understanding of nature. Devotion to God can allow one to see how all creation bears the marks of its creator. In fact, once people truly see, they come to an understanding of how all things, both in the physical world and in one's life, attest to God's larger pattern. The first image included here typifies such a convergence. Theodora and Peregrinus also discuss the reasons for monastic isolation and how true virginity is not mere physical purity but deep spiritual devotion. A key point of their discussion is the fundamental role of pride and humility, a subject visualized in three images. Pride is the "root of all evil," bringing forth its evil fruit, while humility engenders love and the other delightful and nourishing fruits of the Spirit. To make his point to his virgin audience, Peregrinus cites spiritually powerful and virile examples like Semiramis of Babylon, and Thamar, queen of the Scyths. The nuns could also see the illustration of humility overcoming pride, flanked by Jahel conquering the Madianite king and Judith slaying Holofernes. The next logical example of virtue's virgin virility is Mary, and from there the discussion leads to Jesus's parable of the wise and foolish virgins (Matthew 25:1–13). Theodora and Peregrinus then return to a discussion of the relationship between the flesh and the spirit, but this time in order to clarify that, with true devotion, the flesh and spirit can complement one another, leading the soul up the ladder to heaven. Still, as such a soul ascends, that soul must not become careless, less the devil (looking like some crazy, sword-hurling ninja) slay it on the way. This discussion is followed by an extended prayer, emphasizing internal devotion, which is followed by an elaborate discussion of the house of wisdom, the final image included here. The entire work ends with a bridal song celebrating the virgin soul's union with Christ, the groom.

The *Speculum Virginum* includes many metaphorical mirrors. One mirror reflects the original order of things, best exemplified in the *Mystical Paradise* image (Figure 7). At the very center of the image is Christ, holding an open book with the inscription *Si quis sitit, veniat et bibat* ("if any man thirst, let him come unto me, and drink"), from John 7:37. Out from Christ, in a cross pattern, pour forth the four rivers of paradise headed by river-god-like figures representing the Tigris, Gihon, Euphrates, and Pishon. The four figures hold a medallion in each hand. The medallions in the right hands show one of the four evangelists (Matthew, Mark, Luke, or John), and the medallions in the left hands show one of four church fathers: Jerome, Gregory the Great, Augustine, and Ambrose. The same spring of Christ nurtures four trees that also radiate out and culminate in leaves topped by medallions of the four cardinal virtues: Fortitude, Justice, Prudence, and Temperance. With its convergence of evangelists, church fathers, and virtues, this is a theocentric map of the cosmos or of the ultimate order and unity of all things. The natural world (exemplified by the rivers), the word of God in the evangelists, those that elaborated on that gospel in the church fathers, and the four fruits of social and personal virtue all find their original source in Christ.

The *Mystical Paradise* is a synthesizing map where a virgin could look and see her place in God's cosmos. Such a devotee could then look into another set of mirrors to discern the profile of her character. This would be done with the trees of vice and virtue. On the first tree, Pride, holding the golden chalice of Babylon, is the base and source of all vice (Figure 8). Moving up the tree we see six main vice groups (from right to left): Vainglory, Wrath, Envy, Sadness, Greed, and the Sins of Idleness. From each of these branches droop additional limbs budding forth in subsidiary vices. Slithering up the tree are two serpents spitting venom; two griffons perch in the top branches. On the top of the tree is the crowning vice of Indulgence, or, in the Latin, *Luxuria*, with its own set of twelve upward reaching branches and buds of sinful character traits. As the uppermost inscription indicates, this the realm of *vetus adam*, or the "old Adam," whose fall brought about character flaws (vices). If this tree is meant to reflect human frailties, it would seem difficult for a viewer to not find at least a few of the sixty-two named vices in one's own features or character.

The drooping leaves on this tree of death contrast with the upturned leaves of the tree of life, the tree of virtue on the next page (Figure 9). This image is literally on the right side, showing the realm of the *novus adam*, the "new Adam," or Christ, who would restore life through his death. This tree emerges from Humility's breasts, ascending into the branches of Prudence, Justice, Fortitude, Temperance, Hope, and Faith, all of which bring forth seven additional virtues. Charity is this tree's crown, from which two groups of five virtues lift upwards. Christ, as the new Adam, looks out from the top with a blessing gesture. The more colorful image of virtue's tree lists sixty virtues, and though that means that there are two fewer than the sixty-two vices on the other tree, there would still be plenty of good qualities to find in one's soul via this mirror.

Just a few pages later the nuns could see the female face of powerful Humility overcoming Pride (Figure 10). Humility forces the sword down into the chest of Pride, who gestures pitifully, and whose dark hair harkens back to the fiery Fury-like locks of the Group 2 *Psychomachia* illustrations. Judith stands to the right, over the vanquished figure of Holofernes, while Jael, with her mallet still in hand, stands over a Sisera whose head has been staked into the ground. Humility here is not contrition or acquiescence; it is piety's bold victory over vice.

Humility's forceful victory over Pride fits well with the image of the soul's powerful ascent up the ladder (Figure 11). The virgins who climb the rungs must avoid the satanic dragon at the bottom as well as the flying swords of the centrally placed "Ethiopian" guard. The text that accompanies the image explains that the dragon, the spirit of wickedness, diverts the mind from higher things, while the "Ethiopian" uses his terrifying aspect and direct attacks to thwart the virgin's ascent. Though these pitfalls or threats certainly exist, Christ promises a reward in the form of golden branches. In addition, God provides that defensive lance of the cross, and the divine endowment of power allows souls to push away with a finger or casual move of the foot many evil assaults.

With the final image, the final mirror, the virgin could glimpse her soul's rightful home in the Temple of Wisdom (Figure 12). The inscription between the Temple's columns indicates that it is built on the seven pillars of wisdom mentioned in Proverbs 9:1. Those pillars are further explained by the inscription at their bases, which is the first two verses of Isaiah chapter 11 (the description of the root out of the stem of Jesse and the gifts of the Spirit). The lowest central figure is Jesse, the father of David. Above Jesse we find the Virgin Mary's fixed gaze upon us. She holds a book inscribed with the prophetic description from the book of Proverbs of her centrality in time: "The Lord brought me forth as the first of his works, / before his deeds of old; / I was formed long ages ago, / at the very beginning, when the world came to be" (8:22–23). Christ also holds an inscribed book with the first phrase from Isaiah chapter 61: "The Spirit of the Sovereign Lord is on me." Blossoming forth at the top of virtue's tree are the seven Gifts of the Spirit. In the leafy elaborations we find each gift associated with an element of the Paternoster and the Beatitudes. By weaving together the Paternoster, the Beatitudes, and the Gifts of the Spirit, the image combines Old and New Testaments to show Christ, the source of all powers and virtues, as the promised Messiah. The *Speculum Virginum* brings together these different mirrors to give devotees a composite image of God's orderly world and his good news of salvation and virtue for all through Christ. The virgins of Christ could find in this mirror the way up the ladder to Christ and how to properly adorn themselves with true virtue and piety, making them the "fairest of them all."

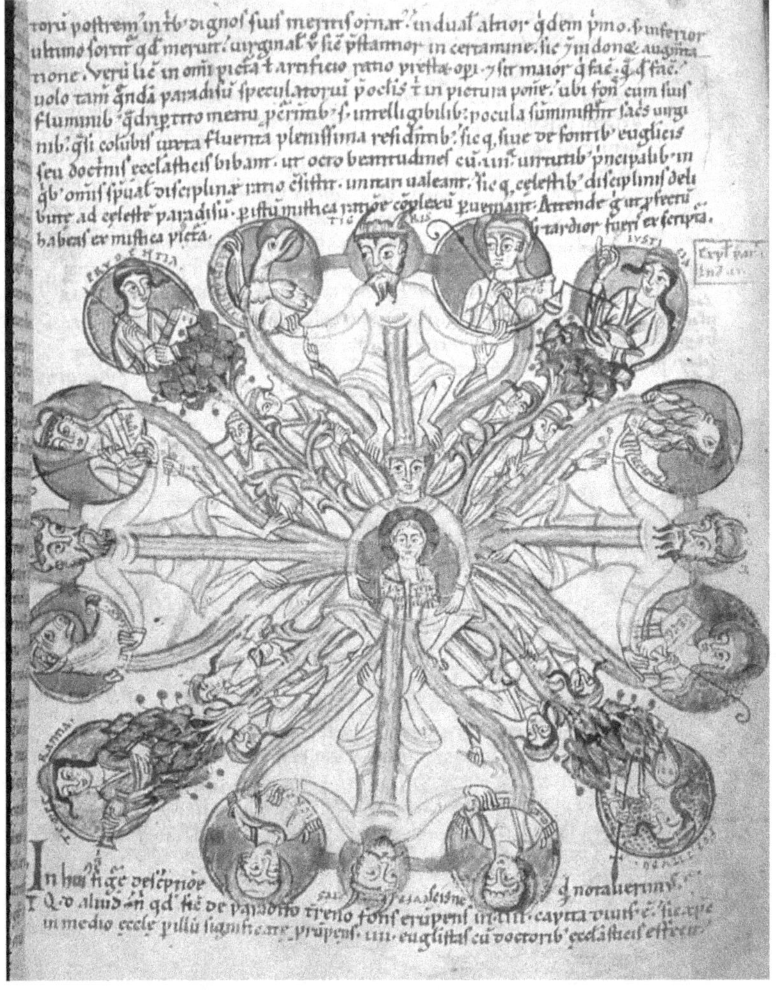

Figure 7. Conrad of Hirsau (?) from Germany, second or third quarter of the 12th century: *Mystical Paradise*. Arundel 44, Folio 13 London: British Library.

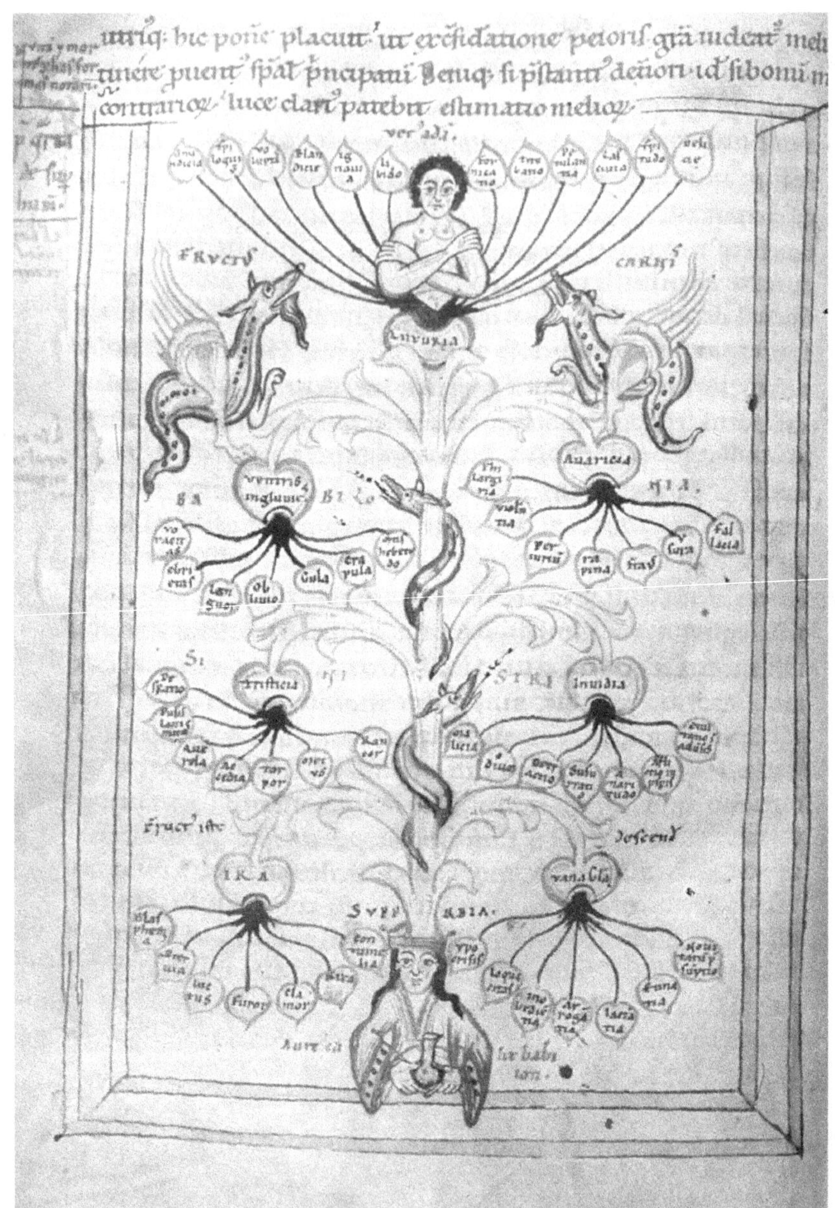

Figure 8. Conrad of Hirsau (?) From Germany, second or third quarter of the twelfth century: *Tree of Vices*. Arundel 44 Folio 13 London: British Library.

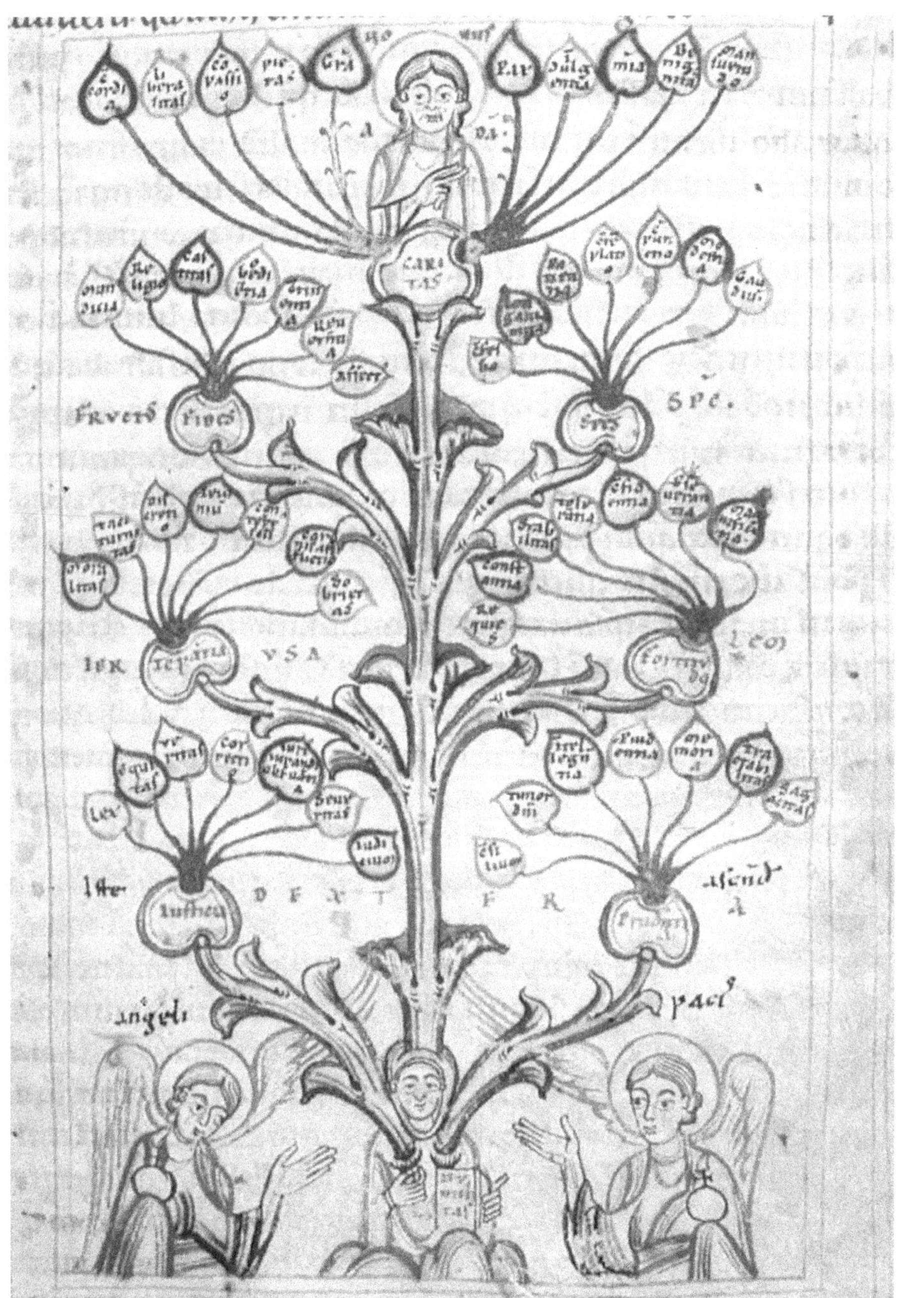

Figure 9. Conrad of Hirsau (?) From Germany, second or third quarter of the twelfth century: "Tree of Virtues." Arundel 44 Folio 29 London: British Library.

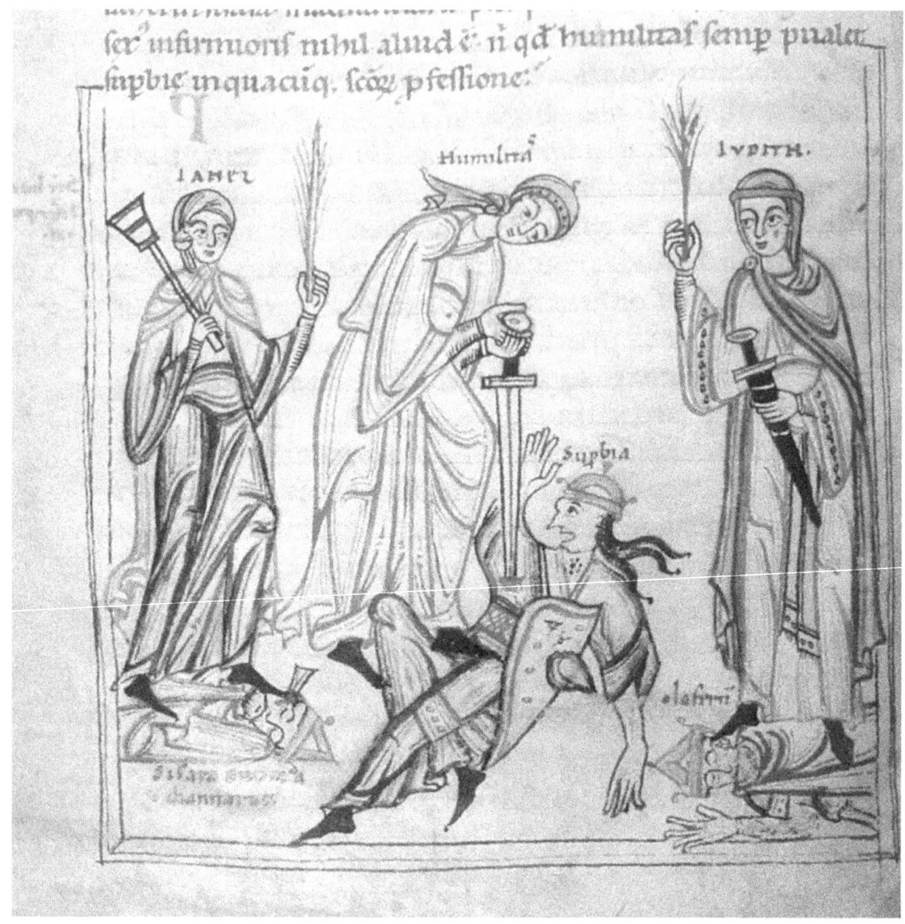

Figure 10. Conrad of Hirsau (?) from Germany, second or third quarter of the twelfth century: "Victory of Humility." Arundel 44 Folio 34 Verso London: British Library.

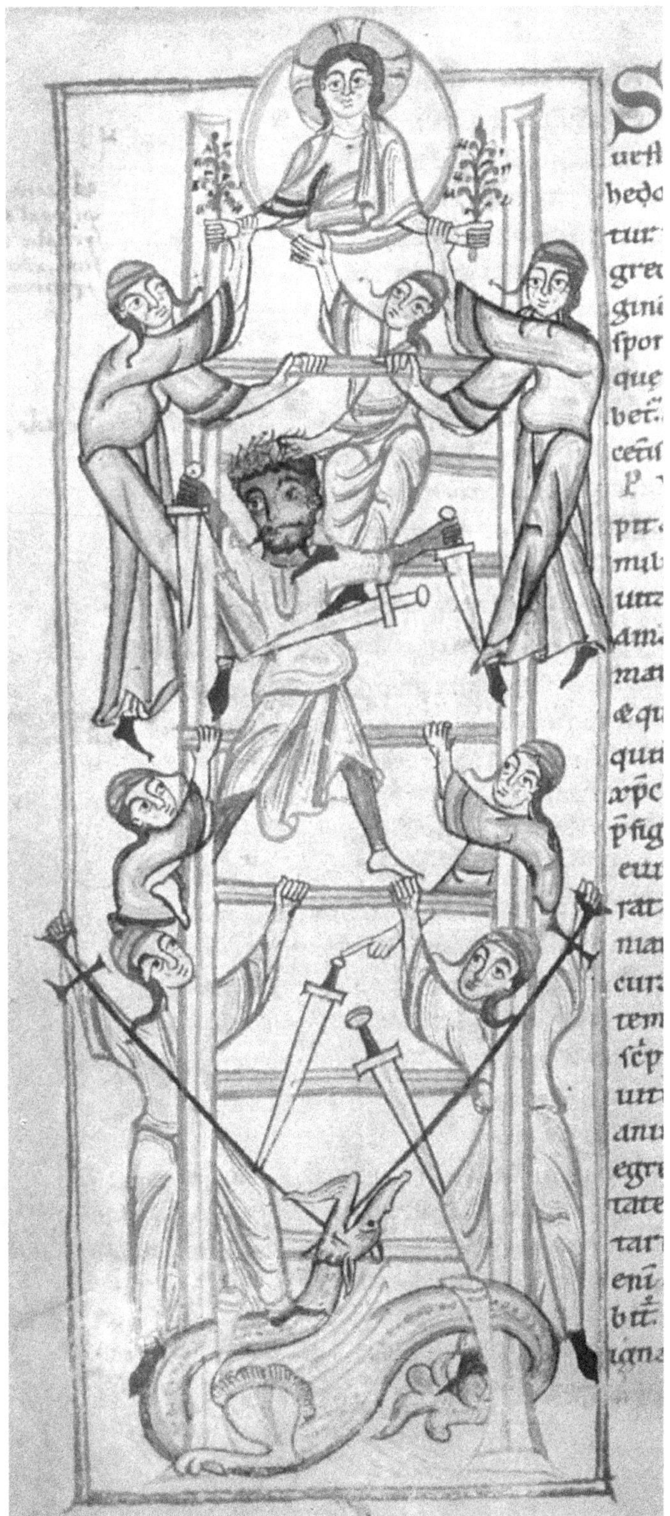

Figure 11. Conrad of Hirsau (?) From Germany, second or third quarter of the twelfth century: *Ladder of Virtue*. Arundel 44 Folio 93 Verso London, British Library.

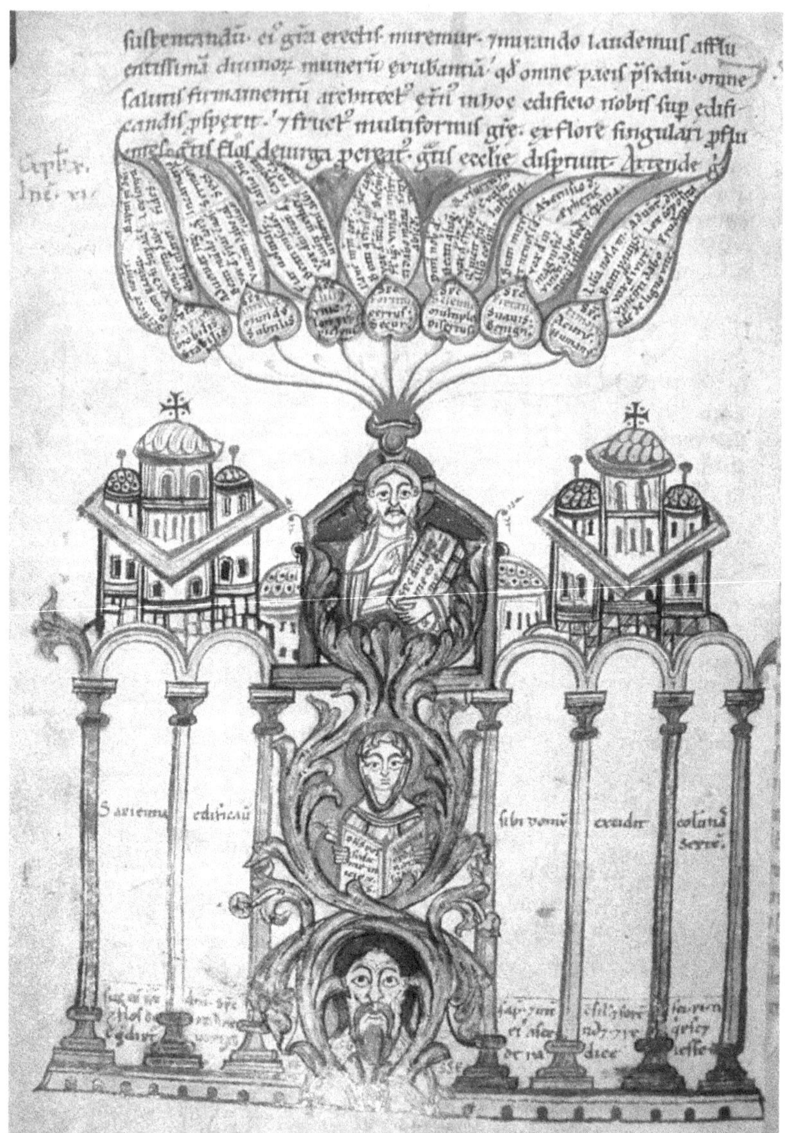

Figure 12. Conrad of Hirsau (?) from Germany, second or third quarter of the 12th century: "Temple of Wisdom." Arundel 44 Folio 114 Verso London, British Library.

HILDEGARD OF BINGEN'S *ORDO VIRTUTUM*

Introduction

Toward the end of Hildegard of Bingen's religious musical drama *Ordo Virtutum* (1151 CE), the devil poses this question to Anima, the work's central figure: Who are you? He (for the devil is the only clearly male character in the work) follows this question up with several others. At this point in the play, Anima is returning to God via the virtues. The devil's questions register his surprise at this, as he had believed that she was under his power. But the devil's questions can also touch on other questions that may have bedeviled the nuns at Hildegard's Rupertsberg convent: who are people to think that they can overcome the devil and who would choose to live a life of cloistered abstinence? Hildegard's dramatization not only shows the power of the virtues in rescuing the fallen human soul, but it speaks in a direct and elegantly poetic manner to the particular struggles of the nuns who would have seen and even performed the *Ordo Virtutum*.

Hildegard of Bingen would have been a remarkable person at any time, and is all the more remarkable as a woman in twelfth-century Europe. Not only did she direct her abbey, but she was also famous as an artist, author, counselor to secular and religious leaders, mystic, physician, and naturalist. She was a polymath or Renaissance woman before the Renaissance even happened. The basic structure of her *Ordo Virtutum* dramatizes fundamental Christian answers to deep human questions. To the question of why there is misery in the world, especially if God is the all-powerful creator, this play reenacts the story of Adam and Eve as the fundamental story of every person's life. Humans, wearing the robe of mortality and distant from God's presence, lose sight of their divine source and potential, are tempted by the devil, and turn toward the world—the here and now of material and mortal life. Each soul or anima becomes lost, not unlike the lost sheep, the lost coin, or the lost (and prodigal) child. God's powers or virtues extend out to the lost soul, encourage its return, and promise the power necessary to make that return possible. God's power comes through Christ's sacrifice, his "wounds." God's power redeems and restores life through Christ, the "New Adam" for the "Old Adam" (all the fallen descendents of Adam and Eve). Anima in the *Ordo Virtutum* is thus every soul, and we could even call the work *Everysoul*. As this work is the first extent morality play, calling it *Everysoul* makes clear its connection with subsequent morality plays like *Everyman*.

In order to show the powers and the works of virtue, the *Ordo Virtutum*, Hildegard makes use of all of the artistic tools at her disposal. Instead of being a closet drama, a play to be read and not performed, Hildegard's is musical theater. All of the players sing their lines with a poetry and music that reveal their character. Since the devil is discordant as well as disagreeable, he can only shout or grunt his lines, where Anima's words and music can reveal, by turns, her optimism, her despair, and her contrition. Hildegard's ethereal music with complex Biblical and natural imagery reveals the verdant power of the virtues. We see this when Humility marshals together all of the virtues to bring Anima back. Each virtue introduces herself, and all of the virtues welcome her. Charity, for example, explains that she can lead "into the radiant light of the flower of the rod." The radiant light, symbol for divine knowledge, warmth, and love (Christ as the light of the world), combines with the marvelous flower of the rod. This evokes images of Aaron's miraculously blossoming rod in Pharaoh's court as well as Isaiah's promise of the "shoot" coming forth from the "stump" of Jesse. Christians like Hildegard understood the "shoot" to be Christ who came from the "stump," or who was a descendent of Jesse's son, David, as well as from His virgin and un-"deflowered" mother Mary. When the Virtues respond to Charity, they echo the love poetry of the *Song of Songs*, saying, "Dearest flower, with ardent longing we run to you." As Hildegard, an artist, mystic, and scientist, uses such a richly complex layering of Biblical and natural imagery, she not only creates a powerful characterization of the virtues, but she also synthesizes the world of God's creations and revelations.

If the *Ordo Virtutum* is a sort of *psychomachia* or battle in and for the soul, it may address conflicts particular to its audience. Toward the end of the work, the devil levels what could have been a difficult question, and while his words are directed against Chastity, they certainly could have been directed at all of the virtues and at the nuns. He accuses Chastity of ignorance and transgression, saying that her "belly is devoid of the beautiful form that woman receives from man," and that she does not heed God's command to "enjoin in the sweet act of love." Following this, the devil says that Chastity, like the virtues and nuns, does not know who she is. Chastity responds that instead of the virtue of chastity being devoid of life, chastity brings the possibility of eternal life for everyone through the Virgin Mary's miraculous, chaste conception of Christ. The virtues then respond by rhetorically turning the devil's accusation of ignorance into praise for God. They ask, reverently, "Who are you, God, who held / such great counsel in yourself, / a counsel that destroyed the draught of hell / in publicans and sinners, / who now shine in paradisal goodness!" They express praise for God's wisdom and his promise to carry them "into a fair wind, sailing the waters" toward a heavenly Jerusalem. Thus all souls in general, and these covenant-bound nuns in particular, know their place and God's promise in the larger context of an unfolding redemptive journey.

Here begins the Play of the Virtues[1]

Prologue

Patriarchs and Prophets:
Who are these, who are like clouds?

1. From Hildegard of Bingen, *Nine Medieval Latin Plays*, trans. Peter Dronke (Cambridge Medieval Classics; Cambridge: Cambridge University Press, 1994), 147–84.

Virtues:
You holy ones of old, why do you marvel at us?
The Word of God grows bright in the shape of man,
and thus we shine with him,
building up the limbs of his beautiful body.

Patriarchs and Prophets:
We are the roots, and you, the boughs,
fruits of the living eye,
and in that eye we were the shadow.

Scene 1

The lament of (a chorus of) embodied Souls:
Oh, we are strangers here!
What have we done, straying to the realms of sin?
We should have been the daughters of the King,
but we have fallen into the shadow of sins.
Oh living Sun, carry us on your shoulders
back to that most just heritage we lost in Adam!
King of kings, we are fighting your battle.

Anima (happily):
Oh sweet divinity, oh gentle life,
in which I shall wear a radiant robe,
receiving that which I lost in my first manifestation—
I sigh for you, and invoke all the Virtues.

Virtues:
You happy Soul, sweet and divine creation,
fashioned in the deep height of the wisdom of God,
you show great love.

Anima (happily):
Oh let me come to you joyfully,
that you may give me the kiss of your heart!

Virtues:
We must fight together with you, royal daughter.
Anima, depressed, laments:

Oh grievous toil, oh harsh weight
that I bear in the dress of this life:
it is too grievous for me to fight against my body.

Virtues (to Anima):
Anima, you that were given your place by the will of God,
you instrument of bliss, why are you so tearful
in the face of the evil God crushed by maidenly being?
You must overcome the devil in our midst.

Anima:
Support me, help me to stay firm!

Knowledge of God (to Anima):
Look at the dress you are wearing, daughter of salvation:
be steadfast, and you'll never fall.

Anima (unhappily)
I don't know what to do
or where to flee.
Woe is me, I cannot complete
this dress I have put on.
Indeed I want to cast it off!

Virtues:
Unhappy state of mind,
oh poor Anima,
why do you hide your face in the presence of your Creator?

Knowledge of God:
You do not know or see or taste the One who has set you here.

Anima:
God created the world:
I'm doing him no injury—
I only want to enjoy it!

Devil (shouting to Anima):
What use to you is toiling foolishly, foolishly? Look to the world: it will embrace you with great honor.

Virtues:
Is this not a plangent voice, of utmost sorrow?
Ah, a certain wondrous victory already
rose in that Soul, in her wondrous longing for God,
in which a sensual delight was secretly hidden,
alas, where previously the will had known no guilt
and the desire fled man's wantonness.
Mourn for this, mourn, Innocence,
you who lost no perfection in your fair modesty,
who did not devour greedily, with the gullet of the serpent of old.

Devil:
What is this power—as if there were no one but God? I say, whoever wants to follow me and do my will, I'll give him everything. As for you, Humility, you have nothing that you can give to your followers: none of you even know what you are!

Humility:
My comrades and I know very well
that you are the dragon of old
who craved to fly higher than the highest one:
but God himself hurled you out of the abyss.

Virtues:
As for us, we dwell in the heights.

Scene 2

Humility:
I, Humility, queen of the Virtues, say:
come to me, you Virtues, and I'll give you the skill
to seek and find the drachma that is lost
and to crown her who perseveres blissfully.

Virtues:
Oh glorious queen, gentlest mediatrix,
gladly we come.

Humility:
Because of this, beloved daughters,
I'll keep your place in the royal wedding-chamber.

Charity:
I am Charity, the flower of love—
come to me, Virtues, and I'll lead you
into the radiant light of the flower of the rod.

Virtues:
Dearest flower, with ardent longing we run to you.

Fear of God:
I, Fear of God, can prepare you, blissful daughters,
to gaze upon the living God and not die of it.

Virtues:
Fear, you can help us greatly:
We are filled with the longing never to part from you.

Devil:
Bravo! Bravo! What is this great fear, and this great love? Where is the champion? Where the prize-giver? You don't even know what you are worshipping!

Virtues:
But you, you were terrified at the supreme Judge,
for, swollen with pride, you were plunged into Gehenna.

Obedience:
I am Obedience, the shining one—
come to me, lovely daughters, and I'll lead you
to your homeland and to the kiss of the King.

Virtues:
Sweetest summoner,
it is right for us to come, most eagerly to you.

Faith:
I am Faith, the mirror of life:
precious daughters, come to me
and I shall show you the leaping fountain.

Virtues:
Serene one, mirror-like, we trust in you:
we shall arrive at that fountain through you.

Hope:
I am the sweet beholder of the living eye,
I am whom no dissembling torpor can deceive.
Darkness, you cannot cloud my gaze!

Virtues:
Living life, gentle, consoling one,
you overcome the deadly shafts of death
and with your seeing eye lay heaven's gate open.

Chastity:
Maidenhood, you remain within the royal chamber.
How sweetly you burn in the King's embraces,
when the Sun blazes through you,
never letting your noble flower fall.
Gentle maiden, you will never know the shadow over the falling flower!

Virtues:
The flower in the meadow falls in the wind, the rain splashes it,
But you, Maidenhood, remain in the symphonies of heavenly habitants:
you are the tender flower that will never grow dry.

Innocence:
My flock, flee from the Devil's taints!

Virtues:
We shall flee from them, if you give us aid.

World-rejection:
I, World-rejection, am the blaze of life.
Oh wretched, exiled state on earth,
with all your toils—I let you go.
Come to me, you Virtues,
and we'll climb up to the fountain of life!

Virtues:
Glorious lady, you that always fight Christ's battles,
great power that tread the world under your feet,
you thereby dwell in heaven, victoriously.
Heavenly Love:
I am the golden gate that's fixed in heaven:
whoever passes through me
will never taste bitter rebelliousness in her mind.

Virtues:
Royal daughter, you are held fast in the embraces the world shuns:
how tender is your love in the highest God!

Discipline:
I am one who loves innocent ways that know nothing ignoble;
I always gaze upon the King of kings
and, as my highest honor, I embrace him.

Virtues:
Angelic comrade, how comely you are
in the royal nuptials!

Shamefastness:
I cover over, drive away or tread down
all the filths of the Devil.

Virtues:
Yours is a part in the building of heavenly Jerusalem,
flowering among the shining lilies.

Mercy:
How bitter in human minds is the harshness that does not soften
and mercifully ease pain!
I want to reach out my hand to all who suffer.

Virtues:
Matchless mother of exiles,
you are always raising them up
and anointing the poor and the weak.

Victory:
I am Victory, the swift, brave champion:
I fight with a stone, I tread the age-old serpent down.

Virtues:
Oh gentlest warrior, in the scorching fountain
that swallowed up the voracious wolf—
glorious, crowned one, how gladly
we'll fight against that trickster, at your side!

Discretion:
I am Discretion, light and moderator of all creatures—
the impartiality of God, that Adam drove away by acting wantonly.

Virtues:
Fairest mother, how sweet you are, how gentle—
in you no one can be confounded.

Patience:
I am the pillar that can never be made to yield,
as my foundation is God.

Virtues:
You that stay firm in the rocky cavern,
you are the glorious warrior who endures all.

Humility:
Daughters of Israel, God raised you from beneath the tree,
so now remember how it was planted.
Therefore rejoice, daughters of Jerusalem.

Scene 3

Virtues:
Alas, alas, let us lament and mourn,
because our master's sheep has fled from life!

Anima (laments, penitent and calling upon the Virtues):
You royal Virtues, how graceful,
how flashing-bright you look in the highest Sun,

and how delectable is your home,
and so, what woe is mine that I fled from you!

Virtues:
You who escaped, come, come to us, and God will take you back.
Anima:
Ah, but a burning sweetness swallowed me up in sins,
so I dare not come in.

Virtues:
Don't be afraid or run away:
the good Shepherd is searching for his lost sheep—it is you.

Anima:
Now I need your help to gather me up—
I stink of the wounds
that the age-old serpent has made me gangrenous.

Virtues:
Run back to us, retrace those steps
where you'll never falter, in our company:
God will heal you.

Anima (penitently, to the Virtues):
I am the sinner who fled from life:
riddled with sores I'll come to you—
you can offer me redemption's shield.
All of you, warriors of Queen Humility,
her white lilies and her crimson roses,
stoop to me, who exiled myself from you like a stranger,
and help me, that in the blood of the Son of God I may arise.

Virtues:
Fugitive Anima, now be strong:
put on the armor of light.

Anima:
And you true medicine, Humility, grant me your help,
for pride has broken me in many vices,
inflicting many scars on me.
Now I'm escaping to you—so take me up!

Humility:
All you Virtues, lift up this mournful sinner,
with all her scars, for the sake of Christ's wounds,
and bring her to me.
Virtues:
We want to bring you back—we shan't desert you,
the whole of heaven's host will have joy in you:
thus it is right for us now to play our symphony.

Humility:
Oh unhappy daughter, I want to embrace you:
the great surgeon has suffered harsh and bitter wounds
for your sake.

Virtues:
Living fountain, how great is your sweetness:
you did not reject the gaze of these upon you—
no, acutely you foresaw
how you could avert them from the fall the angels fell,
they who thought they possessed a power
which no law allows to be like that.
Rejoice then, daughter Jerusalem,
for God is giving you back many
whom the serpent wanted to sunder from you,
who now gleam in a greater brightness
than would have been their state before.

Scene 4:

Devil:
Who are you? Where are you coming from? You were in my embrace, I led you out. Yet now you are going back, defying me—but I shall fight you and bring you down!

Anima (penitently):
I recognised that all my ways were wicked, so I fled you.
But now, trickster, I'll fight you face to face.
Queen Humility, come with your medicine, give me aid!

Humility:
Victory, you who once conquered this creature in the heavens,
run now, with all your soldiery,
and all of you bind this Fiend!

Victory:
Bravest and most glorious warriors, come,
help me vanquish this deceitful one!

Virtues:
Oh sweetest warrior, in the scorching fountain
that swallowed up the voracious wolf—
glorious, crowned one, how gladly
we'll fight against that trickster, at your side!

Humility:
Bind him then, you shining Virtues!

Virtues:
Queen of us all, we obey—
we'll carry out your orders totally.

Victory:
Comrades, rejoice: the age-old snake is bound.

Virtues:
Praise be you, Christ, King of the angels!

Chastity:
In the mind of the Highest, Satan, I trod on your head,
and in a virgin form I nurtured a sweet miracle
when the Son of God came into the world;
therefore you are laid low, with all your plunder;
and now let all who dwell in heaven rejoice,
because your belly has been confounded.

Devil:
You don't know what your are nurturing, for your belly is devoid of the beautiful form that woman receives from man; in this you transgress the command that God enjoined in the sweet act of love; so you don't even know what you are!

Chastity:
How can what you say affect me?
Even your suggestion smirches it with foulness.
I did bring forth a man, who gathers up mankind
to himself, against you, through his nativity.

Virtues:
Who are you, God, who held
such a great counsel in yourself,
a counsel that destroyed the draught of hell
in publicans and sinners,
who now shine in paradisal goodness!
Praise to you, King, for this!
Almighty Father, from you flowed a fountain of fiery love:
guide your children into a fair wind, sailing the waters,
so that we too may steer them in this way
into the heavenly Jerusalem.

Finale

Virtues and Souls:
In the beginning all creation was verdant,
flowers blossomed in the midst of it;
later, greenness sank away.
And the champion saw this and said:
"I know it, but the golden number is not yet full.
You then, behold me, mirror of your fatherhood:
in my body I am suffering exhaustion,
even my little ones faint.
Now remember that the fullness which was made in the beginning
need not have grown dry,
and that then you resolved
that your eye would never fail
until you saw my body full of jewels.
For it wearies me that all my limbs are exposed to mockery:
Father, behold, I am showing you my wounds."
So now, all you people,
bend your knees to the Father,
that he may reach you his hand.

NOTRE DAME OF AMIENS TWELVE VIRTUES AND TWELVE VICES

Between 1220 and 1235 the main entrance for the cathedral at Amiens was decorated with sculpted panels of the virtues and vices. To walk into Our Lady of Amiens, at least through the central portal, is to pass between twelve images of virtue and twelve images of vice. Perhaps it is a little presumptuous (even sinful) to say that they have "pride" of place, but as these images are at about eye level in the main entrance, they are afforded an important role in the overall cathedral decoration. The twenty-four panels at Amiens set up a contrast between the peace that the virtues secure and the mayhem of a life dominated by vice.

The cathedrals in Paris and Chartres have very similar sets of images made around the same time as those at Amiens. I have chosen to include the Amiens images because they seem, for the most part, the best preserved. At all three locations a virtue is paired with a vice to heighten the contrast. The pairings (given from left to right with the virtue above the vice) are Humility and Pride, Prudence and Foolishness, Chastity and Lust, Charity and Greed, Hope and Despair, and Faith and Idolatry on the panel to the left of the doors (Figure 13). To the right of the doors are Fortitude and Cowardice, Patience and Wrath, Gentleness and Harshness, Concord and Discord, Obedience and Contumacy (defiance of authority or flagrant disobedience or rebelliousness), and Perseverance and Inconstancy (Figure 14).

The images at Amiens show continuities and changes in artistic renditions of the virtues and vices. Many of the images hearken back to Prudentius and the illustrations of his *Psychomachia*. The image of Pride falling from her horse is the most striking example. Also echoing back to Prudentius is Hope's optimistic gaze toward a celestial crown, as well as the way most of the virtues are clothed in the style of Roman matrons. There is a suicide at Amiens, but instead of it being Wrath's, it is Despair's. The virtue and vice pairings also echo the victory of the virtues over the vices at Aulney, with some of the same virtues defeating similar vices. Still, at Aulney, virtuous warriors, dressed in contemporary military garb, effortlessly defeat squirming vices, while at Amiens the more stately virtues overcome the vices by their mere placement above them. Amiens's virtues and vices have come down from the archivolts into a more direct human sphere but still feature the elevated and heavenly virtues above the lower and fallen vices.

A close look at these images gives rise to an issue that is threaded throughout this book: how does one show virtue and vice? A quick glance at the virtues reveals that all of the panels include a seated figure holding a shield emblazoned with an attribute. Humility's shield shows a simple, harmless dove, while the emblem on Prudence's shield encourages the wisdom of a serpent. Chastity's figure is somewhat in dispute, as it may be the sexless yet fire-resistant salamander or the immortal and fire-defying phoenix. Chastity is a veiled and virginal figure withstanding lustful burnings. The lamb on Charity's shield evokes not only how such animals offer, for the medieval mind, their milk and flesh for food but also their wool for clothing. As an image of Charity, the lamb may also refer to Christ as the Lamb of God, offering his loving sacrifice to save humanity. Of all the panels for virtues, the Charity panel alone has a second figure, a grateful beggar whose nakedness is being covered. The standard surmounted by a cross on Hope's shield symbolizes Christ's victory over death. An image of a final, hoped-for resurrection is dramatically depicted in the tympanum above these panels. The chalice and cross on Faith's shield reinforces salvation through the death and blood of Christ, as well as the Eucharist as a reminder and guarantee of salvation.

The long-robed female warrior on the right side, Fortitude, not only is dressed in the Pauline "armor of God," but reinforces spiritual power with the lion emblem on her shield. Patience has the slow, plodding ox on her shield, while Gentleness has a meek lamb. Concord has peace's olive branch, and Obedience's shield shows the submissive camel. Perseverance's shield has both the crown that is its reward as well as a lion's tail. This tail matches the head that the figure holds, encouraging the need for a constant and determined resolve from the beginning to the end.

The stateliness and serenity of the virtues contrasts with the pandemonium of the vices. Pride is pitched forward off the horse, while a partly clothed, rock-trotting, and club-carrying idiot makes up the Foolishness panel. A male figure longingly embraces the female embodiment of Lust in the next panel. While Lust looks vainly in a mirror (a common medieval pose for courtesans), the scepter in her right hand and the way her right foot rests on his left foot reveal her seductive control of the man. The figure of Greed clutches money close to her breast, as in the *Psychomachia*, illustrations, while her assertive and miserly left hand closes her strongbox. Next we find Despair's suicide, while the final panel on the left shows Idolatry's worship of a monkey/demon figure.

The images of vice on the right panel are even more dramatic. Cowardice is a knight throwing down his sword in mortal fear of a rabbit. The owl in the tree indicates that his cowardice may come from some ignorance, as it may be nighttime. The "brave" knight running away from a bunny may have struck the initial viewers as comical, and perhaps we can capture some of that humor by comparing the scene with a similar episode in *Monty Python and the Holy Grail.* Wrath is a woman attacking a monk with a sword, while Harshness features a well-dressed lady ungratefully kicking a cup-bearing servant. The image of Discord is a domestic fight with hair-pulling and household-item throwing. A man attacking a cleric, and, by extension, God's authority in the world, constitutes the image of Contumacy or Rebellion, while Inconstancy is a monk abandoning his habit, his monastery, and his vows.

The elevated, serene, and stately images of the virtues demonstrate how these qualities secure peace and harmony for the individual. The peacefulness of the virtues seems to evoke the stillness that spiritual people like Evagrius described and yearned for. It is interesting to note that the decorator did not include the often more social virtue of Justice. This exclusion could show an emphasis on the individual and the internal, or perhaps an image of Justice was unnecessary, since the tympanum decoration above the door gives such a dramatic presentation of divine and eternal justice.

Whereas the virtues have a beneficent and tranquil quality, the vices (performing everyday actions with vividness) may seem more vital, more exciting, and perhaps more real. Does the very chaos of the vices end up making them seem more compelling than the stiff and stale virtues? The decorations above these images, with the writhing demons trampled by Old and New Testament figures and the suffering damned contrasted with the blessed in the tympanum decoration offer a powerful counter-argument to sin's vitality. Still, the very familiar, even narrative quality of the vices could make them more interesting, at least visually, than the more symbolic and spiritual virtues.

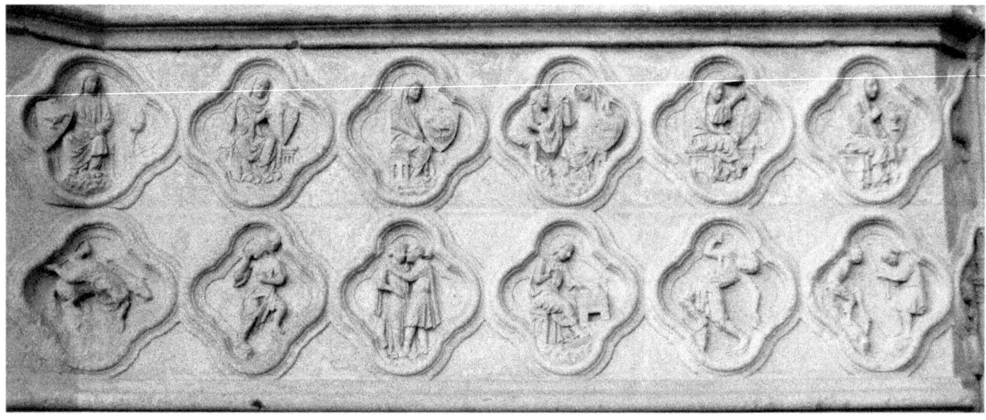

Figure 13. Anonymous from Amiens, about 1220 to 1235: *Six Virtues and Six Vices*, right side of the central portal. Amiens, Amiens Cathedral.

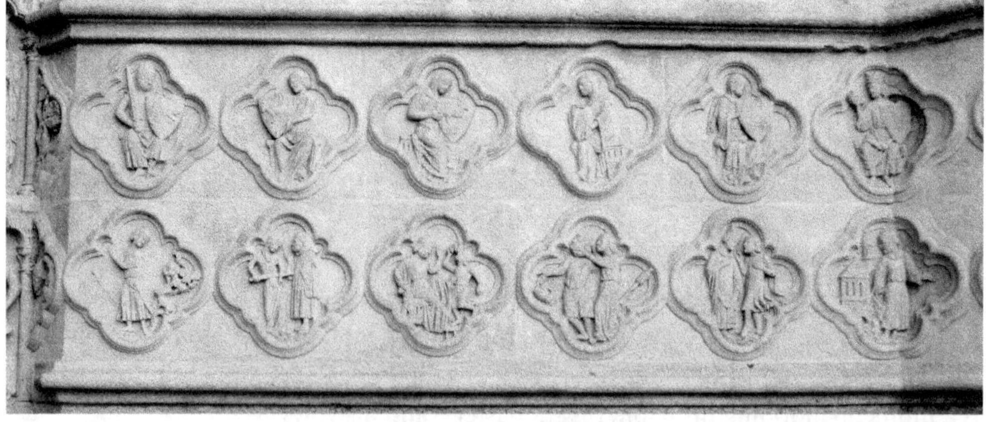

Figure 14. Anonymous from Amiens, about 1220 to 1235: *Six Virtues and Six Vices*, left side of the central portal. Amiens, Amiens Cathedral.

GIOTTO'S VIRTUES AND VICES IN THE ARENA CHAPEL

If there were a recipe for Giotto's work, it might go something like this: take the seven virtues, match them with seven vices, blend in elements of French Gothic, mix with two heaping cups of naturalism, including plenty of trompe l'oeil, stir in some artistic ingenuity and a cup and a half of psychological realism, and bake until it forms a compelling picture of human vice that leads to hell and virtue that prepares one for heaven. Giotto's work has all of these elements, and his depiction of the virtues and vices would be a powerful part of the entire experience of worshiping in the Scrovegni or Arena chapel.

Giotto starts with the seven virtues. Since the vices are not natural opposites for the virtues, Giotto's vices are not the conventional ones, but ones that contrast most clearly and directly with the virtues. The arrangement and placement of those virtues and the vices are very important in the chapel. The focus of the chapel is the image of the *Last Judgment*. Christ's right hand reaches out to lift and bless the righteous, while his left hand is turned down in condemnation of the sinful. The blessed rise from graves at Christ's right side, while the damned suffer a gruesome hell on his left. The images of the virtues and vices are on the side walls that lead up to the Judgment scene, with the vices on the wall to Christ's left and the virtues to Christ's right. Not only are the virtues and vices on these sides, but almost all of them face or lean in toward the Judgment. These images directly address viewers in the chapel itself, worshipers who are as yet still between heaven and hell, stuck in the psychomachia of virtue and vice.

Giotto's naturalism adds to the theatrical quality of the virtues and vices. The images are done in grisaille, meaning that they are mostly done in a monochromatic way so that they look like sculptures that stand (or fly, fall, sit, or hang) in a shallow space. Painted in this way, and placed in conjunction with the Judgment, these eye-level sculptural decorations resemble similar works in French Gothic cathedrals like Amiens. And like Gothic pairings, Giotto's fictive sculptural panels reinforce how virtue and vice are fundamental to human character and destiny.

Giotto uses a number of techniques to make his images of virtue and vice come to life. Closest to Christ we have the figure of Hope reaching toward the crown. Across from Hope, a demon drags the soul from a wretched suicide, and appropriate embodiment of Despair. Next to Hope is Charity (Figure 15), who stands opposite Envy. Charity, like Hope, reaches up, offering her heart to Christ. She wears a crown of roses, creating an association between Charity and the woman who gave her heart for humanity, Mary. With her other hand, Charity offers nurturing and holy gifts, fruits symbolic of Christian service and sacrifice. Classically and modestly dressed, she tramples the money bags symbolic of earthly wealth.

Where Charity gives her heart to God and her abundance to others, her opposite, Envy, is consumed by her own blinding preoccupation (Figure 16). Her turban-like headdress fails to cover her demonic horns. Her face, neck, and hands seem gaunt, and what seems to emaciate the figure, what seems to consume it from the inside out, is the snake coming from her mouth and turning to strike her eyes. Eyes are key for envy, since so much of this vice comes through seeing and craving, a sensory exaggeration reinforced in the animal-sized ears. These eyes and ears are supersensitive to the coveted possessions of others. The tight grip on the money bag and the claw-like quality of the right hand reinforce Envy's grabbing nature. And while Envy seeks more and more, its very obsessions consume it, evidenced by the infernal flames beneath it. Blinded by the snake, the grasping figure gropes its way toward hell. This psychological insight into the nature of this vice makes this image, as well as the whole set of images, powerfully compelling.

Next to Envy is Unfaithfulness or Idolatry, a figure holding aloft a pagan idol, while the chain from the idol holds or chains the figure. Across from her is Faith, bearing a cross-topped staff that smashes an idol. In her other hand is the scroll bearing the Apostles' Creed, while she tramples papers with symbols of heresy on them. Faith looks right at the viewer, while Justice faces out but glances slightly to one side. Justice holds scales with symbols on them of her roles as crowning the righteous and punishing the wicked. Below, on the pedestal beneath her throne, are scenes of the happiness and prosperity that Justice secures. Her opposite is one of the few male figures, a cold and indifferent robber baron with instruments of his cruelty: a sword and grappling hook. The scene below this figure shows how cruelty and violence are the outcomes of his rule. In the next pairing Temperance's firm stance, bridle, and wrapped sword contrast sharply with the wild desperation of Wrath's traumatic fury. Like Temperance, Fortitude stands robustly, holding a rod and shield and the lion-skin headdress that would associated the figure with the virtuous Hercules. Across from Fortitude is Inconstancy, perilously balanced on the orb sliding down a sloped floor. Initial audiences seeing this figure would not have associated her with Cowardice, the common contrast with Fortitude, but with the fickleness of fortune, of a life or character based upon chance instead of strength and integrity.

The final pairing places Prudence against Foolishness. Prudence, a scholar, sits at a desk with an open book in front of her and a mirror (Figure 17). In her hand she holds a compass. A careful look at the figure's head reveals the Janus-head, as there is another profile at the back of the head. This Janus-head, the convex mirror, and the compass, as well as the book, reinforce Prudence's knowledge of things past, present, and future. The unique and humorous figure of Foolishness, adorned with a feathery headdress and weirdly scalloped skirt, brandishes a club. This figure shares two features in common with "fools" in places like the cathedral in Amiens, namely, the club and the gender. But this fool's mock crown and bizarre skirt, with its strange train, could make him the travesty of a king, a baffoon who would lead the band of vices. The place of this mock king is at the end of the procession would add to his embarrassment. It is Giotto's combination of the elements of the virtues and vices tradition, his dynamic use of placement, his naturalism, his ingenuity, and his psychological insights that make this an important contribution to the tradition.

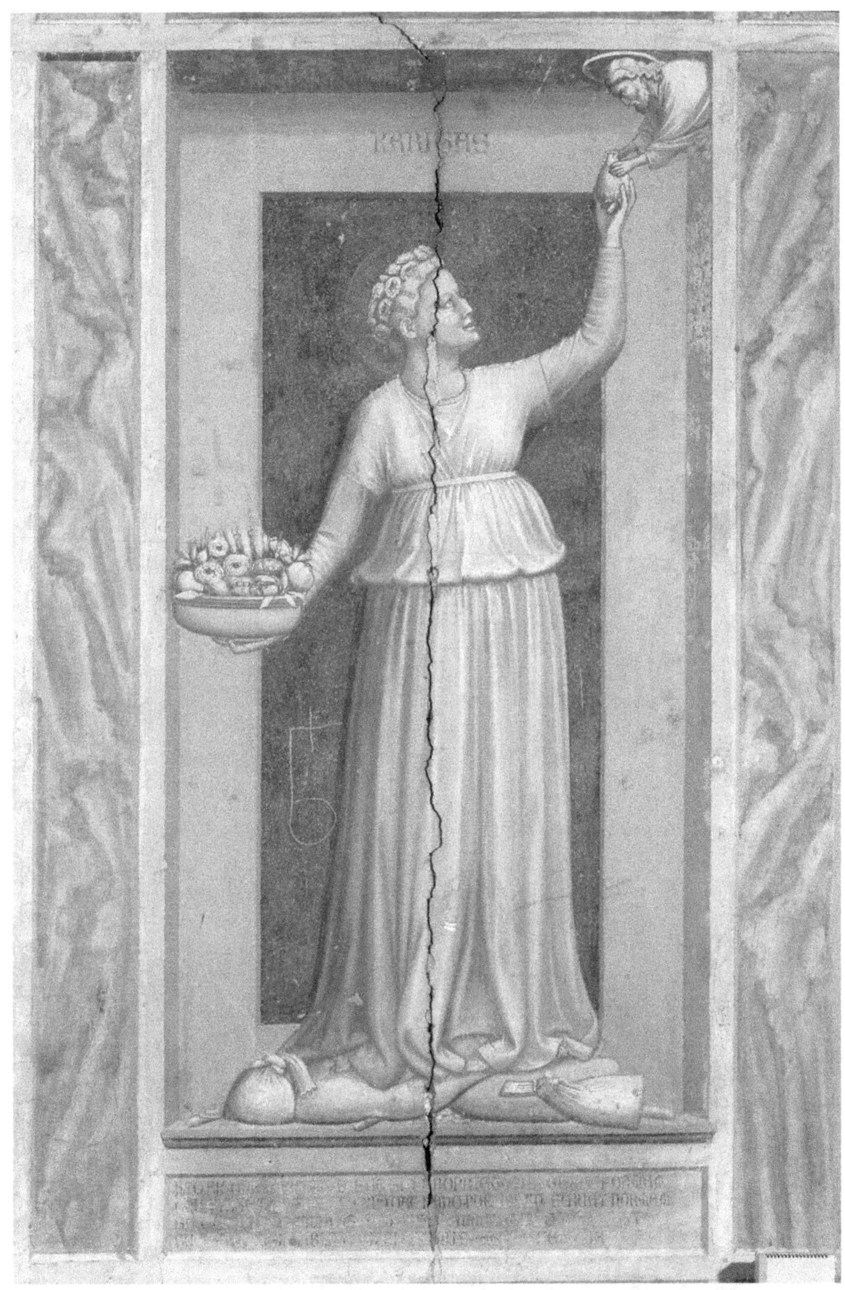

Figure 15. Giotto di Bondone. *Charity*. Grisaille fresco. Scrovegni Chapel, Padua, Italy. Photo Credit: Cameraphoto Arte, Venice / Art Resource, NY.

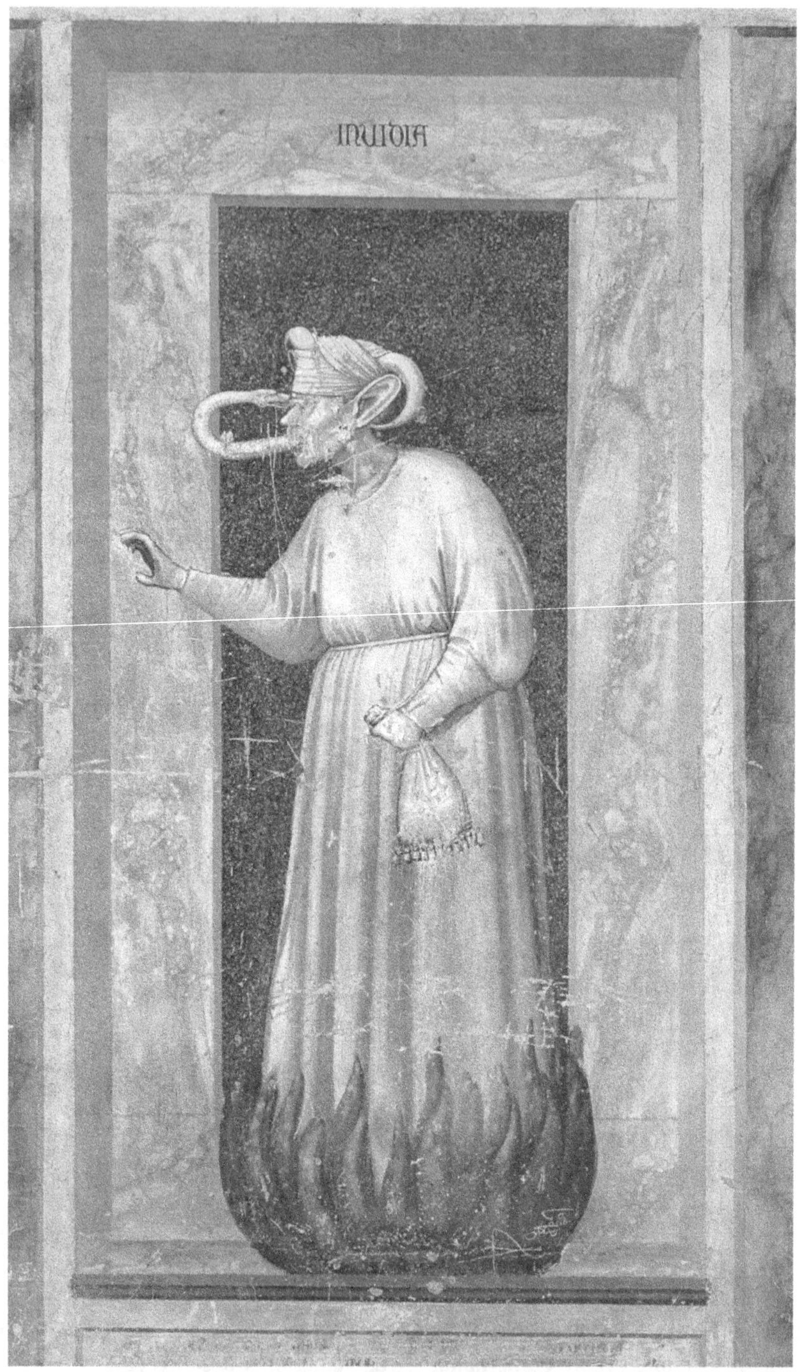

Figure 16. Giotto di Bondone. *Envy*. Grisaille fresco. Scrovegni Chapel, Padua, Italy. Photo Credit: Cameraphoto Arte, Venice / Art Resource, NY.

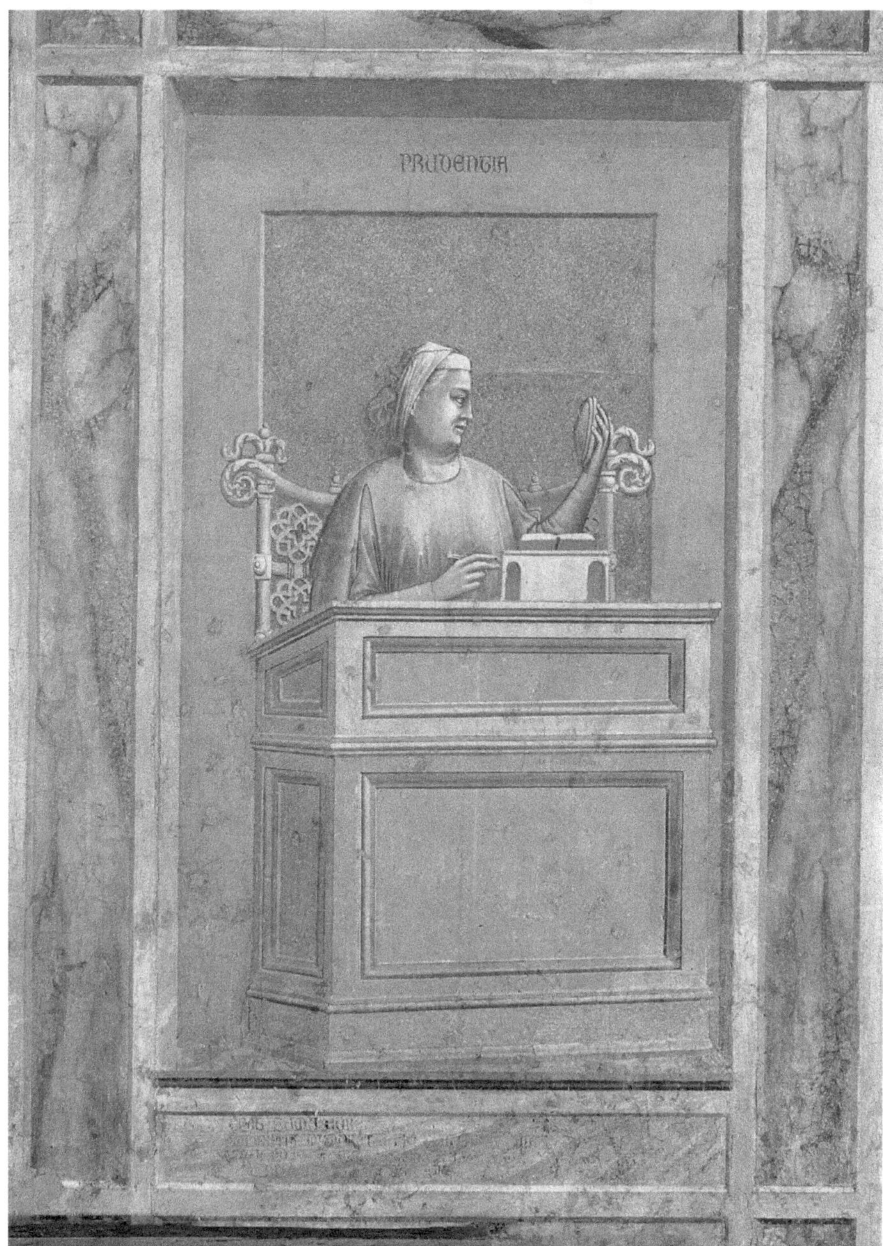

Figure 17. Giotto di Bondone. *Prudence*. Grisaille fresco. Scrovegni Chapel, Padua, Italy. Photo Credit: Cameraphoto Arte, Venice / Art Resource, NY.

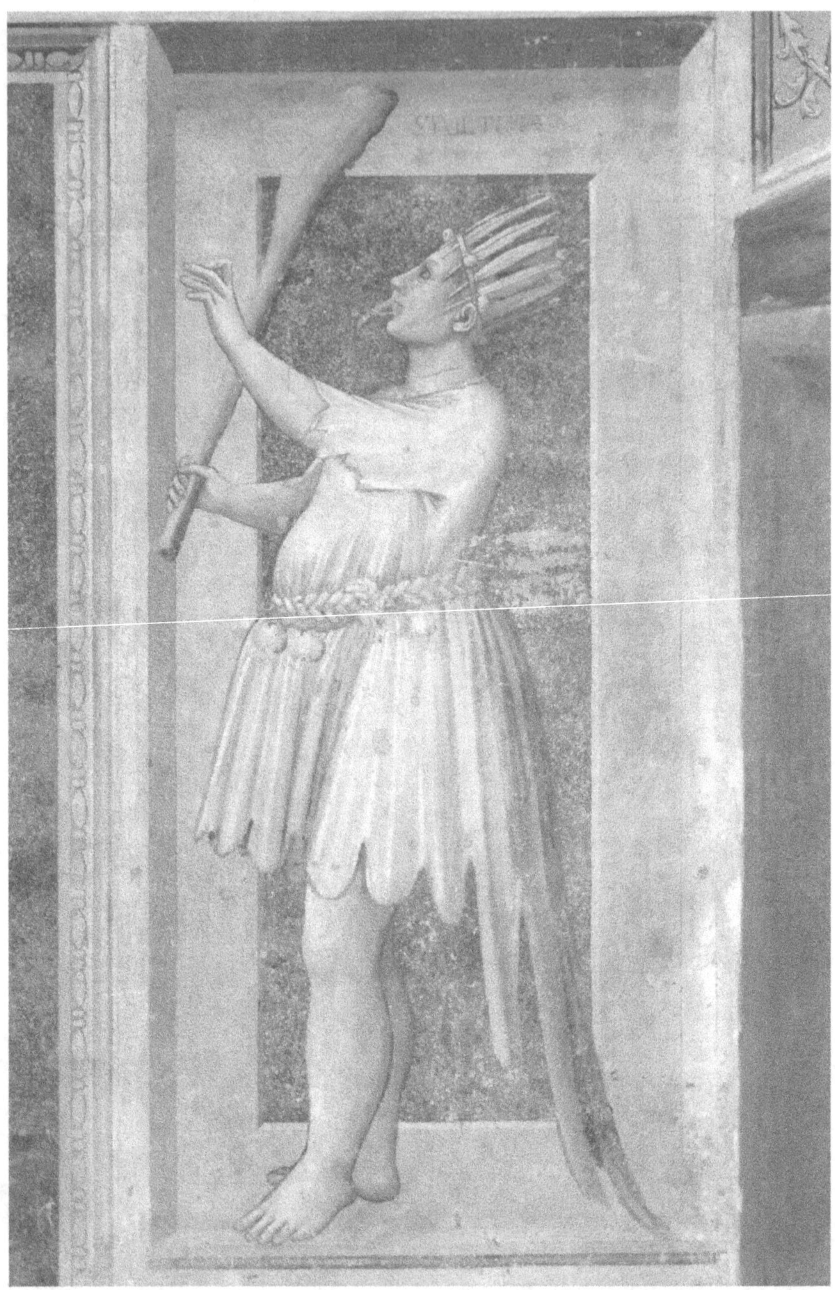

Figure 18. Giotto di Bondone. *Foolishness* (*Folly*). Grisaille fresco. Scrovegni Chapel, Padua, Italy. Photo Credit: Cameraphoto Arte, Venice / Art Resource, NY.

DANTE'S *PURGATORIO*

Introduction

Choosing most of the excerpts for this book was fairly easy. With Plato and Isaiah, Gregory the Great and Benjamin Franklin, all that had to be done was pick the parts that dealt most directly with the virtues and the vices. That is not the case with Dante. All of Dante's *Purgatorio* (if not the entire *Divine Comedy*!) deals with the virtues and vices. If that was not difficult enough, Dante's treatment of the virtues and vices is so profound and compelling that it is tempting to include the entire *Purgatorio*. What the excerpt below gives is a glimpse of Dante's majestic panorama of human virtue and vice. Hopefully the insight of even this glimpse will inspire an examination of the entire *Purgatorio*, and then *Divine Comedy*.

Purgatorio is the second book in Dante's massive *Divine Comedy*. This work is a "comedy" in the sense that, unlike tragedy, it has a happy ending. The work begins with a middle-aged Dante trapped in a dark forest. When three demonic animals block his exit, the spirit of the ancient Roman poet Virgil comes to help. Virgil explains that he has been sent to free Dante, but that the only way out is a long, grueling path. That path turns out to be a journey through all of the postmortal realms. The first book of the *Divine Comedy* describes Dante's journey through the various levels of hell, while the last relates his ascension into paradise. The second book narrates Dante's journey up the mountain of Purgatory.

To purge a metal is to burn off all of the impurities. On the various levels or cornices of Purgatory's mountain the sinful are purged of their sins through the same process: everyone pays penance, expresses contrition, confesses their sins, and seeks absolution. The sinners are purged on levels for the proud, envious, angry, slothful, greedy, gluttonous, and lustful. Each level begins with a "whip" (examples of a virtue that opposes the vice punished on that level). There is also a graphic depiction of the sinner's penance and contrition at that level, their confessions, and a "bridle" (examples of the sin's destructive consequences). These four elements—whip, penance, confessions, and bridle—demonstrate the compelling process by which sinners find absolution, cleanliness, and purity.

What Dante encounters at the beginning of each level can be described as a whip. This metaphorical whip forcefully prompts or moves the sinner to virtue with the presentation of various examples of the virtue that opposes the level's sin. In the excerpt below the "whip" consists in examples of love that oppose envy. The first example is taken from Mary's life, as is the pattern at each level. The envious hear Mary's voice say "Vinum non habent" or "They have no wine." Mary made this sad observation at a wedding feast at Cana. In response to this Jesus performed his first recorded miracle, turning the water into wine. What is significant about this for the envious is that Mary did not rejoice in the misfortune of others. Mary's words express her genuine and heartfelt concern, a concern that inspired the miracle. The second sound the envious hear is "I am Orestes." This refers to the selfless friendship of Orestes and Pylades. When Orestes was condemned to death, Pylades disguised himself as Orestes in order to die in his place. Both friends argue "I am Orestes" in order to save the others's life. The final voice is Christ's command spoken in the Sermon on the Mount, to "Love your enemies." These three voices express of love others, friends, and even enemies in sharp and compelling contrast with envy's self-absorbtion.

What happens next for Dante is what makes *Purgatorio* and the whole *Divine Comedy* so powerfully moving. Dante looks at the bruise-colored, stony ledge and notices people leaning against one another. Each wears a coarse and stiff haircloth cloak, a goat-fur covering that would not only itch but which would scrape the skin to the point of causing running sores. Dante then compares these souls to blind beggars that his audience would have readily recognized. He then notices that they weep through eyes that have been wired shut. These powerful, graphic images of the sinful not only make their penance real and compelling for readers, but they also reveal the nature of their penance. Where the envious had set themselves up in opposition to others in life, now they must lean and support one another. Where they had been internally bruised by the success of others, now they dwell in a place that is and wear clothing that is bruise colored. And where the envious had sinned through their eyes by choosing the see evil, now their eyes are wired shut. In purgatory, not only does the sinner's penance make external the internal pattern of the sin, but that penance seeks to reverse the sinful pattern itself.

The concrete and graphic description of the sinner's penance brings the otherwise abstraction of postmortal suffering into our experience. What makes this description even more real are the confessions. At each level of Purgatory Dante speaks with some of the souls suffering there. In the excerpt we hear from a Sienese woman named Sapia. In the little pun on her name, Sapia was not "sapient," or wise. Sapia was instead foolishly envious of another Sienese family, so when she watched their defeat in the loss and the beheading of Provenzano Salvani at the battle of Colle, she felt such incomparable joy that she concluded that no matter what happened after, she could die a happy woman. The individual and specific confessions of spirits like Sapìa help to flesh out the postmortal world. These confessions also connect abstract principles with everyday life through readily recognized examples.

The last common element for each level is the bridle. Whereas the whip that begins each level scourges the sinner and encourages a virtue opposed to the sin, the bridle restrains or holds back the sinner through images of the vice's devastating results. The envious hear the voice of Cain worried that, now that his envy has compelled him to kill Abel, everyone will seek to kill him. The warning here is not only that envy breeds murder but that it fosters intense fears that others will be just as murderously envious. After the thundering voice of Cain, the envious hear the voice of Aglauros. Aglauros took a bribe from Mercury in order for the god to sleep with Aglauros's sister, but when Aglauros's envy of her sister led her to thwart Mercury's plan, the god turned her to stone. These booming voices of warning show how envy can transform tender feelings of family love first to bitterness and then into stony insensitivity.

Dante's use of positive examples (the whip), negative examples (the bridle), specific and concrete examples (the confessions), and powerful, symbolic images of penance are some of the ways that he makes his description of purgatory so compelling. And the excerpt included here is only part of one level! Each level offers stunning insight into the nature of the vice punished there as well as the virtue that opposes that vice. Dante shows the power of Humility to overcome Pride, and the power of Meekness over Wrath, Zeal over Sloth, Poverty over Greed, Abstinence and Moderation over Gluttony, and Chastity over Lust. He also includes the traditional seven virtues at least twice in the *Purgatorio*. At the beginning of his ascent up the mountain Dante sees four stars, symbols of the four cardinal virtues, which later become three stars, the three theological virtues. Dante sees a whole pageant of symbolic elements at the end of his climb, including the triumphal chariot of the church with the three theological virtues dancing to the right of the chariot and the four cardinal virtues dancing to the left of the chariot. It should also be noted that Dante gives a very interesting explanation for the arrangement of the vices—an explanation rooted in his concept of love. When Dante visits the level where the slothful suffer, we find out that love motivates all human action. When humans desire "the Eternal God" and then use reason to measure or control all secondary desires, "love" never leads to sinful indulgence. When "love" becomes corrupted and turns to evil, by desiring to outdo others (Pride), by desiring ill for others (Envy), or by seeking vengeance (Anger), then such "love" is punished or purified in the lower three levels. When "love" is toward the right thing but is deficient or weak (Sloth) it is corrected in this middle level. Finally, when "love" is pointed at good things but in an excessive way, toward wealth (Greed), or fleshly pleasures (Gluttony and Lust), it is redirected and purified on the upper three levels.

There is so much more that a brief introduction and an excerpt from the *Purgatorio* cannot adequately describe. In its concrete details and its sweeping insights, in its majestic panorama and its intimate portrayal, the *Purgatorio* (as well as the entire *Divine Comedy*) is one of the greatest artistic treatment of the virtues and vices.

Canto 13 and Canto 14 lines 130–151[2]

We were upon the summit of the stairs,
Where for the second time is cut away
The mountain, which ascending shriveth[3] all.

2. From Dante, *The Divine Comedy*, trans. Henry Wadsworth Longfellow (Boston: Ticknor & Fields, 1867), 77–83, 89–90.

3. The mountain of Purgatory is where souls are purified or purged. *To shrive* is to be purified.

There in like manner doth a cornice bind
The hill all round about, as does the first,
Save that its arc more suddenly is curved.

Shade is there none, nor sculpture that appears;
So seems the bank, and so the road seems smooth,
With but the livid color of the stone.

"If to inquire we wait for people here,"
The Poet said, "I fear that peradventure
Too much delay will our election have."

Then steadfast on the sun his eyes he fixed,
Made his right side the center of his motion,
And turned the left part of himself about.

"O thou sweet light! with trust in whom I enter
Upon this novel journey, do thou lead us,"
Said he, "as one within here should be led.

Thou warmest the world, thou shinest over it;
If other reason prompt not otherwise,
Thy rays should evermore our leaders be!"

As much as here is counted for a mile,
So much already there had we advanced
In little time, by dint of ready will;

And tow'rds us there were heard to fly, albeit
They were not visible, spirits uttering
Unto Love's table courteous invitations,

The first voice that passed onward in its flight,
"*Vinum non habent,*"[4] said in accents loud,
And went reiterating it behind us.

And ere it wholly grew inaudible
Because of distance, passed another, crying,
"I am Orestes!"[5] and it also stayed not.

4. This Latin phrase means "They have no wine." This is what Mary said at the wedding at Cana as recorded in John 2:1–11. Mary's words here show her concern for others.

5. This phrase was said by Orestes's friend Pylades, who attempted to take his friend's place and

"O," said I, "Father, these, what voices are they?"
And even as I asked, behold the third,
Saying: "Love those from whom ye have had evil!"[6]

And the good Master said: "This circle scourges
The sin of envy, and on that account
Are drawn from love the lashes of the scourge.[7]

The bridle[8] of another sound shall be;
I think that thou wilt hear it, as I judge,
Before thou comest to the Pass of Pardon.

But fix thine eyes athwart the air right steadfast,
And people thou wilt see before us sitting,
And each one close against the cliff is seated."

Then wider than at first mine eyes I opened;
I looked before me, and saw shades with mantles
Not from the color of the stone diverse.[9]

And when we were a little farther onward,
I heard a cry of, "Mary, pray for us!"
A cry of, "Michael, Peter, and all Saints!"

I do not think there walketh still on earth
A man so hard, that he would not be pierced
With pity at what afterward I saw.

For when I had approached so near to them
That manifest to me their acts became,
Drained was I at the eyes by heavy grief.

die for him.

6. This third phrase also registers compassion for others, and it is taken from the Sermon on the Mount recorded as Matthew 5:43–45.

7. The scourge or whip that compels or moves the envious are the expressions of concern and love for others.

8. The bridle is made up of envious voices, and they are found at the end of the excerpts given here. Those voices are like a bridle in how they hold back the envious impulses of the sinners on this level by providing examples of envy's destructive nature.

9. The spirits on this level are the same color as the rocks that they lean against.

Covered with sackcloth vile they seemed to me,
And one sustained the other with his shoulder,
And all of them were by the bank sustained.

Thus do the blind, in want of livelihood,
Stand at the doors of churches asking alms,
And one upon another leans his head,

So that in others pity soon may rise,
Not only at the accent of their words,
But at their aspect, which no less implores.

And as unto the blind the sun comes not,
So to the shades, of whom just now I spake,
Heaven's light will not be bounteous of itself;

For all their lids an iron wire transpierces,
And sews them up, as to a sparhawk wild
Is done, because it will not quiet stay.

To me it seemed, in passing, to do outrage,
Seeing the others without being seen;
Wherefore I turned me to my counsel sage.

Well knew he what the mute one wished to say,
And therefore waited not for my demand,
But said: "Speak, and be brief, and to the point."

I had Virgilius upon that side
Of the embankment from which one may fall,
Since by no border 'tis engarlanded;

Upon the other side of me I had
The shades devout, who through the horrible seam
Pressed out the tears so that they bathed their cheeks.

To them I turned me, and, "O people, certain,"
Began I, "of beholding the high light,
Which your desire has solely in its care,

So may grace speedily dissolve the scum
Upon your consciences, that limpidly

Through them descend the river of the mind,

Tell me, for dear 'twill be to me and gracious,
If any soul among you here is Latian,
And 'twill perchance be good for him I learn it."

"O brother mine, each one is citizen
Of one true city; but thy meaning is,
Who may have lived in Italy a pilgrim."

By way of answer this I seemed to hear
A little farther on than where I stood,
Whereat I made myself still nearer heard.

Among the rest I saw a shade that waited
In aspect, and should any one ask how,
Its chin it lifted upward like a blind man.

"Spirit," I said, "who stoopest to ascend,
If thou art he who did reply to me,
Make thyself known to me by place or name."

"Sienese was I," it replied, "and with
The others here recleanse my guilty life,
Weeping to Him to lend himself to us.

Sapient I was not, although I Sapia
Was called, and I was at another's harm
More happy far than at my own good fortune.

And that thou mayst not think that I deceive thee,
Hear if I was as foolish as I tell thee.
The arc already of my years descending,

My fellow-citizens near unto Colle
Were joined in battle with their adversaries,
And I was praying God for what he willed.

Routed were they, and turned into the bitter
Passes of flight; and I, the chase beholding,
A joy received unequalled by all others;

So that I lifted upward my bold face
Crying to God, 'Henceforth I fear thee not,'
As did the blackbird at the little sunshine.

Peace I desired with God at the extreme
Of my existence, and as yet would not
My debt have been by penitence discharged,

Had it not been that in remembrance held me
Pier Pettignano in his holy prayers,
Who out of charity was grieved for me.

But who art thou, that into our conditions
Questioning goest, and hast thine eyes unbound
As I believe, and breathing dost discourse?"

"Mine eyes," I said, "will yet be here ta'en from me,
But for short space; for small is the offence
Committed by their being turned with envy.

Far greater is the fear, wherein suspended
My soul is, of the torment underneath,
For even now the load down there weighs on me."

And she to me: "Who led thee, then, among us
Up here, if to return below thou thinkest?"
And I: "He who is with me, and speaks not;

And living am I; therefore ask of me,
Spirit elect, if thou wouldst have me move
O'er yonder yet my mortal feet for thee."

"O, this is such a novel thing to hear,"
She answered, "that great sign it is God loves thee;
Therefore with prayer of thine sometimes assist me.

And I implore, by what thou most desirest,
If e'er thou treadest the soil of Tuscany,
Well with my kindred reinstate my fame.

Them wilt thou see among that people vain
Who hope in Talamone, and will lose there
More hope than in discovering the Diana;

But there still more the admirals will lose."

Canto 14 lines 130–51

When we became alone by going onward,
Thunder, when it doth cleave the air, appeared,
A voice, that counter to us came, exclaiming:

"Shall slay me whosoever findeth me!"
And fled as the reverberation dies
If suddenly the cloud asunder bursts.

As soon as hearing had a truce from this,
Behold another, with so great a crash,
That it resembled thunderings following fast:

"I am Aglaurus, who became a stone!"
And then, to press myself close to the Poet,
I backward, and not forward, took a step.

Already on all sides the air was quiet;
And said he to me: "That was the hard curb
That ought to hold a man within his bounds;

But you take in the bait so that the hook
Of the old Adversary draws you to him,
And hence availeth little curb or call.

The heavens are calling you, and wheel around you,
Displaying to you their eternal beauties,
And still your eye is looking on the ground;

Whence He, who all discerns, chastises you."

AMBROGIO LORENZETTI'S PAINTINGS IN THE PALAZZO PUBBLICO, SIENA

The rule of security or the reign of fear: these are the contrasting dominions that Ambrogio Lorenzetti depicts for Siena's Palazzo Pubblico. In panoramic landscapes, Lorenzetti uses one side to show a hostile world of violence, cruelty, and famine, controlled by fear. The other side shows peace's rich abundance and prosperity. Between these two worlds we find the governments that bring them about. Each government or court has a central ruler, a crowned trinity above that figure, and advisors to each side. Lorenzetti's sumptuous paintings decorate an important meeting room, the Sala dei Nove, in Siena's main government building. The Sienese, both the political officials who worked in this room and the citizens with affairs to conduct here, were confronted with a powerful image of public virtue and vice. This image is specifically tailored to the city-state of Siena, a republic where the harmonious interaction and virtue of its citizens were crucial to its very survival.

Lorenzetti painted two vast, panoramic landscapes. One shows a city and countryside under the control of fear, while the other shows the rule of peace or security. To the right of the peaceful city and countryside is the Court of Justice (Figure 20). The Court of Tyranny is connected with the city and countryside of Fear (Figure 19). At the center of the Court of Tyranny is Tyranny himself. This horned, fanged, and darkly robed figure, reminiscent of medieval depictions of the devil, holds a rock or bludgeon in one hand and a cup in the other. This cup is his sacrilegious and poisonous "holy chalice." Above Tyranny flies his unholy trinity: Avarice, Pride, and Vainglory. The shriveled figure of Avarice holds a hook and money bags, while Vainglory admires herself in a mirror and holds a lifeless dry reed. The bright red and supremely confident looking figure of Pride holds her yoke of subjugation and the spear she uses to intimidate any potential enemies.

Tyranny's other attendants are even more imaginative. At the far left is Cruelty, who nonchalantly wields a snake and strangles a baby. Next to her is Treason, a seemingly placid figure who nonetheless cradles the hybrid animal that represents her nature. Treason's pet is part lamb and part scorpion. The next figure, Fraud, plays an equally important role. This figure, whose gloved hand holds a cudgel, has an angelic face and bat-like wings and claws, attributes that are very appropriate for one who represents duplicity. To the right of Tyranny are Furor, Division, and War. Furor is a malicious combination of a centaur and dog equipped with a stone and snake. Division is perhaps the most imaginative (and inadvertently funny) figure. Dressed in the starkly contrasting white and black, she has "Si" written on one side and "No" on the other. Then, with a saw, she literally cuts herself in half, succinctly representing, among other things, divisive factional infighting. To the far right is War, helmeted and bearing a sword and shield. At the feet of Tyranny we find its worst consequence, the tormented, bound, downcast, and defeated figure of Justice, her scales in pieces beside her.

The utopian and virtuous Court of Justice is structurally identical to the dystopic and vicious Court of Tyranny, with a slight variation. At the center of the Court of Justice is not the figure of Justice, but Common Good. There is a separate space for Justice, which I will discuss in a moment. The figure of Common Good, dressed in the black-and-white colors of Siena, bears a shield with an image and inscription dedicated to the Virgin. In lettering that arcs around the figure are the initials for the city of Siena, CSCCV, meaning "Commune of the City of Siena, City of the Virgin." The image on the shield, inscription, lettering, and trinity of figures above Common Good are some of the few references to religion in the entire work. Above Common Good and to his right is the crowned and modest figure of Faith bearing a cross, while Hope, to the left, looks in positive and reverent anticipation heavenward toward the face of Christ. Directly above Common Good is Charity, with a crown, a dart, an upward gaze, and a flaming heart.

Common Good also has attendants who mirror Tyranny's vicious ministers. To Common Good's far right is the crowned figure of Peace, relaxing serenely above a pile of armor, a shield at her feet, and holding an olive branch. Next to her Fortitude holds a scepter and shield, with mounted knights and foot soldiers below her. Prudence comes next, and in her lap she holds a water clock inscribed "past, present, future," conveying her Janus-like knowledge. To the left of Common Good is Magnanimity. This virtue in particular shows the influence of Aristotle's ideas that effective leaders are generous, a pointed reinforced by the tray of coins in this figure's lap. Temperance, the next figure, uncharacteristically holds a large hourglass. This image may reinforce the need for self-control and discipline since one's resources and time in mortality, as the clock reminds, are limited. And, if we do not have enough images of Justice, there is another one to Common Good's far left. Justice's restrained facial expression, drawn sword, and the severed head at her knee convey her power and control.

Upon close inspection, we can see a cord tied around Common Good's right hand. This cord connects Common Good to the separate image of Justice by way of twenty-four "councilors" and the figure of Concord. These twenty-four councilors represent different Sienese political leaders, including some of the Nine or *Nove* for which the room is named. These citizen-leaders harmoniously move forward, working with one accord. What reinforces the sense of both harmony and justice is the figure of Concord. Not only does she represent this unified harmony, but she holds on her lap a carpenter's plane, a tool used to keep surfaces evenly unified. Above Concord is the bearded and stern yet fatherly figure of Justice seated on his throne with a balance and scales. Hovering above the figure is Wisdom holding a book. Justice exercises distributive justice on one side (as an angel decapitates one figure while crowning another) and commutative justice on the other (as a parallel angel gives a spear and chest). The cord that ends up on Common Good's wrist begins with these angels, running through Concord and the councilors.

Strong contrasts help make the courts of Tyranny and Justice impressive. Beyond obvious differences between Tyranny and Common Good are less obvious ones. Though both Pride and Charity are dressed predominantly in red, Pride's look of disdain and superiority as well as her yoke show her oppressive control, whereas Charity's dart, glance, and flaming heart would turn the audience's mind to Christ's loving sacrifice that made people free. The haggard and hook-bearing Avarice contrasts sharply with the young, cross-bearing Faith. Vainglory carries the lifeless symbol of her vanity and can only look at her reflection in a mirror, while Hope's glance is trained toward the promise of an eternal life in heaven. The beauty and serenity of Peace contrasts sharply with the nonchalant malice of Cruelty, just as the timeless security of Fortitude and Prudence contrasts with the duplicity of Treason and Fraud. Lorenzetti reveals the wild and destructive natures of Furor, Division, and War by contrasting them with the subdued and disciplined renditions of Magnanimity, Temperance, and Justice.

Lorenzetti and whoever else worked on the program for these paintings developed a thought-provoking and ingenious set of contrasting virtues and vices. And like so many works, this one engages traditional elements of the virtues and vices to meet particular needs. Here virtues and vices take the field, not in a personal or strictly internal battle but in the most public of struggles. This work is not about divine gifts of virtue to a particular leader but about a community that either thrives by possessing in common those virtues or is torn apart by their deficiency, their lack. Where the vices create a special threat of division, violence, and fear, so the virtues, in their many manifestations, guarantee prosperity, peace, and survival for this city-state.

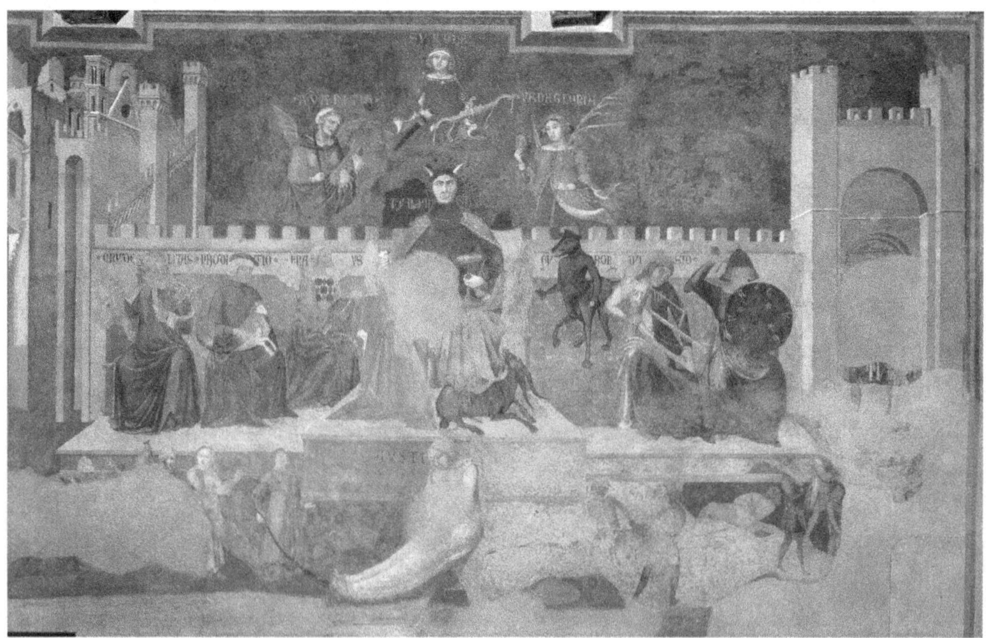

Figure 19. Lorenzetti, Ambrogio. 1338–1339: *Allegory of Bad Government.* Fresco. Palazzo Pubblico, Siena, Italy. Photo Credit: Scala / Art Resource, NY.

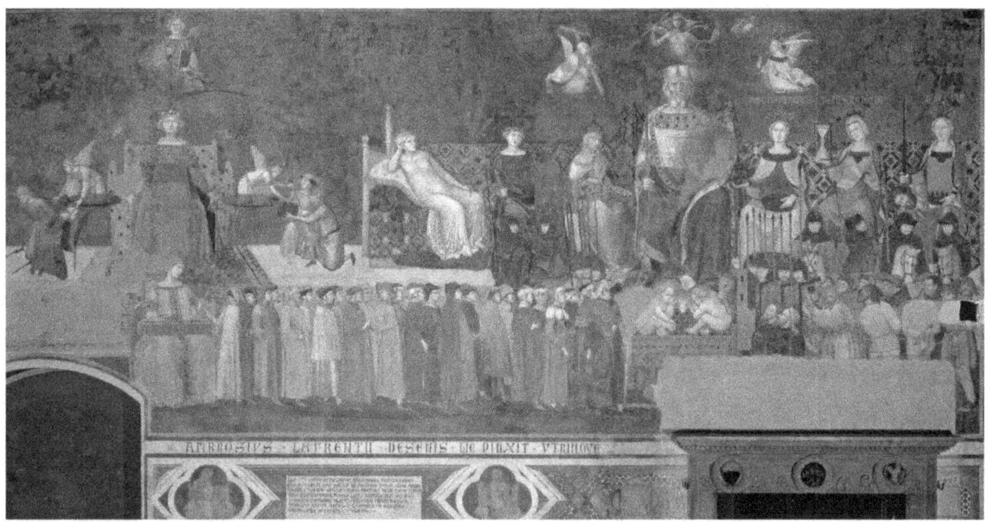

Figure 20. Lorenzetti, Ambrogio. 1338–1339: *Allegory of Good Government*. Fresco. Palazzo Pubblico, Siena, Italy. Photo Credit: Scala / Art Resource, NY.

WILLIAM LANGLAND'S *PIERS PLOWMAN*

Introduction

Pay what you owe. That seems pretty simple, pretty straight forward. You go to the grocery store, you pick up a few items, and, in order to take them home, you must pay what you owe. But this simple phrase has many layers of meaning in the medieval poem *Piers Plowman*. These many layers involve society, the individual, the soul, and virtue and vice.

We do not know very much about the author of *Piers Plowman*. The best scholarly guess is that it was William Langland, who lived between about 1330 and 1387. He seems to have been from the Malvern region of Worcestershire, he spent some time in London, and he may have made his living as a clerk and a psalter—a psalter being one who is paid to pray for the souls of others. He also spent a tremendous amount of time writing *Piers Plowman*. When one examines all the original manuscripts of *Piers Plowman,* (and there are at least more than forty!) the impulse is to exclaim, "Would the real Piers Plowman please stand up!" There are at least three versions of the work, given the imaginative labels A, B, and C, and they were probably made between about 1370 and 1386.

The poem begins with a prologue and then is divided into sections called *passus*, which is Latin for "steps." But do not expect clear, easy-to-follow progressions. The entire work has a fluidity and ambiguity that has led some to compare it to the magical realism of authors like Gabriel García Márquez. There are waking episodes, dream episodes, dream-within-dream episodes, and it is sometimes hard to tell if the speaker is awake or dreaming in any given *passus* or step. One unifying feature is the quest to know how to save one's soul and how to move up the levels or steps of spiritually "doing well" (proper belief and faith), "doing better," (obedience to the law and hope for salvation), and "doing best" (living a charitable life in imitation of Christ). But what makes this otherwise abstract and spiritual quest so compelling is how it is welded to concrete daily realities; this connection of the spiritual to the daily gives the work its pointed social satire and even contemporary resonance.

The poem's blending of the allegorical and even mystical with the concrete makes its treatment of virtue and vice all the more vivid. Two portions of the poem most clearly engage the virtues and the vices. The first of these portions includes both Passus VI and VII of the C version, and in the interest of space it is not excerpted in this book. Just before this section Reason gives a sermon admonishing everyone to repent. The seven vices or deadly sins approach, make confession, and then Repentence makes a reply. While these confessions shed light both on the sinful impulses and on their fruits or deeds, what makes them interesting is how readily one can see oneself (or better, other people!) in these descriptions. Pride, for example, lists her disobedience to parents and to the Church as well as her efforts to one-up and outshine the people around her. Wrath offers a vivid description of how he helped prepare the "squabble-stew" that poisoned the convent. It may be easy to imagine the same dish prepared in your work, school, or home. Lechery's is a rather brief confession, while in Covetousness or Avarice's confession we see one of the humorous puns Langland often employs. Repentence asks Covetousness if he has ever made restitution. Covetousness misunderstands restitution and says that he once stole from some traders while they were "at rest." Gluttony gives a lively account of a binge he went on while he should have been at church, and Sloth's admission shows the vice's physical as well as spiritual inertia. Repentence's statements at the end of the tribunal show the danger of sloth in particular and vice in general. Once overcome by vice, people no longer grieve for their sins, no longer feel spiritual dryness, and instead pursue vanity, become angry at the good, and eventually lose hope entirely.

The second portion of the poem that engages the virtues and vices tradition encompasses the poem's final two sections. It begins with the Dreamer falling asleep in church. In his dream he sees Christ the jouster dressed in Piers Plowman's armor. Conscience explains the shift in meaning between the names Jesus and Christ and that the blood-red jouster, Christ, comes to provide a model for the tempted, an exemplum that can give strength to overcome. What then follows is an allegorical examination of elements of Christ's life that echoes the stages or steps of do-well, do-better, and do-best. After Piers's vision of Christ on the cross, Conscience accompanies him to see the larger world where God's gracious gifts are poured out abundantly. To do his work, Piers is given the four great oxen of the evangelists and four horses of the early church fathers. The seeds that Piers plants are the four cardinal virtues described with insight and economy. Piers then builds a barn to hold the fruits of his labors—a barn made from the wood of Christ's cross and with mortar made with the aid of Christ's baptismal water and blood. This barn is Unity, the Holy Church of England.

Frankly, the first time I read *Piers Plowman*, I thought that it would end here, with a nice triumphal climax. This is about how Prudentius ends his *Psychomachia*. But what Langland gives us is a compelling final battle in and for the soul. Pride and the vices mount a powerful attack and force everyone into the safety of Unity. When Piers reminds them that pardon and safety come through "Redde quod debes" (through paying what one owes), the people balk. Langland uses specific people to voice their sly, subtle rejection of the rule of the cardinal virtues and the demand to pay what they owe. As the last Passus begins, the Dreamer awakes only to be visited by another personification of vice's subtle power, Need. After the brief interview with Need, the Dreamer again falls asleep to witness, in full power, the Antichrist. This mighty figure, using a tremendous twisting or perverting motion, uproots the tree of Truth. The clergy, followed by the rest of the people, soon fall to falsehood and corruption, and finally join Antichrist's ranks, with only the virtuous "fools" holding out. In spite of natural disasters, plagues, famines, and old age, the forces of Conscience cannot gain any headway against Antichrist and the vices. In the end, Conscience tries to close ranks in the safe haven of Unity, only to find that it has been infiltrated by corrupt healers who go so far as to disarm Contrition. Conscience is finally forced to flee as a pilgrim. Langland does not offer a final triumph like the one in *Star Wars*; he shows how the evil empire strikes back, leaving the reader only half awake and still very much in the conflict.

The poem's unresolved ending centers on the difficulty that real people have in paying what they owe. We hear in many places how people in the poem shirk or skirt or outright steal. And this idea of paying what you owe operates on many levels. Christ graciously bestows every needful gift upon every member of society. Priests and clerks get gifts of intelligence, craftspeople are endowed with skills, enforcers of the laws are given strength, and leaders are blessed with wisdom. And for each person, no matter what his or her station, the command is "Redde quod debes:" pay what you owe. This is what gives bite to the poem's social satires, as it explores corruption at all levels born of a failure to use one's gifts properly. Piers the Plowman, in contrast, fully employs his humble gifts as he should and finds God's forgiveness and favor. The obligation to pay what you owe extends to the interpersonal realm as well. Langland's poem does not remain in the lofty heights of social criticism but brings this to the individual level when people like a brewer, an uneducated vicar, or a lord specifically express contrition or corruption. But perhaps the poem's strongest Christian point is that since Christ has suffered and redeemed everyone—since Christ himself has come down, become human, and paid the price for each person's sins—, the only way that one can truly pay what one owes is to give all. In the Christian sense, paying what one owes is using all of one's gifts and abilities, one's passions and faculties, in a way that imitates Christ. Paying what the Christian owes is paying all because Christ gave all.

In *Piers Plowman*, it is only that complete giving that gives power, or virtus, to both avoid vice and to live as the Christian should.

Piers Plowman from Passus XIX[10]

Grace also gave Piers his seeds, the Cardinal Virtues;[11] these he sowed in men's souls, afterwards enumerating their names. The first seed was called 'the Spirit of Prudence.' Whoever ate it would be able to envisage beforehand the way in which a course of action would end, before he actually embarked upon it. This is the virtue that teaches us to buy a long-handled ladle, if our aim is to keep an eye on a pot of broth and keel off the fat from the surface.

The name of the second seed was 'the Spirit of Temperance.' Whoever fed off this seed acquired a temperament of such a kind that he never ended up swollen, whether from over-eating or from stress. No mockery or insult could disturb his self-control; nor could an increase in his fortune, brought about by his success in trade. He would never allow himself to be upset by words thrown out in idle thoughtlessness. Nor would he ever let a suit of clothes artfully tailored and cut be seen on his back, nor spicy food from the hand of a master-chef diffuse its choice flavors on his palate.

The third seed sown by Piers was 'the Spirit of Fortitude.' Anyone who ate that seed always had the stamina to endure every suffering sent by God, every ailment and every other trouble. No false rumours or scandalmongering, and no loss of worldly goods, could plunge him into such deep dejection that he abandoned his cheerful spirit of hope. He remained strong and steadfast in the face of all opprobrium, holding his ground with patience, supported by the prayer, 'Spare me, O Lord!,' and shielding his heart with Cato's sound advice: 'Be of brave heart when you are wrongly blamed!'[12]

The fourth seed Piers planted was 'the Spirit of Justice.' Anyone who ate the fruit of that seed would always remain at rights with God, going in fear of nothing except deceit. Deceit works so darkly, that at times even honesty becomes invisible to the scrutiny of Justice. But, for all that, the Spirit of Justice never jibs at bringing guilty men to the gallows; it will even correct a monarch if he slips off the right path into

10. From William Langland, *Piers Plowman: A New Translation of the B-text*, trans. A. V. C. Schmidt (Oxford World's Classics; Oxford: Oxford University Press, 1992), 235–41. The footnotes are those of the original.

11. *his seeds, the Cardinal Virtues*: those on which natural and social existence was thought to hang (*cardo*, 'hinge') were associated with some at least of the spiritual gifts enumerated in Isa. 1:2–3 (esp. counsel with prudence, piety with justice, and fortitude with the cardinal virtue so named). The importance of temperance has already been stressed by the Holy Church in Passus I, and the special importance of justice is noted by Conscience in his argument with the brewer. These virtues formed the basis on which the specifically spiritual ones, Faith, Hope, and Charity (the 'theological virtues') were built.

12. *Spare me, O Lord! . . . Be of brave heart. . . blamed!*: the prayer, from Job 7:16 occurs in this form in the matins of the Office of the Dead. Its link here with one of Cato's *Distichs* (ii. 14) illustrates Langland's sense of the relatedness of 'secular' and 'religious' virtues in the Christian scheme of things.

criminal ways. For when Justice sits in court in a judge's person, he cares nothing for the anger of a king. Never has he swerved from the letter of the law through fear of some great nobleman's intervention, or even, if it came to it, the threat of death. In spite of bribes, entreaties, or interference from the sovereign, his aim has been to act with impartial fairness, as far as his capacity permitted.

These were the four seeds Piers planted; and after that, he drew his harrow over them—the Old Law and the New. This would enable love to grow up in the midst of these four virtues, and at the same time uproot the vices.

'It's a common thing,' said Piers, 'wherever you go, to see rest-harrow and other weeds choking the crops in the fields where they flourish together. That is just what the vices do to the virtues! And so,' he continued, 'everyone who can should harrow their native understanding of Scripture under the guidance of these doctors of the Church, and cultivate the cardinal virtues in accordance with the tenor of their teaching.'[13]

'Before your seed starts growing towards ripeness,' said Grace, 'erect a building for yourself to store your grain in.'

'I swear to you, Grace!' cried Piers, 'you'll have to provide the wood and plan the construction of that storehouse before you leave.'

So Grace gave Piers the cross on which Christ suffered on Calvary to save mankind,[14] together with our Lord's crown of thorns. And with the baptismal blood he shed on the cross, Grace mixed a kind of cement, and called it 'mercy.' With this, he went on to lay a solid foundation; out of the agony of our Saviour's passion, he now erected a wall of wattle and lime, then raised a roof made up of the whole of Scripture. He called the house Unity—'Holy Church' in English.

After completing this work, Grace built a cart called Christianity,[15] to carry Piers's sheaves of corn back from the fields. To draw the cart, he provided horses, Contrition and Confession, and established Priesthood to oversee the work. He himself, meanwhile, accompanied Piers from one end of the world to the other, cultivating truth, the fields of faith and Holy Church's law.

So now—here Piers is at his ploughing.[16]

13. *cultivate the cardinal virtues... their teaching*: an important passage stressing the need to study the Bible and the works of the moral philosophers alike in the light of the Church's tradition of interpretation. It clearly illustrates the orthodoxy of Langland's religious position. He sees a properly educated mind and heart as the right location for the fruit of charity to grow in (cf. *Anima in Passus* XVI, which anticipates this passage in its reference to hoeing and weeding).

14. *the cross... to save mankind*: the essential point here is that the Church is built on the passion, death, and resurrection of its founder, and unified by the sacrament of the Eucharist, which calls these events to mind each time mass is said.

15. *a cart called Christianity*: the primary sense of 'Christianity' is 'baptism,' the means by which humanity (the corn) is brought from the fields (the world) into the barn (the Church). The baptized Christian is advanced on his journey by the sacrament of penance, administered by a priest.

16. *Piers is at his ploughing*: now has a wider sense—not just St Peter the apostle but all the faithful pastors of Christ throughout history: the siege of Antichrist is both an early historical event (the Neronian persecution) and an ongoing ordeal for the Church facing a hostile and sinful world.

Pride caught sight of him, and assembled a huge army,[17] intending to harass Conscience and the whole community of Christians. The Cardinal Virtues he intended to blow down, breaking them apart and biting their roots in two. Into the field he despatched Presumption, his chief lieutenant, and his spy Kill-Love, otherwise called Backbiter.

This pair approached Conscience and the Christian community, and delivered them a message: the seeds that Piers had planted, the Cardinal Virtues, had no hope of surviving! 'Piers's barn,' they declared, 'is going to be broken into, and everyone inside Unity—including you, Conscience—is going to have to get out! Your pair of horses, Contrition and Confession, and that cart of yours, the Creed, will be given a smart new coat of paint—sophistry, it's called.[18] It will cover them over so effectively that Conscience won't be able to tell, from the evidence of Contrition or Confession, who is a Christian and who is a pagan! For that matter, men of business who handle money won't have the slightest idea whether the profits they make are lawful or unlawful, or tantamount to usury.'

Dressed in the pied paraphernalia of cunning, Pride advanced to battle, by his side a member of the nobility whose sole aim in life was bodily pleasure. 'Let's live a life of unbridled luxury, going through the whole catalogue of the vices!' cried Pride. 'If we use our wits, we can strip society bare and spend the whole lot in one go!'

Then Conscience addressed the whole Christian community.

'This is my advice,' he said. 'Let's make our way into Unity without a moment's delay, and let's remain there. Then let's pray that peace will prevail in Piers Plowman's barn. I know for certain that we haven't the strength to oppose Pride, unless we have Grace with us as our ally.'

At this, Kind Wit came forward, to show Conscience what he should be doing. In ringing tones, he ordered the whole Christian community to dig a deep ditch all around Unity, so that the Church would be able to stand surrounded by holiness, like a fortified tower. So Conscience issued orders to every Christian, to dig a great moat as a protection for Holy Church and its defenders. In response, every kind of Christian repented, and turned away from sin; the only exceptions were the prostitutes, as well as a juror and a summoner who were steeped in habitual perjury. That pair knowingly sided with the guilty, and lied on oath without turning a hair, so long as there was money in it for them.

But apart from those hardened sinners I just mentioned, there was not a single Christian in possession of his faculties who did not help, in some measure, to make holiness grow and increase. Some did this by saying prayers, some by pilgrimages,

17. *Pride . . . assembled a huge army*: the events from here on recapitulate those of the second vision, with the Deadly Sins assaulting the Church in force and eventually prevailing.

18. *a smart new coat of paint—sophistry, it's called*: the key weapon in Antichrist's armoury is religious hypocrisy, the sin warned against by *Anima in Passus* XV. The pretence of real contrition, and the correlative of absolution granted without sincere repentance, combine to corrupt the penitential process on which the preservation of a good conscience and, with it, the growth of holiness, depend.

others by means of private acts of self-denial, or else by giving alms. And then the waters of sorrow for the sinful deeds they had done sprang up like a fountain, a smarting flood that flowed out from men's eyes.[19] It was the sincere piety of ordinary people, and the purity of the clergy, that enabled Unity, the Holy Church, to stand firm, rooted in sanctity.

'What do I care now,' cried Conscience, 'if Pride comes to attack us? I feel confident that the Prince of Pleasure will be stopped dead in his tracks for the season of Lent, at least![20] Come,' he continued, 'Christians all, and eat! You've worked loyally throughout the time of Lent. Now here is the consecrated bread, and under its form the body of Our Lord. Grace has given Piers the power to bring this about through the words of God himself; and people are bidden to eat it as a means to their salvation, once a month or as often as they have need, provided only that they have met the requirements of Piers the Plowman's pardon—"pay what you owe."'

'What is this?' came the general reply. 'Are you telling us we've got to return whatever we owe anybody before we can go to Communion?'

'Yes, indeed!' said Conscience, 'and the Cardinal Virtues agree with me about this. Everyone must forgive one another, as the "Our Father" requires: "And forgive us our trespasses, as we forgive those who trespass against us."[21] Then you can receive absolution, and after that, go to Communion.'

'Oh yes?' exclaimed a brewer.[22] 'Just see if I will! By God, I'm not going to be ordered about by the Spirit of Justice, and I don't care how long you go on about it! Christ Almighty, Conscience—d'you think I'm going to stick to the straight and narrow while I'm able to sell the last mouldy drops at the bottom of the barrel, or pretend there's good strong ale in it when there's nothing there but mild? That's my way—just following my instincts! I've no time to go grubbing about for handfuls of holiness. Stop rabbiting on about this "justice" stuff of yours, Conscience! Stuff it, will you?'

'You damned worthless layabout!' Conscience cried. 'God help you, brewer my friend, or you haven't a hope! The Spirit of Justice is the single most important seed Piers planted; if you don't live by its teaching, your chance of salvation is nil. Unless

19. *the waters of sorrow . . . eyes*: again important as a symbol (now part of an allegorical action) of true inward repentance (cf. the earlier tears of Will, Haukin, and then Will again at the end of *Passus* XVI). The tears fill the defensive moat around the inner fortification of the Christian community, representing the primary bulwark against pride and worldliness.

20. *for the season of Lent, at least!*: Conscience's words make clear the recurrent, cyclical character of Christian penitence, which must exist at all times, but is especially intensified during the liturgical season of Lent, at the end of which all may make their confession, render satisfaction, and receive their Easter Communion with a clear conscience. The terms of the pardon are '"make satisfaction," and then you are at one with God.'

21. *And forgive us . . . against us*: the fifth petition of the Lord's Prayer, which makes unity and peace with God conditional on unity and peace with one's neighbor.

22. *a brewer*: vulgar and mercenary, he represents the recalcitrant worldliness that makes religion into a mere formal show and spiritual values a mockery.

Conscience and the Cardinal Virtues form the food that people live on, just take my word for it, they're utterly lost—every single living soul among them!'

'Then,' piped up an ignorant vicar,[23] 'there're quite a few going to end up "lost," I'll tell you! I'm a parish priest of this Church of ours, and no one's ever knocked on my door who could tell me a single thing about "Cardinal Virtues," or cared a feather for Conscience, I can tell you! I've never known a cardinal who hadn't been sent by the Pope; and when that lot show their faces, it's us—the clergy—who've got to foot the bill: meals, fancy clothes, plus feeding for their horses and the whole crowd of crooks who bring up the rear. "Day by day and every day in the week" the man in the street goes moaning to his neighbor: "What a bloody mess the country gets into every time these cardinals roll in! Wherever they end up, the whole town turns into a brothel overnight. Dear God!' continued the vicar, 'that's why I don't want to see any of your cardinals turning up amongst these good people of mine. Why not let their holinesses carry on hob-nobbing with the hook-nosed fellows at Avignon, eh? You know the old saying, surely: "If you want to be a saint, stick around with the saints!" Or there's always Rome; doesn't their rule actually require them to stay there, and look after the relics in the shrines? As for your good self, Conscience, the right place for you is the royal court; go there, my friend, and stay there. Let this "Grace" that you're always going on about give the clergy a little bit of his guidance. And Piers, with those ploughs of his—the new one and the old—let him be made emperor of the World.[24] Then everyone would really turn into proper Christians!

'There's surely something badly wrong with the Pope, when he should be helping people, saving their immortal souls, not paying mercenaries to kill their bodies![25] I've nothing but goodwill towards Piers, though, because everything that he does is done for God:

> God will send his rain, we trust,
> Both on the wicked and the just.[26]

23. *an ignorant vicar*: his cynicism accompanies a genuine sense of grievance. The cardinals were much resented for their worldly extravagance and interest in collecting money for the pope. During the Avignon papacy (until 1377) many had to engage in raising money from the Jews and other financiers instead of looking after the relics of the martyrs in Rome at the churches for which they were given titular responsibility.

24. *Piers . . . emperor of the World*: the brunt of this remark is that Conscience (perhaps signifying the pious laity of the gentry and knightly classes) should be active in public affairs, while those of the Church are left in the hands of the ordinary people and the clergy who have their interests truly at heart (= Piers); but this may be too specific an interpretation.

25. *the Pope . . . to kill their bodies!*: presumably alludes to the scandalous war between Urban VI and the antipope Clement VII which broke out in 1379 following the Great Schism of 1378. The palpable disunity in Christendom at the highest level doubtless lay behind Langland's choice of 'Unity' as his special name for the Christian Church ideally conceived.

26. *God will send his rain . . . just*: Matt. 5:45, and associating Piers's charitable generosity with that of God himself. Piers here symbolizes both the ideal ploughman and the ideal priest, each of whom works for the good of his fellow Christians.

God's sun shines every bit as brilliantly on a wicked man's fields of wheat as on the crops of the kindest person on earth. Piers, likewise, puts as much effort, I know, into growing food for layabouts and whores as for himself or those who help his labors—the only difference being that he's served first. So, that's why I bless Piers Plowman, who's always sweating and struggling for us all: the dregs of society or the salt of the earth—it makes no difference in the end to him. Worship God, I say! He created everything, the good things and the bad ones alike, and he's willing to put up with sinners until the time is ripe for them to repent. But God, dear God, put the Pope right! He's busy plucking the Church bare! He insists on telling our king that he's the "guardian" of the whole Christian people; yet he doesn't give a damn if Christians are robbed and killed! He even pays armed men to shed Christian blood, in open defiance of what the whole Bible teaches. Look it up in the Gospel of St Luke: "Thou shalt not kill: Vengeance is mine, says the Lord."[27] It looks as though he couldn't care less what happens, just so long as he gets his own way.

'Ah, Christ have mercy, and rescue those cardinals! Change that worldly acumen of theirs into spiritual wisdom to enrich not the body but the soul![28] The ordinary people,' he concluded, 'don't care twopence about what Conscience tells them, or the Cardinal Virtues either, unless they suspect there's something in it for them. But they have no qualms about economizing on truth. Most people now regard the virtue of Prudence as just sharp practice under another name; in fact, it appears that all those illustrious virtues seem to have been transformed into vices. Everyone you meet has hit on some crafty method of concealing sin, and even manages to deck it out as shrewdness combined with straightforwardness!'

Then a nobleman who was there burst out laughing. 'Blow me down!' he exclaimed. 'To my way of thinking, it's perfectly right and proper for my reeve to get his hands on every last thing that's going—whatever my accountant or steward advise me to take, after looking over all the accounts and records. I can tell you, the Spirit of Understanding was hard at work when they looked at the manorial rolls![29] And the Spirit of Fortitude also did its bit when it came to collecting—whatever the tenants may have felt about it!'

At this point, there entered a king, who swore by his crown: 'I was crowned king to govern the people of this land, and defend the Church and the clergy against lawless men. Now, if I'm lacking the wherewithal to do so, it seems to me perfectly lawful to

27. *Thou shalt not kill . . . says the Lord*: the first part of the quotation, from Exod. 20:13, is quoted in Luke 18:20, the second, from Deut. 32:35, in Heb. 10:30.

28. *Change that worldly acumen . . . soul!*: the bad example of the cardinals has led to cynicism about the reality of the cardinal virtues, and the affectation of a mere simulacrum of each of them.

29. *the Spirit of Understanding . . . manorial rolls!*: the virtue of prudence having been corrupted into 'an eye for the main chance,' the nobleman now illustrates the corruption of understanding (the spirit of understanding mentioned in Isa. 11:2) into the quest for profit, and (proper) strength into unjustified coercion.

take it, wherever it lies conveniently to hand. After all, I am "head" of the law![30] The rest of you are just "limbs" of the body politic, but my position is right at the top. And it's because I'm the head of all that I'm able to protect you all: I am the mainstay of the clergy and master of the commons. Now, what I take from you two I take because the Spirit of Justice instructed me to do so. Remember, I am the one who judges you all! So I, at any rate, can go and receive Communion with confidence because I never borrow anything, and the only demands that I make on my subjects are the ones my position entitles me to make.'

'Fair enough,' said Conscience, 'provided you do protect your people and rule this kingdom of yours justly. In that case, it is only right and proper that you should have what you ask for, in accordance with the requirements of law.

> But yet, what's yours is given you in trust,
> Not to be spent to gratify your lust!'[31]

The vicar had a long journey home, and took his leave politely. Just then, I woke from my sleep, and wrote down my dream.

GEOFFREY CHAUCER'S "THE PARSON'S TALE"

Introduction

If you have never read Chaucer, please do not let this stop you. What most people enjoy about Chaucer, especially about his *Canterbury Tales*, are his richly developed characters; the amusing, lively, and sometimes disturbing tales they tell; and the delightful sense of going back into his time and experiencing something so foreign yet familiar. "The Parson's Tale" has almost none of that. This tale is not even a tale; it is a sermon, and instead of sounding like new friends telling great stories, "The Parson's Tale" ends up sounding like some grumpy old man yelling, "you kids get off my lawn!" But—and this is important—the tale also shows that the principal vices became an important part of culture through pastoral sermons.

As I mentioned in the introduction to this section, in 1213 the Church mandated yearly confession on the part of everyone who had reached the years of discretion. As this requirement filtered down into society, it became necessary for church leaders to train people how to confess. This led to an explosion of sermons meant to train people on the principles of penance, contrition, confession, and satisfaction or absolution.

30. *I am head of the law!*: the King's claim to act justly risks the confusion of true justice (rooted in reason and right) and mere power (deriving from his position as the ultimate legal authority in the land). His attitude opens the way to that exploitation of kingdom and people of which Richard II was to be accused in the next decade (by, among others, Langland).

31. *But yet . . . lust!*: the couplet quoted by Conscience is probably some familiar legal dictum of the time, and stands in sharp contrast to the one quoted by the ignorant commons in the Prologue, with which this king would doubtless be willing to agree.

"The Parson's Tale" is an excellent example of all of these elements. It begins with an elaborate description of penance as a whole before focusing on what is proper contrition and what should make people feel contrite or "broken hearted" for their sins. The parson then explains the whys and the hows of confession. The sermon ends with his explanation of satisfaction or the way that sins are permanently removed or expiated.

The excerpt from the tale included here is from the confession section of the sermon. The parson, in order to emphasize the need for confession, gives a sense of the universality of sin through an elaboration on each of the seven principal sins. After discussing them in depth, he further explores each sin's opposing virtue or remedy, following the principle of how contraries cure contraries. His list of principal sins (with their healing virtue or virtues in parentheses) is Pride (Humility or Meekness), Envy (Love), Anger (Gentleness, Patience, or Tolerance), Sloth (Fortitude), Avarice/Covetousness (Mercy and Pity), Gluttony (Abstinence), and Lechery (Chastity and Continence). The discussion of Lechery begins by connecting it with Gluttony, and then gives the scriptural basis for its condemnation. One of the most vivid images the parson presents is the five fingers of the devil's grasp. Each finger of the enslaving satanic hand brings one closer to sin—looking, touching, speaking, kissing, and, finally, the "stinking act of lechery." These are also the very same steps often associated with the stages of courtly love. While the parson's sermon can be understood as a powerful assault on courtly love, an attack further reinforce by his discussion of lust as a form of idolatry, the aim of his sermon is lust's seductive universality.

For a modern audience this sermon poses some interesting questions. We would surely balk at the text's concerns about the maintenance of the "maidenhead." What would we make of the idea of inordinate sexual love within marriage or the links between lust, murder, and theft? An even more interesting set of questions might be how this sermon relates to how people really live. What is the correlation between day-to-day human reality and the world that the sermon evokes? An excellent way to explore how these virtues and vices relate to life, or at least life rendered in stunning artistic detail, is to read the entire sermon and then read the rest of Chaucer's vivid depiction of life in the remaining tales.

From "The Parson's Tale"[32]

SEQUITUR DE LUXURIA (Results of Lust)

After gluttony, then comes lechery; for these two sins are such close cousins that oftentimes they will not be separated. God knows, this sin is unpleasing to God; for He said Himself, "Do no lechery." And therefore He imposed great penalties against this sin in the old law. If a bondwoman were taken in this sin, she should be beaten to

32. From Geoffrey Chaucer *Canterbury Tales*, modernized by J. U. Nicolson (Garden City, NY: International Collectors Library, 1934), 604–14.

death with rods. And if she were a woman of quality, she should be slain with stones. And if she were a bishop's daughter, she should be burnt, by God's commandment. Furthermore, for the sin of lechery, God drowned all the world by the deluge. And after that He burned five cities with thunderbolts and sank them into Hell.

Let us speak, then, of that stinking sin of lechery that men call adultery of wedded folk, which is to say, if one of them be wedded, or both. Saint John says that adulterers shall be in Hell "in the lake which burneth with fire and brimstone"—in the fire for the lechery, in brimstone for the stink of their filthiness. Certainly, the breaking of this sacrament is a horrible thing; it was ordained by God Himself in Paradise, and confirmed by Jesus Christ, as witness Saint Matthew in the gospel: "For this cause shall a man leave father and mother, and shall cleave to his wife; and they twain shall be one flesh." This sacrament betokens the knitting together of Christ and of Holy Church. And not only did God forbid adultery in deed, but also He commanded that "thou shalt not covet thy neighbor's wife." This behest, says Saint Augustine, contains the forbidding of all desire to do lechery. Behold what Saint Matthew says in the gospel: "Whosoever looketh on a woman to lust after her, hath committed adultery with her already in his heart." Here you may see that not only the doing of this sin is forbidden, but also the desire to do that sin. This accursed sin grievously troubles those whom it haunts. And first, it does harm to the soul; for it constrains it to sin and to the pain of everlasting death. Unto the body it is a tribulation also, for it drains it, and wastes and ruins it, and makes of its blood a sacrifice to the Field of Hell; also it wastes wealth and substance. And certainly, if it be a foul thing for a man to waste his wealth on women, it is a yet fouler thing when, for such filthiness, women spend on men their wealth and their substance. This sin, as says the prophet, robs man and woman of good name and of all honor; and it gives great pleasure to the Devil, for thereby won he the greater part of the world. And just as a merchant delights most in that trading whereof he reaps the greater gain, just so the Fiend delights in this filth.

This is the Devil's other hand, with five fingers to catch the people into his slavery. The first finger is the foolish interchange of glances between the foolish woman and the foolish man, which slays just as the basilisk slays folk by the venom of its sight; for the lust of the eyes follows the lust of the heart. The second finger is vile touching in wicked manner; and thereupon Solomon says that he who touches and handles a woman fares like the man that handles the scorpion which stings and suddenly slays by its poisoning; even as, if any man touch warm pitch, it defiles his fingers. The third is vile words, which are like fire, which immediately burns the heart. The fourth finger is kissing; and truly he were a great fool who would kiss the mouth of a burning oven or of a furnace. And the more fools they are who kiss in vileness; for that mouth in the mouth of Hell; and I speak specifically of these old dotard whoremongers, who will yet kiss though they cannot do anything, and so taste them. Certainly they are like dogs, for a dog, when he passes a rosebush, or other bushes, though he cannot piss, yet will he heave up his leg and make an appearance of pissing. And as for the opinion of many that a man cannot sin for any lechery he does with his wife, certainly that opinion is wrong. God knows, a man may slay himself with his own knife, and make himself drunk out of his own tun. Certainly, be it wife, be it child, or any worldly thing that a man loves more than he loves God, it is his idol, and he is an idolater. Man should love his wife with discretion, calmly and moderately; and then she is as it were his sister. The fifth finger of the Devil's hand is the stinking act of lechery. Truly, the five fingers of gluttony the Fiend thrusts into the belly of a man, and with his five fingers of lechery he grips him by the loins in order to throw him into the furnace of Hell; wherein he shall have the fire and the everlasting worms, and weeping and wailing, sharp hunger and thirst, and horror of devils that shall trample all over him, without respite and without end. From lechery, as I said, spring divers branches; as fornication, which is between man and woman who are not married; and this is deadly sin and against nature. All that is an enemy to and destructive of nature is against nature. Faith, the reason of a man tells him well that it is mortal sin, since God forbade lechery. And Saint Paul gives him over to that kingdom which is the reward of no man save those who do mortal sin. Another sin of lechery is to bereave a maiden of her maidenhead; for he that so does, certainly, he casts a maiden out of the highest state in this present life and he bereaves her of that precious fruit that the Book calls "the hundred fruit." I can say it in no other way in English, but in Latin it is called centesimus fructus. Certainly, he that so acts is the cause of many injuries and villainies, more than any man can reckon; just as he sometimes is cause of all damage that beasts do in the field, who breaks down the hedge or the fence, just so does the seducer destroy that which cannot be restored. For truly, no more may a maidenhead be restored than an arm that has been smitten from the body may return thereto to grow again. She may have mercy, this I know well, if she does penance, but it shall never again be that she is uncorrupted. And though I have spoken somewhat of adultery, it is well to show forth more dangers that come of adultery, in order that men may eschew that foul sin. Adultery, in Latin, means to approach another man's bed, by reason of which those that once were one flesh abandon their bodies to other persons. Of this sin, as the wise man says, follow many evils. First, breaking of faith; and certainly, in faith lies the key to Christianity. And when faith is broken and lost, truly, Christianity stands barren and without fruit. This sin is also a theft; for theft commonly is to deprive a person of his own thing against his will. Certainly this is the vilest thievery that can be when a woman steals her body from her husband and gives it to her lecher to defile her; and steals her soul from Christ and gives it to the Devil. This is a fouler theft than to break into a church and steal the chalice; for these adulterers break into the temple of God spiritually and steal the vessel of grace, that is, the body and the soul, for which Christ will destroy them, as Saint Paul says. Truly, of this theft Joseph was much afraid when his master's wife besought him to lie with her, and he said: "Behold, my master wotteth not what is with me in the house, and he hath committed all that he hath to my hand: there is none greater in this house than I; neither hath he kept any thing from me but thee, because thou art his wife: how then can I do this great wickedness and sin against God?" Alas! All too little is such truth encountered nowadays. The third evil is the filth whereby they break the commandment of God and defame the Author of matrimony, Who is Christ. For certainly, in so far as the sacrament of marriage is so noble and honorable, so much the more is it a sin to break it; for God established marriage in Paradise, in the state of innocence, in order to multiply mankind to the service of God. And therefore is the breaking thereof the more grievous. Of which breaking come oftentimes false heirs, that wrongfully inherit. And therefore will Christ put them out of the Kingdom of Heaven, which is the heritage of good folk. From this breaking it happens oftentimes, also, that people wed or sin with their own kindred; and specially the loose-livers who haunt the brothels of prostitutes, who may be likened to a common privy wherein men purge themselves of their ordure. What shall we say, also, of whoremasters who live by the horrible sin of prostitution, yea, sometimes by the prostitution of their own wives and children, as do pimps and procurers? Certainly these are accursed sins. Understand also that adultery is fitly placed in the ten commandments between theft and homicide; for it is the greatest theft that can be, being theft of' body and of soul. And it is like homicide, for it cuts in twain and breaks asunder those that were made one flesh, and therefore, by the old law of God, adulterers should be slain. But nevertheless, by the law of Jesus Christ, which is a law of pity, He said to the woman who was taken in adultery and should have been slain with stones, according to the will of the Jews, as was their law: "Go," said Jesus Christ, "and have no more will to sin," or "will no more to do sin." Truly, the punishment of adultery is given to the torment of Hell, unless it be that it is hindered by penitence. And there are yet more branches of this wicked sin; as when one of them is a religious, or else both; or folk who have entered orders, as a sub-deacon, or deacon, or priest, or hospitaller. And ever the higher that he is in orders, the greater is the sin. The thing that greatly aggravates their sin is the breaking of the vow of chastity, taken when they received the order. And furthermore, the truth is that the office of a holy order is chief of all the treasury of God, and His special sign and mark of chastity, to show that those who have entered it are joined to chastity, which is the most precious kind of life there is. And these folk in orders are specially dedicated to God, and are of the special household of God; for which, when they do deadly sin, they are especially traitors to God and to His people; for they live on the people in order to pray for the people, and while they are such traitors their prayers avail the people nothing at all. Priests are angels, by reason of the dignity of their ministry; but forsooth, as Saint Paul says: "Satan himself is transformed into an angel of light." Truly, the priest that resorts to mortal sin, he may be likened to the angel of darkness transformed into the angel of light; he seems an angel of light, but, forsooth, he is an angel of darkness. Such priests are the sons of Eli, as is shown in the Book of the Kings, that they were the sons of Belial, that is, the Devil. Belial means, "without judge"; and so fare they; they think they are free and have no judge, any more than has a free bull that takes whatever cow pleases him on the farm. So act they with women. For just as a free bull is enough for all a farm, just so is a wicked priest corruption enough for all a parish, or for all a county. These priests, as the Book says, teach not the functions of priesthood to the people, and they know not God; they held themselves but ill satisfied, as the Book says, with the flesh that was boiled and offered to them and took by force the flesh that was raw. Certainly, so these scoundrels hold themselves not pleased with roasted flesh and boiled flesh, with which the people feed them in great reverence, but they will have the raw flesh of laymen's wives and of their daughters. And certainly these women that give assent to their rascality do great wrong to Christ and to Holy Church and all saints and all souls; for they bereave all these of him that should worship Christ and Holy Church and pray for Christian souls. And therefore such priests and their lemans also, who give assent to their lechery, have the cursing of all the Christian court, until they mend their ways. The third kind of adultery is sometimes practised between a man and his wife; and that is when they have no regard to their union, save only for their fleshly delight, as says Saint Jerome; and care for nothing but that they are come together; because they are married, it is all well enough, as they think. But over such folk the Devil has power, as said the Angel Raphael to Tobias; for in their union they put Jesus Christ out of mind and give themselves to all filthiness. The fourth kind is the coming together of those that are akin, or of those that are related by marriage, or else of those whose fathers or other kindred have had intercourse in the sin of lechery; this sin makes them like dogs that pay no heed to relationship. And certainly, kinship is of two kinds, either spiritual or carnal; spiritual, as when one lies with one's sponsor. For just as he that engenders a child is its fleshly father, just so is his godfather his spiritual father. For which reason a woman is in no less sin when she lies carnally with her godfather or her godson than she would be in if she coupled with her own fleshly brother. The fifth kind is that abominable sin whereof a man ought scarcely to speak or write, notwithstanding it is openly discussed in holy writ. This wickedness men and women do with divers intentions and in divers manners; but though holy writ speaks of such horrible sin, holy writ cannot be defiled, any more than can the sun that shines upon the dunghill. Another form of sin appertains to lechery, and that comes often to those who are virgin and also to those who are corrupt; and this sin men call pollution, which comes in four ways. Sometimes it is due to laxness of the body; because the humors are too rank and abundant in the body of man. Sometimes it is due to infirmity; because of the weakness of the retentive virtue, as is discussed in works on medicine. Sometimes it is due to a surfeit of food and drink. And sometimes it comes from base thoughts that were enclosed in man's mind when he fell asleep; which thing may not happen without sin. Because of this, men must govern themselves wisely, or else they may fall into grievous sin.

REMEDIUM CONTRA PECCATUM LUXURIE (Remedy for the Sin of Lust)

Now comes the remedy for lechery, and that is, generally, chastity and continence, which restrain all the inordinate stirrings that come of fleshly desires. And ever the greater merit shall he have who restrains the wicked enkindlings of the ordure of this sin. And this is of two kinds, that is to say, chastity in marriage and chastity in widowhood. Now you shall understand that matrimony is the permitted coming together of man and of woman, who receive, by virtue of the sacrament, the bond of union from which they may not be freed in all their life, that is to say, while they both live. This, says the Book, is a very great sacrament. God established it, as I have said, in Paradise, and had Himself born into wedlock. And to sanctify marriage, He attended a wedding, where He turned water into wine, which, was the first miracle that He wrought on earth before His disciples. The true result of marriage is the cleansing of fornication and the replenishing of Holy Church with believers of good lineage; for that is the end of marriage; and it changes deadly sin to venial sin between those who are wedded, and makes one the hearts of them, as well as the bodies. This is true marriage, which was established by God ere sin began, when natural law occupied its rightful position in Paradise; and it was ordained that one man should have but one woman, and one woman but one man, as Saint Augustine says, and, that for many reasons.

First, because marriage figures the union between Christ and Holy Church. And another is, because the man is the head of the woman; at any rate it has been so ordained by ordinance. For if a woman had more men than one, then should she have more heads than one, and that were a horrible thing before God; and also, a woman could not please too many folk at once. And also, there should never be peace or rest among them; for each would demand his own thing. And furthermore, no man should know his own get, nor who should inherit his property; and the woman should be the less beloved from the time that she were joined with many men.

Now comes the question, How should a man conduct himself toward his wife? and specifically in two things, that is to say, in tolerance and reverence, as Christ showed when He first made woman. For He made her not of the head of Adam, because she should not claim to exercise great lordship. For wherever the woman has the mastery she causes too much disorder; there are needed no instances of this. The experience of every day ought to suffice. Also, certainly, God did not make woman of the foot of Adam, because she should not be held in too great contempt; for she cannot patiently endure: but God made woman of the rib of Adam, because woman should be a companion to man. Man should conduct himself toward his wife in faith, in truth, and in love; as Saint Paul says: "Husbands, love your wives, even as Christ also loved the Church, and gave Himself for it." So should a man give himself for his wife, if there be need.

Now how a woman should be subject to her husband, that is told by Saint Peter. First, by obedience. And also, as says the law, a woman who is a wife, as long as she is a wife, has no authority to make oath or to bear witness without the consent of her husband, who is her lord; in any event he should be so, in reason. She should also serve him in all honor. and be modest in her dress. I know well that they should resolve to please their husbands, but not by the finery of their array. Saint Jerome says that wives who go apparelled in silk and in precious purple cannot clothe themselves in Jesus Christ. Also, what says Saint John on this subject? Saint Gregory, also says that a person seeks precious array only out of vainglory, to be honored the more before the crowd. It is a great folly for a woman to have a fair outward appearance and inwardly to be foul. A wife should also be modest in glance and demeanor and in conversation, and discreet in all her words and deeds. And above all worldly things she should love her husband with her whole heart, and be true to him of her body; so, also, should a husband be to his wife. For since all the body is the husband's, so should her heart be, or else there is between them, in so far as that is concerned, no perfect marriage. Then shall men understand that for three things a man and his wife may have carnal coupling. The first is with intent to procreate children to the service of God, for certainly, that is the chief reason for matrimony. Another is, to pay, each of them to the other, the debt of their bodies, for neither of them has power over his own body. The third is, to avoid lechery and baseness. The fourth is, indeed, deadly sin. As for the first, it is meritorious; the second also, for, as the law says, she has the merit of chastity who pays to her husband the debt of her body, aye, though it be against her liking and the desire of her heart. The third is venial sin, and truly, hardly any of these unions may be without venial sin, because of the original sin and because of the pleasure. As to the fourth, be it understood that if they couple only for amorous love and for none of the aforesaid reasons, but merely to accomplish that burning pleasure, no matter how often, truly it is a mortal sin; and yet (with sorrow I say it) some folk are at pains to do it more and oftener than their appetite really demands.

The second kind of chastity is to be a clean widow and eschew the embraces of man and desire the embrace of Jesus Christ. These are those that have been wives and have lost their husbands, and also women that have fornicated and have been relieved by penitence. And truly, if a wife could keep herself always chaste with leave and license of her husband, so that she should thereby give him never an occasion to sin, it were a great merit in her. These women that observe chastity must be clean in heart as well as in body and in thought, and modest in dress and demeanor; and be abstinent in eating and drinking, in speech and in deed. They are the vessel or the box of the blessed Magdalen, which fills Holy Church with good odour. The third kind of chastity is virginity, and it behooves her to be holy in heart and clean of body; then is she the spouse of Christ and she is the beloved of the angels. She is the honor of this world, and she is the equal of martyrs; she has within her that which tongue may not tell nor the heart think. Virginity bore Our Lord Jesus Christ, and virgin was He Himself.

Another remedy for lechery is, specially to withhold oneself from such things as give rise to this baseness; as ease, and eating and drinking: for certainly, when the pot boils furiously, the best measure is to withdraw it from the fire. Sleeping long in great security from disturbance is also a nurse to lechery.

Another remedy for lechery is, that a man or woman eschew the company of those by whom he expects to be tempted; for though it be that the act itself is withstood, yet there is great temptation. Truly a white wall, though it burn not from the setting of a candle near it, yet shall the wall be made black by the flame. Often and often I counsel that no man trust in his own perfection, save he be stronger than Samson and holier than David and wiser than Solomon.

PART IV

The Transformation of the Virtues and Vices

In 1580, the Italian painter Paolo Veronese produced *The Choice between Virtue and Vice*. This work features a young man poised between Vice and Virtue. The man's ripped sock reveals a bloody wound inflicted by Vice, the figure in the foreground. In response to her assault, the young man moves to the comforting protection of Virtue. Where the aggressive and duplicitous figure of Vice has playing cards and leans against a marble Sphinx (with a dagger), Virtue demurely looks down and wears the verdant green robe and the laurel wreath. This marvelous work gives us a sense of the transformations of the virtues and vices, a transformation that follows these trajectories: Divine Endowment II, Struggle II, the Virtues and Vices in Everyday Life and Death, and the Vitality of Vice.

DIVINE ENDOWMENT II

The transformation of the virtues and vices entails their modification amid shifting contexts. The philosophical, ethical, political, literary, and artistic tradition continued to be strong enough that artists like Veronese could draw upon it. Images of virtue as a gift from God, as we have seen, were a powerful part of that tradition. Veronese embodies Virtue's divinity and beneficence by way of her confident, calm demeanor; the classical serenity of her face, figure, and clothing; and her laurel wreath and green robe. The young man seeks and finds Virtue's compassion and protection.

Where Veronese's man finds virtue, other works engage different aspects of the tradition of virtue as a divine endowment. Piero del Pollaiuolo and Raphael's paintings for the Florence Mercanzia are images of the seven virtues made for a strictly secular and commercial institution. These works create a sort of virtue by association. These paintings do not claim that God endowed the Mercanzia with charity, temperance, or justice; they create an association between such virtues and the group's fundamental qualities. The Mercanzia thereby created an association between virtues usually taken as religious, or at least spiritual, and claimed them for a secular institution. The Mercanzia's move is brilliant public relations—brilliant enough to make contemporary marketing specialists proud.

Some works, especially those for aristocratic audiences, show less of a modification of the tradition. Spenser's *Faerie Queene*, with its allegorical praise of Queen Elizabeth, is an elaborate literary equivalent of the fifth-century portrait of Anicia Julia flanked by the virtues. In the works for her *studiolo*, Isabella d'Este is the face of Minerva casting out the vices and restoring the virtues. In addition, palace architecture all over Europe continued to show allegorical images of monarchs crowned by various virtues well into the eighteenth century. The throne room of the Spanish Royal Palace features just such a mural, Teipolo's *Majesty of the Spanish Monarchy* (1764), as well as statues of the four cardinal virtues. Tapestries provide a particularly strong continuity of this tradition. Bernaert van Orley and Pieter van Aelst's extraordinary series *The Honors* (1517–1525) is an excellent example, as its nine tapestry panels show how rulers who practice the virtues can avoid the twists of fortune and infamy to gain fame, nobility, and honor. This work was done for Charles V, the Hapsberg emperor, to celebrate his coronation. While the panels would instruct the general audience who would attend his coronation or who would later see them in the palace, the panels also praise Charles as the living embodiment of their principles.

STRUGGLE II

Just as the divine-endowment trajectory continues while undergoing modification, so also there is a continuity and modification of the struggle trajectory. The Veronese work also shows an updated *psychomachia*, as the man has been assaulted and injured by Vice and therefore embraces Virtue. Vice has a somewhat seductive look about her, with her beautifully set hair and clothing. Veronese's work is also part of an emerging subset of the struggle trajectory: the choice of Hercules tradition. In 1498, Albrect Dürer created a print called *Hercules at the Crossroads*. This story is taken from Xenephon, relating how Hercules was faced with the choice of a life of pleasure and vice or one of hardship, honor, and virtue. In Dürer's rendition, Hercules seems to want to mediate somewhat between these seemingly extreme positions. In other versions, like Annibale Carricci's *The Choice of Hercules* (1596), Gérard de Lairesse's *Hercules between Virtue and Vice* (1685), or Mariano Salvador Maella's mural in the Spanish Royal Palace of *Hercules between Virtue and Vice* (1765–66), Hercules faces a more straightforward conflict between irreconcilable virtue and vice. The subject is even picked up, though not in a particularly insightful or artistically interesting way, by Johann Sebastian Bach and George Frederic Handel.

Besides these examples of Hercules, the *psychomachia* in allegorical form is perhaps best represented in Spenser's *Faerie Queene*. This is an epic treatment of the struggle between virtue and vice, with countless characters symbolically enacting the many battles within the soul, all of which update Prudentius's work for Spenser's contemporary context.

THE VIRTUES AND VICES IN EVERYDAY LIFE AND IN DEATH

With sermons on the seven deadly sins and images of the virtues and vices on public buildings and in churches, this tradition continued to be part—though a changing part—of everyday life. Moralizing still-life paintings endowed everyday objects with a significance often connected to virtue and vice. Johannes Torrentius's 1614 *Emblematic Still Life with Flagon, Glass, Jug, and Bridle* features temperance imagery. While the vessels are conventional attributes, the bridle is an excellent symbol for temperance's self-restraint, and even the sheet music encourages one to keep a proper "tempo," "harmony," and self-control.

Perhaps the best examples of how art reflects and reinforces the tradition in everyday life are the many prints that make the tradition more readily available to a wider audience. Many artists developed prints of the virtues and vices in the late fifteenth and sixteenth centuries, including Heinrich Aldegrever, Hans Sebald and Barthel Beham, Lucas van Leyden, Jacob Matham, Georg Pencz, and Marcantonio Raimondi. Pieter Brueghel's prints, with their vitality and variety, are excellent examples. These images show the whole gamut of virtue's nobility and vice's depravity in a visually interesting and intellectually rewarding way.

Finally, very finally, the virtues and vices were part of the way people lived in the shadow of inevitable death. Confession, with its basis in penitential manuals and the vices, had always been a part of one's life and one's "departure plans." Thomas More's *The Last Things* (1522) and Hieronymus Bosch's *The Seven Deadly Sins and the Four Last Things* (1500–1510) are excellent examples of this. For both, the four last things are death, judgment, heaven, and hell. By meditating on these realities, one can find focus, purpose, and motivation in life. Both the book and the painting show the seven deadly sins in everyday life in such a way as to allow the viewer or reader to find and root out those sins so as to be prepared for the four last things. While this would indeed prepare one for a proper death, both works are meant to impact the way people lived. Here again Veronese's work is fitting, as the small inscription above the statue reads [HO]NOR ET VIRTUS/[P]OST MORTE FLORET (Honor and Virtue Flourish after Death).

THE VITALITY OF VICE

The many demons and hybrid creatures that torment the vicious in Brueghel's prints create a powerful and terrifying picture of vice. That is not so much the case with Veronese's work. Yes, Vice has claws and we cannot see her face, but she certainly looks alluring from the back. Yes, she does rest on a statue of a Sphinx and that jagged knife cannot be a good sign, but there is still something alluring about her aggressiveness, especially when compared with Virtue's demure posture. Of course if there is to be a struggle, a battle within the soul or conflict for Hercules, vice must have seductive power. But perhaps the greatest modification to the virtues and vices tradition is how artists like Bronzino, Marlow, and especially Machiavelli affirm vice's vitality.

Bronzino's *Venus, Cupid, Folly, and Time* (1545) is a complex and controversial work. While some conclude that its many elements emphasize virtue, others see it as an expression of the vitality of vice. Is Bronzino revealing the painful consequences of fraud, duplicity, time, or lust, or is he playing with vice as a spice for life? Christopher Marlowe's main character in *Doctor Faustus* not only makes a deal with the devil, but he's shown a parade of the seven deadly sins. Faustus, obviously interested in bigger things and not distracted by the sins, is unimpressed.

The clearest example of the vitality of the vices is Machiavelli's *The Prince*. The author makes no excuses for the fact that he believes that knowing the vices of others and productively managing one's own is the best way to keep power. Machiavelli, a Florentine living only a few miles away, would love Lorenzetti's murals in the Palazzo Pubblico. He would admire how they project a powerful image of virtue. But he would also warn that a leader should know how to use the vices, including duplicity, fraud, and fear, when they are necessary. Machiavelli's contribution to the virtues and vices tradition may be an addition or clarification, because surely leaders in the past had understood the value of looking virtuous while being vicious, but his bold-faced affirmation of vice and his refutation of a dogmatic policy of virtue are remarkable and even transformative.

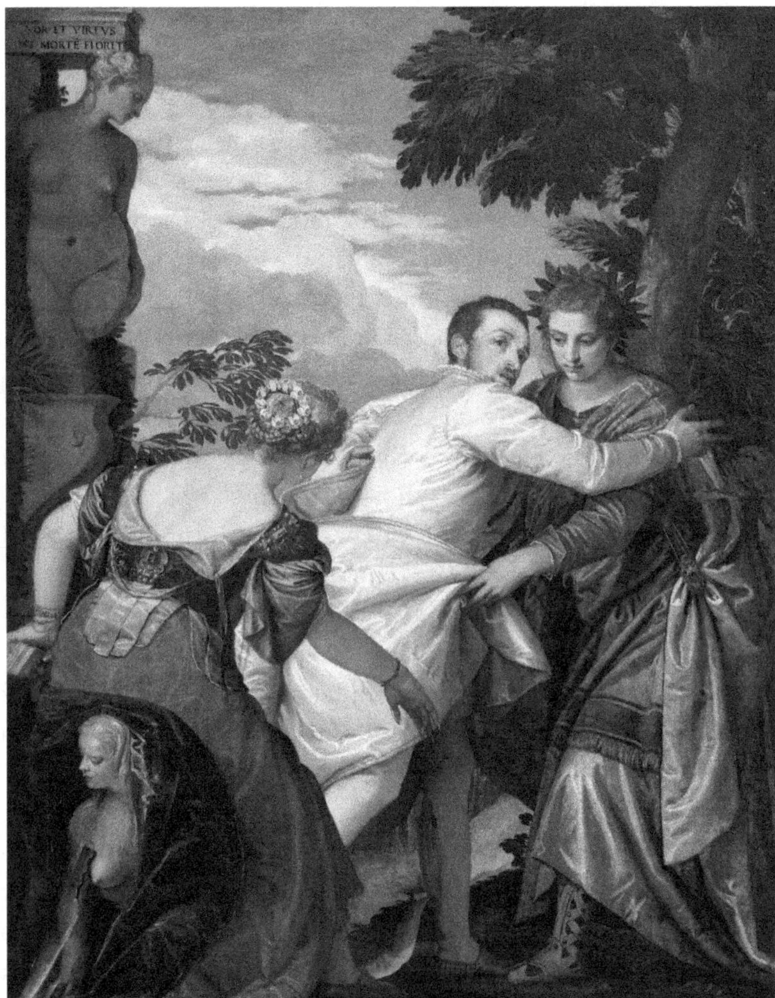

Figure 21. *The Choice between Virtue and Vice* Paolo Veronese, 1580. (Frick Collection, New York. Reproduced with permission.)

PIERO DEL POLLAIUOLO'S *SEVEN VIRTUES*

If there were two things that Florentines of the fifteenth century understood, they were branding and product placement. Florence's guild association, what we might call its chamber of commerce, the Mercanzia, excelled in both. The Mercanzia served as the merchants' tribunal, settling internal and international trade disputes, at the same time that it promoted the city's status and protected its interests. The Mercanzia was organized like the guilds, with five consuls representing the five major guilds, one consul representing the minor guilds, and a seventh member acting as guild prior. In fact, beyond the Mercanzia, all of Florence's guilds knew the value of branding and product placement. When each guild commissioned a work for an important Florentine church, Orsanmichele, they took it as an opportunity to associate themselves with a religious figure. When the armory-and-sword guild commissioned Donatello's statue of Saint George, this famous warrior-saint wore their armor and carried one of their swords. The same artist's statue of Saint Mark sports the woolen cloth of its commissioning guild. It therefore comes as no surprise that when the Mercanzia commissioned Pollaiuolo and Raphael to create panels to be placed behind the consul seats in their meeting hall, the Mercanzia wanted works that would associate the institution with long-standing and sound traditional values: the seven virtues.

In 1469 the Mercanzia commissioned Piero del Pollaiuolo to paint a figure of Charity and subsequently five of the other traditional seven virtues. The Mercanzia decided to begin with the central painting, with the artist creating pairs of paintings moving outward from the central panel. While Piero did six, Raphael did the *Fortitude* panel. The final order of the panels was *Fortitude*, *Temperance*, *Faith*, *Charity*, *Hope*, *Justice*, and *Wisdom*. Most of the panels show each virtue's typical attributes. Fortitude holds a scepter, Temperance dilutes wine in a basin, Charity holds a flaming heart and suckles a child, Hope looks heavenward, and Prudence holds a serpent and mirror. Prudence's reflection in her mirror reinforces her ability to see and know the past, present, and future. Justice holds a sword with her right hand while her left rests on an orb: both objects are symbols associated with her role as protector and enforcer. All the Virtues sit on elaborate thrones placed on a shallow dais with marble canopies over their heads. The Virtues to the left of Charity lean toward her, toward the center, while those to the right lean to the left, with the exception of Hope, who looks heavenward.

An examination of one of the panels from the series reveals how the series engages and transforms the virtues tradition. Pollaiuolo's first panel, *Charity*, uses the traditional symbol of the flaming heart and suckling child. Charity's crown, her bejeweled and embroidered blue mantle, and her red robe give her the regal quality that, combined with the child, associates her with the Queen of Heaven, Mary. Even her otherworldly expression reinforces that she is an embodiment of a celestial love. This panel, like the entire series, draws upon a particularly lively tradition in Florence. Florence had many important, public depictions of these same virtues, including on the Baptistery of Saint John, on the Basilica of Saint Mary of the Flower (the Duomo), and on the Loggia della Signoria. By making these panels of the Virtues, the Mercanzia creates a connection between itself and the entire tradition. Members of the Mercanzia, as well as those who had business to transact or disputes to settle, were addressed by these large, serene, and richly decorated images that drew upon religious and social ideas to reinforce the authority of an economic institution. By creating an association with the Virtues, the Mercanzia effectively made the other Florentine images of the Virtues an extension of themselves. Every image of the Virtues was, in some way, an image potentially associated with, shall we say, the Mercanzia, the Mercanzia brand, and the Mercanzia's product.

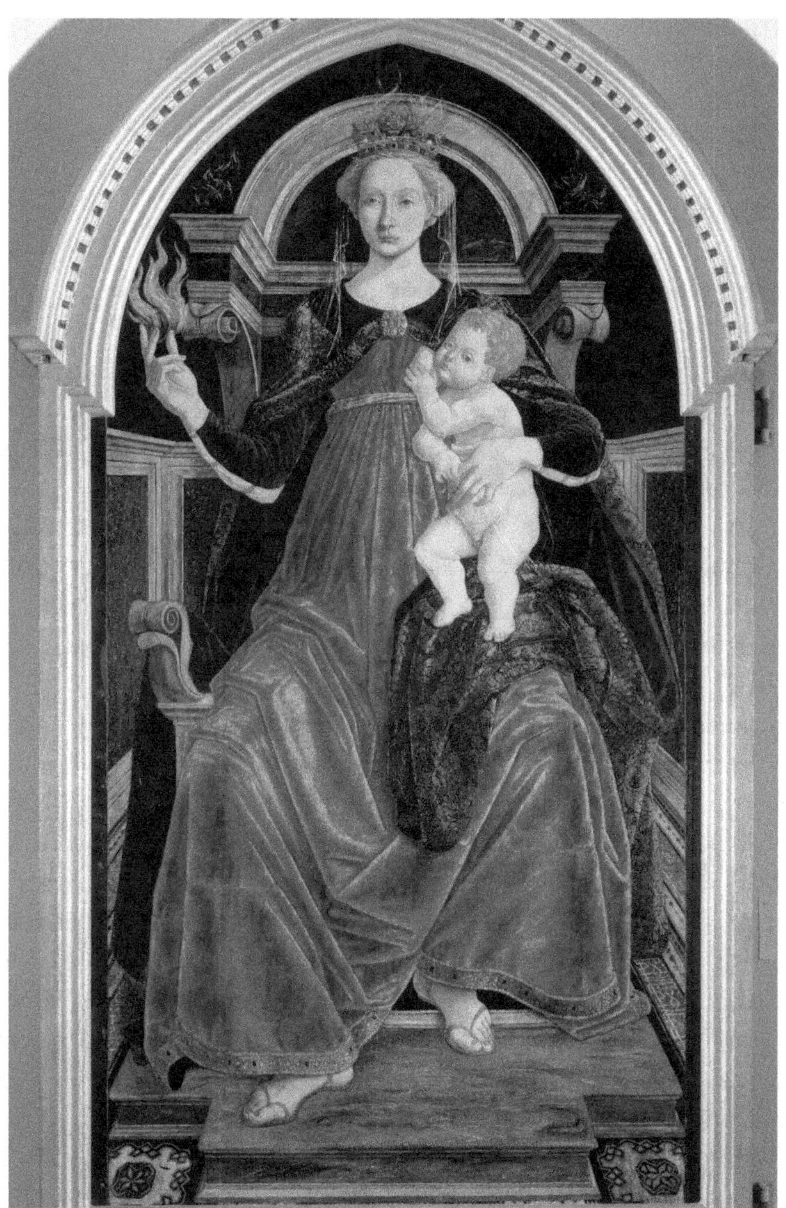

**Figure 22. Pollaiulolo, Piero del. 1469: *Charity*. Uffizi, Florence, Italy.
Photo Credit: Scala/Ministero per i Beni e la Attività culturali / Art Resource, NY.**

ANDREA MANTEGNA'S *MINERVA CHASES THE VICES FROM THE GARDEN OF VIRTUE*

To understand Andrea Mantegna's painting, *Minerva Chases the Vices from the Garden of Virtue*, we must see it as part of a set of pictures. These works were originally intended for a private space, a *studiolo*, which Isabella d'Esta had in Mantua. Working with other thinkers and the artists themselves, Isabella developed the program for the paintings. When all four of the works are taken together, they show a panorama of human conflict, virtue's defeat of vice, and a utopia of human harmony and the flourishing of the arts. At one end is Perugino's *Battle of Love and Chastity*, where the lower impulses of sexual love battle the more elevated and even Platonic ideals. After the conflict in this work and the Mantenga piece we will examine, Isabella had two images of peace and concord. Mantegna's other work for the studiolo shows the mythical Panassus, with Venus and Mars presiding over the dancing muses. The last work is Lorenzo Costa's image of the garden of peaceful arts flourishing under Isabella's patronage. What secures this final serenity and harmony is Minerva's expulsion of the vices, a work that brings together elements of the virtues and vices tradition with the era's renewed classical humanism.

Mantegna's work is a stunning synthesis and extension of the virtues and vices tradition. To the far left of the work is the distraught, human-tree. Winding around this green, hybrid figure is a scroll whose Latin, Greek, and Hebrew inscriptions call for Minerva (Athena), goddess of wisdom and the arts, and Daphne, an embodiment of chastity, to expel the vices that threaten both learning and moral purity. Minerva herself strides powerfully into the garden to do just that. Armed with a shield and broken spear, symbols of knightly victory, she puts the vices to flight. Many are forced to trudge through the swampy water in the foreground. A ragged and foolish figure drags away the bloated and armless figure of Sloth. Next to them a dark, monkey-like figure also flees, with a scroll that identifies it as "Immortal Hatred, Fraud, and Malice." Beside this creature, a centaur flees with a bow-bearing and nude female figure. This figure may be Venus, whom Minerva will free from the centaur, or she may be a consort of the lusty half-human and half-animal. Other composite human-and-animal figures like the fauns and cupids also flee. A final humorous and inventive touch is the three figures who must, with great difficulty, attempt to flee Athena's righteous wrath. Avarice leans forward while Ingratitude leans back, as the figures attempt to carry the fat, crowned figure of Ignorance. Athena herself looks up toward the sky, where Justice with her sword and scale, Fortitude with her club and column, and Temperance with her gesture of diluting wine descend to aid in the fight. Finally, the scroll to the far right indicates that thus far, Wisdom has been trapped in the rocky wall.

Mantegna provided Isabella d'Esta with an updated, Renaissance *psychomachia*. The suffering, living tree, reminiscent of the trees of the Old Adam, looks for the remedy virtue will provide. Not only do we have the tree motif, but this scene also uses the garden image as well, but unlike most medieval works, Mantegna's does not call upon Faith, Hope, or Charity for redemption. In Mantegna's work it is the cardinal, the classical and humanistic virtues and a classical embodiment, Minerva, who defeat the vices. Minerva's face is that of Isabella, and in this transformation of the tradition she does not ascend a ladder toward a Christian paradise but instead secures a humanistic paradise, a Parnassus and a Garden of Peaceful Arts, with Isabella as their guarantor and patron goddess.

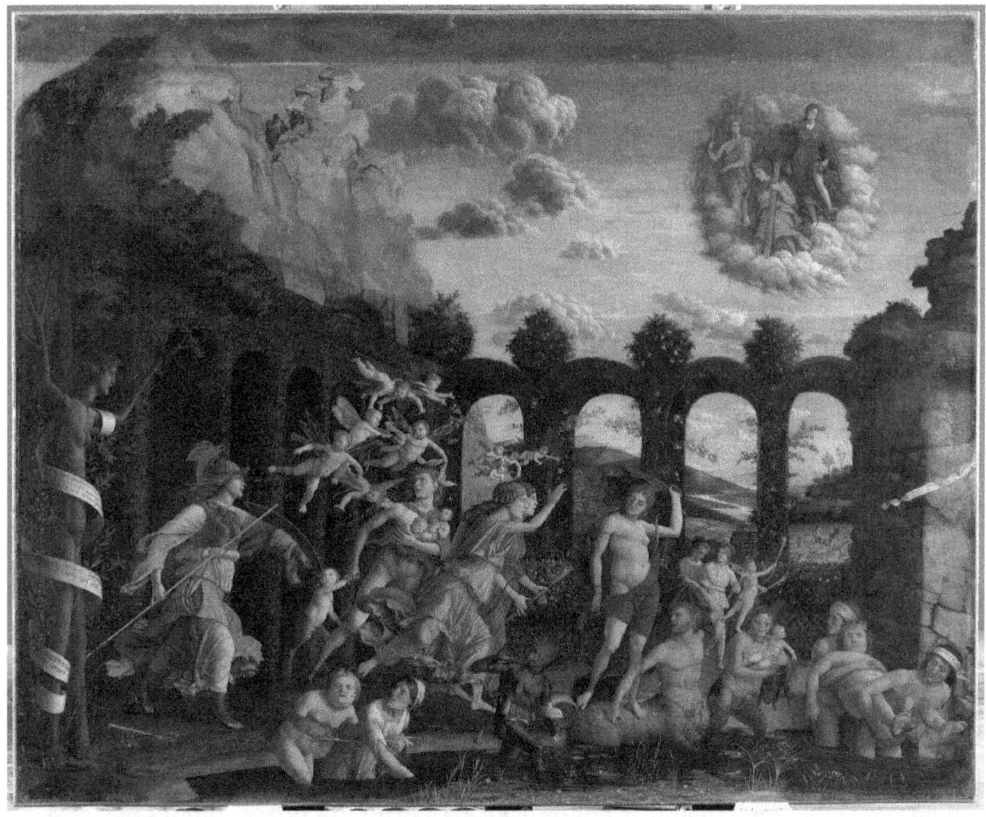

Figure 23. Mantegna, Andrea. 1502: *Minerva Chasing the Vices from the Garden of Virtue.* Paris, Musée du Louvre. ©RMN-Grand Palais / Art Resource, NY.

NICCOLÒ MACHIAVELLI'S *THE PRINCE*

Introduction

As you'll recall from the introduction to Plato's *Republic*, one of the speakers who took exception to Socrates's views of justice was Thrasymachus. According to Thrasymachus, "justice" is the wool leaders pull over the eyes of the people so that they can take advantage of them. If Thrasymachus had been given a chance to develop his political and social insight, he may very well have penned *The Prince*. Machiavelli's famous tract shows the further development and modification of the virtues and vices tradition.

We use the word *Machiavellian* to describe people who ruthlessly use deception and manipulation to achieve their goals. That only partly characterizes the sort of prince that Machiavelli describes and defends. In order to understand *The Prince*, it is important to keep in mind that Machiavelli is not describing a leader with a long tradition to fall back on, nor does he envision someone who has a generally peaceful community to lead. A leader of a chaotic community, and one with no tradition to fall back on, must use all available tools to maintain power.

To understand the tools that Machiavelli's prince has at his disposal, we must first get a sense of Machiavelli's view of humanity. Machiavelli's prince must maintain power over people who are inconsistent, treacherous, selfish, and cowardly. Such people make great promises during times of peace, but will not live up to them in times of crisis. The assumption in *The Prince* is that this is the way people really are. When addressing whether it is better for a prince to be feared or loved, Machiavelli says that fear more reliably controls and motivates people who are fundamentally deceitful and self-interested. If a prince were to rely upon the "love" or "friendship" of such people in times of crisis, he would be ruined.

Since such a prince must impose rule upon the unruly, we can extrapolate four tools that Machiavelli describes as key for such a leader's success: resources, fear, image, and success. A prince has resources at his disposal, including money, positions, and law enforcement. But Machiavelli warns that it is better for a prince to be stingy and even have a reputation for being stingy. A leader who is extravagant in his spending or "liberal" not only risks squandering his resources but could condition his people to expect liberality. When times become difficult for a prince whose people expect liberality, those people soon become irritable, even confrontational. By contrast, a stingy leader who does not take too much of his people's money or goods could be seen as thrifty, and would be greatly praised for any act of generosity.

Another useful tool is fear. Fear can keep a lot of otherwise lawless citizens in line, and it can force factions to work together. If fear prevents seditions, treason, uprisings, and civil wars, then fear not only keeps a prince in power, but it saves lives. A prince should also be conscious of his image as an important tool. Since most people, according to Machiavelli, judge by what they see and not by the evidence, and since it is pretty clear what people wan" to see (that their leader is merciful, faithful, humane, upright, and religious), a prince who can carefully control his public image can keep the public trust.

But perhaps the prince's most important tool is success. A prince who can protect most of the people, who can keep the enemies at bay and the factions in check, who does not tax too severely, and who may have to kill a kinsman but does not touch the family property, and who looks believable doing it, will stay in power. People will prefer this evil—the one that they know and can anticipate—to some ambiguous advantages and an unknown evil. Success in public administration (as in so many things) is the great deodorant: it covers a lot of stink!

The Transformation of the Virtues and Vices—Niccolò Machiavelli's The Prince

Virtues for Machiavelli are whatever faculties, powers, or excellences help a prince maintain control over people in the real world. Machiavelli's plainly stated points, his solid examples from history and from people of his own time, and his clear refutations of possible counterarguments make *The Prince* powerful prose and art. What is also so significant about *The Prince* in the context of the virtues and vices in the arts is how powerfully it questions core values in almost all of the works so far anthologized. Machiavelli takes direct aim at people like Plato and Aristotle. He points out that some people (think Plato) have imagined republics that have never existed and then penned advice based upon those fantasies. He mentions how others (think Aristotle) have described so many different qualities that different leaders may possess, and he says that it would be great to have them, but then, returning to the real world where real leaders live, he asserts that only certain virtues are essential to keeping power. All the rest of those virtues are at least irrelevant if not nonsense. Machiavelli's prince learns from the centaur when to be beastly and when to be human as it suits his purposes. Such a prince knows how to appear God-fearing, how to put on the show of putting on the armor of God, and how to sell his faithfulness to God and his people, but can just as quickly use his own brutish faculties when necessary. The princely centaur commands the world; he does not meekly hope to inherit it.

CHAPTER XV Concerning Things for Which Men, and Especially Princes, Are Praised or Blamed[1]

It remains now to see what ought to be the rules of conduct for a prince towards subject and friends. And as I know that many have written on this point, I expect I shall be considered presumptuous in mentioning it again, especially as in discussing it I shall depart from the methods of other people. But, it being my intention to write a thing which shall be useful to him who apprehends it, it appears to me more appropriate to follow up the real truth of the matter than the imagination of it; for many have pictured republics and principalities which in fact have never been known or seen, because how one lives is so far distant from how one ought to live, that he who neglects what is done for what ought to be done, sooner effects his ruin than his preservation; for a man who wishes to act entirely up to his professions of virtue soon meets with what destroys him among so much that is evil.

Hence it is necessary for a prince wishing to hold his own to know how to do wrong, and to make use of it or not according to necessity. Therefore, putting on one side imaginary things concerning a prince, and discussing those which are real, I say that all men when they are spoken of, and chiefly princes for being more highly placed, are remarkable for some of those qualities which bring them either blame or praise; and thus it is that one is reputed liberal, another miserly, using a Tuscan term

1. From Nicolo Machiavelli, *The Prince*, trans. W. K. Marriott (London: Dent, 1908), 121–45. Notes adapted from the original.

(because an avaricious person in our language is still he who desires to possess by robbery, whilst we call one miserly who deprives himself too much of the use of his own); one is reputed generous, one rapacious; one cruel, one compassionate; one faithless, another faithful; one effeminate and cowardly, another bold and brave; one affable, another haughty; one lascivious, another chaste; one sincere, another cunning; one hard, another easy; one grave, another frivolous; one religious, another unbelieving, and the like. And I know that every one will confess that it would be most praiseworthy in a prince to exhibit all the above qualities that are considered good; but because they can neither be entirely possessed nor observed, for human conditions do not permit it, it is necessary for him to be sufficiently prudent that he may know how to avoid the reproach of those vices which would lose him his state; and also to keep himself, if it be possible, from those which would not lose him it; but this not being possible, he may with less hesitation abandon himself to them. And again, he need not make himself uneasy at incurring a reproach for those vices without which the state can only be saved with difficulty, for if everything is considered carefully, it will be found that something which looks like virtue, if followed, would be his ruin; whilst something else, which looks like vice, yet followed brings him security and prosperity.

CHAPTER XVI Concerning Liberality and Meanness

Commencing then with the first of the above-named characteristics, I say that it would be well to be reputed liberal. Nevertheless, liberality exercised in a way that does not bring you the reputation for it, injures you; for if one exercises it honestly and as it should be exercised, it may not become known, and you will not avoid the reproach of its opposite. Therefore, any one wishing to maintain among men the name of liberal is obliged to avoid no attribute of magnificence; so that a prince thus inclined will consume in such acts all his property, and will be compelled in the end, if he wish to maintain the name of liberal, to unduly weigh down his people, and tax them, and do everything he can to get money. This will soon make him odious to his subjects, and becoming poor he will be little valued by any one; thus, with his liberality, having offended many and rewarded few, he is affected by the very first trouble and imperiled by whatever may be the first danger; recognizing this himself, and wishing to draw back from it, he runs at once into the reproach of being miserly.

Therefore, a prince, not being able to exercise this virtue of liberality in such a way that it is recognized, except to his cost, if he is wise he ought not to fear the reputation of being mean, for in time he will come to be more considered than if liberal, seeing that with his economy his revenues are enough, that he can defend himself against all attacks, and is able to engage in enterprises without burdening his people; thus it comes to pass that he exercises liberality towards all from whom he does not take, who are numberless, and meanness towards those to whom he does not give, who are few.

We have not seen great things done in our time except by those who have been considered mean; the rest have failed. Pope Julius the Second was assisted in reaching the papacy by a reputation for liberality, yet he did not strive afterwards to keep it up, when he made war on the King of France; and he made many wars without imposing any extraordinary tax on his subjects, for he supplied his additional expenses out of his long thriftiness. The present King of Spain would not have undertaken or conquered in so many enterprises if he had been reputed liberal. A prince, therefore, provided that he has not to rob his subjects, that he can defend himself, that he does not become poor and abject, that he is not forced to become rapacious, ought to hold of little account a reputation for being mean, for it is one of those vices which will enable him to govern.

And if any one should say: Caesar obtained empire by liberality, and many others have reached the highest positions by having been liberal, and by being considered so, I answer: Either you are a prince in fact, or in a way to become one. In the first case this liberality is dangerous, in the second it is very necessary to be considered liberal; and Caesar was one of those who wished to become pre-eminent in Rome; but if he had survived after becoming so, and had not moderated his expenses, he would have destroyed his government. And if any one should reply: Many have been princes, and have done great things with armies, who have been considered very liberal, I reply: Either a prince spends that which is his own or his subjects's or else that of others. In the first case he ought to be sparing, in the second he ought not to neglect any opportunity for liberality. And to the prince who goes forth with his army, supporting it by pillage, sack, and extortion, handling that which belongs to others, this liberality is necessary, otherwise he would not be followed by soldiers. And of that which is neither yours nor your subjects' you can be a ready giver, as were Cyrus, Caesar, and Alexander; because it does not take away your reputation if you squander that of others, but adds to it; it is only squandering your own that injures you.

And there is nothing wastes so rapidly as liberality, for even whilst you exercise it you lose the power to do so, and so become either poor or despised, or else, in avoiding poverty, rapacious and hated. And a prince should guard himself, above all things, against being despised and hated; and liberality leads you to both. Therefore it is wiser to have a reputation for meanness which brings reproach without hatred, than to be compelled through seeking a reputation for liberality to incur a name for rapacity which begets reproach with hatred.

CHAPTER XVII Concerning Cruelty and Clemency, and Whether It Is Better to Be Loved Than Feared

Coming now to the other qualities mentioned above, I say that every prince ought to desire to be considered clement and not cruel. Nevertheless he ought to take care not to misuse this clemency. Cesare Borgia was considered cruel; notwithstanding, his cruelty reconciled the Romagna, unified it, and restored it to peace and loyalty. And if this be rightly considered, he will be seen to have been much more merciful than the Florentine people, who, to avoid a reputation for cruelty, permitted Pistoia to be destroyed.[2] Therefore a prince, so long as he keeps his subjects united and loyal, ought not to mind the reproach of cruelty; because with a few examples he will be more merciful than those who, through too much mercy, allow disorders to arise, from which follow murder or robbery; for these are wont to injure the whole people, whilst those executions which originate with a prince offend the individual only.

And of all princes, it is impossible for the new prince to avoid the imputation of cruelty, owing to new states being full of dangers. Hence Virgil, through the mouth of Dido, excuses the inhumanity of her reign owing to its being new, saying:—

> "Res dura, et regni novitas me talia cogunt
> Moliri, et late fines custode tueri."[3]

Nevertheless he ought to be slow to believe and to act, nor should he himself show fear, but proceed in a temperate manner with prudence and humanity, so that too much confidence may not make him incautious and too much distrust render him intolerable.

Upon this a question arises: whether it be better to be loved than feared or feared than loved? It may be answered that one should wish to be both, but, because it is difficult to unite them in one person, it is much safer to be feared than loved, when, of the two, either must be dispensed with. Because this is to be asserted in general of men, that they are ungrateful, fickle, false, cowards, covetous, and as long as you succeed they are yours entirely; they will offer you their blood, property, life, and children, as is said above, when the need is far distant; but when it approaches they turn against you. And that prince who, relying entirely on their promises, has neglected other precautions, is ruined; because friendships that are obtained by payments, and not by greatness or nobility of mind, may indeed be earned, but they are not secured, and in time of need cannot be relied upon; and men have less scruple in offending one who is beloved than one who is feared, for love is preserved by the link of obligation which, owing to the baseness of men, is broken at every opportunity for their advantage; but fear preserves you by a dread of punishment which never fails.

Nevertheless a prince ought to inspire fear in such a way that, if he does not win love, he avoids hatred; because he can endure very well being feared whilst he is not hated, which will always be as long as he abstains from the property of his citizens and subjects and from their women. But when it is necessary for him to proceed against the life of someone, he must do it on proper justification and for manifest cause, but

2. "Pistoia to be destroyed": during the rioting between the Cancellieri and Panciatichi factions in 1502 and 1503. (This note is original to the excerpt.)

3. Virgil: ". . . against my will, my fate / A throne unsettled, and an infant state, / Bid me defend my realms with all my pow'rs, / And guard with these severities my shores." Christopher Pitt. (This note is original to the excerpt.)

above all things he must keep his hands off the property of others, because men more quickly forget the death of their father than the loss of their patrimony. Besides, pretexts for taking away the property are never wanting; for he who has once begun to live by robbery will always find pretexts for seizing what belongs to others; but reasons for taking life, on the contrary, are more difficult to find and sooner lapse. But when a prince is with his army, and has under control a multitude of soldiers, then it is quite necessary for him to disregard the reputation of cruelty, for without it he would never hold his army united or disposed to its duties.

Among the wonderful deeds of Hannibal this one is enumerated: that having led an enormous army, composed of many various races of men, to fight in foreign lands, no dissensions arose either among them or against the prince, whether in his bad or in his good fortune. This arose from nothing else than his inhuman cruelty, which, with his boundless valor, made him revered and terrible in the sight of his soldiers, but without that cruelty, his other virtues were not sufficient to produce this effect. And short-sighted writers admire his deeds from one point of view and from another condemn the principal cause of them. That it is true his other virtues would not have been sufficient for him may be proved by the case of Scipio, that most excellent man, not only of his own times but within the memory of man, against whom, nevertheless, his army rebelled in Spain; this arose from nothing but his too great forbearance, which gave his soldiers more license than is consistent with military discipline. For this he was upbraided in the Senate by Fabius Maximus, and called the corrupter of the Roman soldiery. The Locrians were laid waste by a legate of Scipio, yet they were not avenged by him, nor was the insolence of the legate punished, owing entirely to his easy nature. Insomuch that someone in the Senate, wishing to excuse him, said there were many men who knew much better how not to err than to correct the errors of others. This disposition, if he had been continued in the command, would have destroyed in time the fame and glory of Scipio; but, he being under the control of the Senate, this injurious characteristic not only concealed itself, but contributed to his glory.

Returning to the question of being feared or loved, I come to the conclusion that, men loving according to their own will and fearing according to that of the prince, a wise prince should establish himself on that which is in his own control and not in that of others; he must endeavor only to avoid hatred, as is noted.

CHAPTER XVIII Concerning the Way in Which Princes Should Keep Faith

Every one admits how praiseworthy it is in a prince to keep faith, and to live with integrity and not with craft. Nevertheless our experience has been that those princes who have done great things have held good faith of little account, and have known how to circumvent the intellect of men by craft, and in the end have overcome those who have relied on their word. You must know there are two ways of contesting, the one by the law, the other by force; the first method is proper to men, the second to beasts; but because the first is frequently not sufficient, it is necessary to have recourse to the second. Therefore it is necessary for a prince to understand how to avail himself of the beast and the man. This has been figuratively taught to princes by ancient writers, who describe how Achilles and many other princes of old were given to the Centaur Chiron to nurse, who brought them up in his discipline; which means solely that, as they had for a teacher one who was half beast and half man, so it is necessary for a prince to know how to make use of both natures, and that one without the other is not durable. A prince, therefore, being compelled knowingly to adopt the beast, ought to choose the fox and the lion; because the lion cannot defend himself against snares and the fox cannot defend himself against wolves. Therefore, it is necessary to be a fox to discover the snares and a lion to terrify the wolves. Those who rely simply on the lion do not understand what they are about. Therefore a wise lord cannot, nor ought he to, keep faith when such observance may be turned against him, and when the reasons that caused him to pledge it exist no longer. If men were entirely good this precept would not hold, but because they are bad, and will not keep faith with you, you too are not bound to observe it with them. Nor will there ever be wanting to a prince legitimate reasons to excuse this non-observance. Of this endless modern examples could be given, showing how many treaties and engagements have been made void and of no effect through the faithlessness of princes; and he who has known best how to employ the fox has succeeded best.

But it is necessary to know well how to disguise this characteristic, and to be a great pretender and dissembler; and men are so simple, and so subject to present necessities, that he who seeks to deceive will always find someone who will allow himself to be deceived. One recent example I cannot pass over in silence. Alexander the Sixth did nothing else but deceive men, nor ever thought of doing otherwise, and he always found victims; for there never was a man who had greater power in asserting, or who with greater oaths would affirm a thing, yet would observe it less; nevertheless his deceits always succeeded according to his wishes, because he well understood this side of mankind.

Therefore it is unnecessary for a prince to have all the good qualities I have enumerated, but it is very necessary to appear to have them. And I shall dare to say this also, that to have them and always to observe them is injurious, and that to appear to have them is useful; to appear merciful, faithful, humane, religious, upright, and to be so, but with a mind so framed that should you require not to be so, you may be able and know how to change to the opposite.

And you have to understand this, that a prince, especially a new one, cannot observe all those things for which men are esteemed, being often forced, in order to maintain the state, to act contrary to fidelity, friendship, humanity, and religion. Therefore it is necessary for him to have a mind ready to turn itself accordingly as the winds and variations of fortune force it, yet, as I have said above, not to diverge from the good if he can avoid doing so, but, if compelled, then to know how to set about it.

For this reason a prince ought to take care that he never lets anything slip from his lips that is not replete with the above-named five qualities, that he may appear to him who sees and hears him altogether merciful, faithful, humane, upright, and religious. There is nothing more necessary to appear to have than this last quality, inasmuch as men judge generally more by the eye than by the hand, because it belongs to everybody to see you, to few to come in touch with you. Every one sees what you appear to be, few really know what you are, and those few dare not oppose themselves to the opinion of the many, who have the majesty of the state to defend them; and in the actions of all men, and especially of princes, which it is not prudent to challenge, one judges by the result.

For that reason, let a prince have the credit of conquering and holding his state, the means will always be considered honest, and he will be praised by everybody; because the vulgar are always taken by what a thing seems to be and by what comes of it; and in the world there are only the vulgar, for the few find a place there only when the many have no ground to rest on.

One prince[4] of the present time, whom it is not well to name, never preaches anything else but peace and good faith, and to both he is most hostile, and either, if he had kept it, would have deprived him of reputation and kingdom many a time.

BERNAERT VAN ORLEY (DESIGNER) AND WORKSHOP OF PIETER VAN AELST (WEAVER) *THE HONORS*

Bernaert van Orley and Pieter van Aelst knew that all the world is a stage; they designed its scenery. And none of their stage designs were more important than the ones they created for Emperor Charles V's 1520 coronation. These stage designs, here in the form of nine monumental tapestries, not only provided the ideal imperial backdrop, but illustrated the very qualities, the virtues, a ruler would need in order to reign over such a vast empire.

The tapestries now known as *The Honors* were created for the October 1520 anointing and crowning ceremony of Charles V as King of the Romans and Emperor Elect. While it is unclear if Charles or his court directly commissioned these tapestries, what is clear is how they would form an ideal stage set for the royal theater of Charles's coronation. The nine tapestries, which are all about five meters tall and many are over ten meters long, are complex yet coherent works. The meanings of the separate tapestries become clear when all nine are examined together. The first panel warns of the uncertainties of Fortune, and the second panel displays, in all of her glory, the many aspects of Prudence. Taken together, these works illustrate how wisdom helps a leader see the truth about fickle fortune. The next tapestry reinforces this message, as it shows Divine Wisdom presiding over a scene where Virtue overcomes Vice and Fortitude and

4. Machiavelli here refers to Ferdinand of Aragón (d. 1516); his methods are described in another chapter in *The Prince*.

Temperance control the capriciousness of Fortune. The next panel shows Faith and the other virtues triumphant over vices. The fifth tapestry depicts the triumphal coronation of those worthy of Honor, with the next panel showing the just proclamation of such virtue in the form of Fame. The seventh tapestry shows the "ruler's virtue," Justice, and the last of the public virtues is Nobility, featured in the eighth tapestry. The last panel is a warning, a vast catalogue of personal and public vices that lead to Infamy.

As we can see by their program, *The Honors* tapestries warn against the twin dangers of Fortune and Infamy. Virtue is the cure for both. Virtue, in the form of Wisdom, Fortitude, and Temperance, assures the individual and empire against the vicissitudes of Fortune, while Virtues in all of their varieties defeat the manifold Vices. The scene in the Faith tapestry looks like an elaborate stage, with a central, tiered throne framed by elaborate columns. Seven female Virtues occupy the throne, and at the center is Faith, holding the Old Testament Tablets of Moses, the New Testament Church, and a candle. She treads on the bearded figure of Mohammed, who represents not only heresy but also a dangerous political threat. To her left is Charity, whose heart and radiant mirror exude the warmth of her love, a love contrasting sharply with the figure under her, Herod, the murderer of the innocents. Opposite her, on Faith's right side, is Hope. As the patron virtue of farmers and sailors (people whose livelihoods are out of their control, and who therefore live by her), she carries a boat and spade. She tramples the example of despair, the treacherous and then suicidal Judas. In the tier just below the three theological virtues, Prudence holds her accustomed mirror and serpent, Fortitude is seen with a dragon and anvil, Temperance holds spectacles and a clock, and Justice wields a sword and scales. These figures also overcome symbols of vice such as the foolish indulgence of Saradanapalus, the weakness of Holofernes, the lust and immoderation of Tarquin, and the cruel injustice of Nero. Figures of Reverence or Awe and Religion or Divine Service are seated just below the seven virtues, further introducing and honoring them. Much of the rest of the tapestry is given over to the many historical or mythological figures, dressed in contemporary clothes, who both honor and embody the virtues. There are biblical figures like Joseph, Job, and Jacob, and classical figures like Cassandra, Socrates, the Athenian King Codrus, Solon, Trajan, the Emperor Tiberius, Scripio Africanus, and an impressive figure of Charlemagne. While all of the figures exemplify aspects of the virtues, Charlemagne has a special link with Charles V. Not only was Charles named for Charlemagne, but at the ceremony for which this work was made Charles received Charlemagne's crown. Taken as a whole, these tapestries affirm Charles as a perfect "guardian" in an ideal Platonic republic or empire, as well as a wise ruler in the tradition of Solomon. Their dramatic and powerful affirmation of virtue and condemnation of vice make *The Honors* Charles's mural of good government and bad government like Lorenzetti's murals in Siena. But instead of Charles relying upon others coming to see this work, these portable murals could accompany Charles anywhere, impressing all who see them with the emperor's authority, power, and goodness.

Many problems prevent the reproduction of these tapestries here in this anthology. They are very large, and would be very difficult to see as small, black-and-white reproductions. Reproduction costs and difficulties securing permissions compounded the problem. At press time, and for the foreseeable future, there is an excellent website that reproduces all of the tapestries with images that can be enlarged in order to see all of their rich details. The site also provides additional information. The website is found at http://www.flandesenhispania.org/tapestries/index.php/The_Honours_series_(Los_Honores)/.

PETER BRUEGHEL THE ELDER'S *VIRTUES AND VICES*

Between 1556 and 1560 Peter Brueghel the Elder created drawings of the Seven Vices and the Seven Virtues, plus Patience. These fifteen drawings were almost immediately engraved and published as prints. These drawings (and prints) have such a richness of detail and insight that picking a few to collect here was as difficult as choosing a section from Dante's *Purgatorio*. And not only was it difficult to pick just four, but it is just as impossible to account for the visual and intellectual wealth of even one work, let alone do justice to all of them. It was tempting to try to include all fifteen of them, because these works fit this anthology especially well. Not only do they treat the subject in a way that illuminates both the theme and the other works in this volume, but their original size and graphic nature uniquely fit the format of a book. Where it is hard to believe that almost any of the creators of the works collected in this anthology would even fathom their work presented in the format of this book, Brueghel's drawings (which immediately became prints ready for mass production and general consumption) presented in this book come closest to what the artist's initial ideas may have been about their presentation and reception. And these works speak forcefully yet have so much to say that they reward extended study. Their message can be taken in immediately, yet a deeper inspection reveals details and nuances that yield insight only after one has spent the proper time examining them.

The four images included here, and all fifteen images, share many stylistic features. Front and center of each is a female embodiment of the virtue or vice (and a symbolic animal companion) with its name given in Latin below. Extending across the front foreground are figures and activities associated with that quality. There is generally a middle ground with more figures and activities as well as a deep background. Most of the scenes are incompletely framed by the work itself, giving a sense that these activities extend beyond the window offered by the work. All of the works are filled to overflowing with a wide variety of characters and activities. Inscriptions in Latin and often in Flemish extend and clarify each scene's meaning.

While all of the works of the virtues and vices share these general qualities, each set also has its own shared features. The images of the vices, for example, have cartoonish, fantastic, and phantasmagoric qualities that the images of the virtues lack. With the exception of Temperance, which is included here, and which will be discussed, the people who inhabit the world of the virtues are everyday and even common human beings. The worlds of the vices are populated with naked, strangely costumed, or just weird humans mixed with a menagerie of bizarre hybrid creatures that might fill one's fantasies or nightmares. Such surreal creatures and scenes, inspired by Brueghel's fellow countryman Hieronymus Bosch, convey how the vices are deficiencies or aberrations in one's character. Just as the figures, activities, and even land formations in the vice scenes run counter to nature, so is vice itself unnatural. These scenes are not illustrations of hell itself or hell alone but are imaginative depictions of a particular vice's personal and social consequences. The prints place those consequences in the foreground and middle ground. While the emphasis is on the vice's mortal deformities and aberrations, the fiery (or at least smoky) destruction common in the top and background indicate the vice's long-range outcomes, which, while they may be postmortal, are also outcomes experienced here and now.

The image of Anger (Figure 24) shows many of these qualities. Anger, armor clad, wielding a sword and flaming torch, and accompanied by a bear, leads a charge of figures out of her teetering war tent. Her shock troops use an oversized knife to slice a group of naked human figures. And lest one naked figure get away, a figure with a human body and animal head is ready with a spiked club to finish the job. Above this scene, through the cut-away wall in a nightmarish shed, is another hybrid creature basting a figure that slowly turns on a spit. Brueghel includes an oversized blind figure, holding a vial of poison or a flask of fury, pushing along a barrel that seems to hold a barroom brawl. Above Anger's war tent burns a caldron of what could be marital discord, while to the right two hybrid demons separated by a strange war machine taunt each other, perhaps showing violent human conflict as a demonic game. The inscriptions below express how Anger clogs the faculties and poisons the passions by "swelling the mouth" and "blackening the blood."

The print showing Lust, or sexual excess (Figure 25), also includes bizarre aberrations to show the consequences of a natural impulse that is out of control. At the center of the work, seen through the cutout of a strange cave or hill, Lust, accompanied by a rooster, fondles her genitals and tongue kisses the enthroned demon that caresses her breast. Other hybrid demons attend, perhaps waiting their turn, while one brings in an aphrodisiac. The foreground is filled with a nightmarish zoo of creatures exposing themselves, relieving themselves, castrating themselves, or just plain humping. In the middle ground, to the left of Lust, a naked and handcuffed figure is led away on a hybrid beast. The paper on the figure's hat indicates that this is an adulterer being publicly humiliated and punished. The animals just below the scene reinforce adulterous betrayal, as what seems like a mother bird, her brood in tow, chases down a fleeing father bird. Leading the procession are a self-exposing frog and bagpipe-playing monk, while various demonic and bound human figures are caught up in its pain and exuberance. The entire scene is filled with gardens, fountains, and streams of sexual love, but lurking in them are creatures like the massive pike to the right which can emerge at any time and seize another victim. The print's inscription reinforces how sexual excess destroys human reason and power, or how sexual excess, to use its language, "unmans the man."

If the images of vice are about how these aberrations of natural faculties or impulses dissolve one's integrity, corrupt one's reason, and rob one of power, then the selected images of the virtues show how the various virtues secure power and success. Fortitude (Figure 26) is a fine example of this. The virtue herself, holding a column and caped by an anvil, treads on the demonic vice she controls with a chain. Her breastplate and wings add to the sense of her power, while the anvil shows her strength in withstanding any blow. Around Fortitude's central calm rages a vast battle between virtue and vice. The forces of virtue, all of them human and acting with calm determination, defeat the fantastic army of demonic vices, including Anger's bear, Lust's rooster, Pride's peacock, Envy's turkey, Gluttony's hybrid pig and donkey, and Sloth's ass. Virtue's cavalry charges in powerful, orderly waves, forcing various fleeing demons back toward the pit to the far right from which they've emerged, while other vices retreat back into a hallow egg, another symbol of their abortive decay. At the center of the image is what we might call the castle of the soul. With towers reminiscent of human faces, the castle is guarded by soldiers, at least one bearing a cross, and by winged angels. The Latin inscription brings these many elements together: "To conquer one's impulses, to restrain anger and the other vices and emotion: this is true fortitude."

If Fortitude is restraint and control, then Charity (Figure 27) is using one's energy and time in loving service of others. Charity herself reaches down to care for children, for the innocent and vulnerable. She holds the burning heart of her compassion, while on her head a bird pokes at its breast. This bird is probably a version of a pelican that is often included in images of Charity, because according to the tradition, the pelican would draw its own blood from its breast in order to feed or revive its young. Grouped through the remainder of the scenes are depictions of the seven acts of mercy. To the left the hungry are being fed, above them we see the thirsty being satisfied, and the imprisoned are visited and comforted. At the very back center of the work is the burial of the dead and in front of that strangers are being welcomed. To the right are figures visiting the sick, while in the foreground to the left the naked are being clothed. The inscription points out how charity is making others' problems our own, knowing that one day we may have a similar need. The charitable, free from self-consuming and self-destructive vice, find success in extending themselves for others to relieve pain and suffering.

The calm, down-to-earth, and edifying image of Charity stands in stark contrast with the chaotic, fantastic, and ominous images of the vices. The images of the virtues affirm the power of those qualities to overcome the vices, to succeed in a variety of pursuits, and to make a positive difference in the world. Prints like *Anger* and *Lust* warn, with nightmarish imagery, that excesses and unrestrained passions destroy individuals and society. Yet even here we come back to a common crossroads: the very mayhem and pandemonium of the images of the vices could make them more interesting and even alluring than the images of the virtues. *Charity* might be edifying, but *Lust* is simultaneously repulsive and seductive. While Brueghel himself may have tried to reinforce the value of virtue and the peril of vice, his images, not unlike other images of the virtues and vices, leave open other readings, perceptions, and experiences. Even these superabundant images, complete with inscriptions, cannot speak unambiguously.

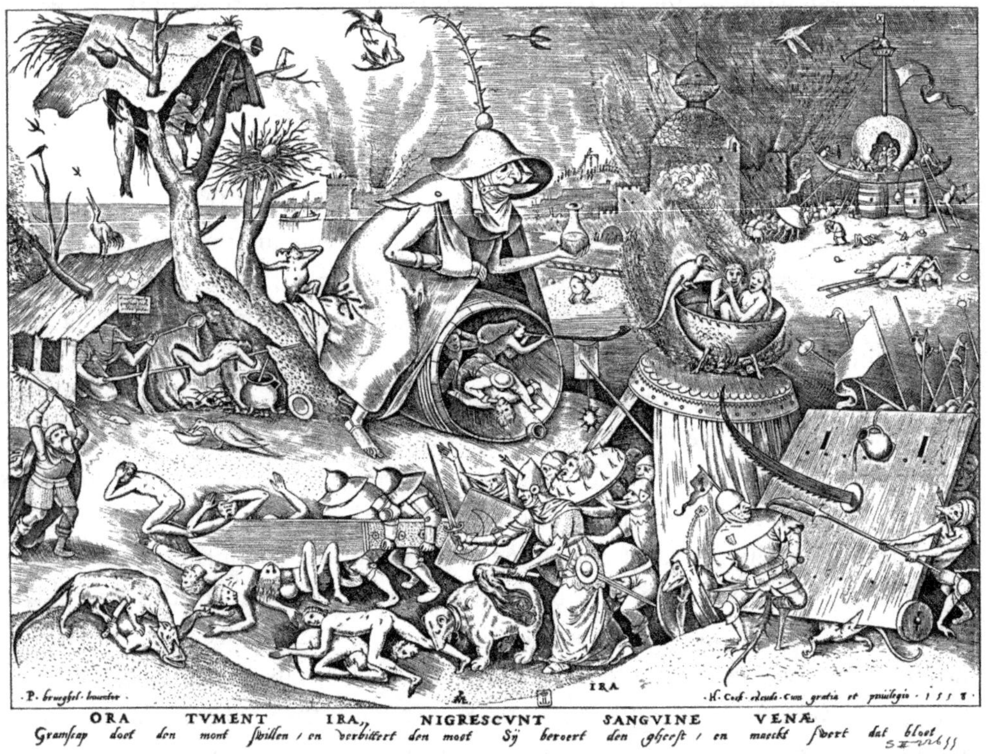

Figure 24. Pieter. Brueghel, 1558: *Anger*. Engraving by Pieter van der Hayden. Engraving, originally published by Hieronymus Cock. Source: http://commons.wikimedia.org/.

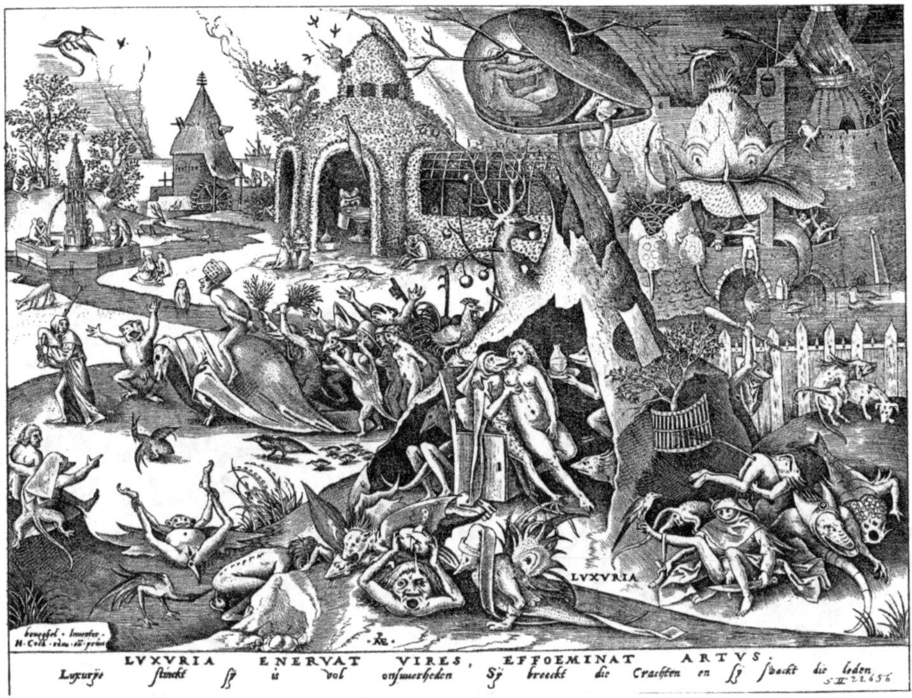

Figure 25. Pieter Brueghel, 1558: *Lust*. Engraving by Pieter van der Hayden. Engraving, originally published by Hieronymus Cock. Source: http://commons.wikimedia.org/.

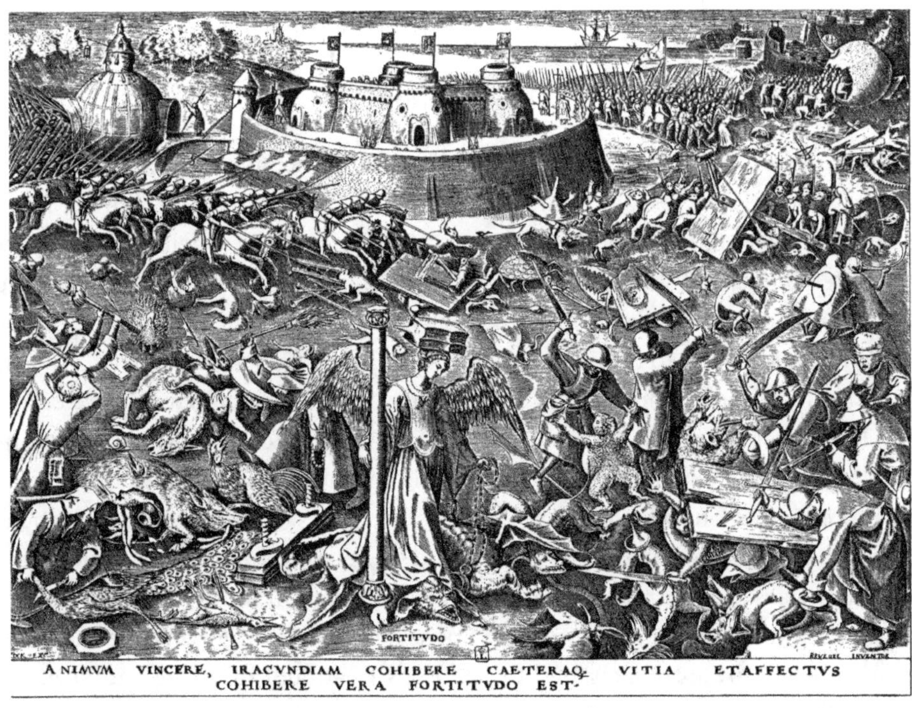

Figure 26. Brueghel, Pieter. 1559: *Fortitude*. Engraving by Pieter van der Hayden. Engraving, originally published by Hieronymus Cock. Source: http://commons.wikimedia.org/.

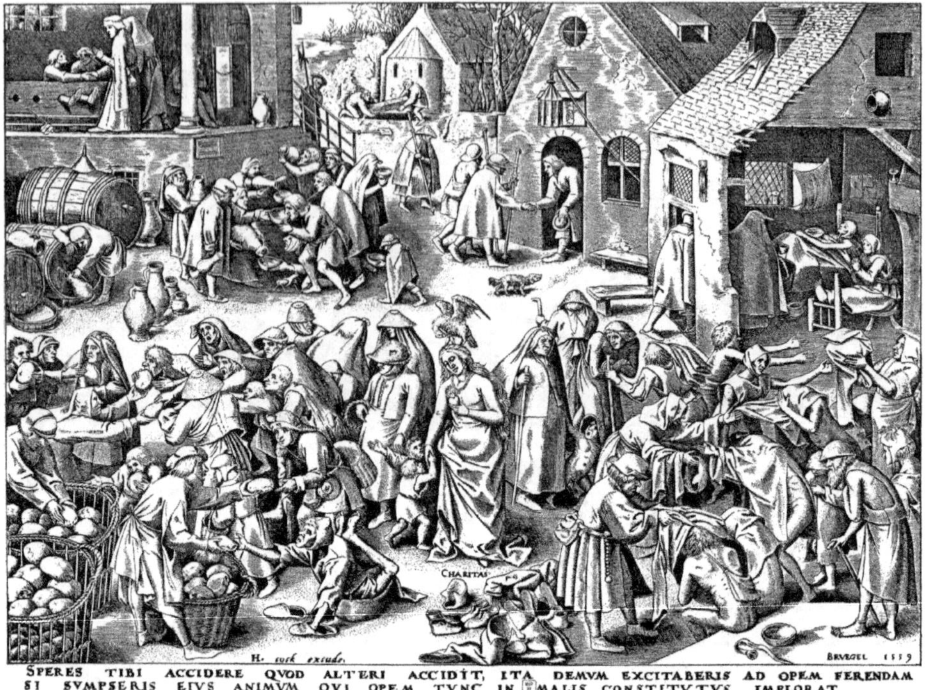

Figure 27. Pieter Brueghel, 1559: *Charity*. Engraving by Pieter van der Hayden. Engraving, originally published by Hieronymus Cock. Source: http://commons.wikimedia.org/.

EDMUND SPENSER'S *THE FAERIE QUEENE*

Introduction

Before there was Oprah Winfrey and school reading-incentive programs, there was Edmund Spenser. And just as Oprah aims to teach and foster reading with her famous and influential book club and programs to get kids to read, Spenser believed that well-written books and stories could improve lives. In 1589, Edmund Spenser wrote a now-famous letter to Sir Walter Raleigh, explaining that the purpose of his epic poem *The Faerie Queene* was "to fashion a gentleman or noble person in virtuous and gentle discipline." In order to fashion such an audience, Spenser created a massive epic, inspired by Homer, Virgil, and others, that tells exemplary stories of King Arthur and a variety of other characters. *The Faerie Queene* is an elaborate allegory that can be read as an expression of Christian theology, as a Protestant assault on Catholicism, and as a celebration of the Tudor dynasty in general and Queen Elizabeth I in particular. As the virtues and vices are central to Spenser's efforts to speak in these many ways at once, they are used to celebrate and condemn Spenser's various targets. While the various allegorical levels are intimately tied to Spenser's treatment of virtue and vice, I will restrict this introduction and excerpt to two portions of the work that are most central to the virtues and vices tradition. These portions are from the poem's first book, cantos IV and X, which deal, respectively, with the House of Pride and the House of Holiness.

Finding a proper excerpt for this anthology is difficult. In the same letter to Raleigh mentioned above, Spenser explained that he conceived of the entire work as twenty-four books dealing with twenty-four virtues. The first twelve books would deal with the "private virtues" as seen in a principal character and number of stories, while the last twelve would deal with the "public virtues" in the stories of King Arthur. Spenser, who drew his virtues from Aristotle and Saint Thomas Aquinas, only completed six books. Those books would "fashion" an audience in the following virtues: holiness, temperance, chastity, friendship, justice, and courtesy.

Spenser's first book deals with the Red Cross Knight's commission to defeat a dragon that scourges Una's homeland. Una signifies unity, the singleness of truth, or even Christianity in its truest form, and for Spenser that truest form is Protestantism. While Red Cross Knight is originally successful in defeating a monster, Error, his gullibility and mistrust of Una make him a victim of an evil magician, Archimago, who passes himself off as a devout hermit. Convinced that Una is a lustful deceiver, Red Cross Knight abandons her and is further deceived by a witch disguised as an innocent damsel. This witch, Duessa, whose name denotes duality, duplicity, and fraud, leads Red Cross Knight to dangers in the form of the Saracen brothers, Sansfoy, Sansloy, and Sansjoy, the evil Lucifera, the House of Pride, and finally the monster Orgoglio. Duessa leaves Red Cross Knight seduced, battered, and imprisoned. Eventually Una is able to enlist the aid of Prince Arthur to free Red Cross Knight, but because of his debilitated state, Una takes him to the House of Holiness to recover. It is during this convalescence that Red Cross Knight learns his true parentage and fate as Saint George, patron saint of England. Fully recovered, Red Cross Knight eventually overcomes the dragon and is betrothed to Una.

While the entire epic is based upon the virtues and their contrary vices, with individual books dealing in elaborate and sophisticated ways with the many aspects of one virtue, the House of Pride and the House of Holiness in book 1 are rich expressions of the tradition. Red Cross Knight is led to the House of Pride by Duessa, who disguises herself as Fidess, or Faith. The approach to the house is the heavily worn and broad path that contrasts with the biblical "straight and narrow." The house itself, built by deceitful magic, features a gold exterior to hide its shabby construction and decay. Spenser connects it with Babylon and pagan capitals in Egypt and Rome. The house, managed by Vanity, is filled with petty, primping courtiers, all of whom sycophantically praise the ruling mistress, Lucifera. Lucifera is associated with Satan, or Lucifer, the light who fell from heaven. This beautiful matron, seated on her throne with a dragon resting at her feet, rules her house with deceitful policies inspired by her six evil counselors. While Lucifera is first in the house and represents Pride, Idleness, Gluttony, Lechery, Avarice, Envy, and Wrath are her advisors. Spenser presents these advisors as a sort of parade, taking three stanzas to describe each vice's dress, object, disease, and beast. As if this parade were not vicious enough, Satan then joins the group and they leave, taking in some fresh air, and moving their party into the broader world.

Whereas the embodiment of duplicity, Duessa, takes Red Cross Knight to the House of Pride, it is Una, the embodiment of unity and the singleness of truth, who takes him to the House of Holiness. And there are a number of other clear contrasts. Where there is a broad road to the sumptuous yet deceitful House of Pride, with Malvenu as the porter, Humility watches the door of the modest House of Holiness, whose entrance is straight and narrow. Red Cross's stay in the house consists of three general stages: purgation, illumination, and union. The wise matron of the house, Caelia, whose name means Heavenly One, has three daughters: Fidelia (Faith), Speranza (Hope), and Charissa (Charity). Fidelia holds the chalice with sacramental wine and baptismal water. In the chalice curls a serpent, recalling Moses's brazen serpent and Aesculapius's healing emblem. She also holds Scriptures in her hands, and it is from that book that she explains Red Cross Knight's need for faith to remedy his inconstancy and sinfulness. As the knight is left despairing over the state of his soul, Speranza, bearing a silver anchor, a biblical sign of her steadfastness and reliability, encourages his hope in Christ. As Fidelia and Speranza have revealed the true state of his soul as well as his source of hope, Red Cross Knight continues his cleansing with the aid of Patience's strict diet and spiritual regimen. With the assistance of Penance, Remorse, and Repentance, Patience helps Red Cross complete his grueling spiritual detoxification.

Red Cross Knight can then move on to proper instruction and illumination in the Christian life, with Charissa as his first teacher. Unlike her sisters, Charissa is married and bears many children. She teaches Red Cross Knight about the active life of righteousness and good works. She introduces Red Cross to Mercy, who takes him up the hill to the house of the seven holy men, embodiments of the Seven Acts of Mercy. Fully illuminated and expert in Christian living, Mercy next leads Red Cross Knight up the very steep climb to the hut where Contemplation dwells. It is there that an initially reluctant Contemplation shows Red Cross Knight the heavenly city, New Jerusalem, and explains his final destiny as Saint George. When Red Cross Knight seeks to start on the narrow path to that destiny, he is reminded of his commission to slay the dragon, a duty he must do before he can achieve complete and final union in the city of God.

Spenser seeks to inspire virtue in his readers from the very first book of *The Faerie Queene*. Red Cross Knight's colorful and gripping adventures describe, according to Spenser's view, the peril of falling pray to vice's deception. As Red Cross Knight finds redemption in the House of Holiness, Spenser demonstrates virtue's healing powers.

Canto IV[5]

To sinful house of Pride, Duessa
Guides the faithful knight,
Where brother's death to wreak,[6] *Sansioy*
Doth challenge him to fight.

Young knight whatever that dost arms profess,
And through long labors huntest after fame,
Beware of fraud, beware of ficklenesses,
In choice and change of thy dear lovèd dame,
Least thou of her believe too lightly blame,[7]
And rash misweening,[8] do thy heart remove.
For unto knight there is no greater shame
Then lightness and inconstancy in love;
That doth this Red Cross Knight's ensample[9] plainly prove.

Who after that he had fair Una lorn,[10]
Through light misdeeming[11] of her loyalty,
And false Duessa in her stead had born[12]—
Callèd Fidess, and so supposed to be—
Long with her traveled, till at last they see
A goodly building, bravely garnishèd[13]—
The house of mighty prince it seemed to be—
And towards it a broad highway that led,
All bare through people's feet, which thither travelèd.

Great troops of people traveled thitherward
Both day and night, of each degree and place,[14]

5. From *The Faerie Queen*, Modernized by Robert Kellogg and Oliver Steele, (New York: Odyssey Press, 1965), 114–23, 188–205. The spelling has been retained from the original, and the notes have been adapted from the original.

6. avenge

7. evil

8. mistaking

9. example

10. lost

11. hastily misjudging

12. placed

13. decorated

14. status

But few returnèd, having scapèd hard[15]
With baleful beggary or foul disgrace,
Which[16] ever after in most wretched case,
Like loathsome lazars[17] by the hedges lay.
Thither Duessa bade him bend his pace;
For she is weary of the toilsome way,
And also nigh consumèd is the lingering day.

A stately Palace built of squarèd brick,
Which cunningly was without mortar laid,
Whose walls were high but nothing strong nor thick,
And golden foil all over them displayed,
That purest sky with brightness they dismayed.[18]
High lifted up were many lofty towers[19]
And goodly galleries far over laid,[20]
Full of fair windows, and delightful bowers;
And on the top a dial told the timely hours.[21]

It was a goodly heap[22] for to behold,
And spake the praises of the workman's wit:[23]
But full great pity, that so fair a mold[24]
Did on so weak foundation ever sit.
For on a sandy hill that still did flit[25]
And fall away, it mounted was full high,
And every breath of heaven shakèd it;
That all the hinder[26] parts, that few could spy,
Were ruinous and old, but painted cunningly.

15. escaped with difficulty

16. who

17. lepers

18. overcame

19. *many lofty towers:* a symbol of presumption since the Tower of Babel: "And they said one to another, go to, let us build us a city and a tower, whose top may reach unto heaven" (Genesis 11:3–4).

20. placed high above

21. The clock is a fit symbol of the City of Man, subject to the ravages of time.

22. structure

23. skill

24. building

25. shift

26. back

Arrivèd there they passèd in forthright;
For still to all[27] the gates stood open wide,
Yet charge of them was to a porter hight,[28]
Called Malvenu,[29] who entrance none denied.
Thence to the hall, which was on every side
With rich array and costly arras[30] dight;[31]
Infinite sorts of people did abide
There, waiting long to win the wishèd sight
Of her that was the lady of that palace bright.

By them they pass, gazing on them round,[32]
And to the presence[33] mount, whose glorious view
Their frail amazèd senses did confound.
In living prince's court none ever knew
Such endless richess and so sumptuous shew;
Ne Persia self, the nurse of pompous pride,
Like ever saw. And there a noble crew
Of lords and ladies stood on every side
Which with their presence fair, the place much beautified.

High above all a cloth of state[34] was spread,
And a rich throne as bright as sunny day,
On which there sat most brave embellishèd
With royal robes and gorgèous array,
A maiden queen, that shone as Titan's ray,
In glistering gold and peerless precious stone.
Yet her bright blazing beauty did assay[35]
To dim the brightness of her glorious throne,
As envying herself,[36] that[37] too exceeding shone.

27. everyone
28. committed
29. *Malvenu:* the opposite of welcome, Fr. *bienvenu.*
30. tapestry
31. furnished
32. from all sides
33. reception hall
34. canopy
35. try
36. her
37. who

Exceeding shone, like Phoebus' fairest child,[38]
That did presume his father's fiery wain,[39]
And flaming mouths of steeds unwonted wild,
Through highest heaven with weaker[40] hand to rein.
Proud of such glory and advancement vain,
While flashing beams do daze his feeble eyne,[41]
He leaves the welkin[42] way most beaten plain,
And rapt[43] with whirling wheels, inflames the skyne[44]
With fire not made to burn, but fairly for to shine.

So proud she shinèd in her princely state,
Looking to heaven—for earth she did disdain—
And sitting high; for lowly[45] she did hate.
Lo, underneath her scornful feet was lain
A dreadful dragon with an hideous train.[46]
And in her hand she held a mirror bright,
Wherein her face she often viewed fain.[47]
And in her self-loved semblance took delight;
For she was wondrous fair as any living wight.

Of grisly Pluto she the daughter was
And sad[48] Proserpina, the queen of hell;
Yet did she think her peerless worth to pass[49]
That parentage, with pride so did she swell;
And thundering Jove, that high in heaven doth dwell,
And wield the world, she claimèd for her sire,
Or if that any else did Jove excel.

38. *Phoebus' fairest child:* Phaëthon, who, like Lucifera, strove to outdo the sun. Ovid's *Metamorphoses* tells the story of Phaëthon's disasterous attempt to drive the chariot of the sun, a story interpreted in medieval tradition as a type of the revolt and fall of Satan. Compare Revelation 9:1.

39. chariot

40. too weak

41. eyes

42. cloudy

43. carried away

44. skies

45. humility

46. tail

47. lovingly

48. dismal

49. surpass

For to the highest she did still aspire,
Or if aught higher were then that, did it desire.

And proud Lucifera men did her call,
That made herself a queen and crowned to be;
Yet rightful kingdom she had none at all,
Ne heritage of native[50] sovereignty,
But did usurp with wrong and tyranny
Upon the scepter which she now did hold;
Ne ruled her realm with laws, but policy[51]
And strong advisement[52]of six wizards old,
That with their counsels bad her kingdom did uphold.

Soon as the elfin knight in presence came,
And false Duessa, seeming lady fair,
A gentle usher, Vanity by name,
Made room, and passage for them did prepare.
So goodly brought them to the lowest stair
Of her high throne, where they on humble knee
Making obeisance did the cause declare
Why they were come her royal state to see:
To prove[53] the wide report of her great majesty.

With lofty eyes, half loath to look so low,
She thankèd them in her disdainful wise,
Ne other grace vouchsafèd them to show
Of princess worthy—scarce them bade arise.
Her lords and ladies all this while devise[54]
Themselves to setten forth[55] to strangers' sight.
Some frounce their curlèd hair in courtly guise,[56]
Some prank[57] their ruffs, and others trimly dight
Their gay attire. Each others' greater pride does spite.

50. inherited
51. cunning
52. advice
53. determine the truth of
54. prepare
55. exhibit
56. elegant style
57. straighten

Goodly they all that knight do entertain,
Right glad with him to have increased their crew.
But to Duess each one himself did pain
All kindness and fair courtesy to shew;
For in that court whilom[58] her well they knew.
Yet the stout faery mongst the middest[59] crowd
Thought all their glory vain in knightly view,
And that great princess too exceeding proud,
That to strange knight no better countenance allowed.[60]

Sudden upriseth from her stately place
The royal dame and for her coach doth call.
All hurtlen[61] forth, and she with princely pace,
As fair Aurora in her purple pall,[62]
Out of the east the dawning day doth call—
So forth she comes. Her brightness broad doth blaze;
The heaps of people thronging in the hall
Do ride each other upon her to gaze.
Her glorious glitterand[63] light doth all men's eyes amaze.

So forth she comes and to her coach does climb,
Adornèd all with gold and garlands gay,
That seemed as fresh as Flora in her prime
And strove to match, in royal rich array
Great Juno's golden chair, the which they say
The gods stand gazing on when she does ride
To Jove's high house through heaven's brass-paved way,
Drawn of fair peacocks, that excel in pride
And, full of Argus' eyes, their tails dispreaden wide.

But this was drawn of six unequal beasts,
On which her six sage counselors did ride,
Taught to obey their bestial behests,
With like conditions to their kinds[64]applied.

58. formerly
59. densest
60. showed
61. rush
62. robe
63. glittering
64. natures

Of which the first, that all the rest did guide,
Was sluggish Idleness, the nurse of sin.
Upon a slothful ass he chose to ride,
Arrayed in habit black and amis[65] thin,
Like to a holy monk, the service to begin.

And in his hand his portess[66] still he bare,
That much was worn but therein little read;
For of devotion he had little care,
Still drowned in sleep and most of his days dead.
Scarce could he once uphold his heavy head
To looken whether it were night or day.
May seem the wain was very evil led
When such an one had guiding of the way,
That knew not whether right he went or else astray.

From worldly cares himself he did esloin,[67]
And greatly shunnèd manly exercise;
From every work he challenged essoin,[68]
For contemplation sake. Yet otherwise
His life he led in lawless riotize,[69]
By which he grew to grievous malady;
For in his lustless[70] limbs through evil guise,[71]
A shaking fever reigned continually.
Such one was Idleness, first of this company.

And by his side rode loathsome Gluttony,
Deformèd creature, on a filthy swine;
His belly was up-blown with luxury,
And eke[72] with fatness swollen were his eyne,
And like a crane his neck was long and fine,[73]
With which he swallowed up excessive feast,

65. hood
66. breviary
67. withdraw
68. claimed exemption
69. riotousness
70. feeble
71. behavior
72. Also—Ed.
73. *Crane:* whose long throat supposedly allows it the maximum pleasurable contact with its food.

For want whereof poor people oft did pine.[74]
And all the way, most like a brutish beast,
He spewèd up his gorge, that all did him detest.

In green vine leaves he was right fitly clad,
For other clothes he could not wear for heat;
And on his head an ivy garland had,
From under which fast trickled down the sweat.
Still as he rode, he somewhat[75] still did eat,
And in his hand did bear a boozing can,
Of which he supposed so oft that on his seat
His drunken corse he scarce upholden can,
In shape and life more like a monster then a man.

Unfit he was for any worldly thing,
And eke unable once[76] to stir or go,
Not meet to be of counsel to a king,
Whose mind in meat and drink was drownèd so
That from his friend he seldom knew his foe.
Full of diseases was his carcass blue,[77]
And a dry dropsy through his flesh did flow,
Which by misdiet daily greater grew.
Such one was Gluttony, the second of that crew.

And next to him rode lustful Lechery,
Upon a bearded Goat whose rugged hair,
And whally[78] eyes (the sign of jealousy)
Was like the person self[79] whom he did bear;
Who rough and black and filthy did appear,
Unseemly man to please fair lady's eye.
Yet he of ladies oft was lovèd dear,
When fairer faces were bid standen by.
O who does know the bent of women's fantasy?

74. starve
75. something
76. at all
77. livid
78. greenish
79. The very person

In a green gown he clothèd was full fair,
Which underneath did hide his filthiness;
And in his hand a burning hart he bare,
Full of vain follies and newfangledness.[80]
For he was false and fraught with fickleness,
And learnèd had to love with secret looks,
And well could[81] dance, and sing with ruefulness,
And fortunes tell, and read in loving[82] books,
And thousand other ways to bait his fleshly hooks.

Inconstant man, that lovèd all he saw
And lusted after all that he did love;
Ne would his looser life be tied to law,
But joyed weak women's hearts to tempt and prove
If from their loyal loves he might then move.
Which lewdness filled him with reproachful pain
Of that foul evil,[83] which all men reprove,
That rots the marrow and consumes the brain.
Such one was Lechery, the third of all this train.

And greedy Avarice by him did ride
Upon a camel loaden all with gold;
Two iron coffers hung on either side,
With precious metal full as they might hold;
And in his lap an heap of coin he told;[84]
For of his wicked pelf[85] his god he made,
And unto hell himself for money sold.
Accursèd usury was his[86] trade,
And right and wrong alike in equal balance weighed.

His life was nigh unto death's door y-placed,
And threadbare coat and cobbled shoes he ware,
Ne scarce good morsel all his life did taste;
But both from back and belly still did spare

80. novelties
81. Knew how to
82. erotic
83. syphilis
84. counted
85. wealth
86. his only

To fill his bags and richess to compare.[87]
Yet child ne kinsman living had he none
To leave them to; but thorough[88] daily care
To get and nightly fear to lose his own,
He led a wretched life unto himself, unknown.[89]

Most wretched wight, whom nothing might suffice,
Whose greedy lust did lack in greatest store,
Whose need had end, but no end covetise,[90]
Whose wealth was want,[91] whose plenty made him poor,
Who had enough, yet wishèd ever more—
A vile disease. And eke in foot and hand
A grievous gout tormented him full sore,
That well he could not touch, nor go, nor stand.
Such one was Avarice, the fourth of this fair band.

And next to him malicious Envy rode,
Upon a ravenous wolf, and still did chaw
Between his cankered teeth a venomous toad,
That all the poison ran about his chaw.[92]
But inwardly he chawèd his own maw[93]
At neighbors' wealth, that made him ever sad;
For death it was when any good he saw,
And wept that cause of weeping none he had;
But when he heard of harm, he waxèd wondrous glad.

All in a kirtle[94] of discolored say[95]
He clothèd was, y-painted full of eyes;
And in his bosom secretly there lay
An hateful snake, the which his tail upties
In many folds and mortal sting implies.[96]

87. acquire
88. through
89. friendless
90. cupidity
91. poverty
92. jaw
93. guts
94. jacket
95. Many-colored wool
96. covers up

Still as he rode, he gnashed his teeth to see
Those heaps of gold with gripple[97] Covetise,
And grudgèd[98] at the great felicity
Of proud Lucifera and his own company.

He hated all good words and virtuous deeds,
And him no less that any like did use;[99]
And who with gracious bread the hungry feeds,
His alms for want of faith he doth accuse;
So every good to bad he doth abuse.[100]
And eke the verse of famous poets' wit
He does backbite, and spiteful poison spews
From leprous mouth on all that ever writ.
Such one vile Envy was, that fifth in row did sit.

And him beside rides fierce revenging Wrath
Upon a lion loath for to be led;
And in his hand a burning brand[101] he hath,
The which he brandisheth about his head;
His eyes did hurl forth sparkles fiery red,
And starèd stern on all that him beheld,
As ashes pale of hue and seeming dead;
And on his dagger still his hand he held,
Trembling through hasty rage when choler[102] in him swelled.

His ruffian[103] raiment all was stained with blood,
Which he had spilt, and all to rags y-rent,
Through unadvisèd rashness woxen wood;[104]
For of his hands he had no government,
Ne cared for blood in his avengèment.
But when the furious fit was overpassed,
His cruel facts[105] he often would repent;

97. grasping
98. grumbled
99. practice
100. twist
101. sword
102. anger
103. disordered
104. grown insane
105. deeds

Yet willful man, he never would forecast
How many mischiefs should ensue his heedless hast.

Full many mischiefs follow cruel Wrath;
Abhorrèd bloodshed and tumultuous strife,
Unmanly[106] murder and unthrifty scath,[107]
Bitter despite, with rancor's rusty knife,
And fretting grief, the enemy of life.
All these, and many evils mo,[108] haunt ire,
The swelling spleen[109] and frenzy raging rife,
The shaking palsy and Saint Francis' fire.[110]
Such one was Wrath, the last of this ungodly tire.[111]

And after all, upon the wagon beam[112]
Rode Satan, with a smarting whip in hand,
With which he forward lashed the lazy team,
So oft as Sloth still in the mire did stand.
Huge routs of people did about them band,
Shouting for joy; and still before their way
A foggy mist had covered all the land;
And underneath their feet all scattered lay
Dead skulls and bones of men whose life had gone astray.

So forth they marchen in this goodly sort,
To take the solace[113] of the open air,
And in fresh flowering fields themselves to sport;
Amongst the rest rode that false lady fair,
The foul Duessa, next unto the chair
Of proud Lucifer,' as one of the train.
But that good knight would not so nigh repair,

106. Inhuman
107. damage
108. more
109. temper
110. *Saint Francis' fire:* probably St. Anthony's fire, erysipelas.
111. procession
112. shaft
113. pleasure

Himself estranging from their joyance vain,
Whose fellowship seemed far unfit for warlike swain.

Canto X

Her faithful knight fair Una brings
To House of Holiness,
Where he is taught repentance and
The way to heavenly bliss.

What man is he that boasts of fleshly might
And vain assurance of mortality,
Which all so soon as it does come to fight
Against spiritual foes, yields by and by,
Or from the field most cowardly doth fly?
Ne let the man ascribe it to his skill,
That thorough grace hath gainèd victory.
If any strength we have, it is too ill,
But all the good is God's, both power and eke will.

By that which lately happened, Una saw
That this her knight was feeble and too faint,
And all his sinews waxen weak and raw[114]
Through long imprisonment and hard constraint
Which he endurèd in his late restraint,
That yet he was unfit for bloody fight.
Therefore to cherish him with diets daint,[115]
She cast to bring him where he cheeren[116] might,
Till he recurèd[117] had his late decayèd plight.

There was an ancient house not far away,
Renowned throughout the world for sacred lore
And pure unspotted life, so well they say
It governed was and guided evermore,
Through wisdom of a matron grave and hoar,[118]
Whose only joy was to relieve the needs

114. out of condition
115. dainty
116. regain cheerfulness
117. recovered
118. grey-haired

Of wretched souls and help the helpless poor.
All night she spent in saying her beads,[119]
And all the day in doing good and godly deeds.

Dame Caelia[120] men did her call, as thought
From heaven to come or thither to arise,
The mother of three daughters, well upbrought
In goodly thews[121] and godly exercise.
The eldest two, most sober, chaste, and wise—
Fidelia and Speranza[122]—virgins were,
Though spoused, yet wanting wedlock's solemnize;
But fair Charissa[123] to a lovely fere[124]
Was linkèd, and by him had many pledges dear.[125]

Arrivèd there, the door they find fast locked;
For it was warely watchèd night and day
For fear of many foes. But when they knocked,
The porter opened unto them straightway.
He was an aged sire, all hoary gray,
With looks full lowly cast and gait full slow,
Wont on a staff his feeble steps to stay,
Hight Humilta. They pass in stooping low;
For straight and narrow was the way which he did show.

Each goodly thing is hardest to begin.
But entered in, a spacious court they see,
Both plain and pleasant to be walkèd in,
Where them does meet a franklin[126] fair and free,[127]
And entertains with comely courteous glee,
His name was Zeal, that him right well became,
For in his speeches and behavior he

119. prayers

120. *Caelia:* "heavenly"

121. manners

122. *Fidelia and Speranza:* "faith" and "hope"

123. *Charissa:* "charity," "spiritual love," "good works." "And now abideth faith, hope, charity, these three; bu the greatest is charity" (I Corinthians 13:13).

124. mate

125. children

126. landowner

127. gracious

Did labor lively[128] to express the same,
And gladly did them guide till to the hall they came.

There fairly them receives a gentle squire,
Of mild demeanor and rare courtesy,
Right cleanly clad in comely sad[129] attire,
In word and deed that showed great modesty
And knew his good[130] to all of each degree,
Hight Reverence. He them with speeches meet
Does fair entreat;[131] no courting nicety,
But simple true and eke unfeignèd sweet,[132]
As might become a squire so great persons to greet.

And afterwards them to his dame he leads,
That aged dame, the lady of the place,
Who all this while was busy at her beads.
Which done, she up arose with seemly grace
And toward them full matronly did pace.
Where when that fairest Una she beheld,
Whom well she knew to spring from heavenly race,
Her heart with joy unwonted inly swelled,
As feeling wondrous comfort in her weaker eld.[133]

And her embracing said, 'O happy earth,
Whereon thy innocent feet do ever tread,
Most virtuous virgin born of heavenly birth,
That to redeem thy woeful parents' head
From tyrant's rage and ever-dying dread[134]
Hast wandered through the world now long a day,
Yet ceasest not thy weary soles to lead,
What grace hath thee now hither brought this way,
Or done[135] thy feeble feet unweeting[136] hither stray?

128. with animation
129. dark-colored
130. the appropriate behavior
131. converse with
132. sweetness
133. old age
134. continual fear of death
135. do
136. unwittingly

'Strange thing it is an errant knight to see
Here in this place, or any other wight
That hither turns his steps. So few there be
That choose the narrow path or seek the right.
All keep the broad highway and take delight
With many rather for to go astray,
And be partakers of their evil plight,
Than with a few to walk the rightest way.
O foolish men, why haste ye to your own decay?'

'Thyself to see and tired limbs to rest,
O matron sage,' quoth she, 'I hither came,
And this good knight his way with me addressed,
Led with thy praises and broad-blazèd fame,
That up to heaven is blown.' The ancient dame
Him goodly greeted in her modest guise,
And entertained them both, as best became,
With all the court'sies, that she could devise,
Ne wanted aught to show her bounteous or wise.

Thus as they gan of sundry things devise,[137]
Lo, two most goodly virgins came in place;
Y-linked arm in arm in lovely wise,
With countenance demure and modest grace,
They numbered even steps and equal pace.[138]
Of which the eldest, that Fidelia hight,
Like sunny beans threw[139] from her crystal face,
That could have dazed the rash beholder's sight,
And round about her head did shine like heaven's light.

She was arrayèd all in lily white,
And in her right hand bore a cup of gold,
With wine and water filled up to the height,
In which a serpent did himself infold,
That horror made to all that did behold;
But she no whit did change her constant mood.
And in her other hand she fast did hold

137. talk
138. Walked in step
139. Threw beams like the sun's

A book, that was both signed and sealed with blood,[140]
Wherein dark things were writ, hard to be understood.

Her younger sister, that Speranza hight,
Was clad in blue, that her beseemèd well.
Not all so cheerful seemed she of sight[141]
As was her sister; whether dread did dwell,
Or anguish, in her heart, is hard to tell.
Upon her arm a silver anchor lay
Whereon she leanèd ever, as befell;
And ever up to heaven as she did pray,
Her steadfast eyes were bent, ne swervèd other way.

They seeing Una, towards her gan wend,
Who them encounters with like courtesy;
Many kind speeches they between them spend,
And greatly joy each other well to see.
Then to the knight with shamefast[142]modesty
They turn themselves, at Una's meek request,
And him salute with well beseeming glee;[143]
Who fair them quites, as him beseemèd best,
And goodly gan discourse of many a noble gest.[144]

Then Una thus: 'But she your sister dear,
The dear Charissa, where is she become?
Or wants she health, or busy is elsewhere?'
'Ah no,' said they, 'but forth she may not come;
For she of late is lightened of her womb
And hath increased the world with one son more,
That her to see should be but troublesome.'
'Indeed,' quoth she, 'that should her trouble sore,
But thanked be God and her increase so evermore.'

Then said the aged Caelia, 'Dear dame,
And you, good sir, I wot that of your toil
And labors long, through which ye hither came,

140. *Signed and sealed with blood:* The New Testament is signed and sealed with Christ's blood.
141. to look at
142. humble
143. proper gladness
144. deed of arms

Ye both forwearied be; therefore a while
I read[145] you rest and to your bowers recoil.'[146]
Then callèd she a groom that forth him led
Into a goodly lodge, and gan despoil[147]
Of puissant arms and laid in easy bed;
His name was meek Obedience, rightfully aread.[148]

Now when their weary limbs with kindly rest,
And bodies were refreshed with due repast,
Fair Una gan Fidelia fair request,
To have her knight into her schoolhouse placed,
That of her heavenly learning he might taste,
And hear the wisdom of her words divine.
She granted, and that knight so much agraced[149]
That she him taught celestial discipline,[150]
And opened his dull eyes, that light mote in them shine.

And that her sacred book, with blood y-writ,
That none could read except she did them teach,
She unto him disclosèd every whit,
And heavenly documents[151] thereout[152] did preach,
That weaker[153] wit of man could never reach—
Of God, of grace, of justice, of free will—
That wonder was to hear her goodly speech.
For she was able with her words to kill
And raise again to life the heart that she did thrill.[154]

And when she list pour out her larger sprite,[155]
She would command the hasty sun to stay,
Or backward turn his course from heaven's height;

145. advise
146. withdraw
147. undress
148. to tell the truth
149. favored
150. divine laws
151. doctrines
152. from it
153. too weak
154. pierce
155. i.e. spiritual power

Sometimes great hosts of men she could dismay;
Dry-shod to pass, she parts the floods in tway;
And eke huge mountains from their native seat
She would command, themselves to bear away
And throw in raging sea with roaring threat.[156]
Almighty God her gave such power and puissance great.

The faithful knight now grew in little space,
By hearing her and by her sister's lore,
To such perfection of all heavenly grace
That wretched world he gan for to abhor
And mortal life gan loathe, as thing forlore,
Grieved with remembrance of his wicked ways,
And pricked with anguish of his sins so sore,
That he desired to end his wretched days.
So much the dart of sinful guilt the soul dismays.

But wise Speranza gave him comfort sweet
And taught him how to take assurèd hold
Upon her silver anchor, as was meet;
Else had his sins so great and manifold
Made him forget all that Fidelia told.
In this distressèd doubtful agony,
When him his dearest Una did behold—
Disdaining life, desiring leave to die—
She found herself assailed with great perplexity.

And came to Caelia to declare her smart,
Who well acquainted with that common plight
Which sinful horror[157] works in wounded heart,
Her wisely comforted all that she might,
With goodly counsel and advisement right;
And straightaway sent with careful diligence
To fetch a leech,[158] the which had great insight
In that disease of grievèd conscience,
And well could cure the same. His name was Patience.

156. threatening roar

157. horror of sin

158. doctor

Who coming to that soul-diseasèd knight,
Could hardly him intreat to tell his grief.
Which known, and all that noyed[159] his heavy sprite
Well searched,[160] eftsoons he gan apply relief
Of salves and med'cines, which had passing prief,[161]
And thereto added words of wondrous might.
By which, to ease he him recurrèd brief,[162]
And much assuaged the passion[163] of his plight,
That he his pain endured, as seeming now more light.

But yet the cause and root of all his ill,
Inward corruption and infected sin,
Not purged nor healed, behind remainèd still;
And festering sore did rankle yet within,
Close[164] creeping twixt the marrow and the skin.
Which to extirp,[165] he laid him privily
Down in a darksome lowly place far in,
Whereas he meant his corsives[166] to apply,
And with strait[167] diet tame his stubborn malady.

In ashes and sackcloth he did array
His dainty corse, proud humors[168] to abate;
And dieted with fasting every day,
The swelling of his wounds to mitigate;
And made him pray both early and eke late.
And ever as superfluous flesh did rot,
Amendment ready still at hand did wait
To pluck it out with pincers fiery hot,
That soon in him was left no one corrupted jot.

159. troubled
160. probed
161. great power
162. quickly
163. suffering
164. Secretly
165. root out
166. remedies
167. strict
168. passions

And bitter Penance with an iron whip,
Was wont him once to disc'ple every day;
And sharp Remorse his heart did prick and nip,
That drops of blood thence like a well did play;
And sad Repentance usèd to embay[169]
His blameful body in salt water sore,
The filthy blots of sin to wash away.
So in short space they did to health restore
The man that would not live, but erst[170] lay at death's door.

In which his torment often was so great
That like a lion he would cry and roar
And rend his flesh and his own sinews eat.
His own dear Una, hearing evermore
His rueful shrieks and groanings, often tore
Her guiltless garments and her golden hair
For pity of his pain and anguish sore.
Yet all with patience wisely she did bear;
For well she wist, his crime could else be never clear.

Whom thus recovered by wise Patience
And true Repentance, they to Una brought.
Who joyous of his curèd conscience,
Him dearly kissed, and fairly eke besought
Himself to cherish,[171] and consuming thought
To put away out of his careful breast.
By this, Charissa, late in childbed brought,
Was waxen strong and left her fruitful nest;
To her fair Una brought this unacquainted guest.

She was a woman in her freshest age,
Of wondrous beauty and of bounty rare,
With goodly grace and comely personage,
That was on earth not easy to compare;
Full of great love, but Cupid's wanton snare
As hell she hated, chaste in work and will;
Her neck and breasts were ever open bare,

169. bathe
170. before
171. cheer up

That aye thereof her babes might suck their fill;
The rest was all in yellow robes arrayèd still.

A multitude of babes about her hung,
Playing their sports, that joyed her to behold,
Whom still she fed whiles they were weak and young,
But thrust them forth still as they waxèd old.
And on her head she wore a tire[172] of gold,
Adorned with gems and ouches[173] wondrous fair,
Whose passing price uneath[174] was to be told;
And by her side there sat a gentle pair
Of turtle doves, she sitting in an ivory chair.

The knight and Una entering, fair her greet,
And bid her joy of that her happy brood;
Who them requites with court'sies seeming meet,
And entertains with friendly cheerful mood.
Then Una her besought to be so good
As in her virtuous rules to school her knight,
Now after all his torment well withstood,
In that sad house of Penance where his sprite
Had passed the pains of hell and long enduring night.

She was right joyous of her just request,
And taking by the hand that faery's son,
Gan him instruct in every good behest:
Of love, and righteousness, and well to done,[175]
And wrath and hatred warily to shun,
That drew on men God's hatred and his wrath,
And many souls in dolors[176] had foredone.[177]
In which when him she well instructed hath,
From thence to heaven she teacheth him the ready path.

Wherein his weaker wandering steps to guide,
An ancient matron she to her does call,

172. head-dress
173. jewels
174. scarcely
175. right doing
176. misery
177. destroyed

Whose sober looks her wisdom well descried.[178]
Her name was Mercy, well known over all
To be both gracious and eke liberal.
To whom the careful charge of him she gave,
To lead aright, that he should never fall
In all his ways through this wide worldès wave,[179]
That Mercy in the end his righteous soul might save.

The godly matron by the hand him bears
Forth from her presence by a narrow way,
Scattered with bushy thorns and ragged breres,[180]
Which still before him she removed away,
That nothing might his ready passage stay.
And ever when his feet encumbered were,
Or gan to shrink, or from the right to stray,
She held him fast and firmly did upbear,
As careful nurse her child from falling oft does rear.

Eftsoons unto an holy hospital[181]
That was forby[182] the way she did him bring,
In which seven beadmen[183] that had vowèd all
Their life to service of high heaven's King
Did spend their days in doing godly thing.[184]
Their gates to all were open evermore
That by the weary way were traveling,
And one sat waiting ever them before
To call in comers-by that needy were and poor.

The first of them, that eldest was and best,
Of all the house had charge and government,
As guardian and steward of the rest.
His office was to give entertainment
And lodging unto all that came and went—
Not unto such as could him feast again

178. made known
179. expanse
180. briers
181. retreat
182. beside
183. men of prayer
184. service

And double quite[185] for that he on them spent,
But such as want of harbor[186] did constrain.
Those, for God's sake, his duty was to entertain.

The second was as almoner[187]of the place.
His office was the hungry for to feed
And thirsty give to drink, a work of grace.
He feared not once himself to be in need,
Ne cared to hoard for those whom he did breed.[188]
The grace of God he laid up still in store,
Which as a stock he left unto his seed;
He had enough, what need him care for more?
And had he less, yet some he would give to the poor.

The third had of their wardrobe custody,
In which were not rich tires[189] nor garments gay,
The plumes of pride and wings of vanity,
But clothès meet to keep keen cold away
And naked nature seemly to array;
With which, bare wretched wights he daily clad,
The images of God in earthly clay.
And if that no spare cloths to give he had,
His own coat he would cut, and it distribute glad.

The fourth appointed by his office was,
Poor prisoners to relieve with gracious aid,
And captives to redeem with price of brass[190]
From Turks and Saracens, which them had stayed.[191]
And though they faulty were, yet well he weighed,
That God to us forgiveth every hour
Much more than that why[192] they in bands were laid;
And he that harrowed hell with heavy stour
The faulty souls from thence brought to his heavenly bower.

185. repay
186. shelter
187. distributer of alms
188. i.e. his family
189. clothes
190. money
191. detained
192. for which

The fifth had charge sick persons to attend,
And comfort those in point[193] of death which lay;
For them most needeth comfort in the end,
When sin, and hell, and death do most dismay
The feeble soul departing hence away.
All is but lost that, living, we bestow,
If not well ended at our dying day.
O man have mind of that last bitter throe;[194]
For as the tree does fall, so lies it ever low.

The sixth had charge of them now being dead,
In seemly sort their corses to engrave,[195]
And deck with dainty flowers their bridal bed,
That to their heavenly Spouse both sweet and brave[196]
They might appear when he their souls shall save.
The wondrous workmanship of God's own mold,[197]
Whose face he made all beasts to fear, and gave
All in his hand, even dead we honor should.
Ah, dearest God, me grant I dead be not defouled.

The seventh, now after death and burial done,
Had charge the tender orphans of the dead
And widows aid, lest they should be undone.[198]
In face of judgment[199] he their right would plead,
Ne aught the power of mighty men did dread
In their defence, nor would for gold or fee
Be won their rightful causes down to tread.
And when they stood in most necessity,
He did supply their want and gave them ever free.

There when the elfin knight arrivèd was,
The first and chiefest of the seven, whose care
Was guests to welcome, towards him did pass.
Where seeing Mercy, that his steps upbare

193. on the point
194. agony
195. bury
196. splendid
197. image
198. harmed
199. the law of court

And always led, to her with reverence rare
He humbly louted[200] in meek lowliness,
And seemly welcome for her did prepare.
For of their order she was patroness,
Albe[201] Charissa were their chiefest founderess.

There she awhile him stays, himself to rest,
That to the rest[202] more able he might be.
During which time, in every good behest
And godly work of alms and charity
She him instructed with great industry.
Shortly therein so perfect he became
That from the first unto the last degree[203]
His mortal life he learnèd had to frame
In holy righteousness, without rebuke or blame.

Thence forward by that painful way they pass
Forth to an hill that was both steep and high,
On top whereof a sacred chapel was
And eke a little hermitage thereby,
Wherein an aged holy man did lie
That day and night said his devotion,
Ne other worldly business did apply.[204]
His name was Heavenly Contemplation;
Of God and goodness was his meditation.

Great grace that old man to him given had;[205]
For God he often saw from heaven's height,
All[206] were his earthly eyne both blunt[207] and bad,
And through great age had lost their kindly[208] sight,
Yet wondrous quick and presant[209] was his sprite,

200. bowed
201. Although
202. in continuing
203. stage
204. carry on
205. had been given
206. Although
207. dim
208. natural
209. piercing

As eagle's eye that can behold the sun.
That hill they scale with all their power and might,
That his frail thighs nigh weary and fordone
Gan fail, but by her help the top at last he won.

There they do find that godly aged sire,
With snowy locks adown his shoulders shed,
As hoary frost with spangles doth attire
The mossy branches of an oak half dead.
Each bone might through his body well be read
And every sinew seen, through[210] his long fast;
For nought he cared his carcass long unfed;
His mind was full of spiritual repast,
And pined[211] his flesh to keep his body low and chaste.

Who when these two approaching he espied,
At their first presence grew aggrievèd sore,
That forced him lay his heavenly thoughts aside.
And had he not that dame respected more,
Whom highly he did reverence and adore,
He would not once have movèd for the knight.
They him saluted standing far afore;
Who well them greeting, humbly did requite,
And askèd to what end they climb that tedious height.

'What end,' quoth she, 'should cause us take such pain
But that same end which every living wight
Should make his mark high heaven to attain?
Is not from hence the way that leadeth right
To that most glorious house that glistereth bright
With burning stars and everliving fire,
Whereof the keys are to thy hand behight[212]
By wise Fidelia? She doth thee require,
To show it to this knight, according[213] his desire.'

'Thrice happy man,' said then the father grave,
'Whose staggering steps thy steady hand doth lead,

210. as a result of

211. starved

212. entrusted

213. granting

And shows the way his sinful soul to save.
Who better can the way to heaven aread[214]
Then thou thyself that was both born and bred
In heavenly throne, where thousand angels shine?
Thou dost the prayers of the righteous seed
Present before the Majesty Divine,
And his avenging wrath to clemency incline.

'Yet since thou bidst, thy pleasure shall be done.
Then come, thou man of earth, and see the way
That never yet was seen of faery's son,
That never leads the traveler astray,
But after labors long and sad delay,
Brings them to joyous rest and endless bliss.
But first thou must a season fast and pray,
Till from her bands the sprite assoilèd[215] is,
And have her strength recured[216] from frail infirmities.'

That done, he leads him to the highest mount;
Such one as that same mighty man of God,[217]
That blood-red billows like a wallèd front[218]
On either side disparted with his rod
Till that his army dry-foot through them yod,[219]
Dwelt forty days upon. Where, writ in stone
With bloody letters by the hand of God,
The bitter doom[220] of death and baleful moan
He did receive, whiles flashing fire about him shone.

Or like that sacred hill whose head full high,[221]
Adorned with fruitful olives all around,
Is—as it were for endless memory
Of that dear Lord who oft thereon was found—
Forever with a flowering garland crowned;

214. point out
215. released
216. recovered
217. Mount Sinai, where Moses received the severe Mosaic law (Exodus 24 and 34)
218. barrier
219. went
220. judgment
221. The Mount of Olives

Or like that pleasant mount, that is for aye[222]
Through famous poets' verse eachwhere[223] renowned,
On which the thrice three learned ladies play
Their heavenly notes and make full many a lovely lay.

From thence, far off he unto him did shew
A little path that was both steep and long,
Which to a goodly city led his view;
Whose walls and towers were builded high and strong
Of pearl and precious stone, that earthly tongue
Cannot describe, nor wit of man can tell—
Too high a ditty[224] for my simple song.
The City of the Great King hight it well,
Wherein eternal peace and happiness doth dwell.

As he thereon stood gazing, he might see
The blessed angels to and fro descend
From highest heaven, in gladsome company,
And with great joy into that city wend
As commonly[225] as friend does with his friend.
Whereat he wondered much and gan inquere
What stately building durst so high extend
Her lofty towers unto the starry sphere
And what unknowèn nation there empeopled[226] were.

'Fair knight,' quoth he, 'Jerusalem that is,
The New Jerusalem, that God has built
For those to dwell in that are chosen his,
His chosen people purged from sinful guilt
With precious blood, which cruelly was spilt
On cursèd tree, of that unspotted lamb
That for the sins of all the world was kilt.

222. *That pleaseant mount:* Mount Parnassus, the seat of the nine muses. All of these are in fact famous examples of divine inspiration and mystical vision. Although Mount Parnassus may seem anticlimactic after the examples from the Old and New Testaments, Spenser is asserting a doctrine of poetry which renaissance critics took seriously. The doctrine goes back to Plato's *Ion*.

223. everywhere

224. subject

225. familiarly

226. settled

Now are they saints all in that city sam,[227]
More dear unto their God then younglings to their dam.'

'Till now,' said then the knight, 'I weenèd well[228]
That great Cleopolis—where I have been—[229]
In which that fairest Faery Queen doth dwell,
The fairest city was that might be seen;
And that bright tower all built of crystal clear,
Panthea, seemed the brightest thing that was.[230]
But now by proof all otherwise I ween;
For this great city that does far surpass,
And this bright angels' tower quite dims that tower of glass.'

'Most true,' then said the holy aged man;
'Yet is Cleopolis for earthly frame[231]
The fairest piece that eye beholden can.
And well beseems all knights of noble name,
That covet in th' immortal book of fame
To be eternizèd, that same to haunt,
And done their service to that sovereign dame,
That glory does to them for guerdon[232]grant.
For she is heavenly born and heaven may justly vaunt.[233]

'And thou, fair imp, sprung out from English race,
However now accounted elfin's son,
Well worthy dost thy service for her grace,[234]
To aid a virgin desolate fordone.
But when thou famous victory hast won,
And high amongst all knights hast hung thy shield,
Thenceforth the suit[235] of earthly conquest shun,
And wash thy hands from guilt of bloody field.
For blood can nought but sin, and wars but sorrows yield.

227. together

228. was sure

229. *Cleopolis:* the Faeryland equivalent of London.

230. *Panthea:* the Faeryland equivalent of Westminster Abbey, the burial place of Britain's illustrious rulers and heroes.

231. as man-made structures go

232. reward

233. claim as home

234. favor

235. pursuit

'Then seek this path that I to thee presage,
Which after all, to heaven shall thee send;
Then peaceably thy painful pilgrimage
To yonder same Jerusalem do bend,
Where is for thee ordained a blessed end:
For thou amongst those saints, whom thou dost see,
Shalt be a saint, and thine own nation's friend
And patron. Thou Saint George shall callèd be,
Saint George of merry England, the sign of victory.'

'Unworthy wretch,' quoth he, 'of so great grace,
How dare I think such glory to attain?'
'These that have it attained were in like case,'
Quoth he, 'as wretched, and lived in like pain.'
'But deeds of arms must I at last be fain,[236]
And ladies' love to leave so dearly bought?'
'What need of arms where peace doth aye remain,'
Said he, 'and battles none are to be fought?
As for loose loves, they're vain and vanish into nought.'

'O let me not,' quoth he, 'then turn again
Back to the world, whose joys so fruitless are;
But let me here for aye in peace remain,
Or straightway on that last long voyage fare,
That nothing may my present hope impair.'
'That may not be,' said he, 'ne mayst thou yit
Forgo that royal maid's bequeathed care,[237]
Who did her cause into thy hand commit,
Till from her cursèd foe thou have her freely quit.'[238]

'Then shall I soon,' quoth he, 'so God me grace,
Abet[239] that virgin's cause disconsolate,
And shortly back return unto this place
To walk this way in pilgrim's poor estate.
But now aread, old father, why of late

236. willing
237. trouble
238. released entirely
239. Support

Didst thou behight[240] me born of English blood,
Whom all a faery's son done nominate?"[241]
'That word[242] shall I,' said he, 'avouchen[243] good,
Sith to thee is unknown the cradle of thy brood.

'For well I wot, thou springst from ancient race
Of Saxon kings, that have with mighty hand
And many bloody battles fought in place[244]
High reared their royal throne in Britons' land,
And vanquished them unable to withstand.
From thence a faery thee unweeting reft,[245]
There as thou slepst in tender swadling band,
And her base elfin brood there for thee left.
Such, men do changelings call, so changed by faery's theft.

'Thence she thee brought into this Faeryland,
And in an heapèd furrow did thee hide,
Where thee a plowman all unweeting fand,[246]
As he his toilsome team that way did guide,
And brought thee up in plowman's state to bide,
Whereof Georgos he thee gave to name.
Till pricked with courage and thy force's pride,
To faery court thou came'st to seek for fame,
And prove thy puissant arms, as seems thee best became.'

'O holy sire,' quoth he, 'how shall I quite
The many favors I with thee have found,
That hast my name and nation read[247] aright,
And taught the way that does to heaven bound?'[248]
This said, adown he lookèd to the ground
To have returned, but dazèd were his eyne,

240. call
241. do call
242. i.e. "English"
243. prove
244. there
245. secretly stole
246. unexpectedly found
247. told
248. go

Through passing[249] brightness, which did quite confound
His feeble sense and too exceeding shine.
So dark are earthly things compared to things divine.

At last whenas himself he gan to find,
To Una back he cast him to retire,
Who him awaited still with pensive mind.
Great thanks and goodly meed[250] to that good sire
He thence departing gave for his pain's hire.[251]
So came to Una, who him joyed to see,
And after little rest gan him desire
Of her adventure mindful for to be.
So leave they take of Caelia, and her daughters three.

249. surpassing
250. gift
251. reward

PART V

The Tradition Extended

The last three hundred years or so have brought a further modification of the virtues and vices tradition. While some past trajectories have fizzled out, others have continued, expanded, and grown. The divine-endowment tradition seems much less vital than it once was, especially with the decline of the aristocracy, the Reformation's democratization of religious authority, and the general decline of religious institutions. Images of the virtues in royal palaces only earn a tourist's passing glance, but those same tourists may debate the virtues and vices of our replacement aristocrats: celebrities. Something about our culture still looks for virtue in powerful and talented people, but we are nevertheless fascinated, like onlookers at a car accident, when we observe their vices. In addition, our culture still seems to hold to certain elements of the "Contraries Cure Contraries" trajectory. The strongest evidence for this might be some practices in modern penance: addiction rehabilitation. The promise of such rehabilitation is that healthy patterns can erase and replace unhealthy ones. A journey through contemporary rehab is not unlike leaving Spenser's House of Pride and entering the House of Holiness, or traveling up Dante's grueling mountain of Purgatory.

Three trajectories that develop and expand the tradition merit further exploration: The Struggle III, the Virtues and Vices in Everyday Life and Death II, and the Vitality of Vice II.

THE STRUGGLE III

Benjamin Franlkin and Oscar Rejlander most clearly engage the continually developing Struggle trajectory of the virtues and vices tradition. Franklin's *Autobiography* shows his best rational attempt to codify, systematize, and implement the virtues. His approach reflects an Enlightenment modification and implementation of the tradition, and his failure may be the most important addition that he made to that tradition. Oscar Rejlander's contribution is not personal but artistic. In 1857 Rejlander created *The Two Ways of Life* (Figure 28). This allegorical work is a montage print that combines thirty-two different images, and it was an incredible technical feat in its time. Thematically, the work follows the choice of Hercules tradition. At the center, framed by the arched doorway, a bearded patriarch leads one son by the hand toward the right, the way of virtue, while cautioning the other son, who hears the left-side's siren call of vice. On the side of virtue are images of piety, penance, study, industry, acts of mercy, and family. Images of the way of vice include seductive women, revelers, gamblers, and wasters like the female figure intemperately emptying a vessel. The veiled nude figure in the foreground could represent Repentance or the artistic convention of Truth. The work was accused of indecency, a charge that largely faded after Queen Victoria bought a copy for Prince Albert.

Rejlander's *The Two Ways of Life* clearly wants to warn and educate those, especially the young, in the struggle between virtue and vice. Education has been central to the struggle since Plato, Aristotle, and Cicero; in Prudentius and Evagrius; in medieval speculum, plays, and sermons; in Brueghel's prints and in Spenser's *The Faerie Queene*. Pedagogy and the struggle between virtue and vice continue today in places like censorship structures as well as Boy Scout and Girl Scout programs. The listed virtues in the Boy Scout and Girl Scout Law statements are perhaps the clearest contemporary extensions of the tradition.

Another strong contemporary element of the struggle trajectory, and one that goes back to *Piers Plowman*, is the powerful element of satire in the arts that engages the tradition. Kurt Weill and Bertolt Brecht's *The Seven Deadly Sins* is a brilliant exploration of how capitalism turns virtue to vice. Prints by artists like Chagall and Ensor, and works like Otto Dix's *Seven Deadly Sins* use the tradition to critique vice in the present. Many of the Mexican Muralists like Diego Rivera use satirical images of the powerful to show their vices, while images of the workers convey their virtue. Finally, Paul Cadmus's powerful images of vice exaggerate and satirize those moral sicknesses in ways that make them strange, yet strangely familiar.

THE VIRTUES AND VICES IN EVERYDAY LIFE AND IN DEATH II

Historically, it was the need for virtuous government (and citizens) and the desire to connect with God that made the virtues and vices an important part of everyday life. They occupied the thoughts of philosophers, prophets, patriarchs, matriarchs, and monks; showed people what to embrace and what to avoid; and were images on religious and political objects. The need to educate people so that they could confess their sins or vices reinforced the place of the virtues and vices, bringing them to the fore in sermons and edifying stories. With the waning of confession came an increase in mass-produced images of the virtues and vices, and defining their role in the diagnostics and improvement of the soul became a personal activity. Benjamin Franklin's *Autobiography* shows this shift from religious confession in search of divine absolution to personal exploration in search of self-improvement.

Two other works of art show a continuity of another aspect of this trajectory. Leo Tolstoy's *The Death of Ivan Ilyich* traces the moral and physical decay of its title character. Ivan's reflections on his life reveal his decline into lust, pride, envy, anger, and greed. Against his conformity to the moral lassitude of his social class stands the compassionate and virtuous servant Gerasim. Faced with death, Ivan discovers how his life had been one of vice and comes to embrace some virtue and forgiveness. Tolstoy's story is a compelling addition to the tradition of how the reality of death can inspire a virtuous life, a tradition exemplified by More's *The Last Things* and Bosch's *The Seven Deadly Sins and the Four Last Things.*

Arthur Miller's *Death of a Salesman*, in a similar way, engages this trajectory. Miller's work can be seen as an inheritor of the tradition of Hildegard's *Ordo Virtutum*, but instead of revealing the redemptive workings of virtue, it shows the all too common and even mundane mechanics of vice. The characters demonstrate how pride, envy, anger, sloth, lust, greed, and gluttony or overindulgence can be subtle, pervasive, and even seemingly permissible elements of everyday life. The cautionary death of the play's "everyman" is just the final logical consequence or step in his vicious undoing.

THE VITALITY OF VICE II

Tolstoy's and Miller's reflections on virtue, vice, and death cast vice as a sickness that is at least difficult to cure if not fatal. The notion of vice in Weill and Brecht's *The Seven Deadly Sins* is far more complicated and interesting. As I mentioned previously, these committed Marxists show how capitalism turns virtues like integrity, anger at social injustice, dignity, and modesty into vices. To the degree that these qualities prevent someone from complete submission or subordination to capitalism's "God Money," these are vices, while anything we would otherwise call a vice, if it is sanctioned by market conditions, becomes a virtue.

Weill and Brecht reveal that virtue and vice are moral codes tied to larger worlviews. When thinkers like Friederich Nietzsche question prevailing worldviews, they also bring into question virtue and vice. Nietzsche extends and modifies the ideas of the "vitality" of vice as developed by people like Machiavelli, exploring how certain notions of virtue and vice may be based on resentment, cowardice, and fear. Nietzsche's critique has since been expanded by other thinkers who examine how racism and sexism could be built into these moral codes. From this perspective, some notions of virtue and vice may work to reinforce forms of privilege and oppression in subtle and not so subtle ways. Such an idea raises again the nightmarish vision of sheep being led to the slaughter, and we may not know who is being led and who is doing the slaughtering, either actively or tacitly.

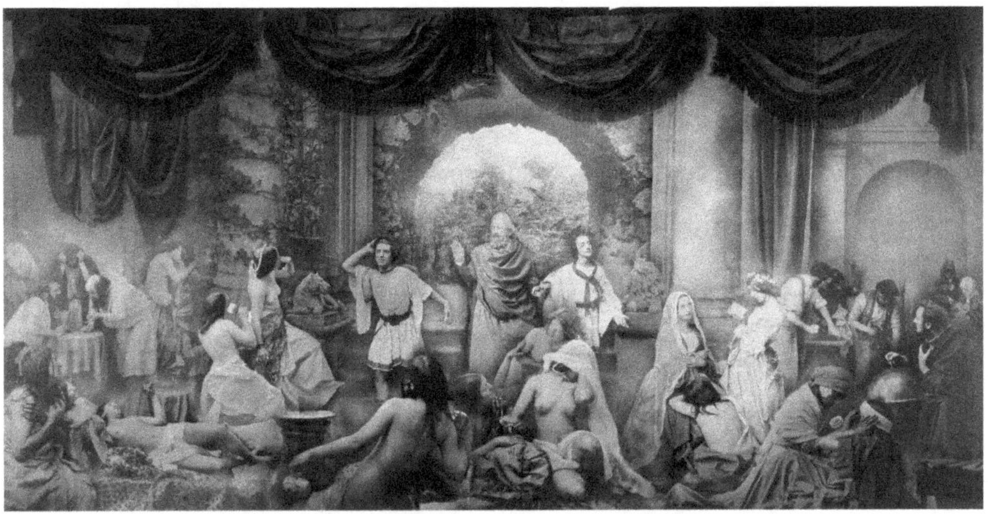

Figure 28. Oscar Gustave Rejlander, 1857: *Two Ways of Life*.
Composite photograph. Royal Photographic Society, Bradford, Great Britain.
Photo Credit: SSPL/National Media Museum / Art Resource, NY.

BENJAMIN FRANKLIN'S *AUTOBIOGRAPHY*

Introduction

Benjamin Franklin invented many things, but he did not invent self-help, Deism, or the Enlightenment. He did not invent the particular American combination of all of these elements with fierce individualism and self-confidence. He did not invent any of these cultural forces, but his *Autobiography* succinctly and powerfully combines them to provide a seminal exploration of the virtues and vices.

If Benjamin Franklin did not invent self-help, he at least seems to have developed it deeply enough to have seen its limitations. The second section of his *Autobiography* begins with two letters, and the remainder of the section is an extended, indirect reply. Both of these letters were written by friends who had read what came to be the book's first section. These letters praise Franklin for what he had put in writing, and strongly encourage him to continue, emphasizing that his work will, in an entertaining way, encourage the virtuous character development of those who read it, and especially the young. The second letter comments that the work will have a personal and a public importance, as it will improve "the features of private character, and consequently of aiding all happiness both public and domestic."[1]

The heavy praise these letters heap on Franklin and on the work he would produce creates an interesting tension with the remainder of the section. The letters say,

1. Benjamin Franklin, *Autobiography* (London: Trübner, 1868), 199.

in essence, "Franklin, you're a virtuous man who is going to tell us all how you did it, so that everyone, and especially the youth, can do the same." A lesser writer, some hack self-help charlatan on a daytime talk show, would have given us something very different from what Franklin wrote. What Franklin says is that he tried it, it seemed like a well-founded and promising plan, and although it was worth trying, it failed.

Franklin had made it known that he would put together a work on the Art of Virtue. We can presume that this would be one of the fruits of his "bold and arduous project of arriving at moral perfection." This project is not spurred by penitential or purgatorial motivations to remove vices from his character; rather it is a moral experiment, a self-help plan developed from his Deist view of God and his self-confidence born of faith in the power of reason. Franklin the Deist does not pray to a miraculous or personal or directly intervening God but instead invokes the Powerful Goodness. He does not seek a Christ who redeems but a "merciful guide" who leads. Surely, he surmised, if he was sufficiently attentive to reason, his rational faculty could overcome what he called "inclination": the propensity to ignore the guidance of reason.

But Franklin the Enlightenment scientist of the soul is humble and honest enough to see the data. What the data reveal is that he failed. Franklin goes so far as to graph the whole project out, transferring his data to different marking systems and trying to make sense of it. In the end he finds that at least with one of his proposed virtues, order, he is incorrigible. And while the noble experiment had some good results, Franklin concludes that he had more faults than he anticipated and that inclination too often trumped reason. After we read about Franklin's best laid plans, it is interesting to hear him try to come to grips with why his plan did not work. He notes his few successes, gives an analogy about preferring a speckled axe to a bright and clean one, and finishes with a discussion of pride. Reading Franklin carefully is to see the Enlightenment promise of character development, to see its best methods employed, and to see the ironic results. Franklin's *Autobiography* is self-help's example and warning.

From Franklin's *Autobiography*[2]

It was about this time I conceived the bold and arduous project of arriving at moral perfection. I wished to live without committing any fault at any time; I would conquer all that either natural inclination, custom, or company might lead me into. As I knew, or thought I knew, what was right and wrong, I did not see why I might not always do the one and avoid the other. But I soon found I had undertaken a task of more difficulty than I had imagined. While my care was employed in guarding against one fault, I was often surprised by another; habit took the advantage of inattention; inclination was sometimes too strong for reason. I concluded at length that the mere speculative conviction that it was our interest to be completely virtuous was not sufficient

2. Ibid., 213–30. The spelling has been modernized.

to prevent our slipping; and that the contrary habits must be broken, and good ones acquired and established before we can have any dependence on a steady, uniform rectitude of conduct. For this purpose I therefore contrived the following method.

In the various enumerations of the moral virtues I had met with in my reading, I found the catalogue more or less numerous, as different writers included more or fewer ideas under the same name. Temperance, for example, was by some confined to eating and drinking; while by others it was extended to mean the moderating every other pleasure, appetite, inclination, or passion, bodily or mental, even to our avarice and ambition. I proposed to myself, for the sake of clearness, to use rather more names, with fewer ideas annexed to each, than a few names with more ideas; and I included under thirteen names of virtues all that at that time occurred to me as necessary or desirable, and annexed to each a short precept, which fully expressed the extent I gave to its meaning.

These names of virtues, with their precepts, were:

1. TEMPERANCE.—Eat not to dullness; drink not to elevation.
2. SILENCE—Speak not but what may benefit others or yourself; avoid trifling conversation.
3. ORDER—Let all your things have their places; let each part of your business have its time.
4. RESOLUTION—Resolve to perform what you ought; perform without fail what you resolve.
5. FRUGALITY—Make no expense but to do good to others or yourself; that is, waste nothing.
6. INDUSTRY—Lose no time; be always employed in something useful; cut off all unnecessary actions.
7. SINCERITY—Use no hurtful deceit; think innocently and justly; and, if you speak, speak accordingly.
8. JUSTICE—Wrong none by doing injuries or omitting the benefits that are your duty.
9. MODERATION—Avoid extremes; forbear resenting injuries so much as you think they deserve.
10. CLEANLINESS—Tolerate no uncleanliness in body, clothes, or habitation.
11. TRANQUILLITY—Be not disturbed at trifles or at accidents common or unavoidable.
12. CHASTITY—Rarely use venery but for health or offspring, never to dulness, weakness, or the injury of your own or another's peace or reputation.
13. HUMILITY—Imitate Jesus and Socrates.

My intention being to acquire the habitude of all these virtues, I judged it would be well not to distract my attention by attempting the whole at once, but to fix it on one of them at a time; and, when I should be master of that, then to proceed to another, and so on, till I should have gone through the thirteen; and, as the previous acquisition of some might facilitate the acquisition of certain others, I arranged them with that view, as they stand above. Temperance first, as it tends to procure that coolness and clearness of head, which is so necessary where constant vigilance was to be kept up, and guard maintained against the unremitting attraction of ancient habits, and the force of perpetual temptations. This being acquired and established, Silence would be more easy; and my desire being to gain knowledge at the same time that I improved in virtue, and considering that in conversation it was obtained rather by the use of the ears than of the tongue, and therefore wishing to break a habit I was getting into of prattling, punning, and joking, which only made me acceptable to trifling company, I gave Silence the second place. This and the next, Order, I expected would allow me more time for attending to my project and my studies. Resolution, once become habitual, would keep me firm in my endeavors to obtain all the subsequent virtues; Frugality and Industry freeing me from my remaining debt, and producing affluence and independence, would make more easy the practice of Sincerity and Justice, etc., etc. Conceiving then, that, agreeably to the advice of Pythagoras in his Golden Verses, daily examination would be necessary, I contrived the following method for conducting that examination.

I made a little book, in which I allotted a page for each of the virtues. I ruled each page with red ink, so as to have seven columns, one for each day of the week, marking each column with a letter for the day. I crossed these columns with thirteen red lines, marking the beginning of each line with the first letter of one of the virtues, on which line, and in its proper column, I might mark, by a little black spot, every fault I found upon examination to have been committed respecting that virtue upon that day.[3]
I determined to give a week's strict attention to each of the virtues successively. Thus, in the first week, my great guard was to avoid every the least offence against Temperance, leaving the other virtues to their ordinary chance, only marking every evening the faults of the day. Thus, if in the first week I could keep my first line, marked T, clear of spots, I supposed the habit of that virtue so much strengthened and its opposite weakened, that I might venture extending my attention to include the next, and for the following week keep both lines clear of spots. Proceeding thus to the last, I could go thro' a course compleat in thirteen weeks, and four courses in a year. And like him who, having a garden to weed, does not attempt to eradicate all the bad herbs at once, which would exceed his reach and his strength, but works on one of the beds at a time, and, having accomplished the first, proceeds to a second, so I should have, I hoped, the encouraging pleasure of seeing on my pages the progress I made in virtue,

3. Franklin included a small chart patterned after the one here described, and, as it is well described, is not reproduced here.

by clearing successively my lines of their spots, till in the end, by a number of courses, I should be happy in viewing a clean book, after a thirteen weeks' daily examination.

This my little book had for its motto these lines from Addison's *Cato*:

> "Here will I hold. If there's a power above us
> (And that there is all nature cries aloud
> Thro' all her works), He must delight in virtue;
> And that which he delights in must be happy."

Another from Cicero,

> "O vitae Philosophia dux! O virtutum indagatrix expultrixque vitiorum! Unus dies, bene et ex praeceptis tuis actus, peccanti immortalitati est anteponendus."[4]

Another from the Proverbs of Solomon, speaking of wisdom or virtue:

> "Length of days is in her right hand, and in her left hand riches and honor. Her ways are ways of pleasantness, and all her paths are peace."(3:16–17)

And conceiving God to be the fountain of wisdom, I thought it right and necessary to solicit his assistance for obtaining it; to this end I formed the following little prayer, which was prefixed to my tables of examination, for daily use.

> "O powerful Goodness! bountiful Father! merciful Guide! Increase in me that wisdom which discovers my truest interest. Strengthen my resolutions to perform what that wisdom dictates. Accept my kind offices to thy other children as the only return in my power for thy continual favors to me."

I used also sometimes a little prayer which I took from Thomson's Poems, viz.:

> "Father of light and life, thou Good Supreme!
> O teach me what is good; teach me Thyself!
> Save me from folly, vanity, and vice,
> From every low pursuit; and fill my soul
> With knowledge, conscious peace, and virtue pure;
> Sacred, substantial, never-fading bliss!"

The precept of Order requiring that every part of my business should have its allotted time, one page in my little book contained the following scheme of employment for the twenty-four hours of a natural day:[5]

I entered upon the execution of this plan for self-examination, and continued it with occasional intermissions for some time. I was surprised to find myself so much fuller of faults than I had imagined; but I had the satisfaction of seeing them diminish.

4. These lines can be translated: O philosophy, life's guide! O searcher of virtues and expeller of vices! One day, well and in accordance with your commands, to a sinful immortality is to be preferred.

5. Here again Franklin reproduces a page from his planner to describe his orderly daily schedule. That planner diagram is not reproduced here.

To avoid the trouble of renewing now and then my little book, which, by scraping out the marks on the paper of old faults to make room for new ones in a new course, became full of holes, I transferred my tables and precepts to the ivory leaves of a memorandum book, on which the lines were drawn with red ink, that made a durable stain, and on those lines I marked my faults with a black-lead pencil, which marks I could easily wipe out with a wet sponge. After a while I went thro' one course only in a year, and afterward only one in several years, till at length I omitted them entirely, being employed in voyages and business abroad, with a multiplicity of affairs that interfered; but I always carried my little book with me.

My scheme of Order gave me the most trouble; and I found that, tho' it might be practicable where a man's business was such as to leave him the disposition of his time, that of a journeyman printer, for instance, it was not possible to be exactly observed by a master, who must mix with the world, and often receive people of business at their own hours. Order, too, with regard to places for things, papers, etc., I found extreamly difficult to acquire. I had not been early accustomed to it, and, having an exceeding good memory, I was not so sensible of the inconvenience attending want of method. This article, therefore, cost me so much painful attention, and my faults in it vexed me so much, and I made so little progress in amendment, and had such frequent relapses, that I was almost ready to give up the attempt, and content myself with a faulty character in that respect, like the man who, in buying an ax of a smith, my neighbor, desired to have the whole of its surface as bright as the edge. The smith consented to grind it bright for him if he would turn the wheel; he turned, while the smith pressed the broad face of the ax hard and heavily on the stone, which made the turning of it very fatiguing. The man came every now and then from the wheel to see how the work went on, and at length would take his ax as it was, without farther grinding. "No," said the smith, "turn on, turn on; we shall have it bright by-and-by; as yet, it is only speckled." "Yes," said the man, "but I think I like a speckled ax best." And I believe this may have been the case with many, who, having, for want of some such means as I employed, found the difficulty of obtaining good and breaking bad habits in other points of vice and virtue, have given up the struggle, and concluded that "a speckled ax was best"; for something, that pretended to be reason, was every now and then suggesting to me that such extream nicety as I exacted of myself might be a kind of foppery in morals, which, if it were known, would make me ridiculous; that a perfect character might be attended with the inconvenience of being envied and hated; and that a benevolent man should allow a few faults in himself, to keep his friends in countenance.

In truth, I found myself incorrigible with respect to Order; and now I am grown old, and my memory bad, I feel very sensibly the want of it. But, on the whole, tho' I never arrived at the perfection I had been so ambitious of obtaining, but fell far short of it, yet I was, by the endeavor, a better and a happier man than I otherwise should have been if I had not attempted it; as those who aim at perfect writing by imitating the engraved copies, tho' they never reach the wished-for excellence of those copies, their hand is mended by the endeavor, and is tolerable while it continues fair and legible.

It may be well my posterity should be informed that to this little artifice, with the blessing of God, their ancestor owed the constant felicity of his life, down to his 79th year, in which this is written. What reverses may attend the remainder is in the hand of Providence; but, if they arrive, the reflection on past happiness enjoyed ought to help his bearing them with more resignation. To Temperance he ascribes his long-continued health, and what is still left to him of a good constitution; to Industry and Frugality, the early easiness of his circumstances and acquisition of his fortune, with all that knowledge that enabled him to be a useful citizen, and obtained for him some degree of reputation among the learned; to Sincerity and Justice, the confidence of his country, and the honorable employs it conferred upon him; and to the joint influence of the whole mass of the virtues, even in the imperfect state he was able to acquire them, all that evenness of temper, and that cheerfulness in conversation, which makes his company still sought for, and agreeable even to his younger acquaintance. I hope, therefore, that some of my descendants may follow the example and reap the benefit.

It will be remarked that, tho' my scheme was not wholly without religion, there was in it no mark of any of the distinguishing tenets of any particular sect. I had purposely avoided them; for, being fully persuaded of the utility and excellency of my method, and that it might be serviceable to people in all religions, and intending some time or other to publish it, I would not have any thing in it that should prejudice any one, of any sect, against it. I purposed writing a little comment on each virtue, in which I would have shown the advantages of possessing it, and the mischiefs attending its opposite vice; and I should have called my book The Art of Virtue, because it would have shown the means and manner of obtaining virtue, which would have distinguished it from the mere exhortation to be good, that does not instruct and indicate the means, but is like the apostle's man of verbal charity, who only without showing to the naked and hungry how or where they might get clothes or victuals, exhorted them to be fed and clothed (see James 2:15–16).

But it so happened that my intention of writing and publishing this comment was never fulfilled. I did, indeed, from time to time, put down short hints of the sentiments, reasonings, etc., to be made use of in it, some of which I have still by me; but the necessary close attention to private business in the earlier part of thy life, and public business since, have occasioned my postponing it; for, it being connected in my mind with a great and extensive project, that required the whole man to execute, and which an unforeseen succession of employs prevented my attending to, it has hitherto remained unfinished.

In this piece it was my design to explain and enforce this doctrine, that vicious actions are not hurtful because they are forbidden, but forbidden because they are hurtful, the nature of man alone considered; that it was, therefore, every one's interest to be virtuous who wished to be happy even in this world; and I should, from this circumstance (there being always in the world a number of rich merchants, nobility, states, and princes, who have need of honest instruments for the management of their affairs, and such being so rare), have endeavored to convince young persons that no qualities were so likely to make a poor man's fortune as those of probity and integrity.

My list of virtues contained at first but twelve; but a Quaker friend having kindly informed me that I was generally thought proud; that my pride showed itself frequently in conversation; that I was not content with being in the right when discussing any point, but was overbearing, and rather insolent, of which he convinced me by mentioning several instances; I determined endeavoring to cure myself, if I could, of this vice or folly among the rest, and I added Humility to my list, giving an extensive meaning to the word.

I cannot boast of much success in acquiring the reality of this virtue, but I had a good deal with regard to the appearance of it. I made it a rule to forbear all direct contradiction to the sentiments of others, and all positive assertion of my own. I even forbid myself, agreeably to the old laws of our Junto, the use of every word or expression in the language that imported a fixed opinion, such as certainly, undoubtedly, etc., and I adopted, instead of them, I conceive, I apprehend, or I imagine a thing to be so or so; or it so appears to me at present. When another asserted something that I thought an error, I denyed myself the pleasure of contradicting him abruptly, and of showing immediately some absurdity in his proposition; and in answering I began by observing that in certain cases or circumstances his opinion would be right, but in the present case there appeared or seemed to me some difference, etc. I soon found the advantage of this change in my manner; the conversations I engaged in went on more pleasantly. The modest way in which I proposed my opinions procured them a readier reception and less contradiction; I had less mortification when I was found to be in the wrong, and I more easily prevailed with others to give up their mistakes and join with me when I happened to be in the right.

And this mode, which I at first put on with some violence to natural inclination, became at length so easy, and so habitual to me, that perhaps for these fifty years past no one has ever heard a dogmatical expression escape me. And to this habit (after my character of integrity) I think it principally owing that I had early so much weight with my fellow-citizens when I proposed new institutions, or alterations in the old, and so much influence in public councils when I became a member; for I was but a bad speaker, never eloquent, subject to much hesitation in my choice of words, hardly correct in language, and yet I generally carried my points.

In reality, there is, perhaps, no one of our natural passions so hard to subdue as pride. Disguise it, struggle with it, beat it down, stifle it, mortify it as much as one pleases, it is still alive, and will every now and then peep out and show itself; you will see it, perhaps, often in this history; for, even if I could conceive that I had compleatly overcome it, I should probably be proud of my humility.

FRIEDRICH NIETZSCHE'S *BEYOND GOOD AND EVIL* AND *THE ANTICHRIST*

Introduction

Whenever I notice that my mood is particularly bad, when I find myself growing grim about the mouth and bringing up the rear of every funeral I meet, I try to picture Nietzsche coaching a young soccer team. Nothing puts a smile on my face more quickly than the thought of his burning eyes and oversized moustache and his shouts of "Get the ball! "Play tough!" and "Stop bunching up!" And thinking of Nietzsche at the team party, some all-you-can-eat pizza buffet where he's passing out team pictures and trophies, makes me laugh out loud.

Given the opportunity, I think that I would be happy to have Friedrich Nietzsche coach my daughter's soccer team. I can imagine that, as the coach, he would have them practice hard and scrimmage against teams that were bigger and better. After the game, he would not let them get away with saying things like, "Well, they're bigger than us," or "We lost, but it was a moral victory." And every season he would inevitably have a game where a girl would get hit by a hard shot or kicked in the leg. He would look carefully, but I doubt he would do anything. He would not yell or run onto the field, and he would discourage parents from going out onto the field as well. After a minute or so, she'd get up, walk it off, and he'd call her name, clap a couple of times, tell her that she's doing a good job and that she needs to keep playing hard. What might make Nietzsche a good coach would be the way he encourages players to be successful, capable, and powerful.

In Nietzsche's writings there is an emphasis on *virtu*, on power, ability, and, to use the old gendered language, manliness. Nietzsche's contribution to the virtues and vices tradition is not a direct engagement. He does not write about any specific lists of virtues or vices or sins, yet much of his writing offers an important and influential critique and expansion of this tradition. Nietzsche's critique is leveled both at institutions like religion, contemporary morality and culture, and philosophy as well as at a more fundamental examination of what he sees as the core values of such institutions. What Nietzsche sees in these values and the institutions that forward them is a world that is topsy-turvy, a world where virtue is called vice and vice is upheld as a virtue.

For Nietzsche, the virtues are character traits or habits of thinking that encourage a sense of power in an individual; vices, on the other hand, rob one of power. Three particularly pernicious vices are resentment, cowardice, and pity. Nietzsche points his most scathing criticism at what he sees as "decadence-values," or traits and thinking patterns that promote decay and loss instead of vibrancy and life. Resentment is at the root of values that destroy life instead of encouraging it. The first excerpt included here is from Nietzsche's section on "The Natural History of Morals" in his book *Beyond Good and Evil*. This quote refers to Nietzsche's view that Jewish resentment of Egyptians and others led them to call evil those things associated with power and success and to call good those things associated with failure. In the same work, Nietzsche calls for a courageous honesty, an honesty that requires one to be every vigilant and hard, especially against the intellectual softness and laxity of his age.

Nietzsche puts forward the idea that there has been a switching of values, what he calls an inversion or a transvaluation of values. This idea of a flipping of values is a key part of Nietzsche's criticism of Christianity in the excerpts from *The Antichrist*. Nietzsche sees in these values resentment on the part of the weak, the poor, and the failures. Since such people cannot have power and control, they designate as evil everything associated with what they cannot have. They simultaneously elevate everything that they are forced to embrace, calling failure and poverty holy and virtuous. When Nietzsche sees the Judeo-Christian emphasis on the other world or God or the true life, he sees the resentment of losers who elevate "loserhood" to place themselves above the true winners in the world.

Just as the world of topsy-turvy values originates in resentment, so do degenerate and "loser" values like cowardice and pity perpetuate that world. When the weak and hopeless look forward to the beyond instead of the here and now, they fearfully seek to escape their own failure. They call their cowardice faith and their fear hope. For Nietzsche even values like love or charity can be decadent values, especially when they take the guise of pity. To pity is to encourage weakness and dependence. Pitying robs or attempts to rob people of power by telling them that they cannot, that they should not, and that they are better off not striving here and now so that they can get some far-off reward. And that reward will come while the seemingly successful suffer.

Nietzsche gives history and society as examples of his principles. I use soccer. A coach's overreaction when something commonplace happens conveys to players that getting kicked or hit by the ball are unusual or terrible things; such a reaction leasd players to believe that they are really injured (when they are not) and that the game is very dangerous (when it is not). Such pity from a soccer coach thus robs the players of power. Coaches who make excuses for players or their teams, or who even allow players to make excuses, communicate to them that this failure is some special case, that it is somehow illegitimate. Forthright coaches, by contrast, show how failures can reveal weaknesses. It is only teams and players that can be honest about failures and weaknesses who can then turn them into strengths.

Nietzsche's ideas about virtue and vice, like just about everything associated with him, are controversial. Where Nietzsche clearly identifies a sort of pride and envy in virtue's resentment, is he really accurate in identifying such resentment as the core of Judeo-Christian ethics? Is faith really just a whitewashed version of cowardice and hope a cover for fear? And what exactly does Nietzsche have in mind when he talks about the *virtu* of the instinct for growth? Does such an instinct have a relation with ideals like compassion and empathy, or are these ideals to be tossed out with pity? What is one's responsibility to others? Could Nietzsche's diatribe be a caustic defense of selfishness, narcissism, and the most destructive and isolating pride? We can even ask these questions in light of this introduction's overall framework: what kind of coach would Nietzsche really be? Would he bench or kick off the team the weaklings instead of pitying them? Would he want to win at all costs? Would winning really be about the success of players and about their empowerment, or would winning be about his success and his feeling of power? Nietzsche's contribution to our notion of virtue and vice proposes many answers to innovative questions at the same time that it raises new questions.

195 from "The Natural History of Morals," from *Beyond Good and Evil*[6]

The Jews–a people "born for slavery," as Tacitus and the whole ancient world say of them; "the chosen people among nations," as they themselves say and believe—the Jews performed a miracle of the inversion of valuations, by means of which life on earth obtained a new and dangerous charm for a couple of millenniums. Their prophets fused into one the expressions "rich," "godless," "evil," "violent," "sensual," and for the first time coined the word "world" as a term of reproach. In this inversion of valuations (in which is also included the use of the word "poor" as synonymous with "saint" and "friend") the significance of the Jewish people is to be found; it is with them that the slave-insurrection in morals commences.

227 from "Our Virtues," from *Beyond Good and Evil*

Honesty, granting that it is the virtue of which we cannot rid ourselves, we free spirits—well, we will labour at it with all our perversity and love, and not tire of "perfecting" ourselves in *our* virtue, which alone remains: may its glance some day overspread like a gilded, blue, mocking twilight this aging civilization with its dull gloomy seriousness! And if, nevertheless, our honesty should one day grow weary, and sigh, and stretch its limbs, and find us too hard, and would fain have it pleasanter, easier, and gentler, like an agreeable vice, let us remain *hard*, we latest Stoics, and let us send to its help whatever devilry we have in us:—our disgust at the clumsy and undefined, our "*nitimur in vetitum*,"[7] our love of adventure, our sharpened and fastidious curiosity, our most subtle, disguised, intellectual Will to Power and universal conquest, which rambles and roves avidiously around all the realms of the future—let us go with all our "devils" to the help of our "God"! It is probable that people will misunderstand and mistake us on that account: what does it matter! They will say: "Their 'honesty'—that is their devilry, and nothing else!" What does it matter! And even if they were right—have not all Gods hitherto been such sanctified, re-baptized devils? And after

6. Friedrich W. Nietzsche, *Beyond Good and Evil*, trans. Helen Zimmern (New York: Modern Library, 1917), 106.

7. This can be translated as "I only love forbidden pleasures" or as "we strive for that which has been forbidden."

all, what do we know of ourselves? And what the spirit that leads us wants to be called? (It is a question of names.) And how many spirits we harbor? Our honesty, we free spirits—let us be careful lest it become our vanity, our ornament and ostentation, our limitation, our stupidity! Every virtue inclines to stupidity, every stupidity to virtue; "stupid to the point of sanctity," they say in Russia,—let us be careful lest out of pure honesty we eventually become saints and bores! Is not life a hundred times too short for us—to bore ourselves? One would have to believe in eternal life in order to . . .

Excerpts from *The Antichrist*[8]

PREFACE

This book belongs to the most rare of men. Perhaps not one of them is yet alive. It is possible that they may be among those who understand my "Zarathustra": how could I confound myself with those who are now sprouting ears?—First the day after tomorrow must come for me. Some men are born posthumously.

The conditions under which any one understands me, and necessarily understands me—I know them only too well. Even to endure my seriousness, my passion, he must carry intellectual integrity to the verge of hardness. He must be accustomed to living on mountain tops—and to looking upon the wretched gabble of politics and nationalism as beneath him. He must have become indifferent; he must never ask of the truth whether it brings profit to him or a fatality to him . . . He must have an inclination, born of strength, for questions that no one has the courage for; the courage for the forbidden; predestination for the labyrinth. The experience of seven solitudes. New ears for new music. New eyes for what is most distant. A new conscience for truths that have hitherto remained unheard. And the will to economize in the grand manner—to hold together his strength, his enthusiasm . . . Reverence for self; love of self; absolute freedom of self . . .

Very well, then! of that sort only are my readers, my true readers, my readers foreordained: of what account are the rest?—The rest are merely humanity.—One must make one's self superior to humanity, in power, in loftiness of soul,—in contempt.

1.

Let us look each other in the face. We are Hyperboreans—we know well enough how remote our place is. "Neither by land nor by water will you find the road to the Hyperboreans": even Pindar, in his day, knew that much about us. Beyond the North, beyond the ice, beyond death—our life, our happiness . . . We have discovered that happiness; we know the way; we got our knowledge of it from thousands of years in the labyrinth.

8. Friedrich W. Nietzsche, *The Antichrist*, trans. H. L. Mencken (New York: Knopf, 1918), 37–52, 67.

Who else has found it?—The man of today?—"I don't know either the way out or the way in; I am whatever doesn't know either the way out or the way in"—so sighs the man of today . . . This is the sort of modernity that made us ill,—we sickened on lazy peace, cowardly compromise, the whole virtuous dirtiness of the modern Yea and Nay. This tolerance and largeur of the heart that "forgives" everything because it "understands" everything is a sirocco to us. Rather live amid the ice than among modern virtues and other such south-winds! . . . We were brave enough; we spared neither ourselves nor others; but we were a long time finding out where to direct our courage. We grew dismal; they called us fatalists. Our fate—it was the fulness, the tension, the storing up of powers. We thirsted for the lightnings and great deeds; we kept as far as possible from the happiness of the weakling, from "resignation" . . . There was thunder in our air; nature, as we embodied it, became overcast—for we had not yet found the way. The formula of our happiness: a Yea, a Nay, a straight line, a goal . . .

2.

What is good?—Whatever augments the feeling of power, the will to power, power itself, in man.

What is evil?—Whatever springs from weakness.

What is happiness?—The feeling that power increases—that resistance is overcome.

Not contentment, but more power; not peace at any price, but war; not virtue, but efficiency (virtue in the Renaissance sense, *virtu*, virtue free of moral acid).
The weak and the botched shall perish: first principle of our charity. And one should help them to it.

What is more harmful than any vice?—Practical sympathy for the botched and the weak—Christianity . . .

3.

The problem that I set here is not what shall replace mankind in the order of living creatures (—man is an end—): but what type of man must be bred, must be willed, as being the most valuable, the most worthy of life, the most secure guarantee of the future.

This more valuable type has appeared often enough in the past: but always as a happy accident, as an exception, never as deliberately willed. Very often it has been precisely the most feared; hitherto it has been almost the terror of terrors;—and out of that terror the contrary type has been willed, cultivated and attained: the domestic animal, the herd animal, the sick brute-man—the Christian . . .

4.

Mankind surely does not represent an evolution toward a better or stronger or higher level, as progress is now understood. This "progress" is merely a modern idea, which is to say, a false idea. The European of today, in his essential worth, falls far below the European of the Renaissance; the process of evolution does not necessarily mean elevation, enhancement, strengthening.

True enough, it succeeds in isolated and individual cases in various parts of the earth and under the most widely different cultures, and in these cases a higher type certainly manifests itself; something which, compared to mankind in the mass, appears as a sort of superman. Such happy strokes of high success have always been possible, and will remain possible, perhaps, for all time to come. Even whole races, tribes and nations may occasionally represent such lucky accidents.

5.

We should not deck out and embellish Christianity: it has waged a war to the death against this higher type of man, it has put all the deepest instincts of this type under its ban, it has developed its concept of evil, of the Evil One himself, out of these instincts—the strong man as the typical reprobate, the "outcast among men." Christianity has taken the part of all the weak, the low, the botched; it has made an ideal out of antagonism to all the self-preservative instincts of sound life; it has corrupted even the faculties of those natures that are intellectually most vigorous, by representing the highest intellectual values as sinful, as misleading, as full of temptation. The most lamentable example: the corruption of Pascal, who believed that his intellect had been destroyed by original sin, whereas it was actually destroyed by Christianity!—

6.

It is a painful and tragic spectacle that rises before me: I have drawn back the curtain from the rottenness of man. This word, in my mouth, is at least free from one suspicion: that it involves a moral accusation against humanity. It is used—and I wish to emphasize the fact again—without any moral significance: and this is so far true that the rottenness I speak of is most apparent to me precisely in those quarters where there has been most aspiration, hitherto, toward "virtue" and "godliness." As you probably surmise, I understand rottenness in the sense of decadence: my argument is that all the values on which mankind now fixes its highest aspirations are decadence-values.

I call an animal, a species, an individual corrupt, when it loses its instincts, when it chooses, when it prefers, what is injurious to it. A history of the "higher feelings," the "ideals of humanity"—and it is possible that I'll have to write it—would almost explain why man is so degenerate. Life itself appears to me as an instinct for growth, for survival, for the accumulation of forces, for power: whenever the will to power fails there is disaster. My contention is that all the highest values of humanity have been emptied of this will—that the values of decadence, of nihilism, now prevail under the holiest names.

7.

Christianity is called the religion of pity.—Pity stands in opposition to all the tonic passions that augment the energy of the feeling of aliveness: it is a depressant. A man loses power when he pities. Through pity that drain upon strength which suffering works is multiplied a thousandfold. Suffering is made contagious by pity; under certain circumstances it may lead to a total sacrifice of life and living energy—a loss out of all proportion to the magnitude of the cause (—the case of the death of the Nazarene). This is the first view of it; there is, however, a still more important one. If one measures the effects of pity by the gravity of the reactions it sets up, its character as a menace to life appears in a much clearer light. Pity thwarts the whole law of evolution, which is the law of natural selection. It preserves whatever is ripe for destruction; it fights on the side of those disinherited and condemned by life; by maintaining life in so many of the botched of all kinds, it gives life itself a gloomy and dubious aspect. Mankind has ventured to call pity a virtue (—in every superior moral system it appears as a weakness—); going still further, it has been called the virtue, the source and foundation of all other virtues—but let us always bear in mind that this was from the standpoint of a philosophy that was nihilistic, and upon whose shield the denial of life was inscribed. Schopenhauer was right in this: that by means of pity life is denied, and made worthy of denial—pity is the technic of nihilism. Let me repeat: this depressing and contagious instinct stands against all those instincts which work for the preservation and enhancement of life: in the role of protector of the miserable, it is a prime agent in the promotion of decadence—pity persuades to extinction . . Of course, one doesn't say "extinction": one says "the other world," or "God," or "the true life," or Nirvana, salvation, blessedness . . . This innocent rhetoric, from the realm of religious-ethical balderdash, appears a good deal less innocent when one reflects upon the tendency that it conceals beneath sublime words: the tendency to destroy life. Schopenhauer was hostile to life: that is why pity appeared to him as a virtue. . . . Aristotle, as every one knows, saw in pity a sickly and dangerous state of mind, the remedy for which was an occasional purgative: he regarded tragedy as that purgative. The instinct of life should prompt us to seek some means of puncturing any such pathological and dangerous accumulation of pity as that appearing in Schopenhauer's case (and also, alack, in that of our whole literary decadence, from St. Petersburg to Paris, from Tolstoi to Wagner), that it may burst and be discharged. . . Nothing is more unhealthy, amid all our unhealthy modernism, than Christian pity. To be the doctors here, to be unmerciful here, to wield the knife here—all this is our business, all this is our sort of humanity, by this sign we are philosophers, we Hyperboreans!—

8.

It is necessary to say just whom we regard as our antagonists: theologians and all who have any theological blood in their veins—this is our whole philosophy . . . One must have faced that menace at close hand, better still, one must have had experience of it directly and almost succumbed to it, to realize that it is not to be taken lightly (—the alleged free-thinking of our naturalists and physiologists seems to me to be a joke—they have no passion about such things; they have not suffered—). This poisoning goes a great deal further than most people think: I find the arrogant habit of the theologian among all who regard themselves as "idealists"—among all who, by virtue of a higher point of departure, claim a right to rise above reality, and to look upon it with suspicion . . . The idealist, like the ecclesiastic, carries all sorts of lofty concepts in his hand (—and not only in his hand!); he launches them with benevolent contempt against "understanding," "the senses," "honor," "good living," "science"; he sees such things as beneath him, as pernicious and seductive forces, on which "the soul" soars as a pure thing-in-itself—as if humility, chastity, poverty, in a word, holiness, had not already done much more damage to life than all imaginable horrors and vices . . . The pure soul is a pure lie . . . So long as the priest, that professional denier, calumniator and poisoner of life, is accepted as a higher variety of man, there can be no answer to the question, What is truth? Truth has already been stood on its head when the obvious attorney of mere emptiness is mistaken for its representative.

9.

Upon this theological instinct I make war: I find the tracks of it everywhere. Whoever has theological blood in his veins is shifty and dishonorable in all things. The pathetic thing that grows out of this condition is called faith: in other words, closing one's eyes upon one's self once for all, to avoid suffering the sight of incurable falsehood. People erect a concept of morality, of virtue, of holiness upon this false view of all things; they ground good conscience upon faulty vision; they argue that no other sort of vision has value any more, once they have made theirs sacrosanct with the names of "God," "salvation" and "eternity." I unearth this theological instinct in all directions: it is the most widespread and the most subterranean form of falsehood to be found on earth. Whatever a theologian regards as true must be false: there you have almost a criterion of truth. His profound instinct of self-preservation stands against truth ever coming into honor in any way, or even getting stated. Wherever the influence of theologians is felt there is a transvaluation of values, and the concepts "true" and "false" are forced to change places: what ever is most damaging to life is there called "true," and whatever exalts it, intensifies it, approves it, justifies it and makes it triumphant is there called "false." . . . When theologians, working through the "consciences" of princes (or of peoples—), stretch out their hands for power, there is never any doubt as to the fundamental issue: the will to make an end, the nihilistic will exerts that power . . .

18.

The Christian concept of a god—the god as the patron of the sick, the god as a spinner of cobwebs, the god as a spirit—is one of the most corrupt concepts that has ever been set up in the world: it probably touches low-water mark in the ebbing evolution of the god-type. God degenerated into the contradiction of life. Instead of being its transfiguration and eternal Yea! In him war is declared on life, on nature, on the will to live! God becomes the formula for every slander upon the "here and now," and for every lie about the "beyond"! In him nothingness is deified, and the will to nothingness is made holy! . . .

KURT WEILL AND BERTOLT BRECHT'S *THE SEVEN DEADLY SINS*

One of my colleagues has such severe nut allergies that she cannot even go into most coffee shops. Even the smell of hazelnut can trigger a powerful allergic reaction, sending her into anaphylactic shock. The central traumatized character in *The Seven Deadly Sins*, a woman named Anna, has a split personality caused by the overwhelming demands of capitalism. Just as my colleague's nut allergy makes dangerous for her the environment of a coffee shop, so for Anna the environment shaped by the machinery of market economics has had such a devastating impact on her that she's crazy, she's nuts—and in my lighter moments I call this work "Anna's Financial Shock." As a powerful satire, *The Seven Deadly Sins* shows how capitalism creates a reversal or inversion of values, elevating to a virtue the otherwise debased qualities that make one marketable or serviceable while transforming character traits like self-respect, modesty, love, and social justice into vices.

The Seven Deadly Sins is a *ballet chanté* or a sung ballet by the composer Kurt Weill and the librettist Bertolt Brecht. Weill and Brecht created this work in Paris, where they had fled to avoid Nazi persecution. It is set in the United States, and the work's prologue includes ragtime rhythms and banjos, musical elements Weill and Brecht's audience would have recognized as American. The entire work shows another important American feature—free-wheeling capitalism. In this same prologue we learn about the central character(s), Anna. Anna's split personalities are identified as Anna 1, level-headed and practical, and Anna 2, beautiful, flighty, and art loving. Anna 1 is by far the dominant narrator, and she explains that both sisters, who share "the same heart and the same savings account,"[9] were sent off by their parents and two

9. Kurt Weill and London Symphony Orchestra, *The Seven Deadly Sins* (New York: CBS Masterworks, 1988), 14.

brothers to spend seven years in seven big cities in order to raise money to build a suitable house on the Mississippi. Anna 1 has been almost (and keep in mind, *almost*) completely taken over or co-opted by capitalism. She says from the start that she must keep an eye on her sister so that Anna 2's whims and vices don't thwart their goals.

Sloth is the first sin Anna encounters. This section's musical and thematic tensions set the tone for the entire work. The driving rhythm and powerful horns set a tense and martial tone to this section. On top of the section's dramatic music we hear a breathtaking call-and-response. One voice expresses the family's concerns about Anna 2, that, if she were not yanked out of bed, the lazy "piece wouldn't get up in the morning."[10] In response to this voice the rest of the family exclaims, "Idleness is the beginning of all vice."[11] Just as idle hands are the devil's playthings, so laziness is the start of all vice, when vice is defined as whatever disobeys capitalism's mandates. In a second verse the voice mentions how Anna 1 is very attentive and obedient. The last verse is a final prayer and admonition, a chilling travesty where the family prays for the "Lord" to look out for Anna and show her the way to prosperity so that she does not "sin against the Laws / which make us rich and happy!"[12] Of course the "Lord" here is capitalism. The driving rhythms in the music and the contrast between the stern first stanza and the compassionate second show how the Anna that is sensitive and free from greedy obsessions is powerfully berated, while the other Anna is carefully conditioned to be an efficient and obedient cog in the capitalist machine. Of course sloth is the first, the most fundamental, and the most grievous transgression against capitalism.

The second section finds Anna in Memphis, working in a cabaret and facing the sin of pride. Anna 1 mentions how much Anna 2 likes her new clothes, but the real problem is that Anna 2 becomes interested in art. Anna 1 must remind her that men do not come to a cabaret for an artist; they have paid their money and they want a good show. Anna must correct her art-loving sister, whose modesty and interest in artistic expression prevent her full, "naked" participation in capitalism. Anna 2 must set aside her selfish and proud interest in art in order to give people what they want. This section also gives one of the small glimpses of the conflict within Anna(s), the subtle *psychomachia* at work, as Anna 1 holds Anna 2, consolingly reminding her of their goal, their "house in Louisiana." Over this faint hint of flagging commitment, of a not completely exhausted flame of real humanity, is the monotone prayer of the demanding family and its capitalist aspirations. When Anna gets to Los Angeles, and, working as an extra in a circus film, sees the cruel treatment of animals, she falls victim to the sin of anger. Here again Anna 1 must restrain Anna 2, reminding her of both the futility of stopping powerful people and the importance of never losing her self-control. As pride is the sin that prevents full

10. Ibid., 15.

11. Ibid.

12. Ibid.

participation in a capitalist system, so anger, directed at powerful forces, is a form of heresy and insubordination to capitalism's principles and authorities.

If this bittersweet work has a particularly hilarious section it is the fourth section. Here the family sings as a barbershop quartet. They are sort of the Capitalist Glee Club from hell. They talk about how Anna 2 has a contract as a solo dancer, yet Anna 1 must keep a very careful watch on Anna 2's diet. In their tender voices, the family reminds us that "they want / no hippopotamus in Philadelphia!"[13] After Anna has spent one year in each of seven cities and thereby has raised the necessary funds, she can enjoy, with her then-relocated family, all of Louisiana's delightful foods, including "Muffins! Cutlets! Asparagus! Chicken! / And the little yellow honey-buns!"[14] The family's last tender caution is "Hold on to yourself, Anna! No good comes from gluttony."[15] When Anna gets to Boston, she must curb her appetite again, but there it is her taste for love. After the hilarity of the previous section, this section has another very touching moment when Anna 1 mentions how much Anna 2 loves the gigolo Fernando. Anna 1's careful conditioning allows for no more than this glimpse of Anna 2's love. Overcoming any detrimental impulses, Anna 1 intercedes in Anna 2's relationship with Fernando, whom she is giving money to, in order to set her straight. Anna 1 gives proper control and focus to Anna 2's "affection," pointing it toward a wealthy benefactor. Love that subverts and jeopardizes their plans is destructive, empty, and sinfully selfish "lust." By the end Anna 2 cannot cope, giving herself cheaply to anyone, while the family pleads and promises that "the one who can triumph over Self / will obtain the Reward."[16]

In Baltimore, the sixth town, Anna's success leads to some bad press. Men are even committing suicide because of her Machiavellian power. The family warns, not unlike how Machiavelli might, that one must be careful to not get a reputation for greed, since that can damage one's future prospects for prosperity. It is in Anna's last town, San Francisco, that Anna 2 meets her final conflict, this time with envy. Anna 1 gives a dramatic catalogue of the sins of San Francisco: people indulge in idleness; they are "not for sale" and are therefore "proud."[17] They are also given to the sin of anger ("raging at every brutality") in their opposition to injustice.[18] Besides the slothful, the proud, and the angry, the city has lustful and greedy folk as well, who are "happy being / loving only to the Beloved" and are "taking openly according to [their] needs."[19] Anna 1's review here of the six previously mentioned sins fits with her warning for Anna 2 not only to avoid such sins but also to avoid envying the sinful. Anna 1

13. Ibid., 20.
14. Ibid., 22.
15. Ibid.
16. Ibid., 24.
17. Ibid., 26, 28
18. Ibid., 28.
19. Ibid.

then employs traditional religious and moral rhetoric to encourage Anna 2's strength in the face of "sin," to encourage Anna 2's dedication to utility, and to help maintain Anna 2's disdain for what other people value; Anna 1 notes that, in the end, those who follow these vices will end up with nothing. This dramatic *dies irae* of capitalism leads right into the work's epilogue, where an exhausted and broken Anna finally "enjoys" the painful and ironic rewards of her toils.

In *The Seven Deadly Sins* Weill and Brecht bring together music and words, ideas and actions, to create a powerful exploration of virtue and vice in contemporary culture. The subtle play between the Annas and the powerful forces that surround them make this both a *psychomachia* and a satire. It is sometimes delightfully funny and at other times darkly sardonic, but it is always compelling.

Just as the size of *The Honors* tapestries prevent them from being presented here, different problems prevent the reproduction of *The Seven Deadly Sins* in this anthology. The most obvious one is that this work is a musical drama, something that does not lend itself to mere text or to still visuals. There are many excellent audio and video reproductions of this work, and one that is highly recommended is Marianne Faithfull's version.

C. S. LEWIS'S *MERE CHRISTIANITY*

Introduction

C. S. Lewis's contribution to the virtues and vices tradition is part of his larger defense of Christianity. Lewis did not return to the faith of his early childhood until later in life. His years of disbelief gave him an inclination to not believe and an outsider's view that served him well when he later defended his convictions. It is his defense of his faith and his thoughtful, well-reasoned appeals to non-believers that earned him the popular title of "The Apostle to the Skeptics." When Lewis defends Christianity to such skeptics (and simultaneously clarifies it for believers), the center of that defense is that God is not really concerned with morality, with right and wrong, or with virtue and vice on a certain level. Yes, God wants people to be good and wise and just, but more important, God wants humans to be radically different. God wants humans to be God-like. Lewis's discussion of virtue and vice is not about doing good and avoiding bad; it is about God sharing divine qualities, abilities, excellences, and powers with human beings.

The excerpt from *Mere Christianity* included here is from the section on Christian behavior. There is only one section from that chapter reproduced here, for reasons later explained, but the entire chapter is a thoughtful meditation on the virtues. Lewis describes Christian behavior with reference to the four cardinal virtues. His depiction of justice harkens back to Plato's *Republic*; justice is knowing and doing one's duty and entails the conventional idea of fairness. Prudence means using one's intellectual capability to the fullest, while temperance is discipline in everything, not just alcohol. Lewis recasts traditional fortitude in a pithy, contemporary word: "guts." Finally, Lewis's tennis-player analogy clarifies how virtue is not a matter of occasional, lucky shots; it is a steady, constant embodiment of characteristics.

The excerpt included here is only one portion of Lewis's examination of the virtues and vices. The Lewis estate would not allow for reproduction of the other sections. One of those sections deals with "The Great Sin," and for Lewis that is pride. Lewis offers a remarkable contribution to the traditional crowning of pride as the sovereign vice. He describes pride's sinful center as enmity that is pointed toward God and toward others. This enmity pits one against God and against everyone else, underwriting one's arrogance, envy, and disdain. It is this fundamental opposition that makes pride the great sin. Pride is the wedge into the heart through which other vices can enter, or, to use Gregory's analogy, pride first takes control of the heart's battlefield and then gives it over to lesser "vice" lieutenants. Lewis even describes how pride may be employed to overcome lesser vices so as to secure pride's place more firmly. Lusts or debaucheries may be illnesses, yet they are minor maladies compared to pride's cancer in the self-righteous or hypocritically chaste or temperate.

For Lewis, whereas the proud set themselves in opposition to God and others, the law of the harvest is at work in the lives of the charitable. Christian charity, treated in his section "Charity" in *Mere Christianity*, is neither mere fond affection nor is it just giving alms; it is an act of will. Those who extend themselves in this willful act find a full harvest of the same generosity and gracious giving, while those who mistreat others reap an equal share of cruelty, hatred, and contemptuous apathy.

Lewis's discussion of hope, also not reproduced here but in the subsequent section of the same chapter of *Mere Christianity*, often confuses my students. It seems odd to assert that if one really wants something, then somehow that desire is good and that one should expect its fulfillment. Does Lewis mean that if I really, really want a Ferrari, then this desire tells me something about my soul and indicates what I should wish for? What Lewis seems to have in mind is that at the center of every human soul is a transcendent longing, or, to use a popular image, there is a "God-shaped hole." Many deep and meaningful human experiences, like the positive ones Lewis mentions, and even negative ones like the loss of a loved one, reveal this transcendent need, this hole. Lewis then gives three possible responses to this emptiness and longing. The fool tries to fill it with the temporal, the temporary, and the transient, while the disillusioned sensible man tries to deny its existence. The hopeful Christian holds fast to this longing, seeking to learn what lessons it may teach about both mortality and eternity.

Added to this hope is faith, treated in the next sections of *Mere Christianity*. For Lewis faith is an action and a commitment instead of a passive belief or mere rational assent. Lewis questions the ability of reason to withstand the pressures, the temptations of everyday life. Reason itself fails to keep otherwise prudent people from doing what they know is foolish. In this respect Lewis provides an interesting response to Benjamin Franklin. The very rational Franklin set up a wise formula for personal improvement, which, if reason were sovereign, should have ensured the intended development. Lewis might describe Franklin as someone who has taken a very important first step in trying as hard as he can. Franklin's failure, for Lewis, would be the very crucial moment when people learn that their own efforts are insufficient. At that point, a person may feel (to use the language of the Beatitudes) "poor in spirit" and may "hunger and thirst for righteousness," the "rightness" that only comes from a relationship with God. Individual failure reveals one's inadequacy, and the realization of one's bankruptcy generates the humility sufficient to seek union with God and thereby gain access to God's power, God's bounty, and the divine endowment of *virtu*.

Of course this idea of a God-shaped hole should give us pause. For thinkers like Nietzsche, such an idea encourages the sense of inadequacy and "poverty" that he traces back to resentment. Nietzsche could take aim at how Lewis celebrates dependence and inadequacy; Lewis calls such God-shaped holes a prerequisite to attaining holiness. Nietzsche could argue his point by making an analogy between humans and circus elephants. The elephants, large, powerful animals that meekly do as they are told and perform as they are instructed, are kept in check by a flimsy chain and stake. Circus elephants have it in their heads that they lack the power to break free from that chain. From a very young age they have been tethered to the chain. When they were young, they were indeed too weak to break free. But now, in adulthood, they do not realize that they no longer need be controlled by the chain. Asks Nietzsche, how is that Christians are not the same: trying when they are weak to live lives of power, and then, when they fail, becoming convinced forever that they cannot live beyond their current expectations? Would Lewis's Christianity really have helped Franklin, or would it have encouraged a new dependence and weakness in him? Of course Lewis could argue that it would have encouraged a new strength in him. Lewis, who himself lived for many years outside the tether of Christianity, might argue that it is only God who can reveal to humans their real power and strength, and that Nietzsche's ideal people of strength are tethered to their merely humanistic and even selfish notions of power and strength.

A careful examination of Lewis's contribution to the virtues and vices tradition shows how he brings together and elaborates upon many elements of that tradition. Such an examination can also reveal the clefts and fissures in the tradition and in our divided cultural house.

The 'Cardinal Virtues'[20]

The previous section was originally composed to be given as a short talk on the air.

If you are allowed to talk for only ten minutes, pretty well everything else has to be sacrificed to brevity. One of my chief reasons for dividing morality up into three

20. From C. S. Lewis, *Mere Christianity*, copyright © C. S. Lewis Pte. Ltd. 1942, 1943, 1944, 1952. Extract reprinted by permission.

parts (with my picture of the ships sailing in convoy) was that this seemed the shortest way of covering the ground. Here I want to give some idea of another way in which the subject has been divided by old writers, which was too long to use in my talk, but which is a very good one.

According to this longer scheme there are seven 'virtues.' Four of them are called 'Cardinal' virtues, and the remaining three are called 'Theological' virtues. The 'Cardinal' ones are those which all civilized people recognize: the 'Theological' are those which, as a rule, only Christians know about. I shall deal with the Theological ones later on: at present I am talking about the four Cardinal virtues. (The word 'cardinal' has nothing to do with 'Cardinals' in the Roman Church. It comes from a Latin word meaning 'the hinge of a door.' These were called 'cardinal' virtues because they are, as we should say, 'pivotal.') They are Prudence, Temperance, Justice, and Fortitude.

Prudence means practical common sense, taking the trouble to think out what you are doing and what is likely to come of it. Nowadays most people hardly think of Prudence as one of the 'virtues.' In fact, because Christ said we could only get into His world by being like children, many Christians have the idea that, provided you are 'good,' it does not matter being a fool. But that is a misunderstanding. In the first place, most children show plenty of 'prudence' about doing the things they are really interested in, and think them out quite sensibly. In the second place, as St. Paul points out, Christ never meant that we were to remain children in intelligence: on the contrary, He told us to be not only 'as harmless as doves,' but also 'as wise as serpents.' He wants a child's heart, but a grown-up's head. He wants us to be simple, single-minded, affectionate, and teachable, as good children are; but He also wants every bit of intelligence we have to be alert at its job, and in first-class fighting trim. The fact that you are giving money to a charity does not mean that you need not try to find out whether that charity is a fraud or not. The fact that what you are thinking about is God Himself (for example, when you are praying) does not mean that you can be content with the same babyish ideas which you had when you were a five-year-old. It is, of course, quite true that God will not love you any the less, or have less use for you, if you happen to have been born with a very second-rate brain. He has room for people with very little sense, but He wants every one to use what sense they have. The proper motto is not 'Be good, sweet maid, and let who can be clever,' but 'Be good, sweet maid, and don't forget that this involves being as clever as you can.' God is no fonder of intellectual slackers than of any other slackers. If you are thinking of becoming a Christian, I warn you, you are embarking on something which is going to take the whole of you, brains and all. But, fortunately, it works the other way round. Anyone who is honestly trying to be a Christian will soon find his intelligence being sharpened: one of the reasons why it needs no special education to be a Christian is that Christianity is an education itself. That is why an uneducated believer like Bunyan was able to write a book that has astonished the whole world.

Temperance is, unfortunately, one of those words that has changed its meaning. It now usually means teetotalism. But in the days when the second Cardinal virtue was christened 'Temperance,' it meant nothing of the sort. Temperance referred not specially to drink, but to all pleasures; and it meant not abstaining, but going the right length and no further. It is a mistake to think that Christians ought all to be teetotallers; Mohammedanism, not Christianity, is the teetotal religion. Of course it may be the duty of a particular Christian, or of any Christian, at a particular time, to abstain from strong drink, either because he is the sort of man who cannot drink at all without drinking too much, or because he wants to give the money to the poor, or because he is with people who are inclined to drunkenness and must not encourage them by drinking himself. But the whole point is that he is abstaining, for a good reason, from something which he does not condemn and which he likes to see other people enjoying. One of the marks of a certain type of bad man is that he cannot give up a thing himself without wanting every one else to give it up. That is not the Christian way. An individual Christian may see fit to give up all sorts of things for special reasons—marriage, or meat, or beer, or the cinema; but the moment he starts saying the things are bad in themselves, or looking down his nose at other people who do use them, he has taken the wrong turning.

One great piece of mischief has been done by the modern restriction of the word Temperance to the question of drink. It helps people to forget that you can be just as intemperate about lots of other things. A man who makes his golf or his motor-bicycle the center of his life, or a woman who devotes all her thoughts to clothes or bridge or her dog, is being just as 'intemperate' as someone who gets drunk every evening. Of course, it does not show on the outside so easily: bridge-mania or golf-mania do not make you fall down in the middle of the road. But God is not deceived by externals.

Justice means much more than the sort of thing that goes on in law courts. It is the old name for everything we should now call 'fairness'; it includes honesty, give and take, truthfulness, keeping promises, and all that side of life. And Fortitude includes both kinds of courage—the kind that faces danger as well as the kind that 'sticks it' under pain. 'Guts' is perhaps the nearest modern English. You will notice, of course, that you cannot practise any of the other virtues very long without bringing this one into play.

There is one further point about the virtues that ought to be noticed. There is a difference between doing some particular just or temperate action and being a just or temperate man. Someone who is not a good tennis player may now and then make a good shot. What you mean by a good player is the man whose eye and muscles and nerves have been so trained by making innumerable good shots that they can now be relied on. They have a certain tone or quality which is there even when he is not playing, just as a mathematician's mind has a certain habit and outlook which is there even when he is not doing mathematics. In the same way a man who perseveres in doing just actions gets in the end a certain quality of character. Now it is that quality rather than the particular actions which we mean when we talk of a 'virtue.'

This distinction is important for the following reason. If we thought only of the particular actions we might encourage three wrong ideas.

1. We might think that, provided you did the right thing, it did not matter how or why you did it—whether you did it willingly or unwillingly, sulkily or cheerfully, through fear of public opinion or for its own sake. But the truth is that right actions done for the wrong reason do not help to build the internal quality or character called a 'virtue,' and it is this quality or character that really matters. (If the bad tennis player hits very hard, not because he sees that a very hard stroke is required, but because he has lost his temper, his stroke might possibly, by luck, help him to win that particular game; but it will not be helping him to become a reliable player.)
2. We might think that God wanted simply obedience to a set of rules: whereas He really wants people of a particular sort.
3. We might think that the 'virtues' were necessary only for this present life—that in the other world we could stop being just because there is nothing to quarrel about and stop being brave because there is no danger. Now it is quite true that there will probably be no occasion for just or courageous acts in the next world, but there will be every occasion for being the sort of people that we can become only as the result of doing such acts here. The point is not that God will refuse you admission to His eternal world if you have not got certain qualities of character: the point is that if people have not got at least the beginnings of those qualities inside them, then no possible external conditions could make a 'Heaven' for them—that is, could make them happy with the deep, strong, unshakable kind of happiness God intends for us.

PAUL CADMUS'S *THE SEVEN DEADLY SINS*

They are the androgynous evil opposites of Pollaiuolo and Raphael's seven virtues. They are Chaucer's Parson's visual aids. They are the worst demon spirits from Evagrius's most satanic nightmare. They are what you'd get if the (unloved) love-child of Hildegard and Brueghel took a huge hit of some bad crack and started to paint. They are Paul Cadmus's paintings *The Seven Deadly Sins*, and they are as gruesome and repulsive as they are powerful and alluring. Paul Cadmus painted this series between 1945 and 1949. While it may not be a coincidence that they were completed just after the human catastrophes of Auschwitz and Hiroshima, these works do not seem to be about group evil. Each of the sins dwells alone, surrounded in its own solipsistic space. Cadmus does not seem interested in the faceless evil of blind masses; he shows vice's twisted visage, warning, perhaps, that we might see some of our own reflected in it.

The overly sweet face of *Envy* (Figure 29) curls with the figure's exaggerated, sycophantic gesture. Everything is appropriately green, and, like Giotto's image, this emaciated figure is consumed from the inside, as a tangle of snakes emerges from its side. One hand reaches out to shake and congratulate, while the other plays with the snaky innards. Even the figure's gauzy green covering turns out to be sloughed snake skin or poison from the headdress snake's fangs. *Envy*'s every step, every movement, is as dangerous and duplicitous as the tall nails protruding from the ground. The dangerous yet relatively clear space *Envy* inhabits contrasts with *Sloth*'s swampy and fetid environment (not reproduced here). This is a figure whose complete inaction has caused it to atrophy to the point that it melts into itself and its surroundings. While part of the figure hardens into a rhino-like shell of skin, the facial features, eyes, ears, tongue, chest, arms, and hands all literally melt from its own lethargy. And where *Sloth* melts or drips into its boggy surrounds, *Gluttony* bloats forth in its intestinal space (not reproduced here). The red, pink, yellow, and purple figure, barely stitched together by the very white, stringy spaghetti that it consumes, desperately stuffs itself to bursting. With only the remnants of recognizable features, a nose, and bloated, club-like hands and feet, it is the living image of self-consuming consumption.

Whereas the image of *Gluttony* orients itself to the top, the orifice from which more is consumed, the image of *Greed* (not reproduced here) has a downward orientation. A ragged, old, miserly, and misanthropic spider grabs a faux jewel that has fallen from the websack on its back. Its boney skeleton and careworn face shows its timeless struggle to possess what it can never hold on to. Its threadbare websack, filled with rags and baubles, so overwhelms the figure that as it reaches for the jewel, it loses its grip and is about to fall into the void of its claustrophobic, jagged, and vertiginous space. Self-destructive longing continues in the *Lust* image (not reproduced here). Everything about this figure, its overall phallic shape, its ripped condom case, the phallic fingers that outline its insatiable pubis, the hypererect nipples and vaginal armpits, screams chaotic and desperate sexual desire. Cadmus seems to have tried to make one half of the face look seductively pleased, while making the other look hopelessly frantic. The panting pinks and reds of the figure match the red flames it exudes, all in an image of sexual immolation, destruction of the individual and everything around it.

Anger (not reproduced here) is the figure with the most dynamic relationship with its space. This dangerously spiked red monster literally flies through the picture plane, breaking the glass and spilling blood as it launches itself into the viewer's space. In fact, the jagged shards of glass that it wrathfully breaks cut the figure so violently that the blood pours out and splatters around. The eyes are slits of rage, and every hair, every joint, and every fold of skin has become razor-blade sharp. With the yellow burst at the bottom of the work and its flying, upward motion, the figure looks like a comic-book or science-fiction cartoon character, but instead of a powerful figure of justice, Cadmus gives us Superfury on speed and steroids. *Pride*, in contrast, shows a haughty restraint, though not without its own dynamism (Figure 30). The semitransparent figure is empty, or filled with the hot air of its own self-importance and self-deception. It bears the peacock imagery common to pride on the headdress, eyes, and breast, with a stuck-up socialite's snobby and condescending glance. One iron-like hand, in mock modesty or self-regard, covers a military-like star emblem over the other breast, another status symbol. The other hand, a tightly clinched iron fist, bespeaks and iron will and iron control, perhaps as compensation for a small purple penis and blue scrotum. Picturing the maxim from Proverbs, "pride goeth before the fall," is a common element in many images of Pride, beginning at least with Prudentius. This inflated image follows in that vein: with the bubbling stew of its own empty gall boiling in its feet, Cadmus's Pride floats along in a space of jagged projectiles. In spite of its imperial purple and imperious look, *Pride* is already beginning to "pass gas" and deflate.

Cadmus's works are alluring and repulsive because of their psychological insight into the nature of vice. From the viewer's first look, these works powerfully confront the viewer; yet in their many complex subtleties they reward the viewer's continued attention with new insights and warnings.

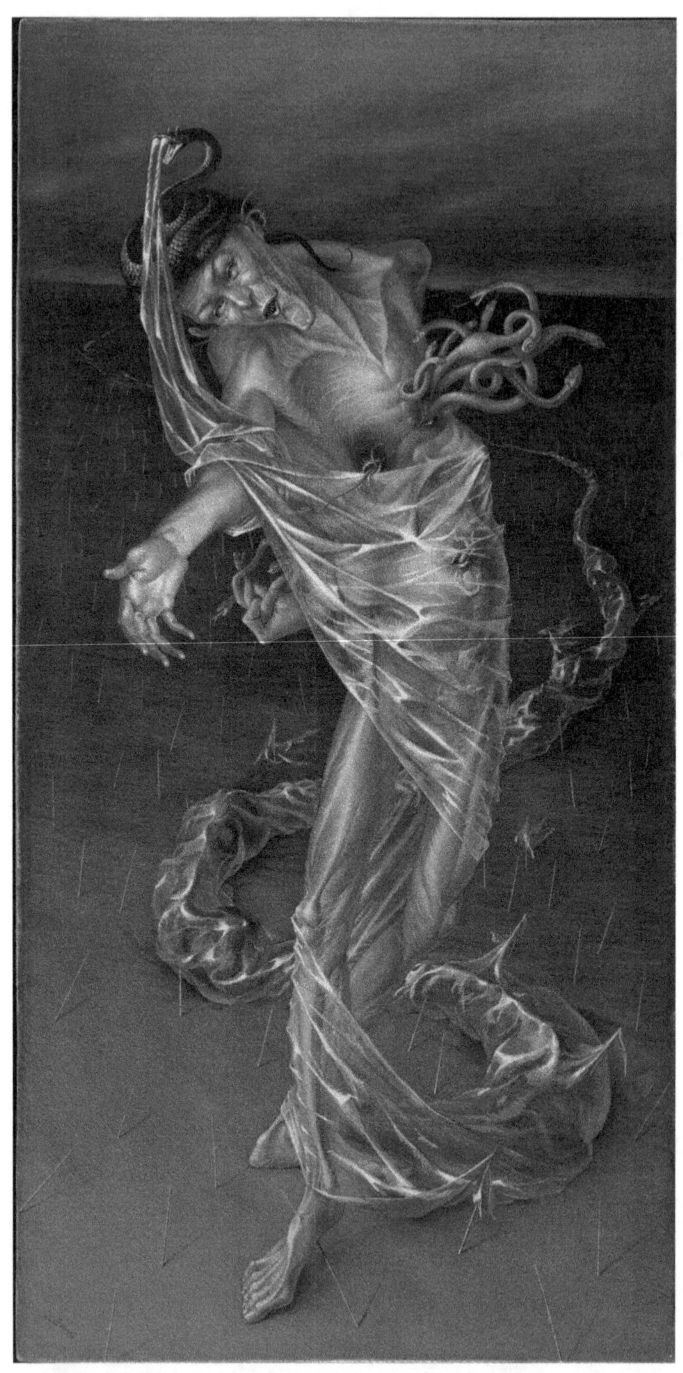

Figure 29: Paul Cadmus, *Envy.* Egg tempera on Masonite. 24 x 12 in. (61 x 30.5 cm).
The Metropolitan Museum of Art, Gift of Lincoln Kirstein, 1993 (1993.87.2).

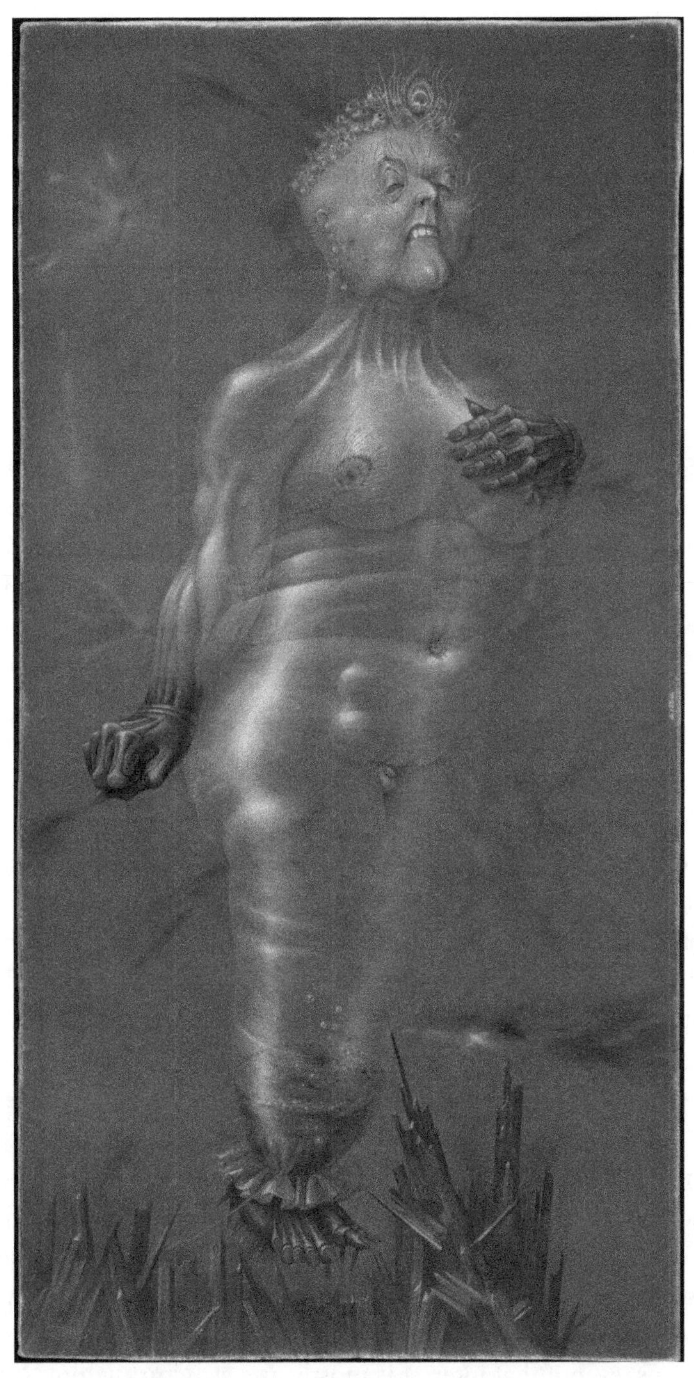

Figure 30: Paul Cadmus, *Pride.* Egg tempera on gessoed linen over Masonite. 24 1/8 x 11 7/8 in. (61x3 x 30.2 cm). The Metropolitan Museum of Art, Gift of Lincoln Kirstein, 1993. (1993.87.2), © VAGA. Image © The Metropolitan Museum of Art.

Epilogue

This book's collection of the key texts of the virtues and vices tradition gives a sweeping view as well as specific, compelling examples of that tradition. Some texts establish the tradition's antecedents and basis, others demonstrate the codification of the virtues and vices, while still others show various trajectories in that tradition like the divine endowment, the struggle, the virtues and vices in everyday life and death, and the vitality of vice. Some of these trajectories continue and flourish, while others reach a peak and seem to fade.

Our present culture's engagement in that tradition shows its continuing vitality and conflicts. We live in a house divided about the description, role, and even meanings of the virtues and vices. If we live in such a divided house, it seems valuable, as an epilogue, to look around that house as with a video camera to glimpse current virtues and vices texts. Panning around in this manner, we can take in what is on television and in magazines, as well as what books and art we might find. No single item will be filmed or examined in depth, as the purpose is to show in the widest sense the continued vitality of the virtues and vices tradition in the present.

Turning the camera first to the television, or the DVD player, one of the most prominent examples is the 1995 movie *Seven*. In this movie a serial killer carries out, directly and indirectly, seven murders based on the deadly sins. Few contemporary works match the brutality of *Seven*, a brutality that seems reminiscent of Cadmus, Brueghel, and Dante. And just as Brueghel's prints presented their horrific view with a mass produced vehicle, thereby bringing that view to a large audience, so *Seven* powerfully exposes the seven deadly sins to many who were previously unaware of them. Other contemporary works also show a continued knowledge of and interest in the seven deadly sins, even if that interest is mostly as a structuring tool. A 1997 episode of *3rd Rock from the Sun* assembles various clips from previous episodes around the theme of the seven deadly sins. The episode uses these vices to satirize human character deficiencies even as those deficiencies are most readily seen in aliens disguised as humans. Such a satire critiques the present by using the normative "building codes" established by the virtues and vices tradition, and continues a satirical trend of *Piers Plowman* as well as Kurt Weill and Bertolt Brecht, though this is a very light approach.

Finally, what we can also find on television is what can only be described as the opposite of Paul Cadmus's view of the seven deadly sins. In a 2005 episode ("The Girl Who Gets Bad News") of the television show *America's Next Top Model*, each contestant dressed, alluringly, as one of the seven deadly sins. Nothing so strikingly shows contrasting depictions of the seven deadly sins as does the comparison of Cadmus's works and these images. One final program is the series on The seven deadly sins broadcast by the History Channel in 2008.

Poised somewhere between *America's Next Top Model* and Paul Cadmus is an interesting 1987 magazine project for *Harper's* titled "You Can Have it All! Seven Campaigns for Deadly Sins."[1] The editors of *Harper's* asked seven advertising agencies to each create an advertisement for one of the seven deadly sins. There are rather satirical swipes at pride and gluttony, wrath's double nature is illustrated by its use in motivating both war and antiwar movements, sloth gets a positive nod for not causing trouble, and lust gets one for perpetuating humanity. Of course one firm was envious of the much more desirable sins that the other six got to promote. An unabashedly satirical response to the seven deadly sins appeared in a December 12, 2001, article "All Seven Deadly Sins Committed at Church Bake Sale" in the *Onion*.[2] Using a journalistic tone, the article plays on the distance between expectations of virtue in the church-going participants of the "twice-annual bake sale at St. Mary's of the Immaculate Conception Church" and their glaring, though all too human, vices.

Book-length discussions in our divided cultural house are as diverse as we might expect. Writers like Robert Solomon, mentioned in this book's introduction, lament our culture's suppression of the unique vitality of the vices. Most of those who presented for the New York Public Library and Oxford University Press in 2002 and 2003, lectures subsequently published by Oxford, also examined each of the seven deadly sins with more of an eye toward how those qualities were misunderstood contributions to life and not debilitating deficiencies. Aviad Kleinberg's *Seven Deadly Sins: A Very Partial List* also explores the limitations of seeing each as something to completely avoid and reject. Kleinberg instead advocates a judicious adaptation of what is lively in the vices. The most laudatory of all recent authors about the relish that the sins give to life is Dan Savage, whose memoir of his adventures in exploring vice is appropriately titled, *Skipping towards Gomorrah: The Seven Deadly Sins and the Pursuit of Happiness in America*.

In the starkest contrast to Savage's work are those that explore the destructive impact of the vices. Whereas the previously mentioned works seem to continue the "vitality of vice" aspects of the virtues and vices tradition, many of these works function like modern-day penitential manuals. Such works also tend to follow the "contraries

1. "You Can Have it All! Seven Campaigns for Deadly Sins." *Harper's*, November 1987, 43–50.

2 http://www.theonion.com/articles/all-seven-deadly-sins-committed-at-church-bake-sal,167/.

cure contraries" tradition, as they encourage a virtue to remedy each vice. This last tendency is especially evident in Jeff Cook's *Seven: The Deadly Sins and the Beatitudes* where Cook insightfully pairs qualities of the blessed against vicious, destructive habits. Kalman Kaplan's title describes a work that takes a similar approach: *The Seven Habits of the Good Life: How the Biblical Virtues Free Us from the Seven Deadly Sins*. Two works that take a bit more of a philosophical approach to describing the "deadliness" of the vices are Ken Bazyn's *The Seven Perennial Sins and Their Offspring* and Rebecca Konyndyk DeYoung's *Glittering Vices: A New Look at the Seven Deadly Sins and Their Remedies*. And finally, André Comte-Sponville's *A Small Treatise on the Great Virtues: The Uses of Philosophy in Everyday Life* is the work of a philosopher, and not really a "small treatise," that takes a humanistic approach to examine how the "great virtues" have a practical impact on improving everyday life.

Finally, looking at the art of our divided cultural house we find perhaps an even greater vitality. Changes in art at the end of the twentieth century have brought changes in artistic approaches to the virtues and vices tradition. Three of the best examples are by Bruce Nauman, Noritoshi Hirakawa, and Diller Scofidio + Renfro. Nauman's 1988 *Vices and Virtues* features all fourteen of the traditional virtues and vices in seven-foot-tall neon signs on the Charles Lee Powell Structural Systems Laboratory on the campus of the University of California, San Diego. The words flash on and off, and the interplay of the names of the virtues and vices inspires audiences to ponder their relationship. What does Faith have to do with Lust, Fortitude have to do with Anger, or Justice have to do with Avarice? A similar approach, one that uses rather limited means to raise critical questions, is employed by both Noritoshi Hirakawa and Diller Scofidio + Renfro. In 1997 Hirakawa produced large photographs, each with a young woman standing outside a church. The series, titled *Virtue in Vice*, seems to show rather banal street pictures or tourist snapshots. The labels accompanying the works clarify that each young woman has, hidden under her skirt, a battery-powered sex toy. Hirakawa's works combine images and ideas of virtue and vice as part of the artist's larger criticism of traditional and unconsciously accepted values. This criticism clearly places his work in the vitality-of-vice trajectory. In the same year as Hirakawa's work, the interdisciplinary design studio of Diller Scofidio + Renfro exhibited four objects in a water-glass series called *Vice/Virtue*. These works present the dual and seemingly mutually exclusive view of what their website describes as the "health and hedonism that characterizes contemporary culture." The four glassworks in the series, which include liquids, hypodermic needles, and pills, are given the titles *The Dispensary*, *The Fountain*, *The Exhaust*, and *The Reservoir*. While they are seemingly simple yet beautifully executed objects, they invite the very questions and engage the very incongruencies and contradictions inherent in the virtues and vices tradition—a tradition that continues to challenge and inspire artists and thinkers today.

APPENDIX 1

Key Virtues and Vices Works

BELOW IS A CHRONOLOGICAL list of key works dealing with the virtues and vices. Works not anthologized are followed by a brief description. There are two books that list and describe many more works in this tradition. *Virtue and Vice: The Personifications in the Index of Christian Art* is a very thorough catalogue listing medieval visual images of the virtues and vices, with an introduction and scholarly essays, edited by Colum Hourihane (Princeton: Index of Christian Art, 2000). Morton Bloomfield's seminal *The Seven Deadly Sins: An Introduction to the History of a Religious Concept, with Special Reference to Medieval English Literature* (Michigan State University Press, 1952, reprinted 1967) gives a thorough historical treatment of the seven deadly sins and explores many of their literary expressions.

Isaiah (*c.* 8th century BCE)

Plato, *The Republic* (*c.* 360 BCE)

Aristotle, *The Nicomachean Ethics* (*c.* 350 BCE)

Proverbs (*c.* 3rd century BCE)

Testament of the Twelve Patriarchs (*c.* 109–106 BCE). These apocryphal scriptures contain Jacob's dying commands to his twelve sons. The second book, the "Testament of Reuben," describes seven spirits of deceit that are close to the seven vices: fornication, gluttony, strife, vainglory, pride, lying, and injustice, with an eighth spirit of sleep added later.

Cicero, *Of Duties* (44 BCE)

Horace, First Epistle to Maecenas (*c.* 20 CE). This epistle mentions various evil passions similar to what would be the seven vices. These vices can grow but can also be assuaged or expiated.

Paul's Letters (*c.* 50–60 CE)

The Gospel of Matthew (between 70 and 100 CE)

The Shepherd of Hermas (or *The Shepherd*) (140–155). This Christian work describes four primary "virgin" virtues on the four corners of a tower: Faith, Continence, Power, and Long-Suffering. Between these virtues are eight other virtues: Simplicity, Guilelessness,

Purity, Cheerfulness, Truth, Understanding, Concord, and Love. In opposition to these are twelve women in black, with the four principals being Unbelief, Intemperance, Disobedience, and Deceit. Their followers are Sadness, Wickedness, Wantonness, Irascibility, Falsehood, Folly, Slander, and Hatred.

Tertullian *The Shows* (207–208)

Ambrose, *Paradise* (375). In this work Saint Ambrose connects the Classical virtues of Prudence, Temperance, Fortitude, and Justice with the Judeo-Christian tradition by comparing them to the four rivers of paradise. This allegorical reading is illustrated in many texts, including the *Speculum Virginum.*

Prudentius, *Psychomachia* (late 4th century)

Evagrius of Pontus, *On the Eight Thoughts* (383–399)

John Cassian, *Institutes* (420–429). This very influential book bridges the Egyptian desert fathers (Evagrius among them) and Europe. While the first four books of *Institutes* deal with the rules of monastic life, the last eight treat the principal vices. The names of the vices are listed here; the Latin vice names are given in parentheses: gluttony (*gula*), lust (*luxuria*), avarice (*avaritia*), anger (*ira*), dejection or sadness (*tristitia*), *acedia*, vainglory (*inanis* or *vana gloria*), and pride (*superbia*). Cassian's *Conferences* also deals with the eight principal spiritual faults or obstacles. While this treatment is not as thorough as the one in *Institutes*, it does introduce the idea of the vices growing out of each other, and it introduces the influential tree and root imagery.

The Vienna Dioscurides (491). This manuscript contains a dedicatory portrait of Anicia Julia with figures of Magnanimity and Prudence on either side.

Gregory the Great *Morals on the Book of Job* (578–595)

John Climacus, *The Ladder of Divine Ascent* (600). This book describes spiritual progression up a ladder with vices to be avoided and virtues that one must acquire.

Cummean, *The Penitential of Cummean* (*c.* 650). This penitential manual is an example of many subsequent manuals based on Cassian's classification of the seven deadly sins. Such manuals established the tradition of using the sins for confession and repentance, a practice later codified at the Fourth Council of the Lateran in 1214.

Virtues Triumphant: Florence, Museo Nazionale (9th century). This ivory shows virtues triumphant over vices.

Psychomachia Illustrations (9th and 10th centuries)

The Ladder of Virtues Klimax Manuscript: Rome, Biblioteca Vaticana (11th century). This illustrates John Climacus's Ladder of Virtues.

Virtues Triumphant: Aulnay (Charent-Inférieure) St. Pierre (1130). One of many Romanesque churches in France along pilgrimage routes that feature *Psychomachia*-inspired images in the archivolts of military-clad Virtues overcoming Vices.

Book cover of the Melisenda Psalter London, British Museum (1131–44). This ivory book cover features *Psychomachia* themes mixed with Bible stories.

Illustrations of the *Speculum Virginum* (1140 CE)

Hugh of Saint Victor, *De frucibus carnis et spiritus* (12th century). Though it may not be a genuine work by Hugh of Saint Victor, this very popular tract seems to be behind some of Herrod's depictions of the virtues and vices and also helped reinforce the tree imagery used in conjunction with the virtues and vices.

Hildegard of Bingen, *Ordo Virtutim* (*c.* 1151)

Floreffe Bible Frontispiece: London, British Museum (*c.* 1155). This frontispiece includes the three theological virtues, the gifts of the Spirit (with six additional gifts), and the acts of mercy, as well as images of Job, David, the apostles, and the Day of Pentecost.

Herrad of Landsberg, *Garden of Delights* (1167–1185) This manuscript is an encyclopedic collection of theology, philosophy, and natural science that includes remarkable *Psychomachia* illustrations as well as images of the Ladder of Virtues.

Notre Dame of Amiens, *Twelve Virtues and Twelve Vices* (1220–1235)

Virtue and Vice cycles on Notre Dame, Paris and Chartres (1220–1230). These two cathedrals have cycles of the virtues and vices similar to the one at Amiens.

Ancren Riwle or *Ancrene Wisse* (*c.* 1225). This monastic manual has an extensive and creative treatment of the virtues and vices, employing animal and castle imagery.

Gullielmus Peraldus *Summa de vitiis et virtutibus* (before 1236). This hugely influential treatment of the virtues and vices includes both traditional and original insights, employing stories and animal types.

Saint Thomas Aquinas, *Summa Theologica* (1265–1274). Like Peter Lombard's *Sentences*, this is an authoritative treatment of virtue and vice.

Laurent Gullas, *Somme le roy* (1279). This very popular compilation of moral teachings draws upon previous works from people like Peraldus, and it was translated and adapted many times.

Virtues Triumphant: Strasbourg Cathedral (*c.* 1280). Four warrior-queen virtues effortlessly overcome and trample small personifications of the vices.

Speculum Theologiae Yale, Beinecke MS 416 (late 13th to early 14th century). This collection of didactic diagrams originated in western Germany, and it includes the Wheel of Sevens, Trees of Virtue and Vice, and the Tower of Wisdom.

Giotto, Virtues and Vices in the Arena Chapel (1303–1308)

Dante, *Purgatorio* (1308–1321)

Gervais de Bus and Chaillou de Pestain, *Le Roman de Fauvel* (1310–1316). What began as a biting underground political and social satire was later expanded into a magnificent edition of the story with illustrations and 167 musical interpolations. The story tells how a fallow-colored horse named Fauvel, whose name stands for Flattery, Avarice, Villainy, Variability (Duplicity), Envy, and Cowardice (*Lascheté*), came to power. When Fauvel attempts to secure his place by marrying Fortune, he's given the hand of Vain Glory instead. While Fauvel and Vain Glory's vicious offspring fill the world, the text ends optimistically with a tournament where the virtues, with angelic help, overcome the vices.

Andrea Pisano, *Eight Virtues* South Doors, Baptistery, Florence (1330–36). Eight virtues, the seven traditional virtues plus Humility, are set within quatrefoil frames on these bronze doors. They are physically close and stylistically related to the *Seven Virtues* on Florence Cathedral's Bell Tower (1337–41), the *Four Cardinal Virtues* on the Loggia del Bigallo (1352–58), and the *Seven Virtues* on the Loggia del Lanzi or Lorgia della Signoria (14th century).

Ambrogio Lorenzetti, Paintings in the Palazzo Pubblico, Siena (1338–1339)

William Langland, *Piers Plowman* (c. 1360–1399)

John Gower, *Confessio amantis* (1386–1393). A lover, called Amans, must confess his sins against love. His confession follows the seven sins and includes a collection of allusions and tales of crimes against love. Gower's French work, *Mirour de l'omme*, is a social satire that pits thirty-five vices against an equal number of virtues.

Geoffrey Chaucer, "The Parson's Tale" (1387–1400)

Cary-Yale Visconti Tarrocchi or Tarot (*c.* 1440). This set of playing cards includes images of the virtues.

Piero del Pollaiuolo and Raphael, *Seven Virtues* (1469)

Albrecht Dürer, *Hercules at the Crossroads* (1498). This print is part of an important subset of the virtues and vices tradition. This story is taken from Xenephon, and it relates how Hercules was faced with the choice of a life of pleasure and vice or one of hardship, honor, and virtue. In Dürer's rendition, Hercules seems to want to mediate somewhat between these seemingly extreme positions. In other versions, like Annibale Carricci's *The Choice of Hercules* (1596), Gérard de Lairesse's *Hercules between Virtue and Vice* (1685), or Mariano Salvador Maella's mural in the Spanish Royal Palace of *Hercules between Virtue and Vice* (1765 - 1766), Hercules faces a more straightforward *psychomachia* between virtue and vice.

Hieronymus Bosch, *The Seven Deadly Sins and the Four Last Things*: Prado Museum, Madrid (1500–1510). As an *ars moriendi* image, or a visual to prepare one for death, this work vividly shows the commonality and infernal consequences of the seven deadly sins set in the all-seeing eye of God.

Andrea Mantegna, *Minerva Chases the Vices from the Garden of Virtue* (1502)

Willaim Dunbar, *Dance of the Seven Deadly Sins* (1507). This carnivalesque poem combines the traditions of depiction of hell and purgatory with the *Danse Macabre* and features Satan entertained by the seven vices and damned sinners.

Niccolò Machiavelli *The Prince* (1513)

Bernaert van Orley, Design and the workshop of Pieter van Aelst, weaver *Honors* (1517–1525)

Thomas More, *The Four Last Things* (1522). This is an *ars moriendi* literary text that parallels Bosch's painting.

Bronzino *Venus, Cupid, Folly, and Time* (1545). Among the many readings of this complex and controversial work are those that explore the many ways it engages the virtues and vices tradition.

Prints of the Virtues, Vices, and Sins (late 15th century through the 16th century). During this time, many graphic artists produced engravings and prints of the virtues, vices, and sins. Some of those artists include Heinrich Aldegrever, Hans Sebald and Barthel Beham, Lucas van Leyden, Jacob Matham, Georg Pencz, and Marcantonio Raimondi. Jacques Callot continued this tradition with a series of *The Seven Deadly Sins* in 1619.

Peter Brueghel the Elder, *Virtues and Vices* (1557–59)

Paolo Veronese *The Choice between Virtue and Vice* (*c.* 1580). A young man, whose ripped sock reveals a bloody wound inflicted by Vice, moves to the comforting protection of Virtue. Whereas the aggressive and duplicitous figure of Vice has playing cards and leans against a marble Sphinx (with a dagger), Virtue demurely looks down and wears the verdant green robe and the laurel wreath. Veronese treated a similar subject in *Youth between Vice and Virtue*, a painting in the Prado.

Edmund Spenser, *The Faerie Queene* (1590–96)

Christopher Marlowe, *The Tragical History of Doctor Faustus* (1594). In this play the devil presents Faustus with a parade of the Seven Deadly Sins for his delight. Ever arrogant, Faustus is not impressed.

Johannes Torrentius, *Emblematic Still Life with Flagon, Glass, Jug, and Bridle*: Rijksmuseum, Amsterdam (1614). This moralizing still life includes images associated with the virtue of temperance, and even the music's lyrics encourage one to keep a proper tempo and control. While this work is late and is more direct than one would expect, it follows a long tradition of moralizing still lifes.

Throne Room of the Spanish Royal Palace, Madrid. This room features René Frémin's large statues of the four cardinal virtues (1721–1738), all with conventional attributes. Giambattista Tiepolo's ceiling painting of the *Majesty of the Spanish Monarchy* (1764) in the same room includes images of Peace, Justice, and other virtues.

Johann Sebastian Bach, *Hercules at the Crossroads* (1733). This secular cantata, composed for the eleventh birthday celebration of the Saxon Prince Frederick Christian, recounts Hercules renunciation of the path of lust to follow that of virtue. George Frideric Handel treated the same subject in his *The Choice of Hercules* (1750), a work that is more developed then Bach's, and one that is also gently self-mocking.

Benjamin Franklin, *Autobiography* (1791)

Oscar Gustave Rejlander, *The Two Ways of Life* (1857). This allegorical photographic montage features a patriarch encouraging the way of virtue and discouraging the way of vice. The way of virtue features images of piety, penance, study, industry, acts of mercy, and family, while images of the way of vice include seductive women, revelers, gamblers, and wasters.

Friedrich Nietzsche, *Beyond Good and Evil* (1886) and *The Antichrist* (1888)

Prints of the Seven Deadly Sins. Twentieth-century graphic artists, including James Ensor and Marc Chagall, have continued the satirical tradition of images of the seven deadly sins.

Diego Rivera, *Orgy—Night of the Rich,* Fresco, Ministry of Education, Mexico City (1926). This portion of Rivera's mural cycle shows the vices of the rich that contrast with the nobility of the common people. Muralists like Rivera, Orozco, and Siqueiros often set the abusive vices of the rich or privileged against the virtues and collectivism of the masses.

Fritz Lang, *Metropolis* (1927). The protagonist Freder is the promised mediating messiah in a futurist world divided between the working class, the "hands," and the intellectual class, the "mind." As the "heart" who would bring the classes together, Freder has a nightmare of the whole society destroyed by the seven deadly sins; in his nightmare, the seven deadly sins foment anger among the workers and apathy and debauchery among the intellectual class.

Kurt Weill and Bertolt Brecht, *The Seven Deadly Sins* (1933)

Otto Dix, *Seven Deadly Sins*: Staatliche Kunsthalle Karlsruhe, Germany (1933). This painting, created shortly after Dix's removal from the Dresden Art Academcy, attacks the vices of both the Nazis and the complacent Germans.

Joseph Pieper, *The Four Cardinal Virtues: Prudence, Justice, Fortitude, Temperance*; and *Faith, Hope, Love* (1934–1965). This philosopher builds on the tradition of Saint Thomas Aquinas to reexamine the seven virtues in the context of his time.

C. S. Lewis, *Mere Christianity* (1943)

C. S. Lewis, *The Great Divorce* (1945). This work can be read as a compelling modern *psychomachia*, as it depicts various characters' struggles with the decisions to embrace virtue or to succumb to vice.

Paul Cadmus, *The Seven Deadly Sins* (1945–1949)

The works below are discussed in the Epilogue

"You Can Have it All! Seven Campaigns for Deadly Sins" (1987)

Seven (1995)
"Seven Deadly Clips." *3rd Rock from the Sun*, season 3, episode 9; airdate: 3 December 1997)
Bruce Nauman, *Vices and Virtues* (1988)
Diller Scofidio + Renfro, *Vice/Virtue* (1997)
Noritoshi Hirakawa, *Virtue in Vice* (1997)
"All Seven Deadly Sins Committed at Church Bake Sale," *The Onion* (2001)
André Comte-Sponville, *A Small Treatise on the Great Virtues: The Uses of Philosophy in Everyday Life* (2002)
Ken Bazyn, *The Seven Perennial Sins and Their Offspring* (2004).
Dan Savage, *Skipping towards Gomorrah* (2003).
The Seven Deadly Sins (Oxford University Press book series, 2003–2006).
"The Girl Who Gets Bad News." *America's Next Top Model*, season 4, episode 8; airdate: April 20, 2005.
Aviad Kleinberg, *Seven Deadly Sins: A Very Partial List* (2008)
Jeff Cook, *Seven: The Deadly Sins and the Beatitudes* (2008)
Kalman Kaplan, *The Seven Habits of the Good Life: How the Biblical Virtues Free Us from the Seven Deadly Sins* (2008)
Rebecca Konyndyk DeYoung, *Glittering Vices: A New Look at the Seven Deadly Sins and Their Remedies* (2009)

Bibliography

Adams, Roger J. "The Virtues and Vices at Aulnay Re-examined." In *The Twelfth Century*, by Bernard S. Levy and Sandro Sticca, 53–73. Acta. Binghamton, NY: Center for Medieval and Early Renaissance Studies, State University of New York at Binghamton, 1975.

Alighieri, Dante. *The Divine Comedy.* Translated by Allen Mandelbaum. Everyman's Library. New York: Knopf, 1995.

"All Seven Deadly Sins Committed at Church Bake Sale." *The Onion*, December 12, 2001. Online: http://www.theonion.com/articles/all-seven-deadly-sins-committed-at-church-bake-sal,167/.

Ambrose, Saint. *Hexameron, Paradise, and Cain and Abel.* Translated by John J Savage. New York: Fathers of the Church, 1961.

Aristotle. *The Nicomachean Ethics of Aristotle.* Translated by J. E. C. Welldon. London: Macmillan, 1920.

Bach, Johann Sebastian. *Secular Cantatas*, BWV 212, 213. "Hercules at the Crossroads," Gächinger Kantorei, Bach-Collegium Stuttgart, et al. Recorded May 1996. Hänssler Edition Bachakademie, vol. 67. Holzgerlingen: Hänssler, 2000, 1 compact disc.

Banks, Tyra, creator. "The Girl Who Gets Bad News." *America's Next Top Model.* Season 4, Episode 8, first broadcast on April 20, 2005.

Bazyn, Ken. *The Seven Perennial Sins and Their Offspring.* New York: Continuum, 2002.

Bejczy, Istvan Pieter, and Richard G. Newhauser, eds. *Virtue and Ethics in the Twelfth Century.* Brill's Studies in Intellectual History 130. Leiden: Brill, 2005.

Biller, Peter, and A. J. Minnis, eds. *Handling Sin: Confession in the Middle Ages.* Woodbridge, UK: York Medieval Press, 1998.

Bloomfield, Morton W. *The Seven Deadly Sins: An Introduction to the History of a Religious Concept, with Special Reference to Medieval English Literature.* Michigan State College of Agriculture and Applied Science. East Lansing. Studies in Language and Literature. East Lansing: Michigan State College Press, 1952.

Bossy, John. "Moral Arithmatic: Seven Sins into Ten Commandments." In *Conscience and Casuistry in Early Modern Europe*, edited by Edmund Leites, 214–34. Ideas in Context. Cambridge: Cambridge University Press, 1988.

Braswell, Mary Flowers. *The Medieval Sinner: Characterization and Confession in the Literature of the English Middle Ages.* Rutherford, NJ: Farleigh Dickinson University Press, 1983.

Campbell, Thomas P. *Tapestry in the Renaissance: Art and Magnificence.* New Haven: Yale University Press, 2002.

Cassian, John. *John Cassian, The Conferences*. Translated by Boniface Ramsey. Ancient Christian Writers 57. New York: Paulist, 1997.

———. *The Institutes*. Translated by Boniface Ramsey. Ancient Christian Writers 58. New York: Paulist, 2000.

Charles, Robert Henry, trans. *The Testaments of the Twelve Patriarchs*. London: Black, 1908.

Chaucer, Geoffrey. *Canterbuy Tales*. Modernized by J. U. Nicolson. Garden City, NY: International Collectors Library, 1934.

Cicero, Marcus Tullius. *Of Duties*. Translated by Walter Miller. Loeb Classical Library 30. Cambridge: Harvard University Press, 1913.

Cole, Bruce. *Giotto: The Scrovegni Chapel, Padua*. Great Fresco Cycles of the Renaissance. New York: Braziller, 1993.

Cook, Jeff. *Seven: The Deadly Sins and the Beatitudes*. Grand Rapids: Zondervan, 2008.

Delmarcel, Guy. *Los Honores: Flemish Tapestries for the Emperor Charles V*. Antwerp: SDZ/Pandora, 2000.

DeYoung, Rebecca Konyndyk. *Glittering Vices: A New Look at the Seven Deadly Sins and Their Remedies*. Grand Rapids: Brazos, 2009.

Diekstra, F. N. M., ed. *Book for a Simple and Devout Woman: A Late Middle English Adaptation of Peraldus's "Summa de vitiis et virtutibus" and Friar Laurent's "Somme le Roi."* Mediaevalia Groningen: Forsten, 1998.

Dixon, Laurinda S. *Bosch*. Art & Ideas. London: Phaidon, 2003.

Dunbar, William. *William Dunbar: The Complete Works*. Edited by John Conlee. Kalamazoo: Medieval Institute Publications, Western Michigan University, 2004.

Dyson, Michael Eric. *Pride: The Seven Deadly Sins*. Oxford: Oxford University Press, 2006.

Evagrius of Pontus. "On the Eight Thoughts." In *Evagrius of Pontus*, translated by Robert E. Sinkewicz, 73–90. Oxford Early Christian Studies. Oxford: Oxford University Press, 2003.

Fairlie, Henry. *The Seven Deadly Sins Today*. Notre Dame, IN: Notre Dame University Press, 1979.

Faithfull, Marianne, singer. *The Seven Deadly Sins*, composed by Kurt Weill and Bertolt Brecht. Audio CD. New York: Reverso, distributed by BMG Entertainment, 1998.

Fincher, David, dir. *Seven*. Los Angeles: Warner Bros., 1997. DVD. United States: New Line Home Video, 2004.

Franklin, Benjamin. *Autobiography*. Philadelphia: Lippincott, 1868.

Gervais, du Bus, and Chaillou de Pesstain. *Le Roman de Fauvel in the Edition of Mesire Chaillou de Pesstain: A Reproduction in Facsimile of the Complete Manuscript, Paris, Bibliothèque Nationale, fonds français 146*. Introduction by Edward H. Roesner et al. New York: Broude Brothers, 1990.

Gower, John. *Confessio Amantis*. 3 vols. Middle English Texts. Kalamazoo: The Consortium for the Teaching of the Middle Ages in association with the University of Rochester by Medieval Institute Publications, Western Michigan University, 2000.

Gregory I, Pope. *Morals on the Book of Job*. Translated by J. H. Parker. Library of Fathers of the Holy Catholic Church 18. Oxford: Oxford University Press, 1844–50.

Herrad of Landsberg. *Hortus Deliciarum*. 2 vols. Studies of the Warburg Institute 36. London: Warburg Institute, 1979.

———. *Hortus Deliciarum*. Strasbourg: Oberlin, 1945.

Hildegard, Saint. *Ordo Virtutum*. In *Nine Medieval Latin Plays*, edited and translated by Peter Dronke, 147–84. Cambridge Medieval Classics 1. Cambridge: Cambridge University Press, 1994.

———. *Ordo Virtutum*. Barbara Thornton, Benjamin Bagby, Elizabeth Gaver, and Sequentia. 2 compact discs. Freiburg: Deutsche Harmonia Mundi. New York: Distributed by BMG Music, 1998.

Horace. *The Epistles of Horace*. London: Macmillan, 1892.

Hourihane, Colum, ed. *Virtue and Vice: The Personifications in the Index of Christian Art*. Index of Christian Art Resources 1. Princeton: Index of Christian Art, Department of Art and Archaeology, Princeton University, in association with Princeton University Press, 2000.

Hughes, Terry, dir. "Seven Deadly Clips." *3rd Rock from the Sun*. Season 3, Episode 9, first broadcast on December 3, 1997.

John Climacus, Saint. *The Ladder of Divine Ascent*. Classics of Western Spirituality. New York: Paulist, 1982.

Jones, Edgar Yoxall. *Father of Art Photography, O. G. Rejlander, 1813–1875*. Greenwich, CT: New York Graphic Society, 1973.

Kaplan, Kalman J., and Matthew B. Schwartz. *The Seven Habits of the Good Life: How the Biblical Virtues Free Us from the Seven Deadly Sins*. Lanham, MD: Rowman & Littlefield, 2008.

Karcher, Eva. *Otto Dix*. Cologn: Taschen, 2002.

Katzenellenbogen, Adolf. *Allegories of the Virtues and Vices in Mediaeval Art from Early Christian Times to the Thirteenth Century*. Translated by Alan J. P. Crick. Medieval Academy Reprints for Teaching. Toronto: University of Toronto Press, 1989.

Kirstein, Lincoln. *Paul Cadmus*. New York: Imago, 1984.

Kleinberg, Aviad. *Seven Deadly Sins: A Very Partial List*. Translated by Susan Emanuel. Cambridge: Harvard University Press, 2008.

Lake, Kirsopp, trans. *The Apostolic Fathers*. Vol. 2, *The Shepherd of Hermas; The Martyrdom of Polycarp; The Epistle to Diognetus*. Loeb Classical Library 24. Cambridge: Harvard University Press, 1913.

Lang, Fritz, dir. *The Complete Metropolis*. 1927. 2 DVDs. New York: Kino Lorber Films, 2010.

Langland, William. *Piers Plowman: A New Translation of the B-Text*. Translated by A. V. C. Schmidt. Oxford World's Classics. Oxford: Oxford University Press, 1992.

Lewis, C. S. *Mere Christianity*. New York: HaperCollins, 2009.

Lightbown, R. W. *Mantegna: With a Complete Catalogue of the Paintings, Drawings*. Berkeley: University of California Press, 1986.

Lozano, Luis-Martín, and Juan Rafael Coronel Rivera. *Diego Rivera: The Complete Murals*. Photography by Rafael Doniz and Francisco Kochen. Edited by Benedikt Taschen. Translated by Mary Blackman and Deirdre MacCloskey. Hong Kong: Taschen, 2008.

Machiavelli. *The Prince*. Translated by W. K. Marriott. Everyman's Library. Essays and belles lettres 280. London: Dent, 1908.

Male, Emile. *The Gothic Image: Religious Art in France of the Thirteenth Century*. Translated by Dora Nussey. Cathedral Library. New York: Harper, 1958.

McNeill, John T. *A History of the Cure of Souls*. New York: Harper, 1951.

McNeill, John T., and Helena M. Gamer. *Medieval Handbooks of Penance*. Records of Civilization, Sources and Studies 29. New York: Octagon, 1965.

Mews, Constant J., ed. *Listen Daughter: The Speculum Virginum and the Formation of Religious Women in the Middle Ages.* New Middle Ages. New York: Palgrave, 2001.

Millett, Bella, ed. *Ancrene Wisse: A Corrected Edition of the Text in Cambridge, Corpus Christi College, ms 402, with Variants from Other Manuscripts.* Early English Text Society Series 325. Oxford: Oxford University Press, 2005.

More, Thomas, Saint. *The Last Things.* In *The Complete Works of St. Thomas More*, edited by Anthony S. G. Edwards et al., 1:128–82. 15 vols. in 21 pts. Yale Edition of the Complete Works of St. Thomas More. New Haven: Yale University Press, 1997.

Newhauser, Richard. *The Early History of Greed: The Sin of Avarice in Early Medieval Thought and Literature.* Cambridge Studies in Medieval Literature 41. Cambridge: Cambridge University Press, 2000.

———, ed. *In the Garden of Evil: The Vices and Culture in the Middle Ages.* Papers in Mediaeval Studies 18. Toronto: Pontifical Institute of Mediaeval Studies, 2005.

———. *The Treatise on Vices and Virtues in Latin and the Vernacular.* Typologie des sources du Moyen Age occidental 68. Turnhout: Brepols, 1993.

———, ed. *The Seven Deadly Sins: From Communities to Individuals.* Studies in Medieval and Reformation Traditions 123. Leiden: Brill, 2007.

Nietzsche, F. W.. *The Antichrist.* Translated by H. L. Mencken. New York: Knopf, 1918.

———. *Beyond Good and Evil.* Translated by Helen Zimmern. New York: Modern Library, 1927.

Norman, Joanne S. *Metamorphoses of an Allegory: The Iconography of the Psychomachia in Medieval Art.* American University Studies. Series IX. History 29. New York: Lang, 1988.

O'Reilly, Jennifer. *Studies in the Iconography of the Virtues and Vices in the Middle Ages.* Outstanding Theses in the Fine Arts from British Universities. New York: Garland, 1988.

Orenstein, Nadine M., ed. *Pieter Bruegel the Elder: Drawings and Prints.* New York: Metropolitan Museum of Art, 2001.

Peraldus, Guillaume. *Summa virtutum.* Antwerp: Nurius, 1588.

———. *Summae virtutum ac vitiorum.* Antwerp, 1571.

Pieper, Josef. *The Four Cardinal Virtues: Prudence, Justice, Fortitude, Temperance.* Translated by Richard Winston et al. New York: Harcourt, Brace & World, 1965.

———. *Faith, Hope, Love.* Translated by Richard Winston et al. San Francisco: Ignatius, 1997.

Plato. *The Republic.* In *The Dialogues of Plato*, vol. 1. Translated by Benjamin Jowett. 2 vols. New York: Random House, 1937.

Prudentius. *Psychomachia.* In *Prudentius*, with an English translation by H. J. Thomson, vol. 1. Loeb Classical Library 387. Cambridge: Harvard University Press, 1949.

Savage, Dan. *Skipping towards Gomorrah: The Seven Deadly Sins and the Pursuit of Happiness in America.* New York: Dutton, 2002.

Serebrennikov, Nina Eugenia. "Pieter Bruegel the Elder's Series of 'Virtues' and 'Vices.'" PhD diss., University of North Carolina, 1986.

Solomon, Robert C., ed. *Wicked Pleasures: Meditations on the Seven "Deadly" Sins.* Lanham, MD: Rowman & Littlefield, 1999.

Spenser, Edmund. *The Faerie Queene.* Modernized by Robert Kellogg and Oliver Steele. New York: Odyssey, 1965.

Spencer, Stephanie. *O. G. Rejlander, Photography as Art.* Studies in Photography 8. Ann Arbor: UMI Research Press, 1985.

Starn, Randolph. *Ambrogio Lorenzetti: The Palazzo Pubblico, Siena*. Great Fresco Cycles of the Renaissance. New York: Braziller, 1994.

Tertullian. *De Spectaculis*. Translated by T. R. Glover. Loeb Classical Library. London: Heinemann, 1931.

Thomas Aquinas, Saint. "Summa Theologica." In *Basic Writings of Saint Thomas Aquinas*, edited by Anton C. Pegis. New York: Random House, 1945.

Tool. *Undertow*. Volcano, 1993. 1 compact disc.

Tuve, Rosamond. "Notes on the Virtues and Vices." *Journal of the Warburg and Courtauld Institutes* 26 (1963) 264–303 and 27 (1964) 42–72.

Weill, Kurt. *Die Sieben Todsünden = The Seven Deadly Sins = Les Sept Peches Capitaux* ; *Kleine Dreigroschenmusik = Little Threepenny Music = Petite Musique de Quat'sous*. London Symphony Orchestra, Michael Tilson Thomas. With Julia Migenes, Robert Tear, Stuart Kale, Alan Opie, and Roderick Kennedy. Recorded 1988. Audio CD. CBS Masterworks, 1988, 1 compact disc. Libretto.

Weill, Kurt, and Bertolt Brecht. *The Seven Deadly Sins*. Marianne Faithfull, Vienna Radio Orchestra, Dennis Russell Davies, Peter Becker, Mark Bleeke, Hugo Munday, and Wilbur Pauley. Recorded June 5, 1997. Audio CD. New York: Reverso, distributed by BMG Entertainment, 1998, 1 compact disc.

Wenzel, Siegfried. "The Seven Deadly Sins: Some Problems of Research." *Speculum* 43 (1968) 1–22.

———. *The Sin of Sloth: Acedia in Medieval Thought and Literature*. Chapel Hill: University of North Carolina Press, 1967.

Wilson, Angus et al. *The Seven Deadly Sins*. Pleasantville, NY: Akadine, 2002.

Woodruff, Helen. *The Illustrated Manuscripts of Prudentius*. Cambridge: Harvard University Press, 1930.

Wright, Alison. *The Pollaiuolo Brothers: The Arts of Florence and Rome*. New Haven: Yale University Press, 2005.

"You Can Have it All! Seven Campaigns for Deadly Sins." *Harper's*, November 1987, 43–50.

Acknowledgment of Copyright

"Sober." Words and Music by Daniel Carey, Paul D'amour, Adam Jones and Maynard Keenan Copyright ©1992 Toolshed Music. All Rights Administered by BMG Rights Management (US) LLC. All Rights Reserved. Used by Permission of Hal Leonard Corporation.

Selections from Plato's *Republic* come from Benjamin Jowett, trans., *The Republic*, in *The Dialogues of Plato*, vol. 1 (2 vols., New York: Random House, 1937), 635–44, 690–99, 705–9.

Selections from *The Nichomachean Ethics* come from J. E. C. Welldon, trans., *The Nicomachean Ethics of Aristotle* (London: Macmillan, 1930), 12–16, 34–36, 43–53, 55–57.

Selections from Cicero come from Walter Miller, trans., Cicero, *Of Duties* (Loeb Classical Library 30; Cambridge: Harvard University Press, 1913), 17–29, 63–71, 95–103, 155–65.

Selections from Proverbs, Isaiah, Matthew, 1 Corinthians, and Ephesians coem from The Holy Bible, New International Version®, NIV® Copyright © 1973, 1978, 1984, 2011 by Biblica, Inc.® Used by permission. All rights reserved worldwide.

Selections from Tertullian come from T. R. Glover, trans., Tertullian, *De Spectaculis* (Loeb Classical Library; Cambridge: Harvard University Press, 1931), 295–97.

Selections from Prudentius come from H. J. Thomson, trans., *Psychomachia*, in *Prudentius* (Loeb Classical Library 387; Cambridge: Harvard University Press, 1949).

Selections from *Evagrius of Pontus*, translated by Robert E. Sinkewicz. copyright © 2003 Oxford University Press. Used by permission.

Selections from Pope Gregory I come from J. H. Parker, trans., Gregory the Great, *Morals on the Book of Job*, vol. 1 (Oxford: Oxford University Press, 1844–50).

Selections from Hildegard of Bingen's *Ordo Virtutum* in *Nine Latin Medieval Plays*, translated and edited by Peter Dronke, copyright © 1994 Cambridge University Press. Used by permission.

Selections from *Purgatorio* come from Henry Wadsworth Longfellow, trans., *The Divine Comedy* (Boston: Ticknor & Fields, 1867), 77–83, 89–90.

Selection from William Langland come from *Piers Plowman: A New Translation of the B-Text*, translated with an introduction and notes by A. V. C. Schmidt, copyright © 2009 Oxford University Press. Used by permission.

Selections from Chaucer come from Geoffrey Chaucer *Canterbury Tales*, modernized by J. U. Nicolson (Garden City, NY: International Collectors Library, 1934), 604–14.

Selections from *The Prince* come from W. K. Marriott, trans. Nicolo Machiavelli, *The Prince* (London: Dent, 1908), 121–45.

Selections from Spenser come from *The Faerie Queen*, Modernized by Robert Kellogg and Oliver Steele (New York: Odyssey, 1965), 114–23, 188–205.

Selections from Franklin come from Benjamin Franklin, *Autobiography* (London: Trübner, 1868).

Selections from Nietzsche come from Helen Zimmern, trans., F. W. Nietzsche, *Beyond Good and Evil* (New York: Modern Library, 1917) and H.L. Mencken, trans., F. W. Nietzsche, *The Antichrist* (New York: Knopf, 1918).

Mere Christianity by C. S. Lewis, copyright © C. S. Lewis Pte. Ltd., 1942, 1943, 1944, 1952. Extract reprinted by permission.

Index

www.ingramcontent.com/pod-product-compliance
Lightning Source LLC
LaVergne TN
LVHW081257100826
845148LV00005B/902

* 9 7 8 1 6 2 5 6 4 7 1 8 4 *